D0208652

BEHAVIORAL STATISTICS IN ACTION

SECOND EDITION

BEHAVIORAL STATISTICS IN ACTION

Mark Vernoy
PALOMAR COLLEGE

Judith Vernoy

Brooks/Cole Publishing Company

I(T)P® An International Thomson Publishing Company

Pacific Grove • Albany • Bonn • Boston • Cincinnati • Detroit • London • Madrid
Melbourne • Mexico City • Paris • San Francisco
Singapore • Tokyo • Toronto • Washington

Sponsoring Editor: *Jim Brace-Thompson*
Marketing Team: *Gay Meixel and Deborah Petit*
Marketing Representative: *Sue Lasbury*
Editorial Assistant: *Terry Thomas*
Production Editor: *Kirk Bomont*
Manuscript Editor: *Carol Reitz*
Permissions Editor: *Cathleen S. Collins*
Interior and Cover Design: *Roy R. Neuhaus*

Interior Illustration: *Lotus Art*
Cover Photo: *Mel Levine/Sports Illustrated*
Art Coordinator: *Lisa Torri*
Typesetting: *Shepard Poorman Communications Corporation*
Cover Printing: *Color Dot Graphics, Inc.*
Printing and Binding: *R. R. Donnelley/Crawfordsville*

For more information, contact:

BROOKS/COLE PUBLISHING COMPANY
511 Forest Lodge Road
Pacific Grove, CA 93950
USA

International Thomson Publishing Europe
Berkshire House 168-173
High Holborn
London WC1V 7AA
England

Thomas Nelson Australia
102 Dodds Street
South Melbourne, 3205
Victoria, Australia

Nelson Canada
1120 Birchmount Road
Scarborough, Ontario
Canada M1K 5G4

International Thomson Editores
Campos Eliseos 385, Piso 7
Col. Polanco
11560 México D. F. México

International Thomson Publishing GmbH
Königswinterer Strasse 418
53227 Bonn
Germany

International Thomson Publishing Asia
221 Henderson Road
#05-10 Henderson Building
Singapore 0315

International Thomson Publishing Japan
Hirakawacho Kyowa Building, 3F
2-2-1 Hirakawacho
Chiyoda-ku, Tokyo 102
Japan

Printed in the United States of America

10 9 8 7 6 5 4 3 2 1

Library of Congress Cataloging-in-Publication Data
Vernoy, Mark W.
    Behavioral statistics in action / Mark Vernoy, Judith Vernoy.—2nd ed.
        p.   cm.
    Includes bibliographical references and index.
    ISBN 0-534-23664-2
    1. Psychology—Statistical methods. I. Vernoy, Judith. II. Title.
BF39.V44   1997
519.5'02415—dc20   96-14983
                                                        CIP

To our parents, who instilled in us the confidence, the perseverance, and the fortitude required to write a statistics book and the sense of humor to survive the ordeal.

Contents

CHAPTER FOUR

Measures of Central Tendency 71

CHAPTER FIVE

Measures of Variability 96

C H A P T E R   S I X

Scaled Scores and Standard Scores: How to Change Apples into Oranges   117

C H A P T E R   S E V E N

The Normal Curve   133

C H A P T E R   E I G H T

Correlation   158

C H A P T E R   N I N E

Regression   179

CHAPTER TEN

Probability Theory and Sampling   202

CHAPTER ELEVEN

Experimental Design   224

CHAPTER TWELVE

t Tests   254

CHAPTER THIRTEEN

One-Way Analysis of Variance   284

CHAPTER FOURTEEN

Factorial Analysis of Variance: Two-Way   308

CHAPTER FIFTEEN

Nonparametric Statistics: Chi-Square, Mann-Whitney *U* Test, Wilcoxon *T* Test, and the Kruskal-Wallis Test   **335**

APPENDIX A

Tables   **372**

APPENDIX B

Solutions to Odd-Numbered Problems   391

Index   422

Preface

Within psychology, statistics is a unique course. It is probably the only course psychology majors take because they are forced to. Other psychology courses, from Introduction to Research Methods to Abnormal, have some face validity—each student can see at a glance why such courses are important. Not so with statistics. Most psych majors can see no reason to study statistics; after all, it's a math course. Thus, it is the task of the statistics professor or the statistics book to help each student grasp that important connection between the study of psychology and the study of statistics. Our major goal in writing *Behavioral Statistics in Action* was to write not only an introductory statistics text that is comprehensive in its basic coverage but also one that continually indicates to students the reasons statistics is essential to all psychological research.

A statistics text can be comprehensive in its coverage, it can provide detailed explanations of concepts, it can reveal a thorough rationale behind the study of statistics. But if it's boring, if it's full of unexplained jargon, no student will read it. Therefore, we wanted to write a book that is easy to read, one that uses free-flowing, almost colloquial language, one that is alluring, interesting, lighthearted—even fun at times. By writing in a conversational tone, as well as by using examples with which students can identify, we feel we created a text that students will find both understandable and exciting to read. If statistical concepts, the logic behind those concepts, and the formulas derived from those concepts are explained in an enjoyable manner and an easy-to-read style, students will be more apt to read the book and therefore more likely to succeed in their study of statistics.

As psychologists, we know that learning is most effective when the student is an active participant in the learning process—hence the name of our text: *Behavioral Statistics in Action*. To enable each student to be an active learner of statistics, we designed special features into the book and structured the entire text around the SQ4R (**S**urvey, **Q**uestion, **R**ead, w**R**ite, **R**ecite, **R**eview) technique. Using the SQ4R technique is difficult and tedious for most students, but *Behavioral Statistics in Action* helps them use the technique with minimum effort by involving them in the study and use of statistical concepts in each chapter.

Several features of the book are designed to support the SQ4R study technique. Each chapter is preceded by a **Chapter Outline** that allows students to *survey* the major topics that will be presented in that chapter. A *questioning* attitude is developed via **Student Questions** found throughout each chapter. A major advantage of a lecture over passive reading is the interaction between professor and student. When students are confused or a topic becomes complex, they can take action and ask questions to clarify the material. Our experience in teaching statistics has allowed us to anticipate questions commonly asked by students; such questions are embedded within the text, and the answers are given.

Reading is facilitated by an informal writing style that introduces each chapter with a provocative psychological research question. These **Chapter Openers** are then integrated into the text and are, in most cases, used as the basis for the majority of examples within the chapter. Although this is a statistics book, the chapters flow easily, and applications of the statistical concepts and methodology abound. We believe that students will find the text interesting and intriguing, as well as instructional.

We encourage students to *write* as they read—jotting notes and summaries next to each concept presented in the text and working each sample problem solved in the text on their own papers. In addition, each chapter has **Problems** at the end that demonstrate and provide practice with the concepts presented in that chapter. The answers to odd-numbered problems are given in Appendix B.

Often, learning the logic behind statistical concepts is more difficult than learning the statistical formulas used to execute the concepts. To help students evaluate their understanding of the concepts covered in the text, we periodically inserted learning checks, which we call **Concept Quizzes**. These are short questions that invite each student to *recite* the conceptual content of the material just covered.

At the end of each chapter there is a **Chapter Summary**, a list of the **Key Terms** in the chapter, and a list of all new **Formulas**. Defining each of the key terms will be an additional opportunity for the student to *recite* the material covered in the chapter. The summaries and formulas serve as *reviews*. Thus, the chapter outlines, chapter openers, student questions, concept quizzes, chapter summaries, list of key terms, list of formulas, and problems all elicit the active participation of the student and facilitate the use of the SQ4R study technique.

During the revision of *Behavioral Statistics in Action*, we have made many changes that we believe will enhance student understanding and make the book easier to use. We changed the notation for the number of scores in a sample to n so it is not confused with the number of scores in a population, N. In addition, we changed the notation for the number of groups in a multilevel design to k. The other major change is the added discussion of the concept of power in Chapter 11. The style and approach of the book remain the same—engaging and easy to understand for beginning behavioral science students.

A student workbook is available to accompany the text. The workbook has more than 400 additional problems with their solutions, as well as an introductory chapter on how to study and learn statistics.

We gratefully extend our thanks to Jim Brace-Thompson, our editor, whose encouragement and well-considered advice helped us through this revision. We also wish to thank our colleagues who reviewed this manuscript and made helpful suggestions: Terry A. Ackerman, University of Illinois; Jay Alperson, Palomar College; Gregory Burton, Seton Hall University; Carol Capelli, Rutgers University-New Brunswick; Jim Juola, University of Kansas; Merle Kelley, Western Oregon State College; William Klein, Colby College; Kathleen Kowal, University of North Carolina at Wilmington; Charles F. Levinthal, Hofstra University; Gerald Peterson, Saginaw Valley State University; Daniel G. Webster, Georgia Southern University; J. Vincent Wisser, Kent State University.

Mark Vernoy
Judith Vernoy

An Introduction to Statistics

A child watches a film of a woman repeatedly kicking and hitting a "Bobo" doll, one of those blow-up clowns that pops back up after someone knocks it down. The woman doesn't just punch it when it swings up; she absolutely batters it, flinging it up into the air and even pouncing on it to thrash it as much as she can. After watching her, the child, alone in the room with the Bobo doll, jumps up, whacks the doll around, and abuses it in precise imitation of the adult in the film. Another child watches a different film of the same woman in the same room with the same toys, including the Bobo doll. But in this film the woman sits passively, ignoring the inflatable doll. At the end of the film, this second child exhibits a similar passive behavior, quite different from the full-blown aggression demonstrated by the first child.

More than 30 years ago, Albert Bandura and Richard Walters (1963) wrote a fascinating book exploring how people learn a repertoire of behaviors through watching and imitating others. One of their research projects, typified by the opening vignette, was a study of how children's aggressive behavior can be shaped by watching aggressive models on film. The design of their experiment was relatively simple. One group of children was shown the film described here of an adult model hitting and kicking a Bobo doll; another group was shown a film of the passive model; and still another group, the control group, was shown no film. When left alone in the room with the inflatable doll and other toys, the children who had seen the violent film tended to display the same violent behavior portrayed in the film. Children who viewed the nonaggressive film and children in the control group rarely committed aggressive acts. In fact, the children who watched the passive models in the film were even more inhibited than those in the control group.

Having read about Bandura and Walters's experiment, what can you conclude? Is watching violence on television or in the movies bad for children? Should violent TV programs be banned? Given the limited amount of information you have about the experiment, you really cannot come to any definite conclusions. Before making judgments based on this research project, you might want to have answers to such questions as these:

1. How many children were in each group?
2. What were the ages of these children?
3. How many aggressive acts were seen by the children who watched the film?
4. How many aggressive acts, on the average, did the children who watched the aggressive film perform?
5. How many aggressive acts, on the average, did the children who watched the passive film perform?
6. How long was the film?

As you may have noticed, all of the preceding questions ask for numbers.

Psychologists who read about or conduct research are constantly bombarded with numbers: "Thirty children in each group," "ages 4 to 7 years," "21 aggressive acts," "28.7 minutes long." These numbers are meant to convey important information about the research. Whenever we use these types of numbers, we are using statistics. **Statistics** is a branch of applied mathematics that psychologists use to plan research; to gather, organize, and analyze data; to present data in research papers; and to make inferences about data. Ultimately, psychologists use statistics to support or refute predictions concerning the behavior of humans and animals.

STATISTICS AND MATH ANXIETY

Statistics. Just the word tends to strike fear into the hearts of most psychology students. In all our years of teaching, we know of not one psychology student who took an introductory statistics class because he or she thought it would be fun. Nevertheless, we do know hundreds of students who found the course both interesting and enjoyable. Most students go into a statistics course with at least a mild amount of dread and very little enthusiasm, but if you've successfully completed an algebra course, there is no reason to fear statistics. The mathematical formulas in this book are no more difficult than those you solved in algebra. (If you have not taken an algebra course, now is the time to talk to your professor.) So using formulas to calculate different kinds of statistics should be relatively easy for you. Often the difficult part of statistics is not the formulas or the calculations but the concepts, the reasons for doing certain operations, the logic behind the computations. Truly comprehending the concepts and the logic behind them is probably more difficult than using the formulas themselves. We kept this in mind when writing this book to make learning both statistical procedures and statistical concepts as simple and as painless as possible.

FEATURES OF THE BOOK

This book should be easy to understand. Our purpose in writing it was to introduce you to the uses of psychological statistics in a friendly, interesting way, using provocative and sometimes amusing examples. We have included several features that should greatly help you to learn statistics if you take advantage of them. These features are: (1) chapter outlines, (2) chapter openers that are either short stories related to psychology or psychology research examples, (3) student questions, (4) concept quizzes, (5) chapter summaries, (6) lists of key terms, (7) lists of formulas used in the chapter, and (8) problems.

The **chapter outline** at the beginning of each chapter provides an overview of that chapter. Reading the outline will let you know what topics will be covered in each chapter, help you keep the material you read in perspective, and aid you in reviewing the chapter.

The short stories and research examples used to open each chapter are also an integral part of that chapter. Each **chapter opener** either is referred to extensively throughout the chapter or is used to introduce the initial statistical concept. These chapter openers also show the interrelationship between statistics and experimental design, as well as illustrate the importance of statistics in the study of behavior.

Student questions are also used throughout the text. How many times have you been listening to a lecture or reading a textbook when a question about the material being covered pops into your mind? Sometimes you need a point clarified, an important concept repeated, or confirmation of whether you are right about an inference you have made or about the way the new concept relates to previous material. Whatever the case, these questions are an important part of the learning process. During a lecture, you and your classmates can ask these questions and your professor can answer them. However, when you are reading it is impossible to get immediate answers. We have drawn on our experience as students and teachers to include, at critical points throughout the text, questions that are frequently asked by students. The number and types of questions vary from chapter to chapter and topic to topic, but each question and answer will enhance your comprehension of the section you're reading.

A course in statistics has two main objectives: (1) to teach you the mathematical formulas for computing statistics, and (2) to teach you the logic underlying the computation and use of those statistics. To reinforce both computational and logical statistical concepts, we have placed **concept quizzes** at vital points throughout the chapter. These quizzes are short-answer fill-ins that review and reinforce critical concepts covered in the chapter. They will also enable you to quickly check whether you know the material you have just finished reading.

A **chapter summary** at the end of each chapter reviews the major mathematical and logical concepts covered in the chapter.

Following each chapter summary are key terms, a list of formulas, and problems. The **key terms** will help you quickly identify and review the important terms and topics covered in the chapter. All new **formulas** used in the chapter are restated. Finally, each chapter ends with **problems** that were carefully chosen to reinforce the material covered in the chapter.

TIPS FOR DOING WELL IN STATISTICS, OR HOW TO SUCCEED IN STATISTICS BY REALLY TRYING

Doing well (i.e., getting good grades) in any college-level class requires a lot of work, and statistics is no exception. Learning statistics and getting a good grade in this course will require a great deal of study and organization on your part. We can't force you to study, but we can suggest ways to go about it, and we can help with the organization.

1. Statistics is cumulative. This statistics class, like most of your classes, consists of a specific body of knowledge. Your job as a student is to master that knowledge. Unlike the content of many other psychology courses, however, the information you learn in statistics is *cumulative*. Thorough comprehension of topics and concepts covered at the beginning of the course is imperative for the understanding of topics and concepts presented later. Missing just one lecture or one page in the textbook may cause you to have difficulty with the rest of the course. First and foremost, you must keep up with the work, attend all lectures, do the homework problems, and read the book consistently. Plan to be sick or go to the beach on your next vacation.

2. Your professor is there to help. As a student you have at least three sources for information about statistics: your professor, the book, and fellow students. All three can be helpful, but your professor can be extremely so. Don't be afraid to approach the professor. Ask for help when you first detect you need it, clear up questions as they arise, ask questions in class if you don't quite understand something. Not only do statistics professors know the material backwards and forwards, but also most of them have lots of experience in pinpointing the causes of students' confusion. Your professor dictates the topics you will cover and the speed at which you will cover them, and your feedback will help him or her to adjust the rate of coverage. Take careful notes in class, work all demonstration problems along with your professor, and ask questions, either in class or in your professor's office, when you don't understand something.

3. Make friends quickly. Other students in your class are another significant source of help in statistics. If you miss a lecture or don't quite understand a small point, a fellow student can often provide just the comment that will eliminate your problem. In turn, helping fellow students will benefit you because, as you shed light on specific concepts for your friends, you further clarify them for yourself. Take time to get to know your fellow students, exchange telephone numbers, and set up study groups.

4. Read the book. This book is also an extremely important part of your statistics course. Think of it as an additional set of lecture notes or a knowledgeable friend. The book is designed to teach you statistics as well as serve as a reference for later years. In our opening comments, we described the main features of the book. Now we will briefly discuss how to use them effectively.

As you might have guessed, reading a statistics book is not like reading a novel. Always have a pencil, paper, and a calculator handy when you start a new chapter. Before you begin to read the body of the chapter, take time to read the outline so that (a) you can get an idea of what topics are going to be discussed and (b) you can gain some notion of the chapter's general organization. As you read the chapter, be sure you understand each new concept or statistical procedure before going on to the next section. Also, as you're reading, don't be afraid of underlining, highlighting, and writing in the margins. After all, this is *your* book that you will refer to again and again, maybe even throughout graduate school.

Make sure you work all the numerical examples in the text. By working the examples using your own paper and calculator, you will get invaluable guided practice. Don't just take the text's word for a sum or a computed value; compute it yourself. Take time to complete the concept quiz at the end of each major section. These quizzes are quick checks to let you know whether you understand the concepts sufficiently to proceed to the next section. Once you have finished a chapter, try to summarize it, and then read the chapter summary to see whether you got it right. Next, see whether you can define each of the key terms. Finally, to reinforce your comprehension, work the problems at the end of the chapter. By utilizing this study system for each chapter, you will maximize your understanding of statistics.

5. Practice helps. This is a fundamental psychological law (Vernoy's Law) that is especially applicable to statistics. The best way to improve your skill is to practice. You practice statistics by working problems. Copy and rework the problems demonstrated in class by your professor. Solve the numerical examples while you are reading the book. Work the problems at the end of each chapter. And make sure you do all the homework as soon as it is assigned. You can also make up problems, by yourself or with your study group, and attempt to solve them.

6. Calculators are necessary. Statistics involves a lot of computation. Computing the sums of columns of numbers, squares, and square roots can be extremely time-consuming without an electronic calculator. In order to do the computations required for this course, you will need the assistance of an electronic calculator or possibly a computer. It is wise to discuss with your professor any calculator or computer you are buying expressly for this course. He or she can tell you exactly what is required and what calculators or computers can meet those requirements. At the very least, you will need a calculator that does addition, subtraction, multiplication, division, and square roots. For a little additional money, you can purchase a statistical or scientific calculator that can be programmed to calculate many of the statistical procedures discussed in this textbook. Before you buy any scientific or statistical calculator, however, take time to read the instruction booklet that goes with it to confirm that it will do what you want it to. Make sure the calculator will compute at least the mean and the standard deviation. It will also be helpful if your calculator computes correlation coefficients. Once you have purchased your calculator, make sure you are thoroughly familiar with it by reading the instruction booklet and working the sample problems in the booklet.

7. Get a "feel" for statistics. As you are learning statistics, try to do more than just memorize the formulas; *try to understand the concepts behind the formulas*. At the end of this course you should know whether a computed value is reasonable. *Think* about the problem you are working or the experiment you are trying to analyze. You already have a feel for some kinds of statistics. For instance, you know that the mean (average) for the numbers 51, 56, 55, 54, and 59 cannot be greater than 60 or less than 50. You *should* know that if a friend tells you the average age of people frequenting bars is 16.5, he or she has to be pulling your leg. Similarly, after having learned that a correlation coefficient can never be more than +1.00 or less than −1.00, you should know that when you compute a correlation of +23, you must have made some kind of mistake. Use your knowledge of mathematics, statistics, and the problem you are working on to decide whether each sum or statistic you compute is reasonable. If there is any doubt, recompute the value. As you work more and more problems, you should get a better feel for statistics. In the next section, we begin to build the foundation you need to develop this statistical sense and to comprehend the *whys* and *wherefores* of statistics.

A NOTE ABOUT NOTATION AND ROUNDING

Statistics, just like algebra or any other form of mathematics, has its own notation. Mathematical or statistical notation is merely a type of shorthand, much of which you already know because statistics shares many of its symbols with algebra, such as +, −, ·, ÷, and =. But some of the notation you encounter will be new. This new notation, as well as how to use it, is discussed in detail when it is introduced, and sufficient examples are given to allow you to master it. For example, in later chapters you will often encounter subscripted variable names such as S_x and S_y or Z_x and Z_y. Remember that the subscripts serve to differentiate one value from another and that they are not the same. For example, S_x would be a value for sample x, and S_y would be a value for sample y.

Careful attention to mathematical notation is vital in statistical work, and so is computational accuracy. Take out your calculator (yes, right now) and divide 1 second by 7 (1 second ÷ 7). What answer did you get? Our calculator said 0.142857142 second. It reported the value in billionths of a second. Do you have any conception of a billionth of a second? Most of us have enough trouble with a thousandth of a second. To remedy this problem, as well as the problem of dealing with so many numbers and decimal places, we can round off our quotient to tenths, hundredths, or thousandths of a second. However, an inherent problem in rounding is that if one person always rounds to the nearest tenth and another person always rounds to the nearest thousandth, there will perpetually be a discrepancy in their answers. To prevent this, there must be some agreement, some ground rules, for rounding numbers. These "rounding rules" are described next.

For most statistical calculations, rounding to the thousandths place (three digits to the right of the decimal point) provides sufficient accuracy. To do this, it is customary to use the following roundoff procedure:

1. Calculate your answer to four decimal places.
2. If the fourth digit is less than 5 (0, 1, 2, 3, or 4), report the first three digits without change.
3. If the fourth digit is 5 or greater (5, 6, 7, 8, or 9), report the first two digits and increase the third digit by 1.

We use this procedure throughout the book. To give you practice, let's work two examples.

As we said earlier, dividing 1 second by 7 results in 0.142857142. To round this result to the thousandths place, or the third digit to the right of the decimal point, we need to consider the fourth digit: 0.142$\underline{8}$. Since this digit is greater than 5, we report the first two digits and add 1 to the third digit to get 0.143. For another example, divide 1 by 3 on your calculator. The result should be 0.333333333. Again, look at the fourth digit: 0.333$\underline{3}$. Because 3 is less than 5, you need report only the original three digits, 0.333. Now let's turn our attention to factors more specifically related to psychological studies.

HYPOTHESES

All psychological inquiry begins with a question about behavior: *What happens to a certain behavior if . . . ? What causes people to . . . ? Can a person's behavior be influenced by . . . ?* In the scientific study of psychology, such a question must be restated in the form of a **hypothesis,** a possible explanation for the behavior being studied that is based on previously gathered facts and theories. Expressed as a prediction, a scientific hypothesis is not always true, but it is stated in such a way that it can be proved false if indeed it is false. For example, Bandura and Walters might have generated the following hypothesis: Children who view a film depicting aggressive adult models will exhibit more aggressive acts than children who see a film depicting passive models. This hypothesis makes a prediction that should be easy to verify.

In most experiments there are two mutually exclusive hypotheses (which means that if one is true, the other can't be). A **research hypothesis** is one that the researcher wishes to support. An example is the hypothesis stated here from Bandura and Walters's study. The **null hypothesis,** on the other hand, is the one the researcher wants to reject because it proposes that there will be no change in behavior, no difference between the groups being measured. In the case of the Bandura and Walters experiment, the null hypothesis might be: The number of aggressive acts performed by children who view a film portraying aggressive adult models will be no greater than the number performed by children who see a film portraying passive models. Because of the way statistical tests are designed, *it is the null hypothesis that is tested in a research study.* If the null hypothesis can be shown to be false, then the research hypothesis is supported.

VARIABLES

After generating a hypothesis, a researcher needs to decide how to test it. Often the test is done via an experiment in which the researcher takes great care to hold everything constant (keep everything the same) except for the factors being investigated. These factors are manipulated, or systematically altered, to see whether they cause any change in the subjects' behavior. By doing this, the researcher can attribute any change in behavior directly to the factors being manipulated, since all other factors have been held constant.

Factors in an experiment are known as variables. **Variables** are events or

ENTER THE VARIABLE.

qualities that can *vary*—they can assume more than one value. Variables include such factors as reaction time, number of subjects in a group, number of aggressive acts, age of the subjects, length of a video program. When researchers decide to conduct an experiment, one of the first things they do is to decide which variable(s) will be manipulated and which variable(s) will be measured for changes that result from the manipulation. These two distinct types of variables are known as *independent* and *dependent variables*.

An **independent variable** is a factor that is selected and manipulated, or controlled, by the experimenter. It is totally independent of anything the subject does. In the Bandura and Walters experiment, the independent variable was the type of film viewed by the child—the aggressive or the passive version. Because the experimenters were solely responsible for determining which film each child viewed, this variable was totally independent of the child's response.

In contrast to an independent variable, a **dependent variable** is a measurable behavior exhibited by the *subject*. It is a result of, or is dependent on, the independent variable. Thus, in an experiment we expect that with any change in the independent variable, there will be a corresponding change in the dependent variable. Since the dependent variable is a measure of each subject's behavior, it is the source of the numbers used in statistics. In the Bandura and Walters experiment, the dependent variable was the number of aggressive acts performed by each child after seeing the film. As it turned out, the children who viewed the violent film performed many aggressive acts, and the children who viewed the passive film performed few, if any, such acts. Thus, the children's behavior was dependent on which film they saw (the independent variable).

A good way to determine which variable is the independent variable and which is the dependent variable is to reword the research question in the form: "What is the effect of (independent variable) on (dependent variable)?" In the case of the Bandura and Walters experiment, the question could be stated: "What is the effect of the type of film viewed on the number of aggressive acts performed by each child?"

In any experiment researchers need to control **extraneous variables,** or "extra" variables, that may affect the outcome of the experiment but are not directly related to the study. For example, if there had been an obnoxious noise from a jackhammer outside the window during or after the children's viewing of the violent film, then their subsequent aggression might actually have been due to the noise rather than to the aggressive behavior of the models in the film. Presumably, Bandura and Walters controlled extraneous variables of noises, personal interruptions, excessively bright lights, and so on.

To research and collect information about human or animal behavior, it is necessary to measure the dependent variable and record the measurement using the same type of scale so that subjects' responses can be compared objectively. Next we take a look at the kinds of measurement scales.

1. Round off the following numbers to the third digit after the decimal:
  a. 3.234473
  b. 5.77377
  c. 2345.2375
  d. 219.3333
  e. 0.3356789
2. A possible explanation for a behavior being studied that is expressed as a prediction is a _____ .
3. The _____ hypothesis is the hypothesis that the researcher wishes to support.
4. The _____ hypothesis is the hypothesis that the researcher wishes to reject.
5. The null hypothesis and the research hypothesis are mutually _____ .
6. In an experiment the _____ variable is manipulated by the experimenter.
7. In an experiment the _____ variable is a measure of the subject's behavior.
8. An experimenter is studying the effect of parenting style on the emotional development of children, as measured by the emotional development rating scale. The independent variable is _____ , and the dependent variable is _____ .

Answers

1. a. 3.234
  b. 5.774
  c. 2345.238
  d. 219.333
  e. 0.336
2. hypothesis
3. research

4. null
5. exclusive
6. independent
7. dependent
8. parenting style; the score on the emotional development rating scale

SCALES OF MEASUREMENT

Because there are countless types of dependent variables, from heartbeats per minute to rankings of tennis players, all kinds of data can be collected to measure them. But no matter what data you collect, they will be recorded on one of four measurement scales: *nominal, ordinal, interval,* or *ratio*. These scales differ in complexity according to how the relationships are described between various points on the scales.

Nominal Scales of Measurement

Are you an introvert or an extrovert? Are you rich or poor? Are you tall or short? Do you have green, blue, or brown eyes? Is your hair black, brown, red, or yellow? Are you a Democrat, an Independent, or a Republican? Often we are placed or place ourselves in a particular category based on a name, a color, or a belief. When we collect data based on a name or a category, we are using a nominal scale of measurement.

A **nominal scale of measurement** is the simplest form of measurement and is used when the variable being measured (the dependent variable) is qualitative as opposed to quantitative. The word *nominal* means *name,* so when researchers use a nominal scale, they assign subjects to a category based on the name of some physical or psychological quality or characteristic, rather than some numerical score. In their study of the effect of television violence, for instance, Bandura and Walters could have used such categories as male/female, aggressive/passive, and tall/short. If they had used the passive/aggressive categories, they could have observed each child during the experiment and assigned him or her to either the passive or the aggressive category. Children with 3 or fewer aggressive acts could have been labeled passive, and those with more than 3 aggressive acts could have been labeled aggressive. Even if one child was only mildly aggressive (4 aggressive acts) and another was extremely aggressive (15 aggressive acts), both would have been assigned to the aggressive category. Countless other behavioral variables can be measured using a nominal scale. Examples are intellectual ability (above normal, normal, below normal) and personality type (introverted, extroverted).

The problem with a nominal scale of measurement is that it can't be used to record anything but qualitative comparisons. Knowing that a child is passive or aggressive does not allow us to make quantitative comparisons; if a child is passive, we don't know whether he or she is bordering on aggressive or near to vegetating. So you see that nominal scales of measurement allow for only the crudest types of comparisons among subjects. If more precision is needed, we must use a more accurate scale of measurement reflecting more quantitative comparisons. The ordinal scale is one of these.

Ordinal Scales of Measurement

Of the quantitative scales, the **ordinal scale of measurement** is the simplest. An ordinal scale requires that we order, or rank, the data from highest to lowest. This tells us whether any one subject ranks higher or lower than any other subject, although it does not tell us how much higher or lower. For example, we could rank all the children who participated in the Bandura and Walters experiment according to the aggressiveness of their behavior after viewing the film. The most aggressive child might get a rank of 7, the next most aggressive a rank of 6, and so on.

Ordinal scales of measurement show relative rankings but reveal nothing about the extent of the differences between the rankings. Equal distances on an ordinal scale do not necessarily represent equal differences between the subjects' qualities. Using an ordinal scale of measurement, we can tell that a child with a rank of 7 is more aggressive than one with a rank of 5, but we cannot determine the difference in the degrees of aggressiveness between the two children. The change in aggressiveness between a child with a rank of 1 and a child with a rank of 2 is not necessarily the same as the change between a child with the rank of 3 and a child with a rank of 4. For more distinct comparisons, we need to use an interval scale of measurement.

Interval Scales of Measurement

An **interval scale of measurement** indicates not only relative ranks of scores but also equal distances or degrees of difference between the scores. Thus, the distance between scores of 1 and 2 is the same as the distance between scores of 3 and 4. For example, Bandura and Walters might have asked their assistants to use an interval scale to rate the aggressiveness of the children that ranged from 1 (least aggressive) to 7 (most aggressive). Had they done so, they would have made sure that the difference in aggressiveness between scores of, say, 1 and 2 was equal to the difference between scores of 4 and 5. In another example, IQ scores compare the intellectual attributes of different people on an interval scale. The distance on a common IQ scale between scores of 110 and 120 is presumed to equal the distance between scores of 80 and 90. Quantitative comparisons can readily be made using an interval scale. Differences between any two subjects are in standard increments, so if on a scale of 1 to 7 one child is rated a 6 in aggressiveness, we know that he or she is just as close to the "most aggressive" rating as another child rated a 2 is to the "least aggressive" rating.

The major disadvantage of the interval scale is that it does not allow us to make ratio types of comparisons. We cannot say that a child who is rated as a 3 in aggressiveness is half as aggressive as a child rated 6, or that a person who has an IQ of 160 has twice the intellectual ability as a person who has an IQ of 80. This difficulty arises because interval scales of measurement have no real, meaningful zero point. In the case of the aggressiveness ratings, it is impossible to set a meaningful zero point: Everyone is capable of at least a mild amount of aggression. Therefore, a rating of zero is not meaningful. Likewise, it is impossible for a person to have an IQ of zero. A ratio scale enables us to make ratio types of comparisons.

Ratio Scales of Measurement

A **ratio scale of measurement** has all the properties of the scales just mentioned, but in addition it has a meaningful zero point—a point at which there is a total absence of the variable being measured. This meaningful zero point makes ratio comparisons possible. If we were to record the number of aggressive acts performed by each child in the Bandura and Walters experiment, we would be using a ratio measurement scale. A child who exhibits ten aggressive acts performs twice as many as a child who exhibits only five. This makes sense because there is a base point, zero, at which no aggressive acts are performed.

Although most of the examples in this book use interval scales or ratio scales of measurement, it is extremely important in the real world of research to be able to identify the measurement scale being used. This is because nominal and ordinal scales require different types of statistical analyses than do interval and ratio scales of measurement. Chapter 15, on nonparametric statistics, is devoted to the analysis of nominal and ordinal data sets.

POPULATIONS AND SAMPLES

No matter what scale is used, they all offer a way of measuring some type of behavior. In most cases a single piece of data represents some behavior or characteristic about an individual person or animal. Although it is sometimes intriguing to know how one particular person behaves in a certain situation, the purpose of psychological inquiry is to determine how *everyone* should behave in that situation. When we speak of everyone, we are referring to all the people in a certain population. A **population** includes *all* members of a certain group. It may be large or small, but it must contain all the members of a defined group. All the people in the world make up a population. All the people in the United States of America are a population. All the people in California, all the people in San Diego County, all the psychology students who attend the University of California at San Diego, all the psychology students who take psychological statistics at the University of California at San Diego—all groups, whether extremely large or relatively small—are separate populations. Most often, the attempt in psychology is to learn about the behavior of relatively large populations, such as all the people in the world, all the people in the United States, or at the very least, all the students in Introduction to Psychology courses in the United States. In statistical notation, a capital italic N is used to denote the number of members in a population.

When a population is large, it is difficult, perhaps even impossible, to measure everyone in that population. To illustrate, suppose we wanted to determine the average IQ of all the people in the United States. To do so, we would have to give an IQ test to all these people. Now, the population of the United States stands at more than 250 million people. (In statistical notation, $N = 250,000,000$.) How could we give a test to every one of these people? Assuming that we could locate the entire population, it would take years to administer the tests, even with the droves of helpers we'd have to hire. How much would all this cost? A *lot* of money!

Question: Couldn't you choose about a thousand people or so, measure their IQs, figure out their average IQ, and then project that average to the entire U.S. population?

Yes, we could, but keep in mind that if we did this, we would not be *measuring* the population; we would be *estimating* the population via a sample. A **sample** is a relatively small representative group selected from a population. The statistical notation for the number of subjects in a sample is a lowercase italic n. Quite often, researchers conduct their experiments with a smaller sample and then generalize their results to a larger population. We could certainly give an IQ test to perhaps a thousand people ($n = 1,000$) and use the average of this sample to estimate the average of the population. When it is too time-consuming or too expensive to collect information from the entire population, the only alternative is to select and measure a sample of the population and use that information to estimate population values.

Statistics that describe population values, such as the mean (average), are called **parameters.** Statistics collected from samples and used to describe population values are called **estimates.** As you work your way through this book, you will be taught how to compute both population parameters and population estimates. Obviously, parameters are more accurate than estimates; therefore, if you have access to both population parameters and population estimates, you should rely on the parameters to give you the most accurate view of the population.

Learning statistics is like learning to play the piano. Almost no one enjoys the initial lessons and the long hours of practice, but everyone appreciates the results. Knowing how to analyze and use statistics is a skill that will always be in demand. During your learning period, remember that when you have mastered the material in this book, you will possess fundamental skills that will serve you for the rest of your professional and personal life.

C O N C E P T   Q U I Z

1. Name the scale of measurement that the following data represent:
   a. the number of automobile accidents a driver has had in the last 10 years
   b. a student's academic rank
   c. whether a person is a Type A or a Type B personality
2. A _____ represents all members of a certain group.
3. A _____ is a small representative group selected from a population.
4. Statistics that describe population values are called _____ , and statistics that are used to describe population values from samples are called _____ .
5. N is the number of subjects in a _____ ; n is the number of subjects in a _____ .

Answers

1. a. ratio
   b. ordinal
   c. nominal
2. population

3. sample
4. parameters; estimates
5. population; sample

S U M M A R Y

Statistics is the branch of applied mathematics that uses numbers to describe and analyze data collected by researchers. Although beginning students are often apprehensive about the mathematics of statistics, anyone who has a solid knowledge of algebra should be successful in the study of statistics.

Behavioral Statistics in Action has been designed to help in your study of statistics. Chapter outlines give you a preview of the chapter, chapter openers show the interrelationship between statistics and experimental design, answers to student questions arise logically at certain points in the discussion, concept quizzes help review and reinforce critical concepts covered in the chapter, and chapter summaries like this one review the major mathematical and logical concepts covered in the chapter. Key terms and formulas that were mentioned in the chapter are listed after the summaries. Finally, each chapter ends with problems that help reinforce the content of the chapter.

Succeeding in statistics will require real effort on your part. You must attend all lectures, read the book, work as many problems as you can, and try to get a feel for the numbers that are generated using statistical procedures. If you are having difficulty, try to get help as soon as possible from your professor or a friend.

Psychological investigations begin with some kind of hypothesis. The research hypothesis expresses the proposition that the researcher wishes to prove true, whereas the null hypothesis usually states that the research will uncover no new findings. When designing an experiment, a researcher needs to identify the independent variable and the dependent variable. The independent variable is a factor selected and manipulated by the experimenter; it is independent of anything the subject does. The dependent variable is a measurable behavior exhibited by the subject. It is the dependent variable measurements that become the data for statistical analysis.

There are four types of measurement scales. A nominal scale of measurement involves assigning subjects to a category based on some physical or psychological assessment. The ordinal scale involves the ranking of data from highest to lowest. An interval scale guarantees equal distances between scores on the scale. Finally, a ratio scale has a meaningful zero point that allows ratio judgments between scores on the scale.

Most psychological investigation is performed to determine what behavior is typical for any particular population. A population consists of all the members of a particular group, whereas a sample is a relatively small representative group selected from a population. Statistical properties of populations are called parameters. Statistics collected from samples that are used to describe population values are called estimates.

KEY TERMS

statistics	variables
chapter outline	independent variable
chapter opener	dependent variable
student questions	extraneous variables
concept quizzes	nominal scale of measurement
chapter summary	ordinal scale of measurement
key terms	interval scale of measurement
formulas	ratio scale of measurement
problems	population
hypothesis	sample
research hypothesis	parameters
null hypothesis	estimates

PROBLEMS

Round off the numbers in Problems 1–5 to three digits to the right of the decimal point.

1. 23,456.5678

2. 890,765.24745

3. 0.2398

4. 2.99213544

5. 93,856.234566

Generate both a research hypothesis and a null hypothesis for the research described in Problems 6–10.

6. Suppose you are a psychologist studying how children acquire language, and you want to see whether a new teaching technique will help children learn faster.

7. You are a military psychologist assigned to test whether the job proficiency of National Guard soldiers is as high as that of soldiers in the regular army.

8. You are a health psychologist interested in knowing whether patients who have undergone knee surgery recover faster if they are released from the hospital 3 days after surgery rather than the customary 5 days.

9. You are the personnel director of a large multinational manufacturing company, and you are interested in measuring the relative effectiveness of two different management training programs.

10. You are a newlywed psychologist, and you are interested in studying the romantic differences between couples that are married and couples that are just living together.

Identify the independent and dependent variables in the experiments described in Problems 11–13.

11. A psychobiologist has two groups of identical nerve cells living in separate dishes. He proposes to apply different concentrations of a nerve-blocking agent to the groups of nerve cells and to measure any change in the number of action potentials (nerve impulses) generated.

12. A psychologist interested in the use of imagery in memory teaches one group of subjects to make mental images of things they are trying to remember. She compares their memories for a list of words to the memories of a group that does not receive imagery training.

13. A school psychologist for a large urban school district believes that temporary forced withdrawal of a student from school (suspension) is more effective than physical punishment in improving the behavior of a disruptive student. The school psychologist assigns 50 disruptive students to the suspension group and 50 disruptive students to the physical punishment group and then counts the number of disruptive acts the children exhibit on the 3 days following their return to the classroom.

Identify the examples in Problems 14–26 as representing the nominal, ordinal, interval, or ratio scales of measurement.

14. Reaction time

15. Skin temperature in degrees centigrade

16. The number of statistics questions answered correctly

17. Class rank

18. Position of a chicken in the current pecking order

19. The name of the EEG tracing exhibited by a sleeping patient (alpha, theta, delta, . . .)

20. The number of errors a rat makes while running a maze

21. The number of errors made on a color vision test

22. The total number of words recalled from a list

23. The number of stressful events you have experienced during the past 6 months

24. The rankings of the ten best movies of last year

25. The number of trials necessary for a pigeon to learn how to press a key

26. The number of people in your class who have red, blond, black, and brown hair

R E F E R E N C E

Bandura, A., & Walters, R. H. (1963). *Social learning and personality development.* New York: Holt, Rinehart & Winston.

Frequency Distributions

The Scholastic Aptitude Test, commonly called the SAT, is taken by most high school seniors who plan to enter a four-year college the following year. The test itself has become extremely controversial because certain subgroups of students tend to score higher on the test than other subgroups. For example, on the average, male students tend to score higher than female students. This can be a real problem because, when the SAT is used to rank students for college admission or for granting scholarships, these low-scoring subgroups are at an obvious disadvantage. Psychometrists, psychologists who specialize in testing and test construction, have recently revised the SAT to address this problem.

Let's say that you are helping to conduct a pilot study for the new SAT, which we'll call the SAT-R (Revised), and you are in charge of making some sense out of the data that others have gathered. You have been handed the list of test scores in Table 2.1. Take a look at the list, and then answer the following questions: Does looking at the table fill you with joyful anticipation for the task ahead of you? How many numbers are in the table? What do the numbers represent? Are there more numbers in the 500s or the 600s? What is the high score? The low score? Are you thinking about dropping this class and selling the book back to the bookstore? The answers to the preceding questions should be: not really; 100; scores from the Scholastic Aptitude Test-Revised; more in the 500s; 800; 219; and not just yet (please!).

Virtually no one would look at the unorganized list of numbers in Table 2.1 and experience any immediate sense of joy (except perhaps accountants and statisticians who are getting paid enormous salaries). The emotions experienced by most of us range from indifference to utter shock and panic. Long lists or large tables of numbers are often like lists of foreign words: They

Table 2.1 Scores from the Scholastic Aptitude Test-Revised (SAT-R), Verbal Subtest

540	432	345	673	740	444	456	732	665	442
437	498	510	522	734	614	623	413	719	750
523	479	463	390	440	457	392	498	685	631
463	442	505	621	577	554	623	444	345	300
496	345	675	620	744	790	562	441	497	472
521	533	667	532	578	599	621	429	468	542
554	476	766	721	645	298	277	346	499	512
512	297	479	505	401	622	771	702	621	234
443	345	489	592	523	532	578	606	432	654
219	800	245	776	523	550	492	472	561	552

have no meaning. And because they have no meaning, they are hard to understand and almost impossible to remember. Yet as a well-informed psychologist, teacher, sociologist, anthropologist, or whatever other professional you may become, you must be able to evaluate the results of any research study and make some sense of the data—in this case the seemingly endless list of SAT scores—collected during that study.

In this chapter, you will learn the basic methods used to decipher the jumble of raw data obtained from research studies, surveys, tests, or other measures employed in gathering information. The term **raw data** refers to scores or numbers that have been collected but not yet organized or summarized. In your role as a psychometrist, the first thing you should do is get a "feel" for the data. The way to do this is to *organize* the raw data in some meaningful way.

Question: But how do I go about organizing such a long list of numbers?

RANKED DISTRIBUTIONS

You need to create a **ranked distribution** by ordering the scores—simply rearranging or listing the data so that the highest number is at the top of the list and the lowest number is at the bottom. Your ranked distribution of the SAT-R scores should look like Table 2.2, which shows an ordered distribution of the same data that appear in Table 2.1. Now it's easier to answer such questions as: What are the highest and lowest scores? and Are there more

Table 2.2   Ranked Distribution of the SAT-R Scores in Table 2.1

800	721	631	599	550	521	496	463	437	345
790	719	623	592	542	512	492	457	432	345
776	702	623	578	540	512	489	456	432	345
771	685	622	578	533	510	479	444	429	300
766	675	621	577	532	505	479	444	413	298
750	673	621	562	532	505	476	443	401	297
744	667	621	561	523	499	472	442	392	277
740	665	620	554	523	498	472	442	390	245
734	654	614	554	523	498	468	441	346	234
732	645	606	552	522	497	463	440	345	219

scores in the 500s or 600s? However, a listing of 100 numbers is still difficult for most people to interpret at a glance. For instance, without actually counting, can you tell whether more students scored in the lower or in the upper 500s? (It's hard, isn't it?) Thus, there is another tool in the organization and summary of large amounts of data: the frequency distribution.

FREQUENCY DISTRIBUTIONS

Simple frequency distributions are created by listing all the possible score values in any distribution and then indicating the frequency (how often each score occurs). Your instructors have probably drawn frequency distributions on the board after exams to show the distributions of grades, like the one in Table 2.3.

Table 2.3 Frequency Distribution of Grades on a Test

Grade	Score	Frequency
	95	1
	93	1
A	92	4
	91	2
	90	4
	89	2
	87	2
B	86	3
	84	4
	82	1
	80	1
	79	3
	78	3
	77	4
C	74	6
	73	7
	72	3
	71	4
	68	2
D	64	1
	63	1
	62	1

As you see, the number of people who received each score (the **frequency**) is listed after the actual score. Scores that are not listed are assumed to have a zero frequency; in other words, it is assumed that no one received those scores. Clearly, it's much easier to find out how well you did on an exam by looking at a frequency distribution than by looking at a long list of raw data. However, if you were to make a frequency distribution of the 100 SAT-R scores in Table 2.1, it would be more than two pages long. As such, it might be just as hard to read as the ranked distribution because nearly every score is unique and occurs only one time (has a frequency of 1). Frequency distributions are useful only if they simplify the data; when they don't simplify the data because of the high number of unique scores, it's a good idea to generate *grouped* frequency distributions.

GROUPED FREQUENCY DISTRIBUTIONS

In a **grouped frequency distribution,** the raw data are combined into equal-sized groups called **class intervals.** Table 2.4 is a grouped frequency distribution of the SAT-R scores in which the 100 scores have been grouped into 13

Table 2.4 Grouped Frequency Distribution of the SAT-R Scores in Table 2.1

Class interval	Frequency
800–849	1
750–799	5
700–749	7
650–699	6
600–649	11
550–599	11
500–549	15
450–499	17
400–449	13
350–399	2
300–349	6
250–299	3
200–249	3

class intervals. When the raw data are summarized in this way, it is easy to see that most of the scores fall between 400 and 600, with the middle of the distribution near 500. Grouped frequency distributions, therefore, can be quite useful in "getting the whole picture" at a glance, which is your goal with the scores from the revised SAT.

Question: You've convinced me, but how do I go about devising a grouped frequency distribution?

Constructing the Class Intervals: How Big and How Many?

The first thing to do is determine the number of intervals needed and the size of the class intervals. Your selection of the former has a direct effect on the latter, and both are related to the range of scores in the raw data. Before making your choices, you must compute the **range,** the full extent of scores from the highest score to the lowest score. The range is computed by subtracting the low score from the high score and adding 1:

$$\text{Range} = \text{high score} - \text{low score} + 1 \tag{2.1}$$
$$\text{Range} = 800 - 219 + 1$$
$$= 581 + 1$$
$$= 582$$

Question: Why do you have to add a 1 to the difference between the high and the low scores?

You have to add a 1 because both the high and the low scores need to be *included* in the range. For example, $4 - 2 = 2$, but if you want to include both 4 and 2 in the range so that all the scores (4, 3, and 2) are counted, then the formula must account for this: $4 - 2 + 1 = 3$.

Having computed the range, you can now select an interval size. Over the years our experience on hundreds of different data sets has shown that it is best to choose an interval size that produces between 10 and 20 intervals. Fewer than 10 intervals result in a loss of information about the original raw data; more than 20 make it difficult to readily comprehend the information. The following two formulas show how to compute the interval size and the number of intervals, where the interval size is represented by i:

$$i \approx \frac{\text{range}}{\text{number of intervals}} \tag{2.2}$$

$$\text{Number of intervals} \approx \frac{\text{range}}{i} \tag{2.3}$$

The squiggly equals sign ($\approx$) means "approximately equals." If you use Formula 2.2 to compute i, you often have to round off the result to a more appropriate number before constructing the grouped frequency distribution. If the range of the raw data in Table 2.1 is 582, and if you decide to have about 12 intervals, you need to make the following calculation:

$$i \approx \frac{582}{12} \approx 48.5$$

Because people generally feel more comfortable working with the number 50 than with 48.5 or 49, you would probably choose 50 for your interval size. It is your choice to round your computed i up or down to a more appropriate interval size. Rounding up leads to fewer intervals than predicted by Formula 2.3, whereas rounding down leads to more intervals. In general, it is best to use numbers such as 2, 5, 10, 25, 50, or 100 if they are appropriate for the interval size because they are easy for most people to count by. It's easier for you to create the frequency distribution with numbers such as these.

To determine the interval numbers and sizes for the SAT-R scores, you might try an interval size of 50 to see whether it leads to between 10 and 20 intervals. Using Formula 2.3, we have:

$$\text{Number of intervals} \approx \frac{582}{50} \approx 11.64$$

Because it is impossible to have a fractional interval, you will have at least 12 intervals. If you look at Table 2.4 and count the number of intervals, you will find that using 50 as an interval size actually produces 13 intervals rather than 12. (Keep in mind that these formulas are rules of thumb or approximations only; the actual number of intervals will depend on where the intervals start and the actual beginning and ending raw scores.) After selecting the interval size, you can begin to construct the class intervals.

Constructing the Class Intervals and Determining Frequency: Setting Limits and Counting Raw Scores

Each class interval is represented by a lower limit and an upper limit. Looking at Table 2.4, you can see that the first column of numbers is labeled "class interval." The lower limit of the top interval is 800; the upper limit of the top interval is 849. Because each class interval is the same size (50), the top interval is constructed so that it contains the highest score in the distribution (800), and the bottom interval contains the lowest score (219).

It is usually best to establish a lower limit that is a multiple of the interval size because this makes the table easier to understand and often simplifies its construction. For instance, because $i = 50$, each lower limit should be a multiple of 50. The choices for lower limits, then, are 0, 50, 100, 150, 200, and so on. If we had selected 25 for an interval size, the choices for lower limits would have been 0, 25, 50, 75, and so on.

After the class intervals have been constructed, the frequency for each interval needs to be counted. To do this, we tally how many raw scores fall within the limits of each interval. Then we count the tallies and record the frequency, or the number of scores, for each interval, as shown in Table 2.4.

To illustrate the entire process of organizing raw data into class intervals, let's use another example. Suppose you invented a driving simulator that enables you to study simple reaction time. A television monitor displays a toddler dashing into the middle of the street; then the simulator measures the amount of time that elapses between the instant the child is first shown on the screen and the point when a driver slams his or her foot on the brake. You recruit 150 Introductory Psychology students to participate in the study. The fastest student responds in 182 milliseconds and the slowest in 433 milliseconds.

In constructing a grouped frequency distribution of these scores, you need to decide what interval size to use and how many class intervals there should be. What do you need to do first? (Try to remember; then read on.) You need to compute the range:

$$
\begin{aligned}
\text{Range} &= \text{high score} - \text{low score} + 1 \\
&= 433 - 182 + 1 \\
&= 252
\end{aligned}
$$

Now use either Formula 2.2 or 2.3 to select the interval size. If you want about ten intervals, then, from Formula 2.2,

$$
i \approx \frac{\text{range}}{\text{number of intervals}} \approx \frac{252}{10} \approx 25.2
$$

Thus an interval size of 25 will produce about ten intervals. Remembering that the lower limit of each interval must be a multiple of 25, you can begin to construct the class intervals. The top interval must contain the highest score in the distribution, which is 433; therefore, the highest interval will be 425–449. Each succeeding lower interval will have a lower limit that is 25 milliseconds less than that of the preceding interval. Now that you have determined the intervals, you are ready to tally the raw scores that fall within each interval and to record the frequency next to each interval. Your frequency distribution ends up looking like Table 2.5.

Before we move on to the next section, we would like to emphasize the advantage of choosing an interval size that is easy to work with. It is easier to work with an interval size of 25 or 50 than with an interval size of 27 or 43. Make it easier on yourself and choose an interval size that makes sense and is easy to work with.

Table 2.5 Frequency Distribution for the Driving Simulator Data

Class interval	Frequency
425–449	5
400–424	11
375–399	7
350–374	15
325–349	6
300–324	32
275–299	24
250–274	21
225–249	17
200–224	9
175–199	3

APPARENT LIMITS AND REAL LIMITS: WHAT YOU SEE VERSUS WHAT IS MEANT

Question: In the list of class intervals in Table 2.5, it looks as if the limits don't include all possible scores. For instance, where would I put a time like 274.8 milliseconds?

If this were a real experiment, you would not obtain a score of 274.8 milliseconds because the upper and lower limits are listed in the actual measurements, which in this case are whole milliseconds. But if there were a time of 274.8 milliseconds, it would fall in the interval 275–299. The limits normally listed are called **apparent limits,** which are in the same units as the original data. However, each interval *really* extends from 0.5 unit below the lower apparent limit to 0.5 unit above the upper apparent limit. Thus, the **real limits** are the lower apparent limit minus 0.5 unit and the upper apparent limit plus 0.5 unit. Table 2.6 shows the grouped frequency distribution for the 100 SAT-R scores, with both the real and the apparent limits listed for each class interval. After examining the table, can you tell where a score of 499.3 would be placed? In the interval with apparent limits of 450–499. The real limits for the driving simulator reaction time data are computed as shown in Table 2.7. A reaction time of 224.9 milliseconds belongs in the interval with the apparent limits of 225–249.

Table 2.6 Grouped Frequency Distribution of SAT-R Scores Showing Real Limits and Apparent Limits

Real limits	Apparent limits	Frequency
799.5–849.5	800–849	1
749.5–799.5	750–799	5
699.5–749.5	700–749	7
649.5–699.5	650–699	6
599.5–649.5	600–649	11
549.5–599.5	550–599	11
499.5–549.5	500–549	15
449.5–499.5	450–499	17
399.5–449.5	400–449	13
349.5–399.5	350–399	2
299.5–349.5	300–349	6
249.5–299.5	250–299	3
199.5–249.5	200–249	3

Table 2.7 Real and Apparent Limits for the Driving Simulator Data

Real limits	Apparent limits
424.5–449.5	425–449
399.5–424.5	400–424
374.5–399.5	375–399
349.5–374.5	350–374
324.5–349.5	325–349
299.5–324.5	300–324
274.5–299.5	275–299
249.5–274.5	250–274
224.5–249.5	225–249
199.5–224.5	200–224
174.5–199.5	175–199

Although grouped frequency distributions are helpful, they do have one major limitation: They are only a *summary* of the raw data. As you can see in Table 2.4 or Table 2.6, there are 17 scores in the class interval 450–499, but the precise scores are not listed, so all 17 scores could be in the 450s, all in the 490s, or all spread evenly throughout the entire interval. The only accurate way of knowing how the scores are actually distributed is by examining the raw data. If the raw data are not available, then one recourse is to specify the center of the interval to represent all the scores in that interval.

MIDPOINT: THE CENTER OF THE INTERVAL

The exact center of an interval is called its **midpoint.** The midpoint is easy to calculate because it is merely the average of the lower and the upper limits of the interval:

$$\text{Midpoint} = \frac{\text{lower limit} + \text{upper limit}}{2} \tag{2.4}$$

No matter whether the apparent or the real limits are summed, they both add up to the same number. Table 2.8 shows a grouped frequency distribution of

Table 2.8   Grouped Frequency Distribution of SAT-R Scores Showing the Midpoint of Each Interval

Real limits	Apparent limits	Frequency	Midpoint
799.5–849.5	800–849	1	824.5
749.5–799.5	750–799	5	774.5
699.5–749.5	700–749	7	724.5
649.5–699.5	650–699	6	674.5
599.5–649.5	600–649	11	624.5
549.5–599.5	550–599	11	574.5
499.5–549.5	500–549	15	524.5
449.5–499.5	450–499	17	474.5
399.5–449.5	400–449	13	424.5
349.5–399.5	350–399	2	374.5
299.5–349.5	300–349	6	324.5
249.5–299.5	250–299	3	274.5
199.5–249.5	200–249	3	224.5

Table 2.9 Real and Apparent Limits and Midpoints for the Driving Simulator Data

Real limits	Apparent limits	Midpoint
424.5–449.5	425–449	437
399.5–424.5	400–424	412
374.5–399.5	375–399	387
349.5–374.5	350–374	362
324.5–349.5	325–349	337
299.5–324.5	300–324	312
274.5–299.5	275–299	287
249.5–274.5	250–274	262
224.5–249.5	225–249	237
199.5–224.5	200–224	212
174.5–199.5	175–199	187

the SAT-R scores with the midpoint calculated for each interval. Note that all the midpoints end in .5. When the interval size (i) is even, the midpoints end in .5. To avoid this, you can select an odd interval size, such as 25, as we did with the scores from the driving simulator study in Table 2.9.

If you wish to avoid fractional midpoints, you must select an interval size that is an odd number (e.g., 3, 5, 25) if it is appropriate for your particular data. But remember, it is most important to choose an interval size that is easy to work with. If you have to choose between interval sizes of 20 and 25, then 25 is the logical choice because, as well as being easy to work with, it is odd. But if you must choose between interval sizes of 45 and 50, then choose 50 because it is much easier to work with—everyone is much more familiar with multiples of 50 than with multiples of 45. Don't choose an interval size just because it is odd.

CONCEPT QUIZ

1. Unorganized data collected from an experiment or research project are called _____ data.
2. A listing of all the possible scores in a distribution is called a _____ distribution.
3. In a grouped frequency distribution, the raw data are combined into groups called _____ .

4. Before you choose the number and size of the class intervals, you must compute the _____ .

5. If the high score in a distribution is 231 and the low score is 54, what is the range?

6. If a distribution has a range equal to 250, what interval size gives approximately ten intervals?

7. Suppose you have a distribution with a range equal to 300. Approximately how many class intervals will there be if you choose an interval size equal to 20?

8. Grouped frequency distribution tables are easier to understand if the lower limit of each class interval is a multiple of the _____ .

9. The top class interval must contain the _____ score in the distribution; the bottom class interval must contain the _____ score in the distribution.

10. If you have a distribution in which the lowest score is 27 and you have chosen to use 4 as the interval size, what should be the lower limit of your lowest interval?

11. In a grouped frequency distribution, the _____ limits are equal to the _____ limits plus or minus 0.5 unit.

12. The real limits of a class interval with apparent limits of 321–323 are _____ – _____ .

13. The midpoint of the class interval 321–323 is equal to _____ .

Answers

1. raw		**8.** interval size	
2. frequency		**9.** highest; lowest	
3. class intervals		**10.** 24	
4. range		**11.** real; apparent	
5. 178		**12.** 320.5–323.5	
6. 25		**13.** 322	
7. 15			

At this point, you should know how to construct a frequency distribution, and you should be able to recognize its basic merit: the organization of data (scores, reaction times, and so on) so that you can readily observe their frequency. In addition, you can acquire other quite helpful information from a frequency distribution: cumulative frequency, relative frequency, cumulative relative frequency, and cumulative percent.

CUMULATIVE FREQUENCY

Frequency, as we have explained, is the total number of scores that fall within a class interval. **Cumulative frequency** is the total number of scores that fall *below* the upper real limit of an interval. It can be particularly helpful when

Table 2.10 Grouped Frequency Distribution of SAT-R Scores Showing Cumulative Frequency

Real limits	Apparent limits	Frequency	Cumulative frequency
799.5–849.5	800–849	1	100
749.5–799.5	750–799	5	99
699.5–749.5	700–749	7	94
649.5–699.5	650–699	6	87
599.5–649.5	600–649	11	81
549.5–599.5	550–599	11	70
499.5–549.5	500–549	15	59
449.5–499.5	450–499	17	44
399.5–449.5	400–449	13	27
349.5–399.5	350–399	2	14
299.5–349.5	300–349	6	12
249.5–299.5	250–299	3	6
199.5–249.5	200–249	3	3

you need to know how many scores in a distribution happen to fall below a particular score.

Question: Why would anyone ever need to know this?

Let's imagine that you are a school counselor. At your school there is a special program called SMART (Students with Magnificently Astute Rare Talents) to which only a small, academically elite group of students who score 700 or higher on the SAT may belong. As a counselor, you want to establish a similar program for the remainder of the students—those who score below 700 on the SAT. You plan to call the second program SMART 2B (Students with Magnificently Astute Rare Talents who need 2 Be stimulated). The first step in setting up the program is to determine how many students are eligible, which you can do by calculating the cumulative frequencies of the SAT-R scores, as shown in Table 2.10. (Remember that the cumulative frequency is the total number of scores below the upper real limit of the interval.) You find that 87 out of 100 students scored below 700 and are thus eligible for SMART 2B.

At times, circumstances arise when people would like to compare the frequencies in one distribution with those in another. Such a comparison is valid only when the number and the range of scores in both distributions are the same. If the number of scores is different, it is necessary to compute *relative frequency* or *cumulative relative frequency* to make the comparison.

Question: I don't understand why you can't just make direct comparisons among grouped frequency distributions.

RELATIVE FREQUENCY AND CUMULATIVE RELATIVE FREQUENCY

Imagine that, in an analysis of the SAT-R, you want to compare scores from your pilot study, involving 100 high school seniors, with data from an all-girls' school with 450 seniors. Although the range of scores in the two distributions is similar, the total numbers of scores are quite different; thus, any differences between frequencies may be due to the different sizes of the samples. In order to make a meaningful comparison, you need to convert all frequencies to **relative frequency,** which is the *proportion* of scores from the distribution that fall within the real limits of an interval. Relative frequency is computed simply by dividing the frequency in the interval by the total number of scores in the distribution. Because frequency distributions are almost always created from samples, the total number of scores in the distribution is denoted by n.

$$\text{Relative frequency} = \frac{\text{frequency}}{n} \tag{2.5}$$

For example, the relative frequency for the interval 500–549 in Table 2.6 is computed as follows:

$$\text{Relative frequency} = \frac{\text{frequency}}{n} = \frac{15}{100} = .15$$

It may help you to comprehend relative frequency as a *proportion* of the scores if you keep in mind that relative frequency is much like a percentage. The difference is that when denoting a percentage, we go one step further and multiply by 100. For instance, in the preceding example we would multiply .15 by 100 to get a percentage of 15%, as opposed to the relative frequency of .15. If you take a moment to consider this idea, you'll see that a percentage *is* a proportion: 15% of all the scores means 15 scores per 100 scores. Relative frequency is merely expressed differently—in terms of hundredths: .15 of all the scores.

To compare the SAT-R scores of the students in the girls' school with those in your pilot study, you need to calculate the relative frequency for each group. (You don't really have to do this; it has been done for you in Tables 2.11 and 2.12.) Even though the relative frequency distributions are not

Table 2.11 Grouped Frequency Distribution of SAT-R Scores for Pilot Group Showing Relative Frequency

Real limits	Apparent limits	Frequency	Relative frequency
799.5–849.5	800–849	1	.01
749.5–799.5	750–799	5	.05
699.5–749.5	700–749	7	.07
649.5–699.5	650–699	6	.06
599.5–649.5	600–649	11	.11
549.5–599.5	550–599	11	.11
499.5–549.5	500–549	15	.15
449.5–499.5	450–499	17	.17
399.5–449.5	400–449	13	.13
349.5–399.5	350–399	2	.02
299.5–349.5	300–349	6	.06
249.5–299.5	250–299	3	.03
199.5–249.5	200–249	3	.03

Table 2.12 Grouped Frequency Distribution of SAT-R Scores for 450 Girls' School Seniors Showing Relative Frequency

Real limits	Apparent limits	Frequency	Relative frequency
799.5–849.5	800–849	7	.02
749.5–799.5	750–799	22	.05
699.5–749.5	700–749	30	.07
649.5–699.5	650–699	26	.06
599.5–649.5	600–649	45	.10
549.5–599.5	550–599	53	.12
499.5–549.5	500–549	66	.15
449.5–499.5	450–499	75	.17
399.5–449.5	400–449	50	.11
349.5–399.5	350–399	20	.04
299.5–349.5	300–349	27	.06
249.5–299.5	250–299	20	.04
199.5–249.5	200–249	9	.02

Table 2.13 Grouped Frequency Distribution of SAT-R Scores for the Pilot Group Showing Cumulative Relative Frequency

Real limits	Apparent limits	Frequency	Cumulative frequency	Relative frequency	Cumulative relative frequency
799.5–849.5	800–849	1	100	.01	1.00
749.5–799.5	750–799	5	99	.05	.99
699.5–749.5	700–749	7	94	.07	.94
649.5–699.5	650–699	6	87	.06	.87
599.5–649.5	600–649	11	81	.11	.81
549.5–599.5	550–599	11	70	.11	.70
499.5–549.5	500–549	15	59	.15	.59
449.5–499.5	450–499	17	44	.17	.44
399.5–449.5	400–449	13	27	.13	.27
349.5–399.5	350–399	2	14	.02	.14
299.5–349.5	300–349	6	12	.06	.12
249.5–299.5	250–299	3	6	.03	.06
199.5–249.5	200–249	3	3	.03	.03

Table 2.14 Grouped Frequency Distribution of SAT-R Scores for 450 Girls' School Seniors Showing Cumulative Relative Frequency

Real limits	Apparent limits	Frequency	Cumulative frequency	Relative frequency	Cumulative relative frequency
799.5–849.5	800–849	7	450	.02	1.00
749.5–799.5	750–799	22	443	.05	.99
699.5–749.5	700–749	30	421	.07	.94
649.5–699.5	650–699	26	391	.06	.87
599.5–649.5	600–649	45	365	.10	.81
549.5–599.5	550–599	53	320	.12	.71
499.5–549.5	500–549	66	267	.15	.59
449.5–499.5	450–499	75	201	.17	.45
399.5–449.5	400–449	50	126	.11	.28
349.5–399.5	350–399	20	76	.04	.17
299.5–349.5	300–349	27	56	.06	.12
249.5–299.5	250–299	20	29	.04	.06
199.5–249.5	200–249	9	9	.02	.02

identical, you can draw meaningful comparisons from the corresponding intervals in each distribution.

> **Question:** Is there some simple check to determine if I have calculated the relative frequencies correctly?

There is no way to determine if each of the individual relative frequencies is correct, short of recalculating each one a second time. But you can check to see if there is a major error by adding all the relative frequencies. The sum of the relative frequencies should equal 1.00. If you take a few seconds to add the relative frequency column in Table 2.11, you will find that the sum is indeed 1.00. Now sum the relative frequencies for Table 2.12. What is your sum? When we did the calculation we computed a sum of 1.01. This is not exactly 1.00: the sum of 1.01 is due to roundoff error. Don't be surprised if the sum of the relative frequencies is off by a hundredth or a few thousandths; small roundoff errors are unavoidable. But if the sum of the relative frequencies is a few hundredths above or below 1.00, you will need to recheck your calculations to find your error.

If the SMART 2B program were available to the pilot group as well as to the girls' school group, you could calculate the *cumulative relative frequency* to find the cutoff point for qualified students in each group. **Cumulative relative frequency** is the total proportion of scores that lie below the real upper limit of the interval. The formula follows:

$$\text{Cumulative relative frequency} = \frac{CF}{n} \qquad (2.6)$$

Cumulative relative frequencies for the girls' school students and for the pilot group are shown in Tables 2.13 and 2.14, where you can see that .87 of the students in both groups scored below 700 (699 or below). To indicate the percentage of students involved, you can multiply the cumulative relative frequency by 100 and thereby determine what is known as the **cumulative percent,** or the *percentile.* As you may have deduced from this example, both cumulative frequency and cumulative relative frequency are particularly useful when trying to determine some type of cutoff score.

C O N C E P T   Q U I Z

1. Cumulative frequency is the total number of scores that fall _____ the _____ real limit of an interval.

2. The proportion of scores from the distribution that fall within the real limits of an interval is called the _____ frequency.

3. The total proportion of scores that lie below the upper real limit of the interval is called the cumulative _____ frequency.

4. _____ frequency is most likely to be used to compare two separate distributions with different numbers of subjects.

5. _____ frequency tells you how many subjects in your distribution scored below the upper real limit of a particular class interval.

6. To find the percentage of subjects scoring below the upper real limit of a class interval, you need to compute the _____ .

Answers

1. below; upper

2. relative

3. relative

4. Relative

5. Cumulative

6. cumulative percent

S U M M A R Y

In statistics, we often encounter sizable amounts of raw data that need to be summarized. The first step in summarizing raw data is to create a ranked distribution where all the scores are arranged in ranked order from highest to lowest. The next step is to create a frequency distribution. In a frequency distribution, each score that occurs is represented along with its frequency, which tells how often that score occurs. In some cases a frequency distribution can adequately summarize and simplify the raw data; however, often it can be nearly as confusing as the raw data themselves. If the data need to be simplified further, a grouped frequency distribution should be created.

In a grouped frequency distribution, the raw data are represented by the number of scores that fall within a set of class intervals. Each class interval has an upper and a lower limit, and the number of scores (frequency) that fall within that interval is listed in a column alongside the class intervals. Each interval has an upper and a lower apparent limit and an upper and a lower real limit. The apparent limits are listed in the same units as the original data, whereas the upper real limit is 0.5 unit above the upper apparent limit and the lower real limit is 0.5 unit below the lower apparent limit.

The size of the class interval (i) is selected so that the total number of intervals is between 10 and 20. The number of intervals can be estimated by dividing the range by the interval size. The lower apparent limit of each class interval should be a multiple of i. In choosing an interval size, you will find it is often best to select an odd number (if that is appropriate to your data) because an even interval size results in fractional midpoints. Always select an interval size that is easy for you to work with, however.

Once the intervals have been constructed, the frequency of each interval

should be computed by tallying how ma[...]
within the limits of each class interval. A[...]
cumulative frequency, relative frequency, cum[...]
midpoint for each interval.

Cumulative frequency is the total number of sco[...]
that fall below the real upper limit of the interval. Re[...]
proportion of scores that fall in an interval and can be co[...]
the frequency by the total number of scores in the inte[...]
relative frequency is the total proportion of scores that fall [...]
upper limit of the interval. It can be computed by dividing the[...]
frequency by the total number of scores. Cumulative percent (the p[...]
of the scores that fall below the exact upper limit of the interval)[...]
cumulative relative frequency times 100.

KEY TERMS

raw data	apparent limits
ranked distribution	real limits
simple frequency distribution	midpoint
frequency	cumulative frequency
grouped frequency distribution	relative frequency
class intervals	cumulative relative frequency
range	cumulative percent

FORMULAS

$$\text{Range} = \text{high score} - \text{low score} + 1 \tag{2.1}$$

$$i \approx \frac{\text{range}}{\text{number of intervals}} \tag{2.2}$$

$$\text{Number of intervals} \approx \frac{\text{range}}{i} \tag{2.3}$$

$$\text{Midpoint} = \frac{\text{lower limit} + \text{upper limit}}{2} \tag{2.4}$$

$$\text{Relative frequency} = \frac{\text{frequency}}{n} \tag{2.5}$$

$$\text{Cumulative relative frequency} = \frac{CF}{n} \tag{2.6}$$

ny scores in the raw distribution fall

this point, we can compute the

ulative relative frequency, and

res in the raw distribution

lative frequency is the

mputed by dividing

val. Cumulative

below the real

cumulative

rcentage

is the

| | | 16 | 18 | 0 | 2 | 4 |
| 7 | 2 | 13 | 21 | 16 | 6 | 5 | 6 | 7 | 8 |

3. The IQ scores of students at Random High School range from a low of 72 to a high of 151. What interval size will produce approximately ten intervals?

4. A cognitive psychologist was interested in the time it took people to rotate a complex object in their minds. She presented each of her subjects with an object. After a brief inspection period, she presented another object and asked whether it was a different object or the same object rotated in space. She recorded the reaction time for each subject and found a low of 235 milliseconds and a high of 623 milliseconds. Approximately how many intervals would she obtain if she decided to make a grouped frequency distribution with each of the following interval sizes:

a. 35

b. 15

c. 20

d. 33

e. 25

f. 40

5. A clinical psychologist recorded the number of negative statements made during 1-hour conversations with 45 people who were depressed. The raw data follow. Create a grouped frequency distribution using 3 as the interval size. Make sure your table includes the real limits, apparent limits, and frequency for each class interval.

```
 3 21 19  7 21 11 12 15 16 11  9  3
 1 12 29 16 28 13 25 18  9  1 29 32
18  6 19 22 19 14 21  4 29 31  2  8
15 19 22 25 31 22 29 14 13
```

6. A sociologist recruited 60 people for a study on personal space, which is the amount of space people need between themselves and others in order to feel comfortable. He asked each person to tell him when to stop as he walked toward him or her. The distances, in centimeters, at which he stopped follow. Generate a frequency distribution with 12 intervals that includes the real limits, apparent limits, frequency, midpoint, cumulative frequency, relative frequency, and cumulative relative frequency for each class interval.

```
116 100 97 85 72 69 54 50 44 37 21 14
114 100 95 85 71 68 52 50 41 34 19 14
112 100 92 84 71 64 52 47 40 33 17 12
106  98 90 81 70 60 52 46 39 27 15 10
103  97 87 74 69 57 51 45 38 24 15  9
```

7. A neuropsychologist was testing the safety of a new drug by injecting it into 40 rats and then measuring their average heart rates over the next hour. Using the heart rates listed here, generate a grouped frequency distribution with 15 intervals. Make sure you include the real limits, apparent limits, frequency, cumulative frequency, relative frequency, cumulative relative frequency, and midpoint for each interval.

```
229 220 210 195 184 176 170 164 160 157
228 217 207 193 182 176 169 162 159 157
222 214 201 190 181 174 165 161 159 156
221 210 198 184 180 173 164 161 158 155
```

8. If the high score in a distribution is 289 and the low score is 16, what is the range?

9. If the high score in a distribution of IQ scores is 147 and the low score is 65, compute the range, choose an appropriate interval size, and create the apparent limits of the class intervals of a grouped frequency distribution that could be used to represent these scores.

10. A developmental psychologist studying nail-biting behavior in small children counted the number of times each child placed at least one finger in his or her mouth. Use the following data to create a grouped frequency distribution, including real limits, apparent limits, frequency, cumulative frequency, relative frequency, and cumulative relative frequency.

```
22 10 23 46 34 56 78 79 98 34 56 10
98 65 23 34 23 34 56 32 96 29 93 83
84 34 56 17 13 14 56 25 29 34 56 67
83 24 45 89 84 88 77 92 23
```

11. If the high score in a distribution is 89 and the low score is 16, what is the range?

12. If the range of a distribution of scores is 275, list all possible interval sizes that will result in no fewer than 10 intervals and no more than 20 intervals.

13. A child psychologist was studying the aggressive behavior of 30 3-year-olds by counting the number of aggressive acts they displayed over a 2-week period. The results of her research follow. Use these data to create a frequency distribution with 7 as the interval size. Include in your frequency distribution the real limits, apparent limits, frequency, and relative frequency.

```
23 36 36 38 43 56 56 56 57 58
59 59 60 65 66 68 70 77 78 80
86 89 90 91 93 97 98 106 113 122
```

14. Another child psychologist was also studying the aggressive behavior of 3-year-olds, but he observed only 25 children. With the following data, create a frequency distribution using 7 as the interval size. Be sure to include the real limits, apparent limits, frequency, and relative frequency.

```
28 29 30 33 34 36 45 46 46
48 50 51 53 53 61 75 79 83
89 93 103 104 107 108 117
```

15. Problems 13 and 14 are both based on research projects studying aggressive behavior in children. If the two distributions have different numbers of children, how can you compare the two studies? What can you conclude from this comparison?

16. A cognitive psychologist interested in chess began to collect data on the amount of time a chess player needs to make a decision on a particular chess move. She asked 40 chess players of equal ability to sit down at the same display of chess pieces and make the next move. The time for the decision, in seconds, for each of the 40 chess players is shown here. Use these scores to create a frequency distribution with 12 intervals. Include the real limits, apparent limits, frequency, and cumulative frequency.

```
37 39 45 54 60 63 75 76 77 77
78 78 78 79 80 80 80 80 83 84
85 86 87 88 88 91 93 95 97 99
102 104 109 113 119 124 132 133 135 135
```

17. Using only the frequency distribution you created in Problem 16, how long do you think the next player will take to make his or her move?

18. A researcher is interested in the types of things that frighten toddlers, so he presents 14-month-old infants with a variety of items and records the number of items feared by each child. The numbers of items feared by 40 children follow. Use these data to create a frequency distribution with an interval size of 2 showing the apparent limits, relative frequency, and cumulative relative frequency.

5	4	2	5	6	8	9	4	2	3
1	0	1	3	6	9	13	23	1	4
16	3	4	5	3	6	4	2	1	1
1	2	3	4	18	19	2	4	11	18

19. A developmental psychologist is interested in smile production in infants. She measures the total numbers of smiles produced by 30 infants during ten 10-minute play periods in a room full of toys. Using the following data, create a frequency distribution with an interval size of 3 smiles. Make sure you include in your frequency distribution the real limits, apparent limits, frequency, cumulative frequency, rela-

tive frequency, and cumulative relative frequency.

5	5	5	6	6	7	7	8	10	13
13	13	14	15	16	18	20	22	24	26
28	30	31	33	34	36	40	42	44	49

20. Forty-one persons were shown a list of 100 words and asked at a later time to recall the list. Use their scores, which follow, to generate a frequency distribution with 16 intervals. Include the apparent limits and the frequency in your frequency distribution.

0	5	6	6	7	9	10	10	11	14	14
15	15	15	16	18	19	22	22	24	25	28
29	29	30	30	33	36	36	36	38	40	42
45	46	51	53	54	59	60	60			

21. Here is a list of the numbers of eye fixations necessary for 24 people to read a 1000-word passage of prose. From this list, create a frequency distribution using an interval size of 25 that contains the real limits, apparent limits, frequency, and cumulative frequency.

100	102	110	114	122	128	132	132
133	135	156	164	183	189	198	207
223	245	252	278	334	387	423	446

Graphs

Y ou are curled up in a corner of your couch, your fingernails nearly bitten to the bone, agonizing as your hero dangles barely a foot above the snapping jaws of the alligators in the pit below, when your tension is relieved by a box of aspirin appearing on the TV screen. Next to it is a graph comparing this product, which gives the "most effective relief," to the other leading brand. Sound familiar? Graphs are used in marketing, research, sports, and industry to visually convey some type of information to us. But do we always comprehend what the graphs are trying to tell us? Are all the graphs we see accurate? Are they useful? This chapter is designed to enable you to understand the properties of common types of graphs, to read graphs effectively, to critically evaluate other people's graphs, and to construct your own graphs from raw data.

Graphs are essentially pictures of numerical data; as such, they tell a story about those data. These "data pictures" can assume various forms, a few of which can be seen in Figures 3.1–3.4. Figure 3.1 is typical of the graphs we see in newspaper and magazine ads and in TV commercials. Truthful or not, it tells quite a tale about the effectiveness of aspirin: Brand A definitely *appears* to be more effective than Brand B. However, several important facts were omitted from this graph:

1. The title doesn't communicate the intent of the graph. Does the graph really show aspirin effectiveness over time, as it leads us to believe?
2. The vertical direction on the graph apparently represents effectiveness, but there are no numbers or labels by which we can compare the two types of aspirin. Is one truly more effective than the other?
3. What were the dosages of the two types of aspirin? Were they equal?
4. What is the time period depicted in this graph? A few minutes? Several hours?

These types of questions should be asked about *all* graphs because some graphs, intentionally or not, are designed in ways that mislead the viewer.

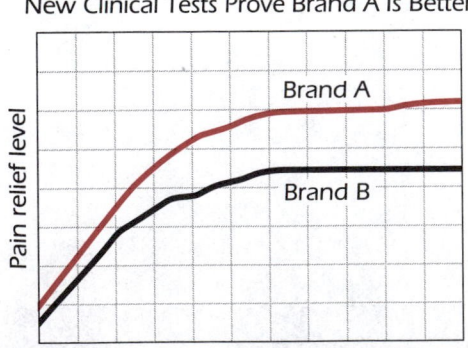

Figure 3.1 Typical graph seen in media ads

Figure 3.2 Yearly tuition at five different universities

Figure 3.2 shows a graph that contrasts not only in form to the one just discussed but also, and particularly, in merit. The title informs us what kind of information is being conveyed; the labels tell us precisely what is being measured; the numbers along the vertical axis tell us in what increments the measurements are being reported; and the vertical bars make it easy for us to determine the tuition for each of the universities.

The graph depicted in Figure 3.3 is called a pie graph or pie chart. This type of graph is helpful for portraying any kind of population distribution or budget allowances. Figure 3.3 illustrates how the tuition at MONYU is apportioned to instruction, administration, and student services. Consider how effective such a chart would be if a MONYU faculty member used it as "ammunition" in an appeal for a salary raise. No administrator would want the university's benefactors to suspect that the amount of money spent on direct instruction is only 10% more than that spent on administration.

Graphs are often used to illustrate trends and to help predict the future. Figure 3.4 shows the history of the price of a single automobile model from 1986 to 1996. As you can see, the price increased from a low of about $8,000

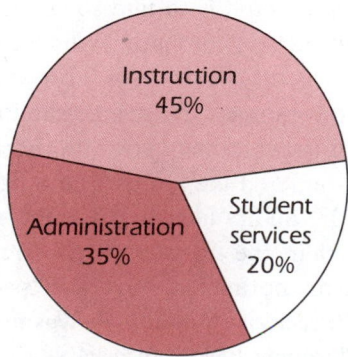

Figure 3.3 Apportionment of tuition at MONYU

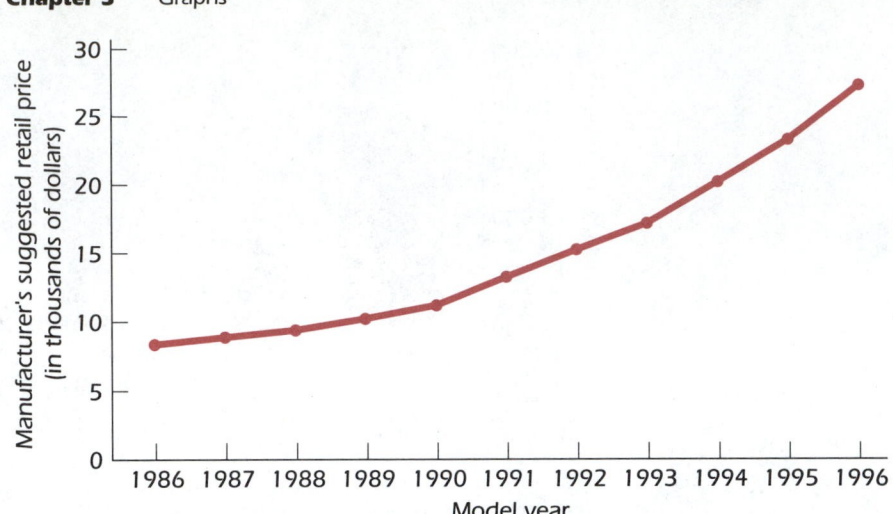

Figure 3.4   Manufacturer's suggested retail prices of a single automobile model from 1986 to 1996

in 1986 to nearly $30,000 in 1996. If this trend continues, we can expect to pay over $50,000 for the same automobile by the year 2010.

BASICS IN CONSTRUCTING A GRAPH

Question: I've seen lots of graphs like these but have never made one myself. If I wanted to graph my own data, where would I start?

The Axes

The first step in creating a graph is to find some graph paper and draw the **axes,** the horizontal and vertical lines along which the labels are placed. The horizontal line is known as the *x*-**axis** or the **abscissa,** and the vertical line is known as the *y*-**axis** or the **ordinate.** These lines can fool the eye, so before you draw them, be aware of the extremely powerful horizontal–vertical illusion, which is shown in Figure 3.5. Take a look at the figure. Does one line look longer than the other? If you are like the "normal" person, you will see the vertical line as longer than the horizontal. (*Digression:* In the behavioral sciences, we often refer to "normal" or "average" people. It is a little-known fact that the National Bureau of Standards in Washington, DC, keeps several "normal" or "average" people locked in a vault for comparison purposes!) Actually, both the horizontal and the vertical lines are the same length, but

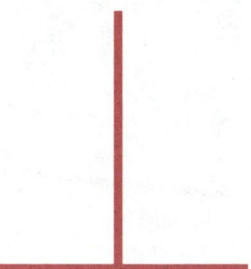

Figure 3.5 *The horizontal–vertical illusion*

perceptually, vertical lines tend to appear longer than horizontal lines. Thus, if you are constructing a graph and want the abscissa to appear as long as the ordinate, you may need to lengthen the horizontal line to counteract this illusion.

In the behavioral sciences, graphs are used to show relationships between independent and dependent variables. In an experiment, the independent variable is manipulated by the experimenter, whereas the dependent variable is some measure of the subject's behavior. The standard procedure is to represent the independent variable along the abscissa, or x-axis, and the dependent variable along the ordinate, or y-axis. For example, suppose a developmental psychologist is interested in the effect of prenatal care on the birth weight of infants. She could assign several mothers to one of three prenatal care conditions: no prenatal care, occasional prenatal care, and regular prenatal care. Then she could average the birth weights for each group and display the results in a graph. To graph the data, she would plot the prenatal care conditions (independent variable) along the abscissa and the average birth weights (dependent variable) along the ordinate (see Figure 3.6).

This same developmental psychologist might want to observe the effects of nutrition as well as prenatal care on the birth weights of children. She could

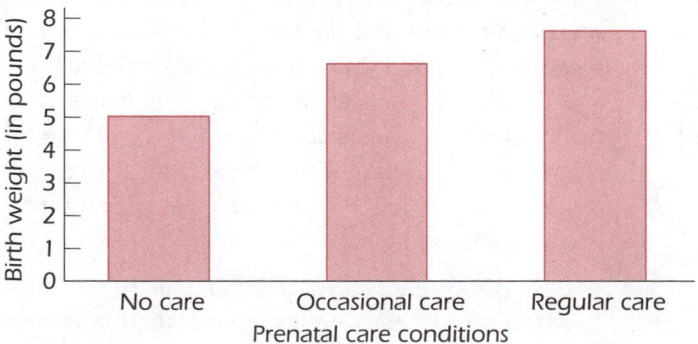

Figure 3.6 *Average birth weights for three different prenatal care conditions*

Figure 3.7   Average birth weights for two different diets and three different prenatal care conditions

have two different diet conditions: one in which mothers eat unhealthy diets full of junk food and lacking in important vitamins and minerals, and another in which mothers eat healthy diets rich with foods recommended by nutrition experts. She could then plot the average birth weights as two separate lines on the graph that has prenatal care conditions as the x-axis and birth weight as the y-axis (see Figure 3.7). In this way, she could observe the three-way relationship among prenatal care, maternal diet, and birth weight.

Graphs can also be used to display information that has been summarized in a frequency distribution, in which case it is customary to represent the dependent variable (the scores) along the abscissa and the frequency along the ordinate. (Because it is easy to illustrate graphing procedures by using information from frequency distributions, we use frequency distributions in the examples throughout the remainder of this chapter. We will discuss other types of graphs in Chapters 9 and 14.) Take a look at Figure 3.8. Each possible score (dependent variable) is represented along the abscissa, with the lower scores on the left and the higher scores on the right. The frequency of each score is represented along the ordinate, with the low frequencies at the bottom and the high frequencies at the top. Frequency is thereby represented by the height of the bar. If you received a score of 21 on this test, you could refer to the graph to find that 15 other students scored the same as you.

In review, a few major points are important to remember in the initial stages of setting up a graph:

- Give the graph a clear, unambiguous title or figure caption.
- Make sure to assign appropriate labels and meaningful numbers to each axis.
- Plot the independent variable along the abscissa and the dependent variable along the ordinate when plotting their relationships. Plot the dependent

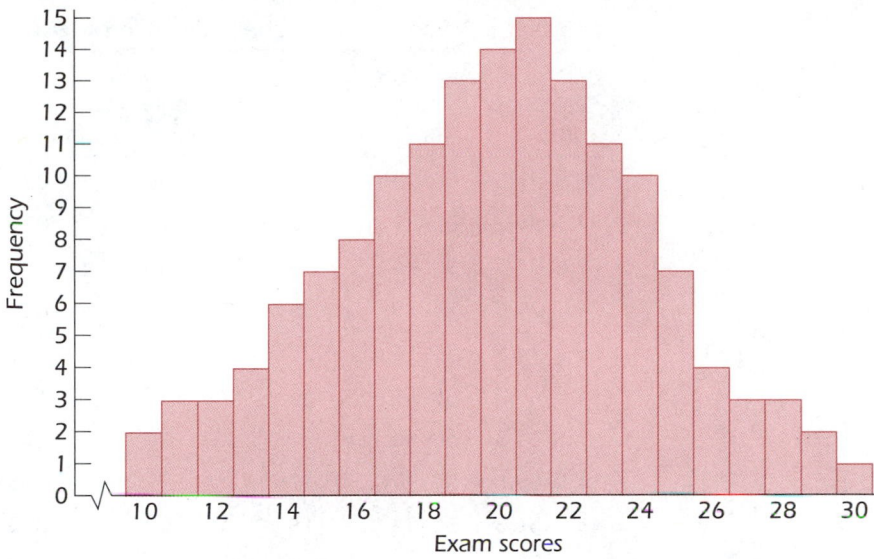

Figure 3.8   Statistics exam scores

variable along the abscissa and the frequency along the ordinate when plotting data from a frequency distribution.

C O N C E P T   Q U I Z

1. On a graph the horizontal or x-axis is called the _____ , and the vertical or y-axis is called the _____ .
2. The horizontal–vertical illusion illustrates the fact that graphs look better if the _____ axis is drawn longer than the _____ axis.
3. The standard procedure when graphing the results of an experiment is to represent the dependent variable long the _____ .
4. In the graph of a frequency distribution, it is customary to represent the _____ along the abscissa and the _____ along the ordinate.
5. It is important to remember that a graph is useful only when the axes have appropriate _____ and meaningful _____ , and the entire graph itself has an unambiguous title.

Answers

1. abscissa; ordinate
2. x; y
3. abscissa
4. dependent variable; frequency
5. labels; numbers

Table 3.1   Speeds of Baseballs Thrown by 200 Padres Fans

Real limits (mph)	Apparent limits (mph)	Frequency	Cumulative frequency	Relative frequency	Cumulative relative frequency	Midpoint
89.5–94.5	90–94	4	200	.020	1.000	92
84.5–89.5	85–89	10	196	.050	.980	87
79.5–84.5	80–84	15	186	.075	.930	82
74.5–79.5	75–79	16	171	.080	.855	77
69.5–74.5	70–74	25	155	.125	.775	72
64.5–69.5	65–69	36	130	.180	.650	67
59.5–64.5	60–64	35	94	.175	.470	62
54.5–59.5	55–59	27	59	.135	.295	57
49.5–54.5	50–54	18	32	.090	.160	52
44.5–49.5	45–49	9	14	.045	.070	47
39.5–44.5	40–44	5	5	.025	.025	42

Plotting the Data: Histograms and Polygons

The next step in graph construction is transferring the data to the graph. To illustrate this procedure, let's use some data we collected last summer during a visit to San Diego's Jack Murphy Stadium, where we witnessed the Padres lose yet another game. Midway into the fourth inning, with the Padres losing 7 to 1, we decided that it might be more fun to get a hot dog and a drink and watch some of the fans test their throwing arms against a radar gun at a charity booth set up just outside the stadium. For $1.00, a person could throw three baseballs at a target, and a radar gun would measure their speeds. The average speeds (in miles per hour) of the baseballs thrown by 200 San Diego Padres fans are listed in the grouped frequency distribution in Table 3.1. The most common graphs of data such as these are a *histogram* (a type of bar graph) and a *polygon* (a type of line graph).

FREQUENCY HISTOGRAM

A **frequency histogram** consists of a number of bars placed side by side, as in Figure 3.2, where the width of each bar indicates the interval size and the height of each bar indicates the frequency of the interval. Follow along as

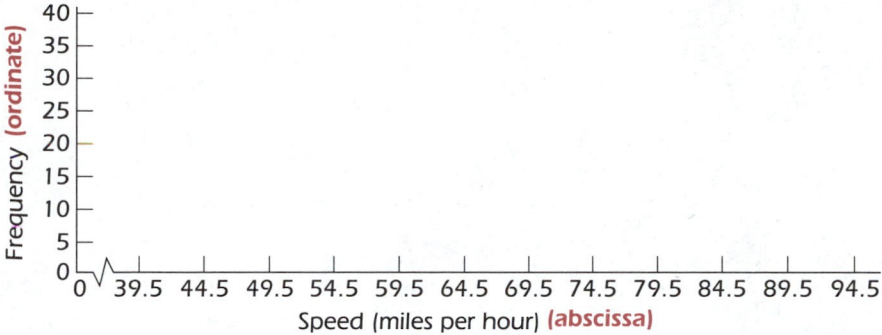

Figure 3.9 The labeling of the axes for the data in Table 3.1

we plot a histogram of the baseball-speed data. First, we determine that the frequency of the intervals will be indicated along the ordinate, and the baseball speeds (the dependent variable) will be indicated along the abscissa. We also need to determine the size and scale of the axes. The ordinate should be labeled so that all possible frequencies are represented. Referring to Table 3.1, we note that these range from 4, the lowest frequency, to 36, the highest frequency. Likewise, the abscissa should be labeled so that the entire range of possible speeds is represented. Looking at Table 3.1, we find that the abscissa labels need to extend from 39.5 miles per hour (mph), the lower real limit of the lowest interval, to 94.5 mph, the upper real limit of the highest interval. Because frequency polygons require that we plot the bars at the real limits, we have labeled Figure 3.9 using real limits to make the building of this graph easier for you to understand. (Most frequency histograms that you see in journals or books will probably not label the abscissa using real limits because it makes the abscissa too busy, but the bars will be placed at the real limits.)

Once the axes have been labeled, the next step is to draw in the bars of the histogram. Beginning at the lower real limit of the lowest interval (39.5 mph), we draw a vertical line up to a frequency of 5, then draw a horizontal line equal to the width of the interval (5 mph) so that it extends to 44.5 mph, and then draw a vertical line down to the abscissa. This single bar represents the interval 39.5–44.5 with a frequency of 5 (see Figure 3.10). The next bar is drawn in the same fashion, beginning at its lower real limit of 44.5 mph, with a height of 9 and a width of 5 mph, and extending out to 49.5 mph (see Figure 3.11). Note that in Figure 3.11 there is no gap between the two bars because the upper limit of the first interval is the same as the lower limit of the second interval: Both are 44.5 mph. Each successive interval is represented by a bar having the appropriate frequency and sharing its limits with the adjacent intervals.

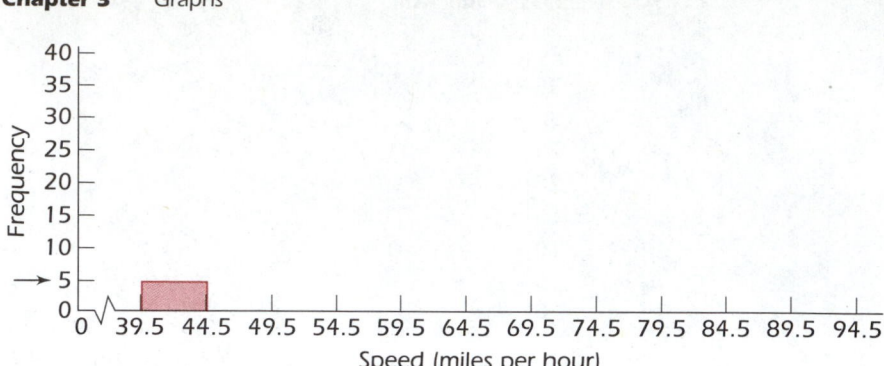

Figure 3.10 The first bar in the histogram for the data in Table 3.1

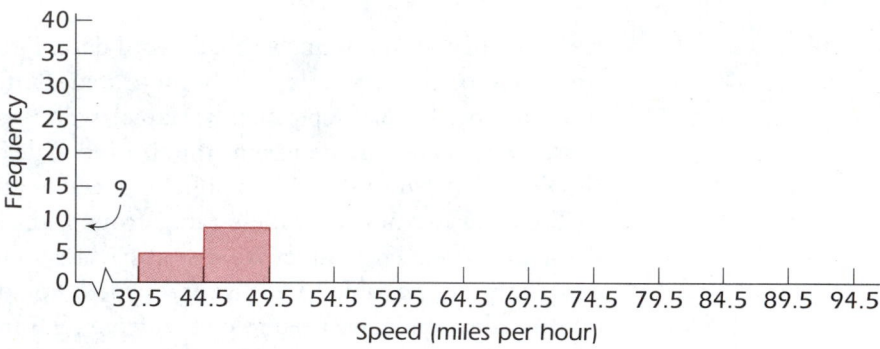

Figure 3.11 The second bar in the histogram for the data in Table 3.1

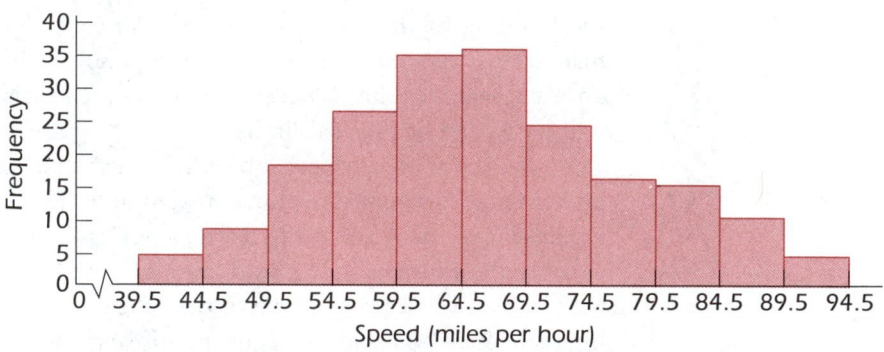

Figure 3.12 A frequency histogram for the data in Table 3.1

The completed frequency histogram illustrating the data from Table 3.1 is shown in Figure 3.12. Take a few minutes to compare the table with the figure. Look at each interval in the table and compare it with the corresponding bar in the figure. Note that the information presented in the table is exactly the same as that presented in the graph.

Just as we can generate a histogram from a grouped frequency distribution, so we can create a grouped frequency distribution from a histogram. The histogram is labeled such that each bar reveals the real limits, the interval size, and the frequency of the interval. If you were given a properly labeled frequency histogram, you could readily regenerate the grouped frequency distribution from which it was created. For this reason, you never find both a grouped frequency table and a frequency graph of that table in the same research report; it would be redundant.

Question: You mentioned that data can be graphed as a histogram or a polygon. What is a polygon and how do I make one?

FREQUENCY POLYGON

A polygon consists of points on a graph with lines connecting them; the lines form an actual geometric polygon when they are connected to the abscissa at the extreme upper and lower ends of the graph. Although there are several types, the simplest is the frequency polygon, which portrays the same information found in a frequency histogram but in a slightly different form. A **frequency polygon** uses a single point rather than a bar to represent an interval on a graph.

Question: If only a single point represents an entire interval, how do you decide which point to use?

The best choice is the midpoint because it is the most representative of all the scores within any interval. If we decide to use one of the lower limits, we will consistently *under*estimate the scores in that interval, whereas if we decide to use one of the upper limits, we will consistently *over*estimate the scores. If we assume that, on average, half the scores fall above the midpoint and half fall below, the best decision is definitely the midpoint. To create a frequency polygon, we determine the midpoint of each interval, plot the midpoints on the graph, and connect them with a straight line.

To illustrate how to construct a frequency polygon, we use the same data we used to construct the histogram (see Table 3.1). First, we need to draw and label the axes. The ordinate can be labeled the same way as in the histogram example, from 0 to 40. The abscissa must be labeled differently because we are now plotting points at the midpoints of the intervals rather than at the real limits, but the labels must still span the entire range of the data. Next, we plot the midpoint of each interval at a height equal to the frequency of that interval. Finally, we connect all the points by straight lines (see Figure 3.13).

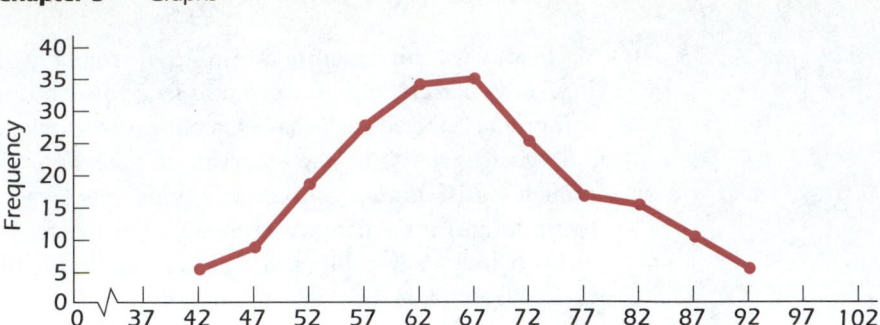

Figure 3.13   An incomplete frequency polygon for the data in Table 3.1

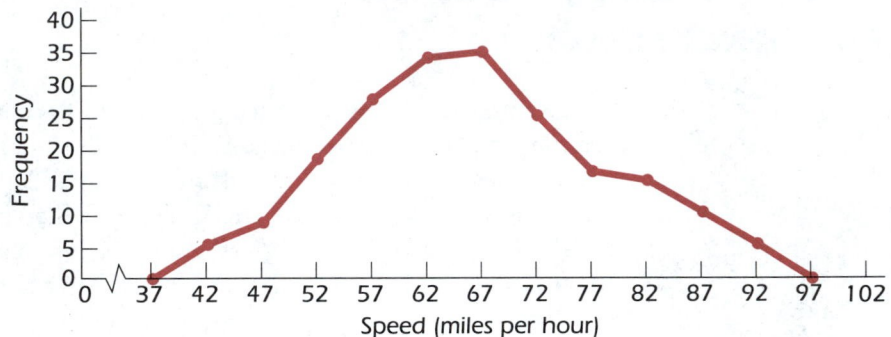

Figure 3.14   A completed frequency polygon for the data in Table 3.1

To complete the polygon, we bring the lines down to the abscissa (zero frequency). The normal practice is to *begin the graph at the midpoint of the interval just below the lowest interval in the grouped frequency distribution*, and to *end the graph at the midpoint of the interval just above the highest interval*. Because there are no scores in either of these intervals, the frequency is zero in each. The lowest interval for the baseball-speed information is 40–44; if there were an interval below that, it would have apparent limits of 35–39 and a midpoint of 37, so in that case we would plot a point at 37 with a frequency of 0. Remember to leave space for this interval to the left of the rest of the graph. The interval above the highest interval would have apparent limits of 95–99, with a midpoint of 97 and a frequency of 0. Figure 3.14 shows the completed frequency polygon of the baseball data.

The baseball-speed information depicted in the frequency histogram (Figure 3.12) is the same as that depicted in the frequency polygon (Figure 3.14). This is illustrated in Figure 3.15, which is a combination of the two figures. Note that the shapes of the two graphs are the same, which is to be

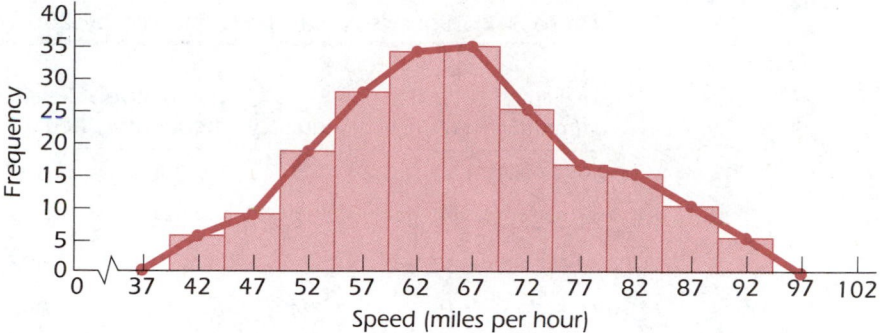

Figure 3.15   A combination of the frequency histogram and the frequency polygon for the data in Table 3.1

expected because the same frequency distribution was used to plot both of them.

RELATIVE FREQUENCY POLYGON

Question: Can I compare frequency polygons of two different distributions?

Yes, you can, as long as the sizes of the distributions are the same. However, if the distributions have different sizes, you cannot compare them directly. For instance, suppose we want to know whether Padres fans are unique in their baseball-throwing ability or whether they are representative of baseball fans throughout the country. We ask Judy's brother who lives in Minneapolis to find out how fast Minnesota Twins fans can throw baseballs, but we forget to tell him to limit his sample size to 200. He goes to a Twins game and collects data from 250 fans. These data are summarized in Table 3.2. Since there are 50 fewer subjects in the Padres study than in the Twins study, the results of the two studies are not directly comparable. There is, however, a way to compare them.

As discussed in Chapter 2, we can compare two distributions that have different numbers of subjects by computing *relative* frequency rather than mere frequency. Similarly, we can compute and graph the relative frequency for the Padres and Twins distributions and compare the resulting relative frequency graphs, or **relative frequency polygons.** Plotting a relative frequency polygon is the same as plotting a frequency polygon, except that instead of using the frequencies, we use the relative frequencies and plot them at the midpoints of the intervals. Thus, by creating relative frequency polygons, we

Table 3.2 Speeds of Baseballs Thrown by 250 Twins Fans

Real limits (mph)	Apparent limits (mph)	Frequency	Cumulative frequency	Relative frequency	Cumulative relative frequency	Midpoint
89.5–94.5	90–94	5	250	.020	1.000	92
84.5–89.5	85–89	18	245	.072	.980	87
79.5–84.5	80–84	23	227	.092	.908	82
74.5–79.5	75–79	24	204	.096	.816	77
69.5–74.5	70–74	30	180	.120	.720	72
64.5–69.5	65–69	39	150	.156	.600	67
59.5–64.5	60–64	37	111	.148	.444	62
54.5–59.5	55–59	33	74	.132	.296	57
49.5–54.5	50–54	26	41	.104	.164	52
44.5–49.5	45–49	12	15	.048	.060	47
39.5–44.5	40–44	3	3	.012	.012	42

can compare similar sets of information that have different numbers of scores. Figure 3.16 does just this. Using relative frequency polygons, it compares the data collected from the Padres fans with those collected from the Twins fans, and we can see that the distributions are quite similar. Most fans, whether they are Padres or Twins fans, can throw a baseball between 60 and 70 mph, and very few can throw it faster than 90 mph.

When we threw the baseballs, the radar gun registered an average speed of 67 mph (one of us threw once and the other threw twice). Is that bad, good, or average? By examining a frequency polygon or a relative frequency polygon, we can get a general impression. On the other hand, if we look at a cumulative frequency or cumulative relative frequency polygon, which we discuss in the next two sections, we can tell at a glance how we compare with others.

C O N C E P T   Q U I Z

1. A frequency histogram is a type of bar graph in which the height of the bar represents the _____ and the width of the bar represents the _____ of an interval in a grouped frequency distribution.

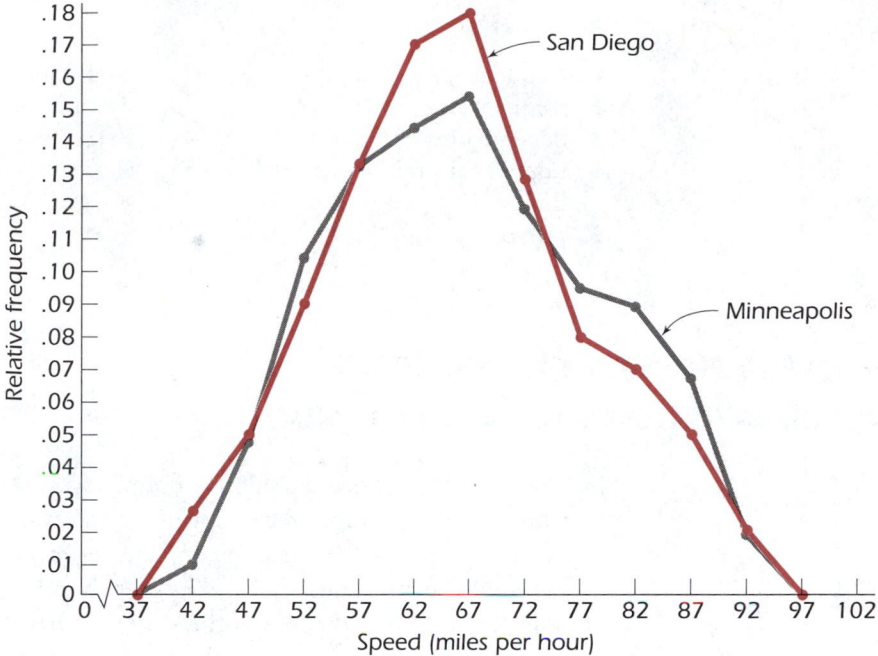

Figure 3.16 A comparison of relative frequency graphs for the data from San Diego and Minneapolis

2. When drawing a frequency histogram, we should label the ordinate with numbers reflecting a range that includes all possible _____ .

3. The abscissa should be labeled to include the entire range of possible _____ variable measures.

4. Since the width of a bar in a frequency histogram represents the width of the entire interval, the right edge of each bar should be plotted at the _____ and the left edge should be plotted at the _____ of the interval.

5. A frequency _____ uses a single point rather than a bar to represent an interval on the graph.

6. The height along the ordinate of each point in a frequency polygon represents the _____ within that interval.

7. The position along the abscissa of each point in a frequency polygon represents the _____ of the interval.

8. The most effective way to graphically compare two distributions with different numbers of subjects is to use a _____ .

9. Plotting a relative frequency polygon is the same as plotting a frequency polygon, except that instead of plotting the frequency at the midpoint, you plot the _____ at the _____ .

Answers

1. frequency; size
2. frequencies
3. dependent
4. upper real limit; lower real limit
5. polygon

6. frequency
7. midpoint
8. relative frequency polygon
9. relative frequency; midpoint

CUMULATIVE FREQUENCY POLYGON

In Chapter 2 we defined cumulative frequency as the total number of scores that fall below the upper real limit of an interval. If we graph cumulative frequency in the form of a polygon, the result is a picture of how many subjects in a distribution fall *below* a particular score, and we can see graphically how we compare to others. In the case of our throwing speed, we can easily see how many people throw slower than we do. In drawing this graph, we don't plot the points in quite the same way as we do in a frequency polygon. True, we plot cumulative frequency along the ordinate and speed in miles per hour along the abscissa, and the height of each point is determined by the cumulative frequency. However, we do not plot the points at the midpoints of the interval.

Question: Why don't we plot the points at the midpoints?

Look again at the definition of cumulative frequency. Cumulative frequency is the number of scores that fall *below the upper real limit,* so in constructing a **cumulative frequency polygon,** we need to plot each point *at* the upper real limit.

There are a few other rather technical factors to remember about constructing a cumulative frequency polygon. (It will be helpful to refer to Figure 3.17 during this discussion.)

1. The first point should be plotted at the upper real limit of the interval below the lowest interval on the cumulative frequency distribution. (In Figure 3.17, this is a speed of 39.5 mph with a cumulative frequency of 0.)
2. The last point represents the cumulative frequency of the last interval, which is equal to n, the total number of scores in the distribution.
3. The cumulative frequency line is *not* brought back down to the abscissa after the last interval but is allowed to hang in the air because all intervals above the last interval have the same cumulative frequency; they are all equal to n.

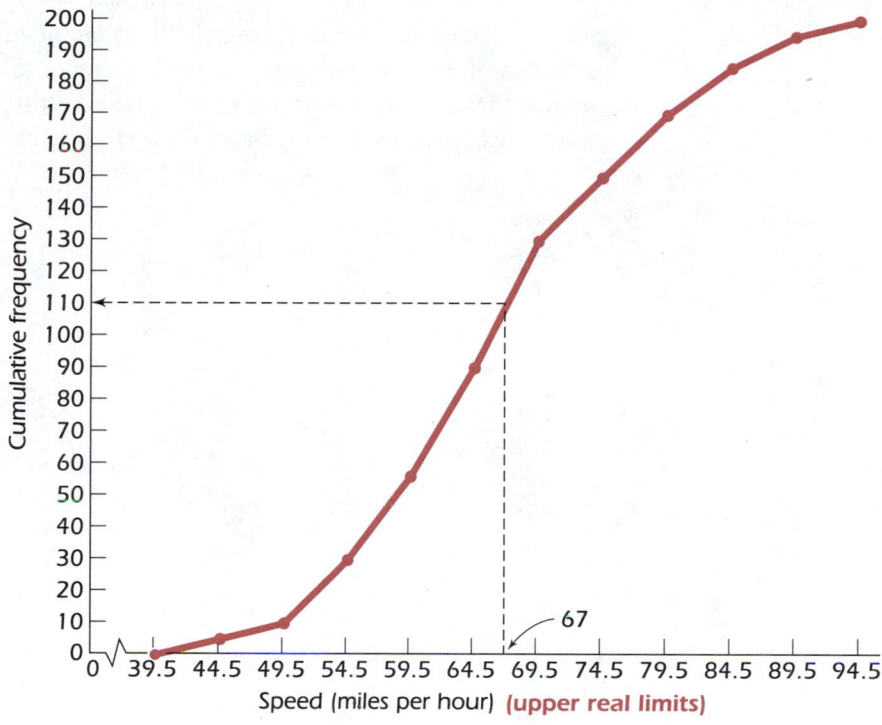

Figure 3.17 A cumulative frequency polygon for the data in Table 3.1

4. The S shape of this curve is called an *ogive* (pronounced "oh-jive").

After studying Figure 3.17, you should be able to readily determine whether our baseball-throwing speed of 67 mph is good or bad. You can see on the graph that the cumulative frequency for 67 mph is approximately 110. That is, of the 200 fans whose speeds were measured, we threw the baseballs faster than 110 of them. If we wanted to make the comparison even clearer, we could convert the cumulative frequency of 110 to a proportion or a percentage by dividing by 200. To compare many scores, however, it is easier to devise a graph that displays proportions of the scores.

CUMULATIVE RELATIVE FREQUENCY POLYGON

The **cumulative relative frequency polygon** is a graph that enables us to read proportions directly. It is plotted in a similar fashion to the cumulative frequency polygon: Cumulative relative frequency is plotted at the upper real limit of the interval. Figure 3.18 is the cumulative relative frequency polygon generated from the data in Table 3.1. By using the same procedure as for the cumulative frequency polygon, we can look up our score of 67 on this graph and find that .55, or 55%, of the Padres fans who threw baseballs were slower than we were (which means that 45% were faster).

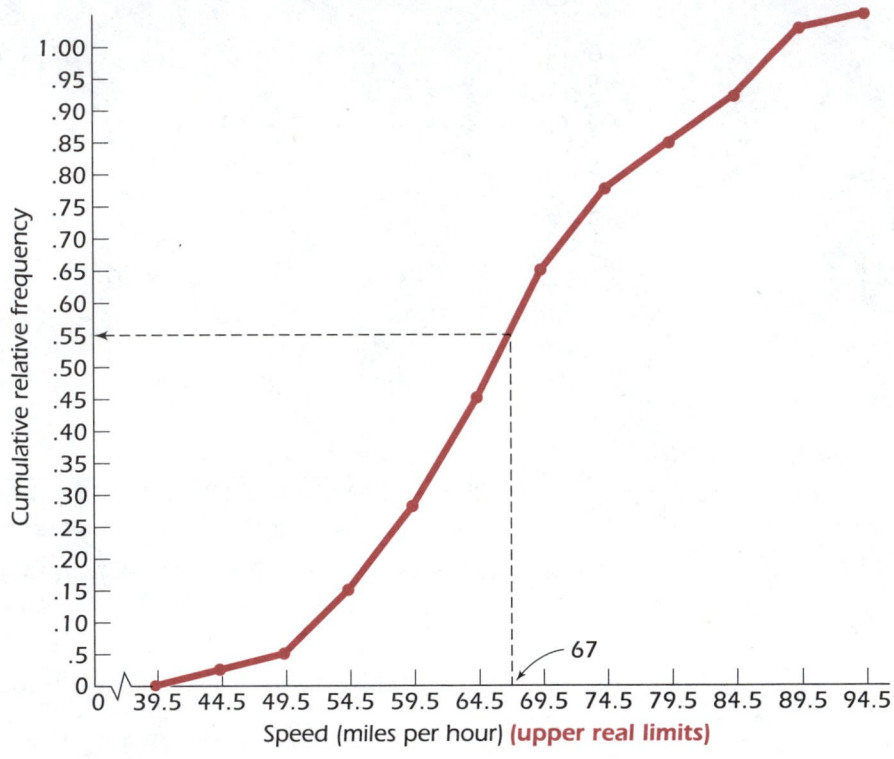

Figure 3.18   A cumulative relative frequency polygon for the data in Table 3.1

STEM AND LEAF DIAGRAMS

Question: *All these graphs use frequency distributions. Is there some kind of graph that displays raw data?*

All these graphs can be used with a simple frequency distribution, which is essentially the same as raw data. In addition, there is a technique similar to a graph, called a **stem and leaf diagram,** that allows us to display raw data visually. In a stem and leaf diagram, each raw score is divided into two parts, a stem and a leaf. The leaf is normally the last digit (or in very large numbers, the last two or three digits) of the score, and the stem is the remaining digit(s) of the score. For example, a raw score of 37 would have a leaf of 7 and a stem of 3. A raw score of 736 would have a leaf of 6 and a stem of 73.

Table 3.3   Speeds (in miles per hour) of Baseballs Thrown by 50 Padres Fans

33	38	39	39	44	44	45	47	48	49
50	53	54	55	56	57	59	59	61	61
63	64	66	67	68	68	68	69	69	69
70	70	71	71	72	76	78	78	79	83
84	84	86	87	89	91	92	92	93	93

If we want to make a stem and leaf diagram from the raw data in Table 3.3, we first create a vertical column that contains all the possible stems in the data:

Stem	Leaf
3	
4	
5	
6	
7	
8	
9	

Then we take each score and list its leaf next to the corresponding stem. For example, the first number in Table 3.3 is 33, which has a stem of 3 and a leaf of 3. We therefore put the 3 leaf next to the 3 stem in the diagram:

Stem	Leaf
3	3
4	
5	
6	
7	
8	
9	

The next score in Table 3.3 is 38, with a stem of 3 and a leaf of 8:

Stem	Leaf
3	3 8
4	
5	
6	
7	
8	
9	

Table 3.4 shows the completed stem and leaf diagram for all 50 scores in Table 3.3. As you can see, all the scores are represented in the diagram without the loss of any information.

Table 3.4   Stem and Leaf Diagram for the Data in Table 3.3

Stem	Leaf
3	3 8 9 9
4	4 4 5 7 8 9
5	0 3 4 5 6 7 9 9
6	1 1 3 4 6 7 8 8 8 9 9 9
7	0 0 1 1 2 6 8 8 9
8	3 4 4 6 7 9
9	1 2 2 3 3

If we rotate the stem and leaf diagram 90 degrees counterclockwise as in Table 3.5, the resulting diagram is very similar to a histogram.

CHANGING THE SHAPE OF A GRAPH

When viewing a graph, we see a picture of data that has been presented by another person in some particular manner for some particular reason. Most often, that reason is to convince people of some belief or conclusion held by

Table 3.5 Rotated
Stem and Leaf Diagram

```
                         9
                         9
                         9
                       8 9
                     9 8 8
                     9 8 8
                 9 7 7 6 9
                   8 6 6 2 7 3
             9 7 5 4 1 6 3
             9 5 4 3 1 4 2
             8 4 3 1 0 4 2
Leaf         3 4 0 1 0 3 1
Stem         3 4 5 6 7 8 9
```

the person who created the graph. Just as any two teachers, conveying the same subject matter, can give two entirely different presentations infused with their own beliefs and opinions, so can any two researchers, using the same data, devise two different graphs infused with their distinctive biases.

Question: You're saying that it's actually "legal" to try to portray data in a way that will convince others of your opinions and beliefs?

Sure. If we were given a certain set of data, we could, without altering the data, vary the type of graph (histogram or polygon), vary the scale along the

Reprinted with special permission of North America Syndicate, Inc.

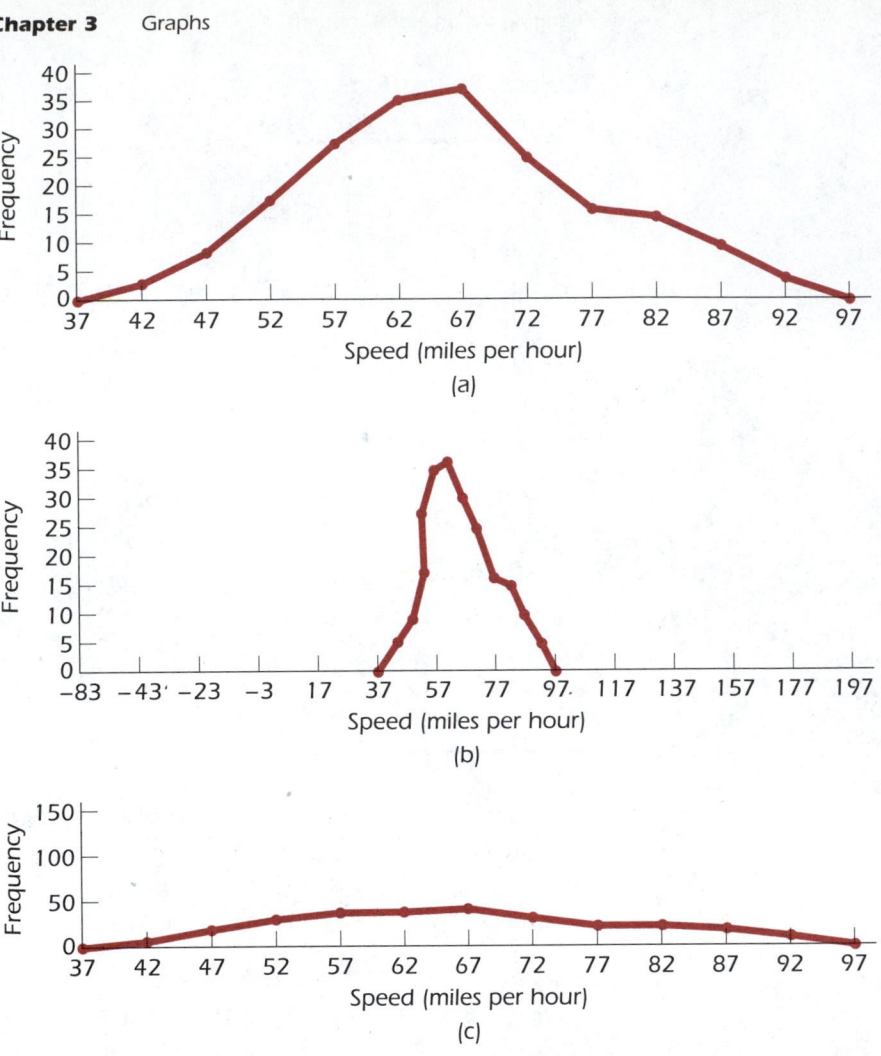

Figure 3.19   Three different frequency polygons for the data in Table 3.1. (a) The graph shows a relatively normal spread of abilities; (b) the data appear to cluster tightly about the center of the graph; (c) the data appear to be widely dispersed.

abscissa, or vary the scale along the ordinate. By modifying any one or all of these factors, we could change the appearance of the entire graph, and such a change might influence the opinions of its viewers. For instance, take a look at the graphs in Figure 3.19. By the way the Padres fans' data are presented in Figure 3.19(a), we are led to believe that there is a spread of abilities, with many people throwing at about the same speed as most others, and that only a few throw either exceedingly fast or embarrassingly slow. Figure 3.19(b) represents the same data, but the abscissa has been lengthened to make the data appear to cluster in the center of the graph. This shape gives the viewer the impression that everyone has similar throwing abilities. The opposite impression is produced by Figure 3.19(c), in which the ordinate has been distorted to make the data appear flat. In this figure, it appears that few people are alike in their baseball-throwing abilities.

When you read someone else's graph, be aware of the point we have just made and take care not to be misled; take the time to study the labels on the axes. If the axes are labeled properly, you can read any graph accurately. Even though the three graphs in Figure 3.19 look different, they all depict the same information, and the original grouped frequency distribution can be precisely reconstructed from any one of them. If you are constructing your own graph, you are free to present it in any way you wish, as long as you remember to label it properly so that the rest of us can see through the smoke.

C O N C E P T   Q U I Z

1. If we plot cumulative frequency in the form of a polygon, the result is a picture of how many people in a distribution fall _____ a particular score.

2. In a cumulative frequency polygon, the height of each point is determined by the _____ of the interval represented by that point.

3. In a frequency polygon, points are plotted at the midpoint of each interval; in a cumulative frequency polygon, the points are plotted at the _____ of each interval.

4. A cumulative frequency polygon is helpful in determining the number of subjects who received scores _____ a particular score in the distribution.

5. A cumulative relative frequency polygon is plotted in the same way as a cumulative frequency polygon except that the height of each point represents the _____ rather than the cumulative frequency of the interval.

6. Because graphs can be misleading, you should always make sure you understand how the graphs are _____ before you attempt to interpret the information displayed in the graph.

Answers

1. below
2. cumulative frequency
3. upper real limit

4. below or lower than
5. cumulative relative frequency
6. labeled

S U M M A R Y

Graphs are visual representations of data collected during some type of research. To be useful, they must be properly titled and labeled. The horizontal line on a graph, or the x-axis, is called the abscissa, whereas the vertical line, or the y-axis, is called the ordinate. When we show relationships between independent and dependent variables, we label the ordinate with some measure of the dependent variable and the abscissa with the independent variable. When we plot data from a frequency distribution, we label the ordinate with some measure of frequency (frequency, relative frequency, cumulative frequency, or cumulative relative frequency) and the abscissa with the dependent variable measure.

This chapter discussed the construction of six types of graphs: frequency histogram, frequency polygon, relative frequency polygon, cumulative frequency polygon, cumulative relative frequency polygon, and stem and leaf diagrams. The frequency histogram is a bar graph, with the width of the bar indicating the interval size and the height of the bar indicating the frequency of the interval. The frequency polygon is a line graph that represents the same information as the frequency histogram. To produce a frequency polygon, we plot points at the midpoint of each interval with their height equal to the frequency of the interval; we then connect the points with straight lines. The frequency polygon always begins one interval below the lowest interval represented in the grouped frequency distribution, and it ends one interval above the highest interval represented. Because the frequency histogram and the frequency polygon depict the same information that a grouped frequency distribution table does, a research report does not usually include both a graph and the table from which it was constructed.

The relative frequency polygon is similar in shape to both the frequency histogram and the frequency polygon. When plotting a relative frequency polygon, we plot relative frequencies at the midpoint of each interval.

Two other graphs discussed in this chapter are the cumulative frequency and the cumulative relative frequency graphs. Because the definition of *cumulative frequency* is "the total number of scores that fall below the upper real limit of the interval," cumulative frequency graphs plot cumulative frequencies at the upper real limit of each interval. The first point that is plotted is the upper real limit of the interval below the first interval. This initial point will have a cumulative frequency equal to zero. The S shape of the cumulative frequency and the cumulative relative frequency graphs is called an ogive.

You can also use a stem and leaf diagram to display raw data visually. To create a stem and leaf diagram, you first need to identify what to use as a stem and what to use as a leaf for each data point in the distribution. The leaf is usually the last digit (in large numbers, the last two or three digits) in the number, and the stem is the remaining digit(s) at the beginning of the number.

For example, the number 223 would have a leaf of 3 and a stem of 22. Next, you create a column at the far left of the diagram containing all possible stems in order, with the smaller stems at the top and the larger stems at the bottom. Finally, each leaf is listed next to its stem, with the smaller leaves at the left and the larger leaves at the right.

The height and width of any graph can be easily modified by changing the scale of the numbers along the ordinate or the abscissa. It is necessary to read and understand the numbers and labels along the axes before trying to interpret the graph. As long as the numbers used to label the axes are accurate, it should be possible to read the graph accurately. Graphs that are not appropriately labeled can be extremely misleading; therefore, you should avoid drawing any conclusions from unlabeled or mislabeled graphs.

K E Y   T E R M S

axes
x-axis
abscissa
y-axis
ordinate
frequency histogram

frequency polygon
relative frequency polygon
cumulative frequency polygon
cumulative relative frequency
    polygon
stem and leaf diagram

P R O B L E M S

One hundred students at the University of Perfectly Average Yuppies (UPAY) were asked to swim as many laps of the pool as possible in 60 minutes. The raw data on the numbers of laps are listed here:

8	20	35	40	45	55	59	65	68	70
9	20	36	41	45	55	61	65	68	71
9	22	36	42	45	56	63	65	69	71
11	27	38	42	45	56	63	66	69	74
14	29	38	42	46	56	63	66	69	74
16	31	39	42	46	57	63	67	69	75
18	33	39	43	48	58	64	67	69	75
18	34	40	43	50	58	64	67	70	76
19	34	40	44	51	58	64	67	70	77
20	34	40	44	54	59	64	68	70	83

1. Using the UPAY data, generate a grouped frequency distribution with an interval size equal to five laps.

2. Use the frequency distribution that you created in Problem 1 to plot a frequency histogram.

3. Use the frequency distribution that you created in Problem 1 to plot a frequency polygon.

4. Plot a cumulative frequency polygon using the frequency distribution from Problem 1.

5. Plot a relative frequency polygon using

the frequency distribution from Problem 1.

6. Plot a cumulative relative frequency polygon using the frequency distribution from Problem 1.

Use the following frequency distribution of scores on a personality questionnaire to do Problems 7–12.

7. Plot a frequency histogram of the personality questionnaire data.

8. Plot a frequency polygon of the personality questionnaire data.

9. Plot a cumulative frequency polygon using the personality questionnaire data.

10. Plot a relative frequency polygon using the personality questionnaire data.

11. Plot a cumulative relative frequency polygon using the personality questionnaire data.

12. Compare the table of personality questionnaire data with the following table of personality questionnaire data from a different group of subjects by plotting the relative frequency polygons of both on the same axes

Apparent limits	Frequency	Relative frequency
500–549	130	.033
450–499	220	.055
400–449	317	.079
350–399	423	.106
300–349	545	.136
250–299	684	.171
200–249	516	.129
150–199	422	.106
100–149	386	.097
50– 99	222	.056
0– 49	135	.034

Personality Questionnaire Scores (for Problems 7–12)

Apparent limits	Frequency	Cumulative frequency	Relative frequency	Cumulative relative frequency
500–549	17	500	.034	1.000
450–499	25	483	.050	.966
400–449	37	458	.074	.916
350–399	56	421	.112	.842
300–349	73	365	.146	.730
250–299	94	292	.188	.584
200–249	82	198	.164	.396
150–199	49	116	.098	.232
100–149	38	67	.076	.134
50– 99	22	29	.044	.058
0– 49	7	7	.014	.014

Two hundred fifty students were asked to rate the level of student services at their college or university. Students who thought that their student services represented the best in the nation were to rate their school a 100; those who believed their student services to be nonexistent were to rate their school a 0. The results of this survey are given in the following frequency distribution. Use this to do Problems 13–20.

Apparent limits	Frequency
90–99	10
80–89	16
70–79	28
60–69	34
50–59	49
40–49	25
30–39	39
20–29	32
10–19	11
0– 9	6

13. Plot a frequency histogram.

14. Plot a frequency polygon.

15. Generate a cumulative frequency column and then plot a cumulative frequency polygon.

16. Generate a relative frequency column and then plot a relative frequency polygon.

17. Generate a cumulative relative frequency column and then plot a cumulative relative frequency polygon.

18. Plot a frequency histogram of the survey results, but this time change the scale of the y-axis to make it appear that there is little or no difference between the frequencies of the class intervals.

19. Plot a relative frequency polygon of the survey results, but this time change the scale of the y-axis to accentuate the differences in relative frequencies between the class intervals.

20. Plot a frequency polygon that makes it appear that all the ratings are grouped in the middle of the distribution.

21. Use the accompanying frequency polygon of test scores to re-create the frequency distribution that was used to generate the graph. You need only re-create the apparent limits and the frequency for each interval.

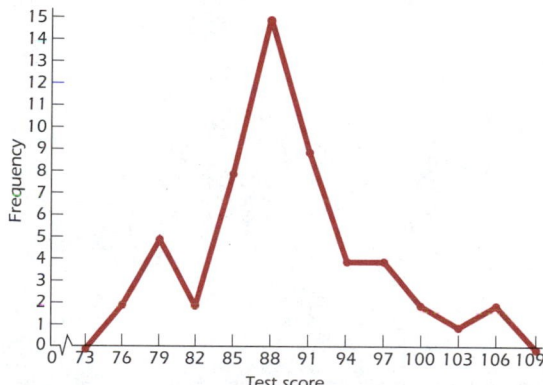

22. Use the accompanying frequency polygon of reaction times to re-create the frequency distribution that was used to generate the graph. Re-create the real limits, the apparent limits, the frequency, and the midpoint for each interval.

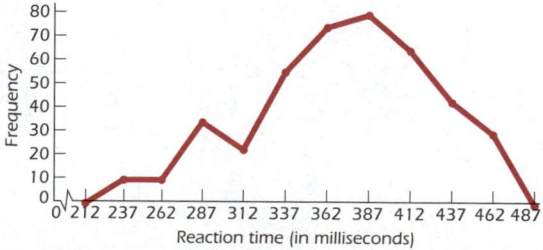

The midterm exam scores for 500 statistics students at a major university are shown in the following frequency distribution. Use this frequency distribution to do Problems 23–29.

Apparent limits	Frequency
95–99	6
90–94	9
85–89	55
80–84	67
75–79	189
70–74	47
65–69	29
60–64	22
55–59	21
50–54	22
45–49	13
40–44	9
35–39	7
30–34	3
25–29	1

23. Plot a frequency histogram.

24. Plot a frequency polygon.

25. Plot a relative frequency polygon.

26. Plot a cumulative frequency polygon.

27. Plot a cumulative relative frequency polygon.

28. If you were the instructor, which type of graph would you show to the class to best illustrate the distribution of scores on this exam?

29. If you were the instructor, which type of graph would you use to compare the performance of this class with the performance of your statistics class of the previous semester in which you had 695 students?

30. Use the following grades on a statistics exam to create a stem and leaf diagram.

45 47 49 49 54 55 55 57 59 61 62
65 67 69 70 77 78 78 79 82 82 83
84 85 85 85 89 90 91 94 95 97 99

31. Use the following reaction time scores (in milliseconds) to create a stem and leaf diagram.

374 379 379 381 382 384 385 392 392
395 397 398 399 399 400 401 402 403
404 404 404 407 409 412 413 415 417
418 418 419 421 422 422 422 425 428
430 437 438 449 456 457 459 459

Measures of Central Tendency

Because he would be graduating in a couple of weeks from the University of Popular and Original Programs (UPOP), Roy Babbins had been interviewing for a job with a number of companies. His current interview was with a recruiter from Rat Race, Incorporated (RRI), which produces Skinner boxes, rat mazes, and other equipment used in psychological studies with animals. Roy felt the interview was going remarkably well. Having worked in the psychology lab at the university, he was well versed in the uses for RRI's products, and he was sure he was conveying his knowledge to the recruiter. In turn, Roy was quite impressed with the company. Toward the end of the interview, Roy asked, "What is the average salary at RRI?"

The recruiter replied, "It's quite high, more than $4,000 per month. Of course, new employees begin at the bottom and work up. We are willing to pay you $900 a month to start, and if you work hard, you can expect that to increase after you've been with us for a short while."

This beginning salary was much lower than those of other companies, but the average salary was much higher. After some consideration, Roy accepted a position at RRI because of the presumed potential for rapid salary advancement.

Although Roy worked hard, after nearly a year at RRI, his salary had risen to only $950 a month, still thousands away from the average of $4,000. Aware that fellow employees seldom discussed their paychecks with one another, Roy patiently kept his mouth shut until one day, out of desperation, he began asking his colleagues how much they received each month. The more employees he approached, the angrier he became, until he finally stormed into the office of the recruiter who had convinced him to come to RRI.

"You told me at my interview a year ago that the average RRI salary is more than $4,000 a month," Roy bellowed. "I've talked to most of my fellow workers, and not one of them gets more than $1,500 a month."

"Nearly everyone makes exactly $1,250 a month," the recruiter calmly replied.

"Then why did you lie to me and tell me that the average salary was $4,000 a month?" blared Roy.

"I never lied to you," said the recruiter. "The average salary at RRI *is* more than $4,000 per month. Here, take a look at my computer screen. We'll list all the employees in this company along with their salaries and then compute the average salary. As you can see, the average is more than $4,000 a month." (See Table 4.1.)

"Sure, the average is more than $4,000 a month because you included the salary of the company president and a few other bigwigs, and each one of them makes around $20,000 a month!" Roy was furious. "You yourself admitted that most employees make only $1,250 a month."

"That's true," agreed the recruiter, "and if you had asked me the median, I would have told you it was $1,250 a month. That's the reason I like to recruit students from UPOP—they aren't required to take a statistics class before graduating."

Table 4.1 Monthly Salaries for All Employees at RRI

Employee	Position	Monthly salary
HBJ	President	$ 25,000
JBJ	Vice-president	21,000
TBJ	Vice-president	20,000
TBQ	Recruiter	15,000
MMP	Manager	1,500
CAF	Manager	1,500
DUD	Worker	1,250
MOG	Worker	1,250
DDP	Worker	1,250
MNN	Worker	1,250
MNP	Worker	1,250
KMD	Worker	1,250
OFT	Worker	1,250
DGA	Worker	1,250
CST	Worker	1,250
ZAS	Worker	1,250
KIP	Worker	1,250
DUN	Worker	1,250
RGB	Worker	950
TLC	New worker	900
MBD	New worker	900
MFP	New worker	900
DDK	New worker	900
POP	New worker	900
MIP	New worker	900
	Total	$105,350

Obviously, the recruiter *had* taken a statistics course and had chosen to use his statistical knowledge to deceive Roy Babbins and probably many other recruits. By asking for the "average" salary, what Roy really wanted to know was the most representative salary. The recruiter was aware of this, but he was also aware that there were several salary figures he could provide to denote the "average" salary; he decided to furnish Roy with the one that best suited his recruiting purposes.

Every day we hear people refer to a single number falling somewhere around the center of a distribution that best represents that distribution: "The normal weight of a 5′5″ woman is . . . ," "The average number of college students who achieve their B.A. degree is . . . ," "The Dow Jones average is. . . . " Scores that represent the center of the distribution are called **measures of central tendency.** In this chapter we discuss the three most common measures: the arithmetic mean (hereafter referred to as the *mean*), the median, and the mode. As illustrated by Mr. Babbins's unfortunate employment decision, it is important for you to know which measure best represents your data and best serves your purposes.

THE MEAN

Raw Scores

The mean is the most commonly used measure of central tendency. People often ask about the average of a certain group of scores; almost invariably, what they really want to know is the mean. The **mean** of any set of raw scores is the sum of all the scores divided by the total number of scores. The formulas for calculating both a sample mean and a population mean follow. To understand the formulas, you need to know that Σ (the Greek capital letter *sigma*) tells us to add all the scores represented by the symbol following it and that the symbol X represents the scores in either a sample or a population. Thus, ΣX means to add all the scores in the sample or the population. You also need to know that n represents the total number of scores in a sample and N represents the total number of scores in a population.

Now let's take a look at the formulas. First, the formula for the sample mean, which is usually designated by the symbol $\overline{X}$, known as "X-bar," is:

$$\text{Mean of a sample} = \overline{X} = \frac{\Sigma X}{n} \qquad (4.1)$$

Next, the formula for the mean of a population, which is designated by the Greek letter μ (mu), is:

$$\text{Mean of a population} = \mu = \frac{\Sigma X}{N} \qquad (4.2)$$

As you can see, the formulas for the sample mean and the population mean are nearly identical. The only difference is that the sample mean is computed by summing all the scores in the sample and dividing by the total number of scores in the sample, whereas the population mean is computed by summing all the scores in the entire population and dividing by the total number of scores in the population.

From the formula for the mean of a sample, the mean of the numbers 1, 2, 3, 4, and 5 is the sum of the numbers (15) divided by n (the number of scores in the sample, which is 5). Fifteen divided by 5 is 3. The mean, then, is 3.

HERMAN®

**"There we are. What's 350
pounds divided by two?"**

Herman © 1984 Jim Unger. Reprinted with permission of Universal Press
Syndicate. All rights reserved.

To check whether the RRI recruiter was telling the truth, let's compute the
mean salary at his company. The salaries of all 25 employees are listed in
Table 4.1. We will use Formula 4.2 because we are dealing with a population—the population of people who work at RRI. According to the formula,
we first sum all 25 salaries. As you can see from the bottom of the table, the
total is $105,350. Then we divide this sum by the total number of salaries,
which is 25:

$$\mu = \frac{\Sigma X}{N} = \frac{\$105,350}{25} = \$4,214$$

Thus, the recruiter was absolutely correct. The mean salary at RRI *is* more
than $4,000 per month.

Grouped Frequency Distributions

Often raw data are not available. In research reports and newspaper articles,
for instance, experimental results are often reported in graphs or in frequency
distributions. Suppose you ran across a study having to do with personal

Table 4.2 Interpersonal Distance (in Centimeters) for 75 College Sophomores

Apparent limits	Frequency
150–164	6
135–149	6
120–134	5
105–119	7
90–104	9
75– 89	12
60– 74	15
45– 59	7
30– 44	6
15– 29	1
0– 14	1

space—the amount of space people need between themselves and another person in order to feel comfortable. You were particularly interested in the results of this experiment because you thought they would be helpful in a project of your own that involved interpersonal exchanges. Specifically, you wanted to know the mean interpersonal distance with which people feel comfortable, but the only data reported were in a frequency distribution, like the one in Table 4.2.

Question: Could I find the mean even if no raw data are included in the report? If so, how?

Sure, if you are willing to settle for an estimate that, though not exact, is very close to the mean of the raw data. When no raw data are reported, you merely have to reconstruct them. Of course, without serious ESP powers, it is impossible to reconstruct the actual raw data; however, it *is* possible to make some well-founded guesses. For example, take the interval 15–29, which has only one score. If you had to select a number within this interval to represent that score, what would you choose? The midpoint, 22? Yes; in general, the midpoint is always your best choice. By computing the midpoint for each interval (six 157s for the interval 150–164, nine 97s for the interval 90–104, and so on), we can effectively reconstruct a "raw" distribution for the data (see Table 4.3).

Table 4.3 Midpoints of the Data in Table 4.2

157	127	97	67	52
157	127	97	67	52
157	112	97	67	52
157	112	82	67	52
157	112	82	67	52
157	112	82	67	52
142	112	82	67	52
142	112	82	67	37
142	112	82	67	37
142	97	82	67	37
142	97	82	67	37
142	97	82	67	37
127	97	82	67	37
127	97	82	67	22
127	97	82	67	7

Now that we have reconstructed the "raw" data, we can sum the scores and use the raw-data formula (Formula 4.1) to compute the mean:

$$\overline{X} = \frac{\Sigma X}{n} = \frac{6690}{75} = 89.2$$

Question: Isn't there an easier way to do this? Wouldn't this be awfully time-consuming if you had a thousand scores?

Yes. It's quite time-consuming with only 75 scores; it would be extremely so if there were a thousand. Fortunately, there is a faster, simpler method. Take a look at Table 4.4, which is made up of 1000 people's estimates of the length (in meters) of the painted dashed lane-divider lines on highways. These lines produce a remarkably potent modern-day illusion—nearly everyone greatly underestimates their length. (Most lane lines are well over 250 centimeters, or longer than 8 feet. See Harte, 1975.) To determine the mean of these estimates, we could proceed as we did earlier and list the midpoints according to their frequency, but this would be rather ridiculous considering that we'd have to write down the midpoint of the interval 200–224 (which is

Table 4.4   Estimated Lengths of Highway Divider Lines (in Centimeters)

Apparent limits	Frequency	Midpoint	Frequency × midpoint
300–324	10	312	3,120
275–299	25	287	7,175
250–274	69	262	18,078
225–249	146	237	34,602
200–224	247	212	52,364
175–199	206	187	38,522
150–174	147	162	23,814
125–149	104	137	14,248
100–124	32	112	3,584
75– 99	14	87	1,218
$n = \Sigma F = 1000$			Σ(Frequency × midpoint) = 196,725

212) 247 times. It makes much more sense to multiply the midpoint of each interval by the number of scores (the frequency) in that interval and then sum the resulting values over all the intervals. This is what we have done (we've multiplied the frequency of each interval by its midpoint) in the "Frequency × midpoint" column in Table 4.4. With this method, the formula for obtaining the mean of a frequency distribution is:

$$\text{Mean of a frequency distribution} = \overline{X} = \frac{\Sigma(\text{Frequency} \times \text{midpoint})}{n} \qquad (4.3)$$

A note of caution: Make sure you use the total number of scores for n, not just the number of intervals.

Using Formula 4.3, we can compute the mean of the frequency distribution in Table 4.4:

$$\overline{X} = \frac{\Sigma(\text{Frequency} \times \text{midpoint})}{n} = \frac{196,725}{1,000} = 196.725 \text{ centimeters}$$

Thus, the average, or mean, estimate of the length of the highway divider lines from our sample is 196.725 centimeters.

Formula 4.3 is an easy one that can be used to compute the mean of any grouped frequency distribution. Keep in mind, however, that when you are dealing with data that have been summarized into a grouped frequency distribution, you no longer know the original raw data. Because the mean of the grouped frequency distribution has not been computed from the raw data, it is usually slightly different from the mean of the actual raw data. The point to remember is that the mean of the raw data is more accurate and should be used if at all possible.

CONCEPT QUIZ

1. Scores that represent the center of the distribution are called _____ .

2. The symbol for the mean of a population is _____ ; the symbol for the mean of a sample is _____ .

3. The _____ of any set of raw data is the sum of all the scores divided by the total number of scores.

4. The mean of the scores 22, 36, 42, 55, and 60 is _____ .

5. You have collected the following six scores: 236, 247, 296, 307, 325, and 286. Without actually calculating the mean, estimate which of the following numbers will be closest to the actual mean: 236, 325, 280, or 250.

Use the following frequency distribution to answer questions 6–8. (We purposely show only five intervals to make the calculations easier, but remember, when you make your own frequency distributions, you should have between 10 and 20 intervals.)

Apparent limits	Frequency	Midpoint
225–249	4	237
200–224	5	212
175–199	1	187
150–174	3	162
125–149	2	137

6. In the frequency distribution, what does n equal?

7. In the frequency distribution, what does Σ(frequency × midpoint) equal?

8. Compute the mean of the frequency distribution.

Answers

1. measures of central tendency

2. μ; $\overline{X}$

3. mean

4. 43

5. 280

6. 15

7. 2955

8. 197

THE MEDIAN

Raw Scores

The **median** is the middle score, with half the scores being above and half the scores below, when all the scores have been ranked, or placed in numerical order. If there are five ranked scores, the middle score is the third score; if there are 25 ranked scores, the median is the 13th score. The monthly salaries for the 25 RRI employees are listed here. Note that the 13th salary is the median.

1.	$25,000
2.	$21,000
3.	$20,000
4.	$15,000
5.	$ 1,500
6.	$ 1,500
7.	$ 1,250
8.	$ 1,250
9.	$ 1,250
10.	$ 1,250
11.	$ 1,250
12.	$ 1,250
13.	$ 1,250 ← Median
14.	$ 1,250
15.	$ 1,250
16.	$ 1,250
17.	$ 1,250
18.	$ 1,250
19.	$ 950
20.	$ 900
21.	$ 900
22.	$ 900
23.	$ 900
24.	$ 900
25.	$ 900

Question: Picking the middle score is easy when the number of scores is odd because there is a middle score, but how do you pick the median when there is an even number of scores?

When there is an even number of scores, the median is the average of the two middle scores. This means, of course, that there is no actual "middle score" in the data; the median is merely the value halfway between the two middle scores. The heights of the eight players on the local college basketball team are listed here. Because there is an even number of players, the median is the average between the two middle heights.

79 inches
78 inches
76 inches
76 inches ← Middle score
74 inches ← Middle score
72 inches
72 inches
69 inches

Raw

$$\text{Median} = \frac{76 + 74}{2} = 75$$

The challenge in determining the median lies in finding the middle score(s). In smaller distributions the middle score is obvious by inspection, but in large distributions it is not so obvious. For instance, which is the middle score of 325 scores? 11,346 scores? 241,523 scores? Fortunately, when faced with large distributions, we can rely on the following formulas, one for odd numbers of scores and one for even numbers, to help us determine the median:

$$\text{Median}_{\text{odd no. of scores}} = \left[\frac{n + 1}{2} \right] \text{th score} \tag{4.4}$$

$$\text{Median}_{\text{even no. of scores}} = \frac{\left[\dfrac{n + 2}{2} \right] \text{th score} + \left[\dfrac{n}{2} \right] \text{th score}}{2} \tag{4.5}$$

The median for a distribution with 325 scores can be computed using Formula 4.4 because there is an odd number of scores:

$$\text{Median} = \left[\frac{n + 1}{2} \right] \text{th score} = \left[\frac{325 + 1}{2} \right] \text{th score} = 163\text{rd score}$$

The median for a distribution with 11,346 scores is the average of the two middle scores because it is an even number. Using Formula 4.4, we have:

$$\text{Median} = \frac{\left[\dfrac{n + 2}{2} \right] \text{th score} + \left[\dfrac{n}{2} \right] \text{th score}}{2}$$

$$= \frac{\left[\dfrac{11{,}346 + 2}{2} \right] \text{th score} + \left[\dfrac{11{,}346}{2} \right] \text{th score}}{2}$$

$$= \frac{5{,}674\text{th score} + 5{,}673\text{rd score}}{2}$$

In this example, the median is not the 5,673.5th score. It is the average of the 5,674th score and the 5,673rd score, whatever they are.

In summary, to find the median score in all but the smallest distributions, you need to rank all scores, determine the middle score using one of the preceding formulas, and then count down to that score. This process is relatively straightforward; finding the median from a grouped frequency distribution is a bit more complicated.

Grouped Frequency Distributions

Take a look at Table 4.5, which has the same distribution as Table 4.4. Can you tell which score is the median? Probably not, although you may be able to figure out which interval contains the median (particularly because that interval is in boldface type). You know that the median is the middle score and that the number of scores in the distribution is 1000. You also know from Chapter 2 that the cumulative frequency is the total number of scores below the real upper limit of the interval. So, starting with the lowest interval in the cumulative frequency column, scan each successively higher cumulative frequency until you find the first value that is greater than or equal to 500—in our example it is 503 in the interval 175–199. This, then, is the interval that contains the median. But how can you determine which single score is the median?

Question: Couldn't you just make an educated guess that the median score would be the midpoint of the interval?

There is a much more accurate way of estimating the median from a frequency distribution. Even though we do not know the exact median, we do

Table 4.5   Estimated Lengths of Highway Divider Lines (in centimeters)

Real limits	Apparent limits	Frequency (F)	Cumulative frequency (CF)
299.5–324.5	300–324	10	1000 ← n
274.5–299.5	275–299	25	990
249.5–274.5	250–274	69	965
224.5–249.5	225–249	146	896
199.5–224.5	200–224	247	750
$L \rightarrow$ **174.5–199.5**	**175–199**	**206** ← F_i	**503**
149.5–174.5	150–174	147	297 ← CF_b
124.5–149.5	125–149	104	150
99.5–124.5	100–124	32	46
74.5– 99.5	75– 99	14	14

know several things. We know the real limits of the interval (174.5–199.5), we know the size of the interval (25), we know the number of scores within the interval (206), and we can compute how far up into the interval the median resides if we assume all 206 scores are evenly distributed within the interval. Given this information, we can use the following formula to estimate the median from a frequency distribution:

$$\text{Median} = L + \left[\frac{(n/2) - CF_b}{F_i} \right] \cdot i \tag{4.6}$$

algebraically formula

where

L = the lower real limit of the interval that contains the median
n = the number of scores in the entire distribution
CF_b = the cumulative frequency in the interval *below* the interval that contains the median
F_i = the frequency in the interval that contains the median
i = the interval size

$$\text{Median} = 174.5 + \left[\frac{(1000/2) - 297}{206} \right] \cdot 25$$

$$= 174.5 + \left[\frac{500 - 297}{206} \right] \cdot 25$$

$$= 174.5 + \left[\frac{203}{206} \right] \cdot 25$$

$$= 174.5 + 0.985 \cdot 25 = 174.5 + 24.625$$

$$= 199.125$$

The most critical factor in obtaining the median of a grouped frequency distribution is locating the interval that contains the median. Once you have found the interval, you can readily locate the necessary information to "plug into" the formula, and then proceed to estimate the median.

CONCEPT QUIZ

1. After all the scores have been ranked, the median is the score above which _____ the scores will fall and below which _____ the scores will fall.

2. If there are 13 scores in a ranked raw-data distribution, the median will be the _____ score.

3. If there are 24 scores in a ranked raw-data distribution, the median will be the _____ .

Use the following frequency distribution to answer questions 4–7.

Apparent limits	Frequency (F)	Cumulative frequency (CF)
1200–1299	2	165
1100–1199	7	163
1000–1099	9	156
900– 999	12	147
800– 899	17	135
700– 799	22	118
600– 699	23	96
500– 599	29	73
400– 499	21	44
300– 399	14	23
200– 299	7	9
100– 199	2	2

4. How many scores are represented by this frequency distribution? (What is n?)
5. What are the apparent limits of the interval that contains the median?
6. What is the size of each interval in this frequency distribution?
7. What is the estimated median of this frequency distribution?

Answers

1. half; half
2. seventh
3. average of the 12th and 13th scores

4. 165
5. 600–699
6. 100
7. 640.804

THE MODE

Raw Scores

The easiest to compute of all the measures of central tendency is the **mode,** which is simply the most frequent score. To determine the mode, you need only look at the ranked distribution of scores and find the most frequent one. Look at the following simple distribution. The score 9 is represented three times, whereas all other scores are represented only once; therefore, the mode is equal to 9.

$$\left.\begin{array}{c} 9 \\ 9 \\ 9 \end{array}\right\} \text{Mode} = 9$$

$$\begin{array}{c} 8 \\ 6 \\ 1 \end{array}$$

Take a look at Table 4.1. Can you pick out the mode? Twelve of the 25 workers make $1,250 a month, so $1,250 is the mode for the salaries at RRI.

Question: That seems easy enough, but what if there are two scores that have the highest frequency? Or what if there is only one of each score in the distribution?

In cases where two different scores tie for the most frequent score, there are two modes. Although most distributions are unimodal, having only one mode, it is not uncommon for distributions to be bimodal with two modes, or multi-modal with more than two modes. A bimodal distribution often occurs in tests that are exceedingly difficult because there are normally some people who know the material being tested very well, resulting in a cluster of high scores, and others who know the material barely at all, resulting in a separate cluster of low scores. This situation is illustrated in the following data from a highly challenging mechanical aptitude test given to a sample of 25 college students:

95	87	75	45	10
90	86	73	45	9
90	84	70	45	9
90	77	60	45	8
90	76	53	25	8

(90, 90, 90, 90, 90) Mode   (45, 45, 45, 45) Mode

In answer to the second question, a distribution that consists of only one of each score has n modes. In other words, there are as many modes as there are scores. As you have seen, the mode is quite easy to find when you are dealing with raw data; it is just as easy when you are dealing with a grouped frequency distribution.

Grouped Frequency Distributions

The mode in a grouped frequency distribution is the midpoint of the interval with the highest frequency. Take a look at Table 4.4 (estimated lengths of highway divider lines) and find the interval that has the highest frequency; then determine the midpoint of that interval. You should have selected the interval 200–224 and found a midpoint of 212. Thus, the mode for Table 4.4 is 212

Table 4.6 Interpersonal Distance (in Centimeters) for 75 College Sophomores

Apparent limits	Frequency	Midpoint
150–164	6	157
135–149	6	142
120–134	5	127
105–119	7	112
90–104	9	97
75– 89	12	82
60– 74	15	67
45– 59	7	52
30– 44	6	37
15– 29	1	22
0– 14	1	7

centimeters. For a little more practice, look at Table 4.6, a repeat of Table 4.2, and see if you can figure out the mode. Do you see that the mode is 67?

MEAN, MEDIAN, OR MODE: A QUESTION OF SKEW

You are now familiar with three measures of central tendency, but how do you know which one to use in any one circumstance? How do you avoid a problem like the one faced by Roy Babbins when you need to know which "average" score best represents a particular set of data? For the most part, the answer lies in knowing the skew of a distribution.

The term **skew** refers to the general shape of a distribution when it is graphed. A distribution is *not* skewed when it is symmetrical; a distribution *is* skewed when it has most of the scores at one end and very few at the other. Figure 4.1 illustrates the three types of skew: Figure 4.1(a) shows a symmetrical distribution with no, or zero, skew; Figure 4.1(b) shows a distribution with a positive skew; and Figure 4.1(c) shows a distribution with a negative skew.

Question: The scores in Figure 4.1(b) are all clustered at the low end of the graph, and we generally consider low scores to be negative. Why is this distribution said to have a positive skew?

The skew of a distribution has nothing to do with the area that contains the

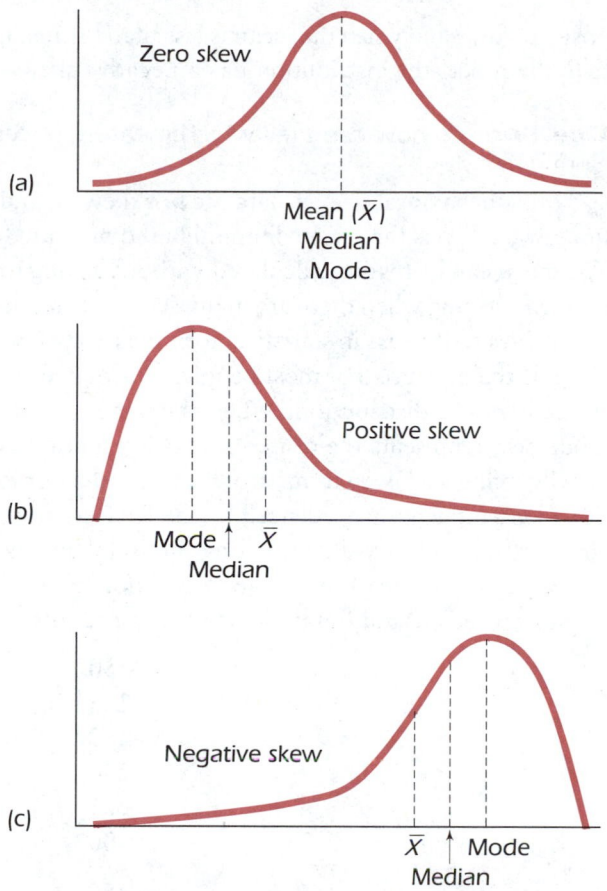

Figure 4.1 Graphs indicating the three different types of skew:
(a) zero skew (the distribution is symmetrical); (b) positive skew (the tail
points in the positive direction); and (c) negative skew (the tail points in
the negative direction)

most scores; it has to do with the direction in which its tail is pointing. Tails of
distributions are the areas at the extreme high or extreme low end where the
data frequency taper off to zero—where the graph approaches the abscissa.
When the tail is to the right of the distribution [pointing in the positive direction
as in Figure 4.1(b)], the skew is positive; when the tail is to the left of the
distribution [as in Figure 4.1(c)], the skew is negative. A symmetrical distribution has two tails and, as previously mentioned, is not skewed. Note that in a
perfectly symmetrical distribution with absolutely no skew [see Figure 4.1(a)],
the mean, median, and mode are all equal. On the other hand, in a skewed
distribution, the mean, median, and mode are all different. In fact, we can
determine the skew of any distribution by comparing the measures of central
tendency. When they are the same, there is no skew; when the mean is greater
than the median and the median is greater than the mode, the distribution has a

positive skew; and when the mean is less than the median and the median is less than the mode, the distribution has a negative skew.

Question: So how can I tell which measure of central tendency to use?

Most behavioral science data are not skewed, and in nonskewed distributions, the mean is the most commonly used measure for a number of reasons: The mean can be readily calculated without having to rank the data, which is time-consuming when there are many scores; its mathematical properties lend themselves well to use in statistical formulas, as you will see in future chapters; and it is the measure that most people immediately think of when referring to the center of a distribution. When the data *are* skewed, the median or the mode best represents the center of the distribution because the mean can be heavily influenced by extreme scores at the upper or lower end of the distribution. Such influence is evidenced by the RRI example at the beginning of this chapter and is clearly illustrated by the following example.

Suppose you measure a subject's reaction time to the same stimulus on six consecutive trials and obtain the following results (in milliseconds):

$$250$$
$$225$$
$$250$$
$$250$$
$$275$$
$$300$$

$$\overline{X} = 250$$
$$\text{Median} = 250$$
$$\text{Mode} = 250$$

This distribution of reaction times is symmetrical—the mean, the median, and the mode are all equal to 250 msec—and because it is not skewed, the mean is the best choice to represent the central score. But suppose the subject had become distracted on her last trial and her reaction time was 1800 msec rather than 300 msec.

$$250$$
$$225$$
$$250$$
$$250$$
$$275$$
$$1800$$

$$\overline{X} = 500$$
$$\text{Median} = 250$$
$$\text{Mode} = 250$$

Calvin and Hobbes

by Bill Watterson

The change to the new high score, 1800, has no effect on the median or the mode—they both remain 250—but the mean has changed drastically, doubling from 250 to 500. Obviously, the measure that best represents the center of this revised distribution is the median or the mode. In such cases, the median is normally selected over the mode because there can be only one median but more than one mode and because the mode is fickle: It can change significantly whenever a score that just happens to duplicate another score is added.

You also must consider the scale of measurement being used. The only valid measure of central tendency for nominal scales of measurement is the mode. The best measure of central tendency for an ordinal scale is the median. And, as mentioned above, either the mean, the median, or the mode might be the most appropriate score for an interval or ratio scale of measurement. In general, however, choose a measure of central tendency that best represents the distribution and the scale of measurement. In most cases, the most representative score is the mean.

CONCEPT QUIZ

1. The _____ score in a raw-data distribution is the mode.
2. It is possible for a distribution to have _____ mode.
3. If the numbers 2, 33, 33, 45, 67, 78, and 92 are all the scores in a distribution, what is the mode?
4. In a grouped frequency distribution, the mode is the _____ .
5. In a symmetrical distribution, the mean, the median, and the mode are all _____ .

6. In a skewed distribution, the mean, the median, and the mode are all
_____ .

7. In most cases the most representative measure of central tendency is the
_____ .

Answers

1. most frequent

2. more than one

3. 33

4. midpoint of the interval with
the greatest frequency

5. equal

6. different

7. mean

S U M M A R Y

This chapter discusses the computation of the three measures of central tendency—the mean, the median, and the mode. If the distribution is skewed, the median or the mode is the best representation of the center of the distribution. The mean is the most widely used of the three measures because most social science data are not skewed.

When people hear or read about an "average," they almost invariably think of the mean. To compute the mean from a distribution of raw scores, you simply add all the scores and divide by the total number of scores. To compute the mean from a grouped frequency distribution, you multiply the frequency by the midpoint for each interval, add those values, and then divide by the total number of scores.

The median is the middle score. To find the median in a distribution of raw scores, rank all the scores; then, if the number of scores is odd, identify the middle score, and if the number of scores is even, average the two middle scores.

Computing the median from a grouped frequency distribution is a little more complicated. Initially, you need to identify the interval that contains the median. Since the median is the middle score, find the interval that contains the $n/2$th score by starting at the bottom of the cumulative frequency column and then scanning upward until you reach the first cumulative frequency that is greater than or equal to $n/2$. That interval is the one that contains the median. Once you know which interval contains the median, you can use Formula 4.5 to compute the median. The values you need to use this formula include the lower real limit of the interval that contains the median, the cumulative frequency of the interval below the interval that contains the median, the frequency in the interval that contains the median, and the interval size.

The mode is defined as the most frequent score. In a raw distribution, the mode is merely the score that is represented most often. In a grouped frequency distribution, the mode is the midpoint of the interval with the greatest frequency. Unlike the mean and the median, there can be more than one mode. Because there can be multiple modes, the mode is normally not as good a representative of the central tendency of a distribution as the mean or the median.

KEY TERMS

measures of central tendency   mode
mean   skew
median

FORMULAS

$$\text{Mean of a sample} = \overline{X} = \frac{\Sigma X}{n} \tag{4.1}$$

$$\text{Mean of a population} = \mu = \frac{\Sigma X}{N} \tag{4.2}$$

$$\text{Mean of a frequency distribution} = \overline{X} = \frac{\Sigma(\text{Frequency} \times \text{midpoint})}{n} \tag{4.3}$$

$$\text{Median}_{\text{odd no. of scores}} = \left[\frac{n+1}{2}\right] \text{th score} \tag{4.4}$$

$$\text{Median}_{\text{even no. of scores}} = \frac{\left[\dfrac{n+2}{2}\right] \text{th score} + \left[\dfrac{n}{2}\right] \text{th score}}{2} \tag{4.5}$$

$$\text{Median} = L + \left[\frac{(n/2) - CF_b}{F_i}\right] \cdot i \qquad algebaically \tag{4.6}$$

where
    L = the lower real limit of the interval that contains the median
    n = the number of scores in the entire distribution
  CF_b = the cumulative frequency in the interval *below* the interval that
        contains the median
    F_i = the frequency in the interval that contains the median
    i = the interval size

PROBLEMS

1. Find the mean, the median, and the mode of the following sample of IQ scores:

120	134	74	93	103	123
124	119	106	129	93	74
134	97	88	74	93	99

2. Find the mean, the median, and the mode of the following sample of welding aptitude test scores:

23	25	27	22	35	45
29	26	33	34	25	27
25	29	33			

3. Find the mean, the median, and the mode of the following sample of the numbers of items answered correctly in a memory test:

49	46	43	40	38	37
48	45	43	39	38	37
48	44	42	38	38	36
47	44	41	38	37	34
46	43	41	38	37	33

4. Compute the mean, the median, and the mode of the following sample of the annual salaries of 15 psychology professors:

$55,000	$50,000	$40,000	$30,000	$25,000
$54,000	$49,000	$38,000	$29,000	$24,000
$52,000	$49,000	$33,000	$27,000	$22,000

5. Compute the mean, the median, and the mode of the frequency distribution of IQ scores at top right.

6. Compute the mean, the median, and the mode of the frequency distribution of welding aptitude test scores at bottom right.

IQ Scores (for Problem 5)

Apparent limits	Frequency (F)	Cumulative frequency (CF)	Midpoint
150–159	3	173	154.5
140–149	5	170	144.5
130–139	9	165	134.5
120–129	18	156	124.5
110–119	26	138	114.5
100–109	36	112	104.5
90– 99	34	76	94.5
80– 89	23	42	84.5
70– 79	13	19	74.5
60– 69	5	6	64.5
50– 59	1	1	54.5

Welding Aptitude Test Scores (for Problem 6)

Apparent limits	Frequency (F)	Cumulative frequency (CF)
45–47	3	88
42–44	5	85
39–41	10	80
36–38	14	70
33–35	22	56
30–32	15	34
27–29	10	19
24–26	7	9
21–23	2	2

7. Compute the mean, the median, and the mode of the following frequency distribution of the numbers of items answered correctly on a memory test:

Apparent limits	Frequency (F)
48–49	2
46–47	4
44–45	5
42–43	9
40–41	13
38–39	11
36–37	8
34–35	5
32–33	1

8. Compute the mean, the median, and the mode of the following frequency distribution of professors' annual salaries (in dollars):

Apparent limits	Frequency (F)
56,000–59,999	2
52,000–55,999	5
48,000–51,999	11
44,000–47,999	14
40,000–43,999	27
36,000–39,999	35
32,000–35,999	29
28,000–31,999	18
24,000–27,999	14
20,000–23,999	6

In Problems 9–11, find the mean, the median, and the mode.

9. The following is a frequency distribution of student rankings of student services at their university:

Apparent limits	Frequency (F)
90–99	10
80–89	16
70–79	28
60–69	34
50–59	49
40–49	25
30–39	39
20–29	32
10–19	11
0– 9	6

10. These 11 scores are the result of a simple reaction time experiment (in milliseconds):

240	356	277	835	277	354
456	789	923	235	456	

11. The following data represent the number of times that 15 patients of a psychoanalyst used the defense mechanism of regression:

23	25	17	11	11	23	6	6
6	7	22	45	21	56	67	

12. Given that the mean, the median, and the mode of a distribution of ten scores all equal 15, what would be the effect on the mean, the median, and the mode of adding an additional score of 37 to the distribution?

13. Suppose we have a distribution with the mean equal to 34, the median equal to 50, and the mode equal to 75. Which measure

of central tendency best represents this distribution? What kind of skew does this distribution have?

14. Suppose we have a distribution with the mean equal to 123, the median equal to 124, and the mode equal to 122. Which measure of central tendency best represents this distribution? How would you describe the skew of this distribution?

15. Suppose we have a distribution with the mean equal to 123, the median equal to 84, and the mode equal to 22. Which measure of central tendency best represents this distribution? How would you describe the skew of this distribution?

16. A distribution with most of the scores at the low end and very few scores at the high end has what kind of skew?

17. How would you describe the relationship between the mean, the median, and the mode in a distribution that has no skew?

18. A distribution with the tail pointing in the positive direction has a _____ skew.

In Problems 19–27, find the mean, the median, and the mode of the data presented.

19. A cognitive psychologist interested in short-term working memory has measured the capacity of short-term memory for 18 subjects.

9	3	5	6	7	7	7	6	8
9	10	13	5	6	4	7	7	7

20. A psychobiologist has been studying the density of neurons in a structure called the *hippocampus* in the brain of the rat and has found that the density of neurons varies from rat to rat. The following data are the numbers of neurons found in equal-sized tissue samples from the brains of 13 rats:

88	93	65	77	77	106	123
139	142	190	97	143	88	

21. A psychologist studying the sensation of touch uses a vibrator to stimulate the nerve endings in the fingers of 11 subjects. Because the rate of vibration can be changed, she is able to find the number of vibrations per second to which each subject is most sensitive. The data follow:

234	254	266	250	231	245
300	222	250	245	231	

22. The midterm exam scores for 500 statistics students at a major university are shown in the following frequency distribution:

Apparent limits	Frequency (F)
95–99	6
90–94	9
85–89	55
80–84	67
75–79	189
70–74	47
65–69	29
60–64	22
55–59	21
50–54	22
45–49	13
40–44	9
35–39	7
30–34	3
25–29	1

23. The following distribution summarizes the numbers of errors made by 294 new student drivers in their first attempt at a driving simulator:

Apparent limits	Frequency (F)
70–76	12
63–69	23
56–62	24
49–55	43
42–48	56
35–41	54
28–34	44
21–27	23
14–20	12
7–13	3

24. The chairs of 118 psychology departments in the United States were asked how many students were employed by their departments as undergraduate research assistants. A frequency distribution of the results is given here:

Apparent limits	Frequency (F)
22–23	1
20–21	3
18–19	3
16–17	4

(continued)

Apparent limits	Frequency (F)
14–15	5
12–13	6
10–11	8
8– 9	13
6– 7	14
4– 5	17
2– 3	20
0– 1	24

25. A drug rehabilitation center has kept records of the number of days that 20 former patients have remained drug-free.

21 35 78 90 123 121 88   17   19 123
45 45 67 78   72   89 78 122 180   87

26. As the pressure to publish increases at colleges and universities, many psychologists meet this pressure by working with co-authors on more and more papers. Following is a list of the numbers of authors for all the research reports published in the journal *Psychological Science* for the year 1990:

3 2 3 5 4 4 4 2 2 2 2 5
4 1 5 3 4 3 1 2 1 3 1

27. The work performance ratings (1 to 10) for 18 employees of a small business are listed:

2 4 5 5 6 6 6 6   6
6 7 7 8 9 9 9 9 10

R E F E R E N C E

Harte, D. B. (1975). Estimates of the length of highway guidelines and spaces. *Human Factors, 17,* 455–460.

CHAPTER FIVE

Measures of Variability

Humans seem to have a built-in need for competition. The legendary Green Bay Packers coach Vince Lombardi once said, "Winning isn't everything; it's the only thing." Many people agree wholeheartedly with his statement, and even the most noncompetitive find themselves acceding to it in at least some circumstances. We compete in myriad aspects of our lives—in business to earn a living, in research to make the first discovery, in school to get the highest grades, in shopping to find the shortest line, in sports to have fun.

Even though humans spend much of their lives competing, it is not clear that competition always brings out the best in people. Indeed, most of the psychological literature on games stresses cooperation rather than competition to improve performance (Buskist & Morgan, 1988). Still, there is something about competition that incites some people to new heights of performance, particularly in sports. What makes competition so compelling is that even heavily favored people or teams often lose. They lose because people's behavior, whether it be academic, athletic, or cooperative team behavior, is not always the same; it varies. With this in mind, see if you can answer the following questions.

Raya Rayavich, with a diving average of 5.8, and Jamie Fowler, who averages 5.7, are vying for the world diving championship. Who will win? An academic college bowl team that averages 150 points per game is competing against a team that averages 140 points. Which one do you think will win? The water polo teams from Cucamonga College and Buckaroo University both average 6 points per game. What are the chances that their game, scheduled for this afternoon, will end in a 6–6 tie? To project the outcomes of these matches, it is certainly helpful to know the competitors' averages. But just because Raya *averages* 5.8, does it mean that she *always* gets a 5.8? Just because a team *averages* 6 points per game, does it mean that the team's final score is *usually* 6? People aren't perfect, and they certainly aren't perfectly consistent. Some, however, are more consistent than others. For example, let's take a look at the Cucamonga and Buckaroo water polo teams.

Knowing the average scores of the Cucamonga and Buckaroo water polo teams leads you to assume that the game will be a close one. But look at their scores in Table 5.1. Cucamonga College unfailingly scores just about 6 goals in every contest, whereas Buckaroo University scores either a lot of goals or none at all, and it has never scored exactly 6. Knowing the point spread for each team, what do you think about the question we asked earlier? Do you think the match will end in a 6–6 tie?

There are statistical tools that can be used to measure the spread of scores in such distributions as the water polo teams' performances; they are called *measures of variability*. When used in conjunction with measures of central tendency, they disclose valuable information about any distribution.

Measures of central tendency yield a single average score that represents

Table 5.1 Goals Scored in the Past Ten Games by the Cucamonga College and Buckaroo University Water Polo Teams

Game	Cucamonga College X	Buckaroo University X
1	6	0
2	5	11
3	6	13
4	7	0
5	6	12
6	6	0
7	6	0
8	8	14
9	5	10
10	5	0
	$\Sigma X = 60$	$\Sigma X = 60$
	$\bar{X} = 6$	$\bar{X} = 6$

an entire distribution. **Measures of variability** give us an idea of how much scores in the distribution *vary* from one another or from that one average score. For instance, by knowing that Rayavich averages 5.8 on her dives, we known that, over all, she is a better diver than Fowler, who averages 5.7. If we also know that each diver's scores almost never vary by more than 0.1 point, we can safely assume that Rayavich will have a better chance of winning the diving championship. Thus, measures of variability can reveal the consistency or similarity of the scores in a distribution. They can also indicate just how much the average score truly represents all the scores in the distribution. If we know that there is a large spread among the scores, as with Buckaroo's water polo scores, we have quite a different picture of the team's performance than we would if the scores clustered around the average, as do Cucamonga's.

We discuss four basic measures of variability in this chapter: the range, the average mean deviation, the variance, and the standard deviation. The range, though by far the easiest to compute, is quite fickle because one extreme score can have a radical effect on it. Therefore, it is seldom used as a measure of variability. By comparison, the variance and the standard deviation, though more complicated than the range, are less affected by extreme scores and are much more widely used.

THE RANGE

The **range** is a measure of the full extent of the scores in a distribution, from the highest to the lowest. It is computed by subtracting the low score from the high score, and adding 1:

$$\text{Range} = \text{high score} - \text{low score} + 1 \qquad (5.1)$$

Question: Why do you have to add the 1?

As we mentioned in Chapter 2, you add 1 to the difference between the scores because both the high score and the low score need to be included in the range: If the scores range from 2 to 5 and we don't add 1 when we calculate the range, then we will get 3 because $5 - 2 = 3$; but the range spans four scores (2, 3, 4, and 5), so the formula must account for this: $5 - 2 + 1 = 4$. As you can see, adding 1 changes the range significantly when the range is small; when the range is large, however, one extra unit has very little effect. (If the high score is 1,000,100 and the low score is 100, adding 1 merely changes the range from 1,000,000 to 1,000,001.) From another point of view, the range can be considered as the difference between the upper real limit of the highest score and the lower real limit of the lowest score. In our example, the range computed this way would be $5.5 - 1.5 = 4$.

The range is extremely easy to compute. Quite often, in fact, you can compute it in your head. For example, look at the data in Table 5.1 and calculate the range of scores for the Cucamonga water polo team and for the Buckaroo team. If you need help, use Formula 5.1:

$$\text{Range}_{\text{Cucamonga}} = 8 - 5 + 1 = 4$$

$$\text{Range}_{\text{Buckaroo}} = 14 - 0 + 1 = 15$$

Even if you didn't have access to the actual scores, knowing the range would tell you that Cucamonga's team must be pretty dependable because all its final scores vary within only 4 points of one another. Buckaroo's team is much more unpredictable because its scores are highly scattered and vary quite a bit. But what if Cucamonga played one team that not only was the worst team in the league but also had an exceptionally bad day, and what if Cucamonga scored 19 points on that one day? Then its distribution of points would look like this:

6	5	6	7	6
6	6	8	5	19

Compare the preceding distribution to the one shown in Table 5.1:

6	5	6	7	6
6	6	8	5	5

The distributions are identical except for that single 19, which changes Cucamonga's range from 4 to 15 and makes it the same as Buckaroo's. If you were shown the means and the revised ranges for the two teams, you would assume that their performances were quite similar. You can see by this example that even though the range is easy to compute, it is severely affected by extreme scores; just one score can alter the range to a large degree. Thus, although the range is sometimes used to gain a quick and easy picture of the spread of scores, it is not used as a reliable measure of variability.

MEAN DEVIATIONS

Question: Is there some measure of variability that takes into account each of the scores so that one extreme score doesn't have so much influence?

Yes, the other measures of variability do just this: They incorporate all the scores in their calculations. Using the mean as a sort of reference point, they determine how much the other scores differ from the mean.

Average Mean Deviation: It All Adds Up to Nothing

The **average mean deviation** is the average deviation of each score from the mean of the distribution. To compute the average mean deviation, first find the mean; then subtract it from each of the scores. This will give you the **deviation scores,** or the mean deviations, which are represented by the symbol x (we call them "little x's"). Next, sum the deviation scores and divide that sum by the total number of scores. Thus, you compute the average mean deviation as you would any average, but instead of computing an average of several numbers or scores, you are computing an average of the deviations from the mean. Here is the formula:

$$\text{Average mean deviation} = \frac{\Sigma(X - \overline{X})}{n} = \frac{\Sigma x}{n} \qquad (5.2)$$

To illustrate the calculation of the average mean deviation, let's pretend you are conducting a preliminary study on conformity. In conformity experiments it is customary to place subjects in situations where a group of confederates (people hired by the experimenter) try to convince the subject to give a response that he or she knows is wrong or false. Suppose that there are five groups, each group consisting of one subject and three confederates. The task of each subject is to determine which of three lines displayed on a computer

Table 5.2 Computation of the Deviation Scores for the Study on Conformity

X	$X - \bar{X}$	x
1	$1 - 3$	-2
2	$2 - 3$	-1
3	$3 - 3$	0
4	$4 - 3$	1
5	$5 - 3$	2
$\Sigma X = 15$		$\Sigma x = 0$
$\bar{X} = 3$		

$$\text{Average mean deviation} = \frac{\Sigma(X - \bar{X})}{n} = \frac{\Sigma x}{n} = \frac{0}{5} = 0$$

screen is the same as a line previously displayed. Everyone in the group sees the same computer screen, and the experimenter asks each person in turn which of the lines on the screen matches the line previously displayed. The confederates are always asked for their opinion before the subject, and the confederates always agree on the same line. During eight of the trials, the critical trials, the confederates name the wrong line as matching the previous line. The dependent variable in this research project is the number of conforming trials: the number of times the subject agrees with the confederates on the critical trials. Table 5.2 lists the number of conforming trials for each of the five subjects in this study.

The average mean deviation is equal to zero. Compare this to the average mean deviation for the two water polo teams, which we have computed in Table 5.3. Do you notice the similarity? These are not special cases. *The average mean deviation is always equal to zero.* Because we are computing the average deviation, about half of the deviation scores are positive; these are counterbalanced by the other half, which are negative. When added together, they equal zero.

The basic idea of finding the average amount each score deviates from the mean is quite sound. But when the end result always equals zero, the procedure is worthless as a measure of variability because it does not allow for any meaningful comparisons between different distributions. If all distributions have the same average mean deviation, then we must find another way to compute the variability of scores within a distribution. The way out of this dilemma is to eliminate the minus signs of the deviation scores. But how can we do this? One way is to use absolute value: Sum the absolute values of the

Table 5.3   Computation of the Deviation Scores for the Cucamonga College and Buckaroo University Water Polo Teams

Game	Cucamonga College			Buckaroo University		
	X	$X - \bar{X}$	x	X	$X - \bar{X}$	x
1	6	6 − 6	0	0	0 − 6	−6
2	5	5 − 6	−1	11	11 − 6	5
3	6	6 − 6	0	13	13 − 6	7
4	7	7 − 6	1	0	0 − 6	−6
5	6	6 − 6	0	12	12 − 6	6
6	6	6 − 6	0	0	0 − 6	−6
7	6	6 − 6	0	0	0 − 6	−6
8	8	8 − 6	2	14	14 − 6	8
9	5	5 − 6	−1	10	10 − 6	4
10	5	5 − 6	−1	0	0 − 6	−6
	$\Sigma X = 60$		$\Sigma x = 0$	$\Sigma X = 60$		$\Sigma x = 0$

mean deviations; then divide by the total number of scores. Absolute value is quite arbitrary, however, and is almost never used in statistics.

C O N C E P T   Q U I Z

1. Distributions with the same means are not necessarily identical because having the same mean does not guarantee that the scores within the distribution have the same _____ .
2. The measure of the spread of the scores within any distribution is called the _____ .
3. The problem with using the range as a measure of variability is that it can be unduly influenced by _____ scores.
4. Subtracting the mean from each score creates _____ scores.
5. The average mean deviation for any distribution is equal to _____ .

Answers

1. variability
2. range
3. extreme
4. deviation
5. zero

THE VARIANCE: THE MEAN OF THE SQUARED DEVIATIONS

Question: How about squaring the deviation scores? When you square negative numbers, the results are positive.

This is exactly what we do when we compute the variance and the standard deviation. Both measures take advantage of the fact that whenever any number, positive or negative, is squared, the resulting value is positive. The **variance**, in fact, is simply the mean of the squared deviations. It is represented by σ^2 (lowercase Greek letter sigma squared) or by S^2, where σ^2 signifies the variance of an entire population of scores and S^2 signifies the variance of a sample. The procedure for computing the variance follows:

1. Compute the mean.
2. Subtract the mean from each score to find the deviation scores.
3. Square each deviation score.
4. Sum the squared deviations.
5. Divide this sum by the total number of scores.

The formulas for this procedure follow. Note that Formula 5.3 is for the variance of a population and Formula 5.4 is for the variance of a sample. Also note that μ represents the mean of a population.

$$\text{Variance of a population} = \sigma^2 = \frac{\Sigma(X - \mu)^2}{N} = \frac{\Sigma x^2}{N} \qquad (5.3)$$

$$\text{Variance of a sample} = S^2 = \frac{\Sigma(X - \overline{X})^2}{n} = \frac{\Sigma x^2}{n} \qquad (5.4)$$

The population variance is the actual computed variance of the population, whereas the sample variance is the actual computed variance of the sample. (There is some disagreement among statisticians regarding the sample variance. Some feel that the sample variance, S^2, should represent the actual computed variance of the sample. Others feel that S^2 should represent an estimate of the population variance using the scores from the sample by substituting $n - 1$ for n in the formula for the sample variance. We have chosen to discuss the estimation of the population variance in Chapter 10 where you learn to compute est. σ^2.) Because it is rare to have access to scores from an entire population, the variance of the sample is more widely used than the variance of the population. Thus, when we use the term *variance* in the rest of this chapter, we are referring to the variance of the sample. In Table 5.4, the variance is computed from the distribution of scores from the conformity study. In Table 5.5, we have calculated the variance for the water polo data.

Table 5.4   Computation of the Variance in the Study on Conformity

Subject	X	$X - \bar{X}$	x	x^2
A	1	1 – 3	−2	4
B	2	2 – 3	−1	1
C	3	3 – 3	0	0
D	4	4 – 3	1	1
E	5	5 – 3	2	4

$\Sigma X = 15$ $\Sigma x^2 = 10$

$\bar{X} = 3$

$$S^2 = \frac{\Sigma x^2}{n} = \frac{10}{5} = 2$$

Table 5.5   Computation of the Variance and Standard Deviation Using Deviation Scores for the Cucamonga College and Buckaroo University Water Polo Teams

Game	Cucamonga College			Buckaroo University		
	X	x	x^2	X	x	x^2
1	6	0	0	0	−6	36
2	5	−1	1	11	5	25
3	6	0	0	13	7	49
4	7	1	1	0	−6	36
5	6	0	0	12	6	36
6	6	0	0	0	−6	36
7	6	0	0	0	−6	36
8	8	2	4	14	8	64
9	5	−1	1	10	4	16
10	5	−1	1	0	−6	36

Cucamonga College:

$\Sigma X = 60$ $\Sigma x^2 = 8$

$\bar{X} = 6$

$$S^2 = \frac{\Sigma x^2}{n} = \frac{8}{10} = 0.8$$

$$S = \sqrt{0.8} = 0.894$$

Buckaroo University:

$\Sigma X = 60$ $\Sigma x^2 = 370$

$\bar{X} = 6$

$$S^2 = \frac{\Sigma x^2}{n} = \frac{370}{10} = 37$$

$$S = \sqrt{37} = 6.083$$

You may have noticed that there is a problem with the variance: It is not in the same units as the original scores. Because all the deviations are squared, the variance is in squared units; this fact can be quite misleading when you try to relate the variance to the raw scores. The solution to this dilemma is quite simple: Compute the square root of the variance, which is the standard deviation.

STANDARD DEVIATION: THE SQUARE ROOT OF THE VARIANCE

The **standard deviation** is the square root of the variance, and it is represented by either σ or S. Thus, the standard deviation is in the same units as the original scores. The formula for the standard deviation of a population is

$$\sigma = \sqrt{\frac{\Sigma(X - \mu)^2}{N}} = \sqrt{\frac{\Sigma x^2}{N}} \quad \text{or} \quad \sigma = \sqrt{\sigma^2} \tag{5.5}$$

The formula for the standard deviation of a sample is

$$S = \sqrt{\frac{\Sigma(X - \overline{X})^2}{n}} = \sqrt{\frac{\Sigma x^2}{n}} \quad \text{or} \quad S = \sqrt{S^2} \tag{5.6}$$

To find the standard deviation of the conformity distribution from Table 5.4, you merely calculate the square root of its variance:

$$S = \sqrt{S^2} = \sqrt{2} = 1.414$$

Table 5.5 shows the calculation of the standard deviation for the water polo teams' scores.

Question: *I still don't really understand the variance and the standard deviation. Without using formulas, can you tell me what they are?*

Both the standard deviation and the variance are averages. The variance is the average of the squared deviations from the mean. And because the standard deviation is the square root of the variance, it represents an average measure of the amount each score deviates from the mean.

COMPUTATIONAL FORMULAS

Question: *Computing the variance and standard deviation is so complicated and time-consuming! Isn't there an easier way to calculate them?*

There are several alternative methods for computing the variance and standard deviation. One of these is to use computational formulas rather than the deviation score formulas we gave earlier. Computational formulas are designed to make calculations faster when you use an electronic calculator, but they are dreadfully tedious when done with paper and pencil because of the large numbers involved. Therefore, you should use them only when you have a calculator. The following computational formulas are for the variance and standard deviation:

$$\text{Variance} = S^2 = \frac{\Sigma X^2}{n} - \left[\frac{\Sigma X}{n}\right]^2 = \frac{\Sigma X^2}{n} - \overline{X}^2 \qquad (5.7)$$

$$\text{Standard deviation} = S = \sqrt{\frac{\Sigma X^2}{n} - \left[\frac{\Sigma X}{n}\right]^2} = \sqrt{\frac{\Sigma X^2}{n} - \overline{X}^2} \qquad (5.8)$$

These formulas introduce a new term: ΣX^2. We read this as "the sum of the X squared," and it equals $X_1^2 + X_2^2 + X_3^2 + \cdots + X_n^2$. It means that you should square each original score and then compute the sum of these squared scores. In Table 5.6, we compute the variance and the standard deviation for the scores from the conformity study using Computational Formula 5.7. Table 5.7 illustrates how the computational formulas are used to calculate the variance and standard deviation of the water polo data for Cucamonga College and Buckaroo University.

Table 5.6 Calculation of the Variance and Standard Deviation Using Computational Formulas for the Study on Conformity

Subject	X	X^2
A	1	1
B	2	4
C	3	9
D	4	16
E	5	25
	$\Sigma X = 15$	$\Sigma X^2 = 55$
	$\overline{X} = 3$	

$$S^2 = \frac{\Sigma X^2}{n} - \overline{X}^2 = \frac{55}{5} - 3^2 = 11 - 9 = 2$$

$$S = \sqrt{S^2} = \sqrt{2} = 1.414$$

Table 5.7 Calculation of the Variance and Standard Deviation Using Computational Formulas for the Cucamonga College and Buckaroo University Water Polo Teams

Game	Cucamonga College X	X^2	Buckaroo University X	X^2
1	6	36	0	0
2	5	25	11	121
3	6	36	13	169
4	7	49	0	0
5	6	36	12	144
6	6	36	0	0
7	6	36	0	0
8	8	64	14	196
9	5	25	10	100
10	5	25	0	0

Cucamonga College:

$$\Sigma X = 60 \qquad \Sigma X^2 = 368$$
$$\bar{X} = 6$$
$$S^2 = \frac{\Sigma X^2}{n} - \bar{X}^2 = \frac{368}{10} - 6^2 = 36.8 - 36 = 0.8$$
$$S = \sqrt{S^2} = \sqrt{0.8} = 0.894$$

Buckaroo University:

$$\Sigma X = 60 \qquad \Sigma X^2 = 730$$
$$\bar{X} = 6$$
$$S^2 = \frac{730}{10} - 6^2 = 73 - 36 = 37$$
$$S = \sqrt{37} = 6.083$$

The easiest alternative to computing any statistics is to use a computer program or a calculator that will compute the values for you. But before you use computer programs or calculators to compute the variance or standard deviation, make sure you know which formulas the machines use. The formulas shown here for the population variance and the sample variance are, for all practical purposes, identical. Oftentimes, however, computers or calculators compute a variance or standard deviation that is an *estimate* of the population value. These estimates (we mentioned this previously) involve formulas that are slightly different from those shown here; therefore, they may return values for the variance and standard deviation that are different from your sample values. An estimate of the population standard deviation is always larger than the sample standard deviation. It is a good idea to read the instruction manuals that come with computer programs and calculators to be sure that your machine uses formulas that will compute the statistics you want.

CALCULATING VARIABILITY FROM GROUPED FREQUENCY DISTRIBUTIONS

Question: Not that I want to have to learn another formula, but is it possible to compute the variance and standard deviation from a grouped frequency distribution?

It is always preferable to use raw data to compute means, variances, and standard deviations; nevertheless, it is possible to compute these values from a grouped frequency distribution if the raw data are not available. The procedure for computing the variance and standard deviation from a grouped frequency distribution is similar to that used to compute the mean from a grouped frequency distribution. Assume that the scores within each interval are represented by the midpoint of that interval. Using the midpoints, follow these steps:

1. Compute the mean.
2. Compute the deviation score for each interval by subtracting the mean from the midpoint ($x = \text{midpoint} - \bar{x}$)
3. Square each deviation score.
4. Multiply each squared deviation score by the frequency in that interval.
5. Sum these products.
6. Divide the sum by the number of scores.

The formula for the variance of a grouped frequency distribution is

$$S^2 = \frac{\Sigma(Fx^2)}{n} \qquad (5.9)$$

Because the standard deviation is the square root of the variance, the formula for the standard deviation of a grouped frequency distribution is

$$S = \sqrt{S^2} = \sqrt{\frac{\Sigma(Fx^2)}{n}} \qquad (5.10)$$

Table 5.8 uses these formulas to compute the variance and standard deviation from the frequency distribution of the highway divider line estimates we discussed in Chapter 4. In Table 5.9, we have computed the variance and standard deviation of a simplified grouped frequency distribution.

Question: I got so caught up in the mathematical formulas and calculations for the variance and standard deviation that I lost sight of what they are all about. Can you explain why we would use them without using mathematical jargon?

In plain terms, the variance and the standard deviation are statistics that

Table 5.8 Computation of the Variance and Standard Deviation from Estimated Lengths of Highway Divider Lines (in Centimeters)

Apparent limits	F	Midpoint	Frequency × midpoint	Midpoint − $\bar{X}$ = x	x^2	Fx^2
300–324	10	312	3,120	115.275	13,288.326	132,883.26
275–299	25	287	7,175	90.275	8,149.576	203,739.40
250–274	69	262	18,078	65.275	4,260.826	293,996.99
225–249	146	237	34,602	40.275	1,622.076	236,823.10
200–224	247	212	52,364	15.275	233.326	57,631.52
175–199	206	187	38,522	−9.725	94.576	19,482.66
150–174	147	162	23,814	−34.725	1,205.826	177,256.42
125–149	104	137	14,248	−59.725	3,567.076	370,975.90
100–124	32	112	3,584	−84.725	7,178.326	229,706.43
75– 99	14	87	1,218	−109.725	12,039.576	168,554.06

$n = \Sigma F = 1{,}000$ $\Sigma(\text{Frequency} \times \text{midpoint}) = 196{,}725$ $\Sigma Fx^2 = 1{,}891{,}049.74$

$$\bar{X} = \frac{196{,}725}{1{,}000} = 196.725$$

$$S^2 = \frac{\Sigma(Fx^2)}{n} = \frac{1{,}891{,}049.74}{1{,}000} = 1{,}891.050$$

$$S = \sqrt{S^2} = \sqrt{1{,}891.050} = 43.486$$

measure how much the scores in a distribution deviate from the mean. They indicate whether the scores are clustered close to the mean, as were the Cucamonga water polo team's, or spread out far from the mean, as were Buckaroo's. As standards, the variance and the standard deviation can readily be used to compare the variability of different distributions. For example, you could use them to compare the variability of a conformity study involving a heterogeneous sample of people with a separate study involving a sample of high-anxiety people

The difference between the variance and the standard deviation is that the latter is the square root of the former. This difference is quite helpful when you are discussing the characteristics of various distributions because it would be extremely confusing to relate the variability to the raw scores if the variability were in squared units. For instance, suppose you were scouting out information to help you predict the outcome of the water polo match and someone told you that the variance of Buckaroo's scores was 37. This wouldn't help

Table 5.9 Computation of the Variance and Standard Deviation from a Grouped Frequency Distribution

Apparent limits	F	Midpoint	Frequency × midpoint	x	x^2	Fx^2
12–14	1	13	13	6	36	36
9–11	2	10	20	3	9	18
6– 8	4	7	28	0	0	0
3– 5	2	4	8	−3	9	18
0– 2	1	1	1	−6	36	36

$$n = 10$$
$$\bar{X} = \frac{70}{10} = 7$$

$$\Sigma(\text{Frequency} \times \text{midpoint}) = 70$$

$$\Sigma Fx^2 = 108$$

$$S^2 = \frac{\Sigma(Fx^2)}{n} = \frac{108}{10} = 10.8$$

$$S = \sqrt{S^2} = \sqrt{\frac{\Sigma(Fx^2)}{n}} = \sqrt{\frac{108}{10}} = \sqrt{10.8} = 3.286$$

you much, especially in light of the fact that Buckaroo's scores range from 0 to 14. But if you were told that the standard deviation of their scores was about 6 as opposed to 0.89 for Cucamonga, it would be easy to compare the two distributions, and you'd almost certainly *not* bet on a 6–6 tie.

C O N C E P T   Q U I Z

1. The variance is simply the _____ of the squared deviations from the population mean or the sample mean.
2. The standard deviation is the _____ of the variance.
3. Which of the following groups of scores has the greatest variance?
   a. 2, 3, 4, 5, 6
   b. 2, 2, 2, 3, 6
   c. 2, 6, 6, 6, 6
4. Why is the standard deviation normally preferred over the variance for describing the variability of a distribution of scores?
5. The value ΣX^2 is one of the terms used in the computational formula for the standard deviation. How do you compute ΣX^2?

Answers

1. mean
2. square root
3. c: the variance equals 2.56
4. The standard deviation is in the same units as the scores in the original distribution, whereas the variance is in squared units.
5. First square each score in the distribution and then sum those squared scores.

S U M M A R Y

This chapter has focused on measures of variation: the range, the average mean deviation, the variance, and the standard deviation. The range is simply the difference between the high and the low scores in the distribution, plus 1. Although it is easy and quick to compute, the range can be overly influenced by extreme scores.

The computation of the other measures of variation begins with calculating the deviation scores. Deviation scores are computed by subtracting the mean from each score in the distribution. They are used when calculating the average mean deviation and when calculating the variance and the standard deviation. The variance and the standard deviation are the most widely used measures of variation.

The average mean deviation is the average deviation of the scores from the mean. It is found by summing the deviation scores and then dividing the result by the number of scores in the distribution. Although by its nature it is always equal to zero, it is the basis for computing the variance and the standard deviation; it was presented in this chapter because of its value in helping to conceptualize the rationale for calculating these other more commonly used measures.

The variance is computed by squaring each deviation score and then computing the mean of the squared deviations. The standard deviation is the square root of the variance. The major advantage of the standard deviation over the variance is that the standard deviation is in the same units as the original scores.

It is also possible to compute the variance and the standard deviation from a grouped frequency distribution. To compute the variance from a grouped frequency distribution, it is necessary to find the mean. Then, using the midpoint of each interval, compute the deviation score for each interval. Next, multiply the frequency of each interval by the squared deviation score for that interval. Sum these products, and divide the sum by the total number of scores. To find the standard deviation from a grouped frequency distribution, merely find the square root of the variance.

KEY TERMS

measures of variability
range
average mean deviation

deviation scores
variance
standard deviation

FORMULAS

$$\text{Range} = \text{high score} - \text{low score} + 1 \tag{5.1}$$

$$\text{Average mean deviation} = \frac{\Sigma(X - \overline{X})}{n} = \frac{\Sigma x}{n} \tag{5.2}$$

Deviation Formulas

$$\text{Variance of a population} = \sigma^2 = \frac{\Sigma(X - \mu)^2}{N} = \frac{\Sigma x^2}{N} \tag{5.3}$$

$$\text{Variance of a sample} = S^2 = \frac{\Sigma(X - \overline{X})^2}{n} = \frac{\Sigma x^2}{n} \tag{5.4}$$

$$\sigma = \sqrt{\frac{\Sigma(X - \mu)^2}{N}} = \sqrt{\frac{\Sigma x^2}{N}} \tag{5.5}$$

$$S = \sqrt{\frac{\Sigma(X - \overline{X})^2}{n}} = \sqrt{\frac{\Sigma x^2}{n}} \tag{5.6}$$

Computational Formulas

$$\text{Variance} = S^2 = \frac{\Sigma X^2}{n} - \left[\frac{\Sigma X}{n}\right]^2 = \frac{\Sigma X^2}{n} - \overline{X}^2 \tag{5.7}$$

$$\text{Standard deviation} = S = \sqrt{\frac{\Sigma X^2}{n} - \left[\frac{\Sigma X}{n}\right]^2} = \sqrt{\frac{\Sigma X^2}{n} - \overline{X}^2} \tag{5.8}$$

Grouped Frequency Distributions

$$S^2 = \frac{\Sigma(Fx^2)}{n} \tag{5.9}$$

$$S = \sqrt{S^2} = \sqrt{\frac{\Sigma(Fx^2)}{n}} \tag{5.10}$$

P R O B L E M S

Seven aircraft accident investigators were asked to rate the severity of a light plane crash. Use their ratings, listed in the table, for Problems 1–5.

Investigator	Severity rating
M. P.	2
J. T.	3
K. T.	5
B. D.	4
J. B.	2
M. K.	3

1. What is the mean for the ratings?

2. Compute the range of the rating scores.

3. Compute the variance of the ratings using Formula 5.3 (the deviation formula).

4. Compute the variance of the ratings using Formula 5.7 (the computational formula).

5. What is the standard deviation of the ratings scores?

The following table lists the numbers of errors for two groups of students on a test of complex mechanical reasoning. Use the data in Problems 6–8.

Engineering majors	History majors
9	14
12	13
14	1
15	19
15	18

6. Use Formula 5.6 (the deviation formula) to compute the standard deviations for both groups.

7. Use Formula 5.8 (the computational formula) to compute the standard deviations for both groups.

8. What do the standard deviations tell you about the two distributions, given that the means for both distributions are 13?

Suppose we conduct an experiment in which we vary the brightness contrast on a video monitor and measure how many words a person can read from that screen in 1 minute. Use the following results of that experiment to do Problems 9–11.

Low brightness contrast	High brightness contrast
Mean = 150 words	Mean = 175 words
Standard deviation = 50 words	Standard deviation = 10 words

9. Which brightness contrast produced the most consistent results? Why do you say that?

10. Of the two brightness contrast conditions, which one do you think will contain the *single subject* who read the most words in 1 minute? Why do you think so?

11. If you were to choose between these two brightness contrast conditions for use on your computer, which one would you choose and why?

In Problems 12–14, use the following frequency distribution of personality test scores.

Apparent limits	Frequency (F)	Midpoint
147–153	5	150
140–146	10	143
133–139	15	136
126–132	20	129
119–125	25	122
112–118	25	115
105–111	20	108
98–104	15	101
91– 97	10	94
84– 90	5	87

12. Compute the mean.

13. Compute the variance.

14. Compute the standard deviation.

In Problems 15–17, use the following frequency distribution of the numbers of errors made by mice running a maze.

Apparent limits	Frequency (F)
33–35	3
30–32	6
27–29	8
24–26	7
21–23	13
18–20	23
15–17	29
12–14	12
9–11	8
6– 8	5
3– 5	1

15. Compute the mean.

16. Compute the variance.

17. Compute the standard deviation.

In Problems 18–29, compute the mean, the variance, and the standard deviation of the scores.

18. The following are block design test scores:

6	3	5	7	3	1	5	4	3
4	4	4	2	2	3	4	5	5

19. A clinical psychologist has recorded the numbers of compulsive acts performed each day during the last week by a person with obsessive-compulsive disorder.

23	34	24	18	23	26	20

20. The following are the biofeedback-assisted changes in blood pressure recordings for 13 people who have hypertension:

5	10	–7	8	12	22	5
0	–3	5	6	12	3	

21. A cognitive psychologist interested in short-term working memory has measured the capacity of short-term memory for 18 respondents.

9	3	5	6	4	7	7	3	8
9	10	13	2	6	4	7	7	7

22. A psychobiologist has been studying the density of neurons in a structure called the *pons* in the brain stem of the rat and has found that the density of neurons varies from rat to rat. The following data are the number of neurons found in equal-sized tissue samples from the brains of 13 rats:

99	93	76	77	77	106	145
183	242	190	97	156	98	

23. A psychologist studying the sensation of touch uses a vibrator to stimulate the nerve endings on the tips of the noses of 11 subjects. Because the rate of vibration can be changed, she is able to find the number of vibrations per second to which each subject is most sensitive. These numbers of vibrations follow:

265	254	297	250	231	232
310	225	240	245	221	

24. The midterm exam scores for 450 statistics students at a major university are shown in the frequency distribution.

Apparent limits	Frequency (F)
95–99	6
90–94	9
85–89	55
80–84	67
75–79	172
70–74	47
65–69	29
60–64	22
55–59	21
50–54	22

25. The following frequency distribution summarizes the numbers of errors made by 275 new student drivers in their first attempt at a driving simulator.

Apparent limits	Frequency (F)
70–76	12
63–69	23
56–62	25
49–55	43
42–48	50
35–41	54
28–34	42
21–27	20
14–20	6

26. The chairs of 100 psychology departments in the United States were asked how many students were employed by their departments as graduate research assistants. A frequency distribution of the results follows.

Apparent limits	Frequency (F)
18–19	4
16–17	4
14–15	7
12–13	6
10–11	6
8– 9	10
6– 7	14
4– 5	10
2– 3	20
0– 1	19

27. A drug rehabilitation center has kept records of the numbers of days that 20 former patients have remained drug-free:

21	35	78	90	113	121	88	17	19	103
45	95	67	78	52	89	78	122	170	87

28. As the pressure to publish increases at colleges and universities, many psychologists meet this pressure by working with co-authors on more and more papers. Following is a list of the number of authors for all the research reports published in the journal *Psychological Science* for the year 1990:

3	2	3	5	4	4	4	2	2	2	2	5
4	1	5	3	4	3	1	2	1	3	1	

29. The work performance ratings (1 to 10) for 15 employees of a small business are:

5	6	6	6	6	6	6	7
7	8	9	9	9	9	10	

REFERENCE

Buskist, W., & Morgan, D. (1988). Method and theory in the study of human competition. In G. Davey & C. Cullen (Eds.), *Human operant conditioning and behavior modification* (pp. 167–195). New York: John Wiley & Sons.

Scaled Scores and Standard Scores: How to Change Apples into Oranges

One of the major uses of statistics is making comparisons. Indeed, we humans are constantly making comparisons. Employees compare their salaries to co-workers' salaries to see whether they are being paid fairly. Students compare their exam grades to other students' to see how they are doing in their classes. Parents compare the age their child first said "Dada" to the age at which other babies accomplished this common but victorious feat. (Parents claim they do this to assure themselves of their child's normal development, but we all know that they're just trying to find another reason to brag.)

The preceding comparisons are simple because we are comparing similar factors—in a figurative sense we are comparing apples to apples. But what if the things we want to compare are dissimilar? Remember back to your elementary school days. Your arithmetic teachers told you it is quite all right to add, subtract, or in some way compare apples to apples. But woe to the pupil who attempts to compare apples to oranges. If you have to work with apples and oranges, your teachers proclaimed, you must find a common denominator. Well then, you reason, how about converting both to pears? If we change the apples into pears and the oranges into pears, we can compare the pears. The only problem is that in the world of fruit, such a conversion is quite impossible unless you happen to be an enchantingly clever magician. In the world of statistics, however, such conversions are totally possible. In this chapter, we lead you first through the rationale, and then through the procedures, for changing distributions in such a way that they can be compared with other previously dissimilar distributions.

Question: So how do you convert apples and oranges into pears in the world of statistics?

SCALED SCORES

Let's start with something a little easier than converting both apples and oranges to pears. Let's just convert apples to oranges. And let's begin with a more (or actually, less) "fruitful" example. Suppose that the professor for your advanced personality course, Dr. Easyone, is subpoenaed to testify about the personality of a defendant in a murder trial, and she is replaced for 2 weeks by Dr. Ardtest. At the end of the 2 weeks, you are tested on the material covered by Dr. Ardtest, and the entire class does very poorly. The scores on this exam for the five students in your class are listed in Table 6.1. The mean is 35 out of 100, which is 45 points below normal for this class. The standard deviation is 7.071, which is exactly the same as that for Dr. Easyone's tests. Because Dr.

Table 6.1   Test Scores

Student	X	x	x^2
A	45	10	100
B	40	5	25
C	35	0	0
D	30	−5	25
E	25	−10	100

$$\Sigma X = 175 \qquad\qquad \Sigma x^2 = 250$$

$$\bar{X} = 35$$

$$S^2 = \frac{250}{5} = 50$$

$$S = \sqrt{50} = 7.071$$

Easyone always grades on a straight percentage (90 = A, 80 = B, etc.), this one test is likely to cause many of the students in the class to fail the course, or at least to fall a couple of grades, when this score is averaged with those of the tests given earlier. Faced with this situation, what do you do if you are a student in this class?

Question: How do you drop this personality class?

If it is too late in the semester to drop the course, there is only one alternative: Get Dr. Easyone to change apples to oranges. In more practical terms, get her to adjust the scores on the test so that you will not be penalized for this overly difficult and unfair test. She can do this by converting the test scores to **scaled scores.** These are scores that are adjusted via some type of scale, through applying (adding, multiplying, subtracting, or dividing) the same constant to all the scores in the distribution. Be aware that when raw scores are transformed to scaled scores, the distribution is invariably modified in some way. The mean, the variance, and the standard deviation may change depending on how the scores are modified. We look first at the effect of adding or subtracting a constant to each score in the distribution.

Adding or Subtracting a Constant: No Change in Variability

If we add a constant to each score in any distribution, we in effect create a new distribution based on the original one. Because the scores on Dr. Ardtest's exam were 45 points below normal for this class, Dr. Easyone could just add

Table 6.2   Test Scores with 45 Points Added

Student	X_{orig}	$(X_{original} + 45)$ X_{new}	x_{new}	x_{new}^2
A	45	90	10	100
B	40	85	5	25
C	35	80	0	0
D	30	75	−5	25
E	25	70	−10	100

$$\Sigma X_{orig} = 175 \qquad \Sigma X_{new} = 400 \qquad \Sigma x_{new}^2 = 250$$

$$\bar{X}_{orig} = 35 \qquad \bar{X}_{new} = \frac{400}{5} = 80$$

$$S_{orig}^2 = 50 \qquad S_{new}^2 = \frac{250}{5} = 50$$

$$S_{orig} = \sqrt{50} = 7.071 \qquad S_{new} = \sqrt{50} = 7.071$$

45 points to each student's test score to make up the difference. If she does this, it will result in the distribution shown in Table 6.2. The new distribution has a new mean that is 45 points higher than in the original distribution; thus, this new mean is increased by exactly the same number of points as the constant that was added to each score. The variance and the standard deviation have not changed at all.

Question: Why does the mean change and not the standard deviation?

Obviously, adding a constant to each score raises the value of each score; therefore, the sum of the scores is increased, as is the mean. However, adding the constant does not affect the spread of the scores. The highest score is still 5 points higher than the next highest score, and so on. Since the general spread of all the scores is not affected, this simple transformation does not change the variance or the standard deviation.

Question: Is the same thing true when you subtract a constant from each score?

Yes; when you subtract a constant from each score, you again change the mean without affecting the variance or the standard deviation. Table 6.3 shows the scores for 25 college students on a test measuring their need for affiliation. A high score (25) indicates that the student has personality traits

Table 6.3 Need for Affiliation Scores for 25 College Students

X_{orig}	$(X_{orig} - \bar{X}_{orig})$ X_{new}	x	x^2
7	−8	−8	64
10	−5	−5	25
25	10	10	100
21	6	6	36
9	−6	−6	36
2	−13	−13	169
13	−2	−2	4
25	10	10	100
15	0	0	0
17	2	2	4
15	0	0	0
11	−4	−4	16
7	−8	−8	64
19	4	4	16
23	8	8	64
8	−7	−7	49
17	2	2	4
17	2	2	4
22	7	7	49
21	6	6	36
12	−3	−3	9
24	9	9	81
10	−5	−5	25
10	−5	−5	25
15	0	0	0

$\Sigma X_{orig} = 375$ $\qquad$ $\Sigma X_{new} = 0$ $\qquad\qquad\qquad$ $\Sigma x^2 = 980$

$\bar{X}_{orig} = 15$ $\qquad\quad$ $\bar{X}_{new} = 0$

$S^2_{orig} = 39.2$ $\qquad\quad$ $S^2_{new} = \dfrac{980}{25} = 39.2$

$S_{orig} = 6.261$ $\qquad\quad$ $S_{new} = \sqrt{39.2} = 6.261$

associated with people who like to be with other people, whereas a low score (2) indicates that the student is a loner. The mean affiliation score for this group of college students is 15. Rather than subtract a random constant from each of these scores, we decided to subtract 15, the mean, from each score. It is clear from an inspection of Table 6.3 that when 15 was subtracted from each score, the mean decreased by the same amount, whereas the variance and the standard deviation remained the same. To summarize, *if you add or subtract a constant from each score in the distribution, the mean changes by the amount that was added or subtracted and the variance and the standard deviation stay the same.* Stated more succinctly:

$$\overline{X}_{new} = \overline{X}_{orig} \pm constant \tag{6.1}$$

and

$$S_{new} = S_{orig} \tag{6.2}$$

Multiplying or Dividing by a Constant: A Concurrent Change in Mean and Standard Deviation

Question: If you multiply each score by the same number—say, 2—what happens to the mean and the standard deviation?

If we double each score, the sum of the scores will of course increase, resulting in a change in the mean. Multiplying each score by 2 will also change the spread of the scores, thus affecting the variance and the standard deviation. Table 6.4 shows what happens when we double our sample of five test scores. If you compare both the original mean and standard deviation to the new ones, it is evident that the new mean is twice the original mean and the new standard deviation is twice the original standard deviation. The variance

Table 6.4   Test Scores Multiplied by 2

Student	X_{orig}	$(X_{orig} \times 2)$ X_{new}	x_{new}	x_{new}^2
A	45	90	20	400
B	40	80	10	100
C	35	70	0	0
D	30	60	−10	100
E	25	50	−20	400

$$\Sigma X_{orig} = 175 \qquad \Sigma X_{new} = 350 \qquad \Sigma x_{new}^2 = 1000$$

$$\overline{X}_{orig} = 35 \qquad \overline{X}_{new} = \frac{350}{5} = 70$$

$$S_{orig}^2 = 50 \qquad S_{new}^2 = \frac{1000}{5} = 200$$

$$S_{orig} = \sqrt{50} = 7.071 \qquad S_{new} = \sqrt{200} = 14.142$$

Table 6.5 Need for Affiliation Scores Divided by a Constant

X_{orig}	$(X_{orig} \div S_{orig})$ X_{new}	x	x^2
7	1.118	−1.276	1.628
10	1.597	−0.797	0.635
25	3.993	1.599	2.557
21	3.354	0.960	0.922
9	1.437	−0.957	0.916
2	0.319	−2.075	4.306
13	2.076	−0.318	0.101
25	3.993	1.599	2.557
15	2.396	0.002	0.000
17	2.715	0.321	0.103
15	2.369	0.002	0.000
11	1.757	−0.637	0.406
7	1.118	−1.276	1.628
19	3.035	0.641	0.411
23	3.674	1.280	1.638
8	1.278	−1.116	1.245
17	2.715	0.321	0.103
17	2.715	0.321	0.103
22	3.514	−1.120	1.254
21	3.354	0.960	0.922
12	1.917	−0.477	0.228
24	3.833	1.439	2.070
10	1.597	−0.797	0.635
10	1.597	−0.797	0.635
15	2.369	0.002	0.000

$\Sigma X_{orig} = 375$ $\Sigma X_{new} = 59.840$ $\Sigma x^2_{new} = 25.012$

$\bar{X}_{orig} = 15$ $\bar{X}_{new} = \dfrac{59.840}{25} = 2.394$

$S^2_{orig} = 39.2$ $S^2_{new} = \dfrac{25.012}{25} = 1.000$

$S_{orig} = 6.261$ $S_{new} = \sqrt{1} = 1$

also changes, but it is multiplied by the square of the constant rather than just the constant itself.

Table 6.5 shows the effect of dividing each score in the distribution by a constant. In Table 6.5, which uses the same scores as Table 6.3, each original score is divided by the original standard deviation. This results in a new mean that equals the original mean divided by the original standard deviation and in a new standard deviation that equals the original standard deviation divided by itself. From these two examples it is easy to see that if you multiply or divide each score in the distribution by the same constant, then

$$\overline{X}_{new} = \overline{X}_{orig} \times \text{or} \div \text{constant} \tag{6.3}$$

and

$$S_{new} = S_{orig} \times \text{or} \div \text{constant} \tag{6.4}$$

CONCEPT QUIZ

1. If we add, subtract, multiply, or divide each score in a distribution by the same constant, we create a new distribution of _____ scores.
2. If we add 10 to each score in a distribution, we create a new mean equal to the old mean _____ and a new standard deviation equal to

   _____ .
3. Adding or subtracting a constant from each score in the distribution has what effect on the mean and standard deviation?
4. If we create a new distribution by dividing all the scores in a distribution by 3, we create a new distribution with a new mean equal to the old mean _____ and a new standard deviation equal to the old standard deviation _____ .
5. Multiplying or dividing each score by a constant has what effect on the mean and standard deviation?

Answers

1. scaled
2. plus 10; the old standard deviation
3. It changes the mean of the distribution by the amount added or subtracted from each score, but the standard

deviation remains the same.
4. divided by 3; divided by 3
5. It either multiplies or divides both the mean and the standard deviation by the constant.

Question: Now I know how to change test scores into larger or smaller scores. When am I going to learn how to change apples and oranges into pears?

As any magician will tell you, changing is the hard part. Once you change one score by making it larger or smaller, it is not difficult to convert it into something else. The goal of this chapter is to show you a way to *standardize* any distribution by transforming a distribution of scores so that you can compare it with any other distribution. Figuratively speaking, this involves transforming apples into pears and oranges into pears, and then comparing them. Statistically speaking, it involves transforming scores from two dissimilar distributions into those ultimate common denominators known as **standard scores,** or z scores.

STANDARD SCORES (Z SCORES)

If Dr. Ardtest's exam had produced a distribution similar to Dr. Easyone's distributions with the same mean and standard deviation, then Dr. Ardtest's scores could be considered comparable to the scores on the other tests. Unfortunately, when we want to compare two distributions, the means and standard deviations are often *not* the same. We need to convert raw scores to standard z scores, which makes it possible to compare disparate distributions, such as apples and oranges, SAT scores and ACT scores, dollars and rubles. z scores are standard, uniform values to which any raw-score value can be converted. **The z-score distribution has a mean of 0 and a standard deviation of 1.** Any distribution, regardless of its original mean and standard deviation, can be converted into the z-score distribution through a simple transformation of the scores using the rules given in Formulas 6.1–6.4.

To transform a distribution of scores into z scores, the first step is to create a new distribution with a mean of 0. Take a look at Formula 6.1. It states that the new mean is equal to the original mean plus or minus the constant used to transform the scores. Thus, if the original mean is 35, what value must we subtract in order for the new mean to equal 0? Of course: 35, the original mean. And because we are subtracting 35 from the mean, we also need to subtract 35 from each of the other scores in the distribution. We have devised a mnemonic (memory technique) to help you remember that the first step in creating z scores is to subtract the mean from each score. Think of the z as representing "zero." This will remind you that you must bring the mean down to 0 by subtracting the mean from itself and then from the other scores.

If Dr. Easyone were to devise a z-score distribution for the low test scores, she would first subtract the original mean, 35, from each score and obtain the distribution listed in Table 6.6.

To review, a z-score distribution has a mean of 0 and a standard deviation of 1. We have discussed how to transform a group of scores so that their mean is 0; now we show you how to transform their standard deviation so that it equals 1. If you recall from Formula 6.4, the new standard deviation equals the original standard deviation multiplied or divided by a constant. The second step in creating z scores requires that we change the spread of the scores by multiplying or dividing each score by a constant such that the standard deviation will be equal to 1. What is this constant? If the original standard deviation is 7.071, by

Table 6.6   Test Scores with 35 Points Subtracted

Student	X_{orig}	$\dfrac{(X_{orig} - \bar{X}_{orig})}{X_{new}}$	x_{new}	x_{new}^2
A	45	10	10	100
B	40	5	5	25
C	35	0	0	0
D	30	−5	−5	25
E	25	−10	−10	100

$$\Sigma X_{orig} = 175 \qquad \Sigma X_{new} = 0 \qquad \Sigma x_{new}^2 = 250$$

$$\bar{X}_{orig} = 35 \qquad \bar{X}_{new} = \frac{0}{5} = 0$$

$$S_{orig}^2 = 50 \qquad S_{new}^2 = \frac{250}{5} = 50$$

what number can you divide it to make it equal 1? The answer is: itself. Thus, z scores are produced by subtracting the original mean from each score and then dividing by the original standard deviation. The formula using the sample mean and the sample standard deviation is

$$z = \frac{X - \bar{X}}{S} \tag{6.5}$$

The formula for z using the population mean and the population standard deviation is

$$z = \frac{X - \mu}{\sigma} \tag{6.6}$$

Although z scores can be computed using the population mean and population standard deviation, these are rarely available. Thus, the mean and the standard deviation of the *sample* are most commonly used. In the following table, Dr. Ardtest's scores have been converted to z scores by using Formula 6.5:

Student	X	z
A	45	1.414
B	40	0.707
C	35	0.000
D	30	−0.707
E	25	−1.414

Table 6.7 Computation of the Mean and Standard Deviation of z Scores

Student	z	x_z	x_z^2
A	1.414	1.414	2.0
B	0.707	0.707	0.5
C	0.000	0.000	0.0
D	−0.707	−0.707	0.5
E	−1.414	−1.414	2.0

$$\Sigma z = 0.000 \qquad\qquad \Sigma x_z^2 = 5.0$$

$$\bar{z} = \frac{0}{5} = 0 \text{ (mean)}$$

$$S_z^2 = \frac{5}{5} = 1$$

$$S_z = \sqrt{1} = 1 \text{ (standard deviation)}$$

To prove to you that these are true z scores and to illustrate that z scores do indeed have a mean of 0 and a standard deviation of 1, we have computed the mean and standard deviation for the preceding scores in Table 6.7.

By now you may be able to appreciate that once a distribution has been converted to z scores, it can be compared to any other distribution that has also been converted to z scores. So it is possible to compare apples to oranges.

Question: I'm still a little fuzzy about what a z score actually represents. What does a z score tell you?

The next chapter is dedicated to discussing the normal curve, and after reading that chapter you'll have a much clearer comprehension of the value of z scores. Basically, however, a z score tells you how many standard deviation units above or below the mean your original score lies. A z score of +2 means that the original score is two standard deviations above the mean; a z score of −1 means that the original score is one standard deviation below the mean. A z score of +0.27 indicates that the raw score is 27/100 of a standard deviation above the mean; a z score of −0.84 indicates that the raw score is 84/100 of a standard deviation below the mean.

Let's use an example to clarify this point. Suppose you want to compare the IQ scores of two individuals. This may seem simple until you realize that there are several types of IQ tests, and the two people took different tests. Mark took the Stanford-Binet Intelligence Scale and scored 145, and Judy took the Wechsler Adult Intelligence Scale and scored 144. Mark's score was higher than Judy's, but if we assume that IQ tests actually do measure intelligence (and this is an extremely controversial subject right now), who is *really* more intelligent?

The way to answer this question is to find the mean and standard deviation of each test, convert each IQ score to a z score, and then determine who has the higher z score. Let's assume that the mean of Mark's test is 100 and the standard deviation is 16 IQ points; the mean of Judy's test is 100 and the standard deviation is 15 points. Using Formula 6.5, we can convert the two IQ scores to z scores and then make our comparison:

$$z_{\text{Mark}} = \frac{145 - 100}{16} = \frac{45}{16} = 2.813$$

$$z_{\text{Judy}} = \frac{144 - 100}{15} = \frac{44}{15} = 2.933$$

These calculations show that Judy has a slightly higher z score than Mark. Judy's IQ score was 2.933 standard deviations above the mean; Mark's was only 2.813 standard deviations above the mean. Thus, assuming that these IQ tests really do measure intelligence, it looks as if Judy's IQ score of 144 on the Wechsler test indicates a slightly higher intelligence than Mark's 145 on the Stanford-Binet test. We really can compare apples to oranges if we first convert them both to z scores.

C O N C E P T   Q U I Z

1. If we want to compare the scores in two different distributions, we must first transform each distribution into _____ or _____ scores.
2. The z distribution has a mean of _____ and a standard deviation equal to _____ .
3. A z score of 2.0 indicates a raw score that is two _____ above the mean.

Answers

1. standard; z
2. 0; 1

3. standard deviations

S U M M A R Y

It is possible to transform distribution scores in several ways. The simplest is to merely add or subtract a constant from each score in the distribution, which causes the mean to increase or decrease by the amount of the constant without affecting the variance or the standard deviation. It is also possible to multiply or divide each score by a constant, which results in both the mean and the standard deviation changing by the value of the constant used in the multiplication or division process.

Knowing these rules of transformation, we can create a new distribution that has a mean of 0 and a standard deviation of 1. This new distribution is called a *z*-score distribution, and the scores that make up this distribution are known as standard scores, or *z* scores. *z* scores are computed by subtracting the mean of the distribution from the original score and then dividing that result by the standard deviation.

KEY TERMS

scaled scores

standard scores

z scores

z-score distribution

FORMULAS

$$\overline{X}_{new} = \overline{X}_{orig} \pm constant \tag{6.1}$$

$$S_{new} = S_{orig} \tag{6.2}$$

$$\overline{X}_{new} = \overline{X}_{orig} \times or \div constant \tag{6.3}$$

$$S_{new} = S_{orig} \times or \div constant \tag{6.4}$$

$$z = \frac{X - \overline{X}}{S} \tag{6.5}$$

$$z = \frac{X - \mu}{\sigma} \tag{6.6}$$

PROBLEMS

Suppose we were examining the lengths of positive interactions between siblings in various environments during a 3-hour period. In a classroom environment, we found that the mean length of positive interactions was 100 minutes and the standard deviation was 20 minutes.

1. Calculate the new mean and the new standard deviation of this distribution if you add 10 to each score.

2. Calculate the new mean and the new standard deviation of the distribution if you subtract 20 from each score.

3. If you multiply each score in the original distribution by 7, what are the new mean and the new standard deviation?

4. If you divide each score in the original distribution by 5, what are the new mean and the new standard deviation?

5. What is the effect on the mean and the standard deviation of the original distribution if you subtract the mean from each score?

6. What are the resultant mean and standard deviation if you first subtract the mean from each score and then divide each of those scores by the standard deviation?

7. What is the effect on the mean and the standard deviation if you divide each score by the standard deviation?

8. In a duplication of Pavlov's classic conditioning experiment, we obtained the following amounts of saliva when dogs were presented with meat powder. Compute the mean and the standard deviation for the distribution, and then convert each score to a z score.

Dog	Amount of saliva (in milliliters)	z score
Spot	250	_____
Rover	240	_____
Blackie	280	_____
Ginger	190	_____
Gus	300	_____
Scruffy	200	_____
Digger	230	_____
Muffin	180	_____
Sandy	160	_____
Tiger	280	_____

9. A psychiatrist who was particularly interested in the use of defense mechanisms recorded the numbers of defense mechanisms used by her clients during their sessions with her over a month. Find the mean and the standard deviation for her distribution, and then convert the individual clients' scores to z scores.

Client	Number of defense mechanisms	z score
L. V.	0	_____
P. D.	3	_____
O. S.	6	_____
T. J.	7	_____
T. V.	11	_____
M. Q.	18	_____
I. S.	21	_____
B. J.	26	_____
K. S.	28	_____
L. B.	30	_____

10. Given that the mean of a statistics test is 84 and the standard deviation of this test is 4, convert the following test scores to z scores:

94   97   88   85   84   80   77   74   76

11. Given that the mean number of secondary reinforcements each day in a psychiatric hospital token economy is 10 tokens and the standard deviation is 4.5 tokens, convert the following to z scores:

16 tokens
19 tokens
8 tokens
9 tokens
10 tokens

12. Given that the mean response time to a very complex visual display is 825 milliseconds (ms) with a standard deviation of 186 milliseconds, convert the following response times to z scores:

700 ms
1000 ms
900 ms
950 ms
745 ms

The mean on a personality test given to 100 people is 345 and the standard deviation is 27. Use these values to solve Problems 13–17.

13. What are the new mean and the new standard deviation if you add 50 to each score?

14. What are the new mean and the new standard deviation if you divide each score by 23?

15. What are the new mean and the new standard deviation if you subtract 100 from each score?

16. What are the new mean and the new standard deviation if you multiply each score by 19?

17. What are the new mean and the new standard deviation if you add 25 to each score and then divide each score by 6?

A football coach gives a motivation index to each of his players and finds that his team averages 37, with a standard deviation of 13. Use these values to answer Problems 18–21.

18. What would the new mean and the new standard deviation be if the coach could motivate each player to increase his score by 13 points?

19. What would the new mean and the new standard deviation be if the coach could motivate each player to double his motivation score?

20. What would the new mean and the new standard deviation be if the coach could motivate each player to decrease his motivation score by 13?

21. What would the new mean and the new standard deviation be if the coach could motivate each player to divide his motivation score by 4?

22. The following are key-pecking rates for eight pigeons at the local psychology lab. Compute the mean and the standard deviation for the eight pigeons and then convert each pigeon's rate to a z score.

Pigeon	Pecking rate	z score
A	22	_____
B	23	_____
C	20	_____
D	24	_____
E	21	_____
F	21	_____
G	24	_____
H	25	_____

23. The following are the self-esteem scores for the nine members of a women's basketball team. Compute the mean and the standard deviation of the nine scores, and then convert each woman's score to a z score.

Woman	Self-esteem score	z score
T. D.	94	_____
B. C.	68	_____
D. D.	78	_____
P. F.	93	_____
N. Q.	85	_____
O. T.	80	_____
N. G.	75	_____
V. C.	77	_____
R. C.	69	_____

24. Patients with bipolar affective disorder alternate between mania and depression. The following data are the number of days between manic and depressed phases of the disorder for five patients with this disorder. Compute the mean and the standard deviation for the five patients, and then convert each patient's score to a z score.

Patient	Number of days	z score
O. D.	16	_____
B. G.	10	_____
I. D.	37	_____
P. C.	43	_____
G. Q.	56	_____

25. The mean for all students who took the College Aptitude Test in 1995 was 476, and the standard deviation was 104 points. Using the preceding information, convert the following CAT test scores to z scores:

290
735
666
450
476

26. The mean for a group of people on a delayed recall task is 12 items, and the standard deviation is 3.7 items. Convert the following delayed recall scores to z scores:

14   17   9   7   8   15   12

27. A statistics professor always converts every test score to a z score. In the fall of 1996, Ralph received a raw score of 91 on the midterm with a z score of +1.7. In the spring of 1997, Mary received a raw score of 97 on the same midterm with a z score of +1.65. Which of these students received the higher score compared to fellow students? Explain why you believe this is true.

The Normal Curve

I n 1894 Mark Twain observed:

We should be careful to get out of an experience only the wisdom that is in it—and stop there; lest we be like the cat that sits down on a hot stove lid. She will never sit down on a hot stove lid again—and that is well; but also she will never sit down on a cold one any more.

Mark Twain earned his acclaim through his exceptional ability to fathom human, and in this case animal, behavior and then write about it in a way that prompts us to laugh at our shortcomings and ponder our antics. Observations similar to Mark Twain's about the cat learning not to sit on a hot stove lid have been scientifically explored in psychological research on classical conditioning, which was begun at the turn of the century by Ivan Pavlov. Any stimulus, such as heat, that causes a reflex response can be paired with a neutral stimulus, such as a stove lid, so that eventually the neutral stimulus will cause the response. In this way, the cat is conditioned—it learns—to avoid hot stove lids.

Mark Twain notes not only the conditioning but also another interesting phenomenon associated with classical conditioning. He admonishes us to beware of our tendency to generalize. Once a person or an animal has learned a conditioned response to a conditioned stimulus, stimuli similar to the conditioned stimulus may also cause that same response. Through generalization, the cat learns to avoid not only *hot* stove lids, but cold stove lids as well. Likewise, much as Mark Twain warned against it, through generalization some of us learn to stereotype all homeless people as being lazy and good-for-nothing and all people who have schizophrenia as being dangerous to society. We learn to fear all snakes, not just those with rattles on their tails. We lump all art history professors into the dull and boring category. We react to all bells as if they are attached to phones or doors that need to be answered.

Speaking of bells, Ivan Pavlov first used bells and then tones to study conditioning. While conditioning his dogs to salivate to a specific tone—for example, a tone with a pitch of 1000 cycles per second—he noticed that he could also cause salivation in the dogs if he used a slightly lower pitch, such as 900 cycles per second, or a slightly higher pitch, such as 1100 cycles per second. As a matter of fact, the amount of salivation was directly related to the similarity between the tone presented and the original tone. The more closely the tone resembled the original tone, the more the dogs salivated; the less the tone resembled the original tone, the less the dogs salivated. When Pavlov graphed the amount of salivation on the y-axis and the tone on the x-axis, he noticed a bell-shaped curve with its center at the original 1000-cycle tone.

Typical of most generalization experiments, the results of Pavlov's experiments illustrate the **normal curve,** which is in essence a graphic picture of the bell-shaped normal distribution. In a **normal distribution,** most of the scores are clustered around the middle, around the mean/median/mode (these measures are all equal in a normal distribution), with the frequency of the other scores gradually lessening on either side. When a normal distribution is graphed, it takes on the shape of a bell, with a large center hump where the highest frequency of scores is located. The curve gradually descends on either side and flattens out as it approaches either end, indicating that there are progressively fewer scores at the extremes. Much of the data collected in any scientific discipline—be it chemistry, biology, or psychology—tend to be normally distributed and can be described by a normal curve. For instance, if during Pavlov's experiment he had measured the activity level of each dog and graphed the numbers of times the dogs moved, he would have inevitably graphed a normal curve. A few dogs would have made few movements, most of them would have made a moderate number of movements, and a few would have jumped and moved around a lot. Likewise, if he had measured the dogs' eating behavior by counting the number of bits of dog chow each dog consumed and then graphed these data, the resulting graph would probably have assumed a normal curve similar to the activity graph. Something to remember when working with the normal curve is that real data can only approximate the normal curve because the perfect normal distribution exists in theory only.

CHARACTERISTICS OF THE NORMAL CURVE

The shape of the normal curve reflects the fact that most behavior is "normal," with the extremes of behavior being rare and found at either end of the curve. This is evident when we graph any behavioral variable, from scores on personality tests to reaction times to the numbers of nonsense words remembered in a memory task. For the most part, behavior tends to be normally distributed across most populations. Depending on the behavior being measured and the individual performances of the members of the population or sample, normal curves can assume various shapes with an endless variety of means and standard deviations, as illustrated in Figure 7.1. Nevertheless, all normal curves share some common characteristics:

1. The curve is bell-shaped and symmetrical.
2. The mean, the median, and the mode are all equal.
3. The highest frequency is in the middle of the curve.
4. The frequency gradually tapers off as the scores approach the ends of the curve.
5. The curve approaches but never meets the abscissa at both the high and low ends.

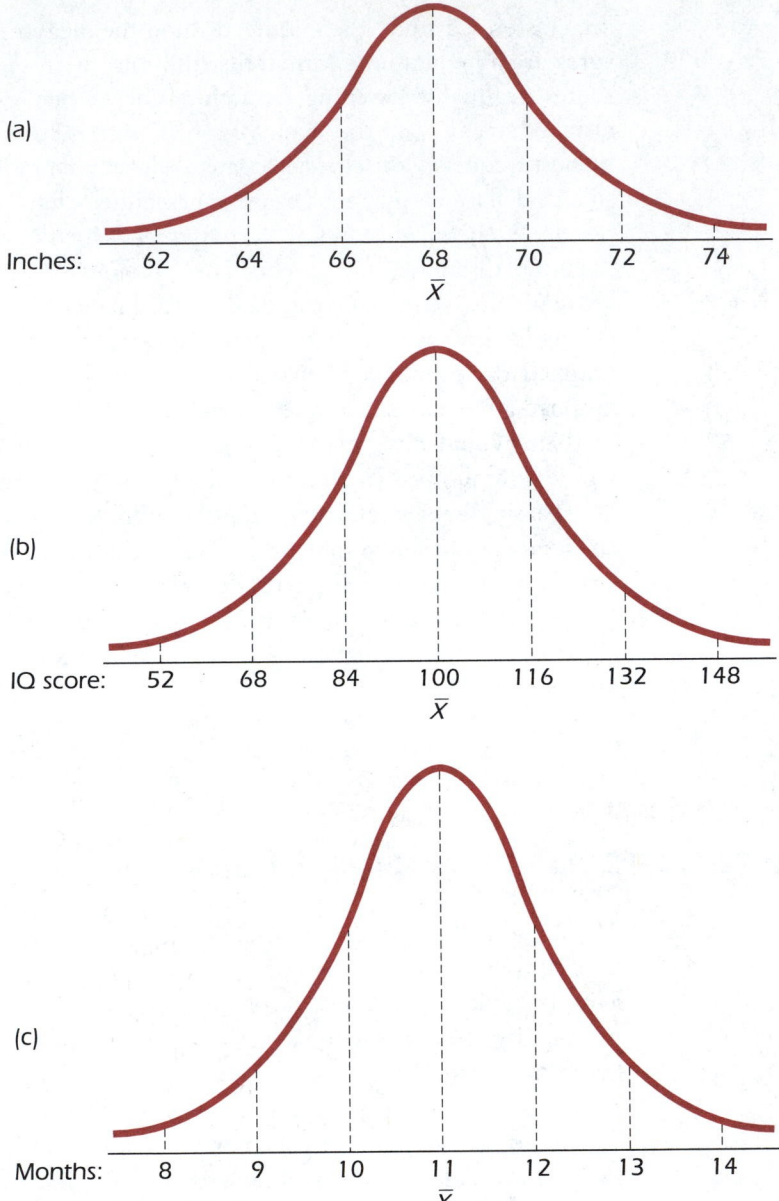

Figure 7.1 Examples of three normal curves: (a) the heights of students in a psychological statistics class, (b) scores on the Stanford-Binet IQ Scale, and (c) the ages when children took their first steps at the Midtown Child Care Center

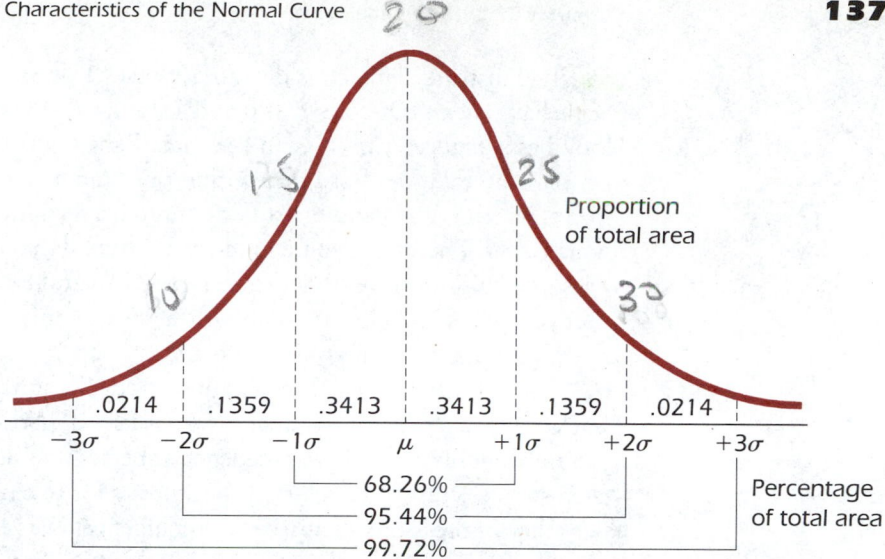

Figure 7.2 Areas under the normal curve

The normal curve can be envisioned as a picture of the proportion of the total number of scores lying under the curve. The entire area under the curve is equal to 1. Imagine a line drawn from the precise center at the top of the curve straight down to the horizontal axis. Exactly .50 (50%) of the total scores in the distribution lie above, or to the right of this line, and 50% lie below, or to the left. The score at this precise center is the mean. As you can see in Figure 7.2, 34.13% (about one-third) of the scores can be found from the mean to the point that is one standard deviation unit *above* the mean (+1σ). The same amount, 34.13%, can be found from the mean to one standard deviation unit *below* the mean (−1σ), so it follows that 68.26% (a little more than two-thirds) of the scores lie between −1σ and +1σ. Figure 7.2 illustrates the proportions of scores lying under the entire normal curve. Note that the curve never touches the horizontal axis. This is because, conventionally, normal curves are used to describe populations, and they must be open-ended to allow for the rare scores that do not fall within three standard deviation units of the mean.

Question: I don't understand. What if the mean is 100 and the standard deviation is 16? Your figure shows only three standard deviation units; it doesn't go up to 16.

When we say that the standard deviation is equal to 16, we mean that *one* standard deviation unit (1σ) equals 16 points. Remember that one standard deviation unit is also equal to a *z* score of 1. So one standard deviation unit above the mean would be equal to the mean, 100, plus 1 × 16, or 116; two standard deviation units *below* the mean would equal 100 minus 2 × 16, or

68. To illustrate, let's consider an IQ test. The Stanford-Binet Intelligence Scale has a mean IQ score of 100 and a standard deviation of 16 IQ points. By looking at Figure 7.2, you can see that slightly more than two-thirds of the people who take the test score within one standard deviation unit above the mean, which is 116, and within one standard deviation unit below the mean, which is 84. Therefore, you would expect to find that two-thirds of the people who take this test have IQ scores between 116 and 84. Moreover, if you know that your IQ is 132 (132 is 2σ above the mean), only 2.28% of the population has an IQ higher than yours. (Dream on . . .)

This information can have highly practical applications. For instance, we know a teacher with a student who seemed particularly bright but was virtually unable to read at grade level, subtract double-digit numbers, or spell even simple words. She referred the student for testing in order to confirm or deny her impressions of his basic intelligence. Was he intelligent enough to excel in school? Or was he in fact a dull child without the capacity to perform at grade level? Assuming that the tests were valid, she could answer the following questions merely by knowing her student's score: Is the student about average in intelligence? Is he above average, as she suspected? What percentage of the population scores better than this student? Worse? Even if the teacher were not told the student's exact score but only that he scored, say, in the top 9% of the population, she could figure out the exact score.

Question: You mean that there's actually a way to figure out a student's exact score just by knowing the percentage?

Yes, by knowing the percentage, as well as knowing the mean and standard deviation of the test. In fact, a great many questions can be answered about how an individual's behavior compares to a population's by using the normal curve. These questions are answered next.

C O N C E P T   Q U I Z

1. The normal curve has a _____ shape.
2. In the normal curve, the mean, the median, and the mode are all _____ .
3. In a normal curve, the frequency of scores gradually tapers off as the scores approach the _____ of the curve.
4. In a normal curve, _____ of the scores lie above the mean and _____ of the scores lie below the mean.
5. In a normal curve, approximately _____ % of the scores lie

between one standard deviation unit below the mean and one standard deviation unit above the mean.

6. If the mean for a test equals 80 and the standard deviation for that test equals 10, use Figure 7.2 to determine the percentage of students taking this test who score between 60 and 100.

7. Given that a test has a mean of 20 and a standard deviation of 5, use Figure 7.2 to determine what test scores represent the limits of the middle 68.26% of the scores in the distribution.

Answers

1. bell

2. equal

3. ends

4. 50% or half; 50% or half

5. 68

6. 95.44%

7. 15 and 25

FINDING PROPORTIONS AND PERCENTAGES

As we have mentioned, normal curves have countless shapes and sizes, depending on the data collected and how the scores are distributed. Their means as well as their standard deviations can vary widely. In Chapter 6 you learned that in order to compare two completely different sets of scores, you can standardize the scores by converting both sets to z scores. Two separate tables based on z scores—Table Z and Table P—have been devised to help people answer questions about proportions of scores. *Both Tables Z and P are found in Appendix A at the back of this book.*

Using Table *Z*: Finding Areas Under the Curve

You should use Table Z when you know a particular score or scores and you want to determine the proportion or percentage of scores lying above or below that one score or between two known scores. Table Z is divided into three columns. So that you won't have to turn back to the appendix each time, we have excerpted a section of Table Z in Figure 7.3 so you can refer to it while we describe it.

- **Column 1** lists positive z scores from 0 to 3.70. The normal curve is symmetrical, so to find a negative z score, look up the corresponding positive score.
- **Column 2** lists the area between the mean (which corresponds to a z of 0) and the z score listed in column 1. If the z score is positive, this area is just to the right of the mean [see Figure 7.4(a)]; if the z score is negative, the area is just to the left of the mean [see Figure 7.4(b)].

Column 2 gives the proportion of the area under the entire curve that is between the mean ($z = 0$) and the positive value of z. Areas for negative values of z are the same as for positive values because the curve is symmetrical.

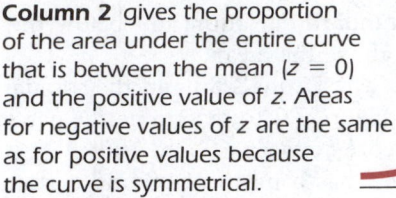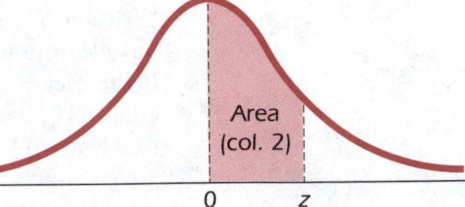

Column 3 gives the proportion of the area under the entire curve that falls beyond the stated positive value of z. Areas for negative values of z are the same because the curve is symmetrical.

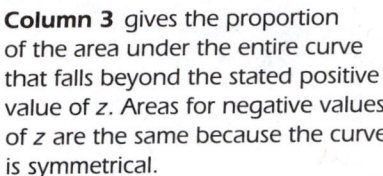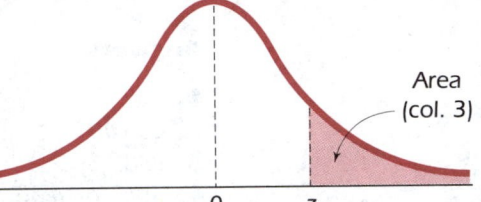

z	Area between mean and z	Area beyond z	z	Area between mean and z	Area beyond z
1	2	3	1	2	3
1.25	.3944	.1056	1.30	.4032	.0968
1.26	.3962	.1038	1.31	.4049	.0951
1.27	.3980	.1020	1.32	.4066	.0934
1.28	.3997	.1003	1.33	.4082	.0918
1.29	.4015	.0985	1.34	.4099	.0901

Figure 7.3   A portion of Table Z in Appendix A

- **Column 3** lists the area beyond the z score in column 1. If the z score is positive, this is the area in the entire remainder of the curve above the z score [see Figure 7.5(a)]; if the z score is negative, this is the area in the entire remainder of the curve below the z score [see Figure 7.5(b)].

The areas given in columns 2 and 3 are proportions of the total area under the normal curve; as such, they are listed in ten-thousandths of the total area. To convert the areas to percentages, simply multiply the figures by 100. As we mentioned previously, the normal curve is symmetrical, so .50, or 50%, of the scores lie above the mean and .50 lie below. Knowing this, you should be able to add any column-2 area to its corresponding column-3 area, and the result should always equal .50. Try it: From columns 2 and 3, add both areas that correspond to a z score of +1.25. Now do the same with both areas that correspond to a z score of -1.25 (they are, of course, the same numbers). Each adds up to .50, and when they are added together, they equal 1.00, or 100% of the total area.

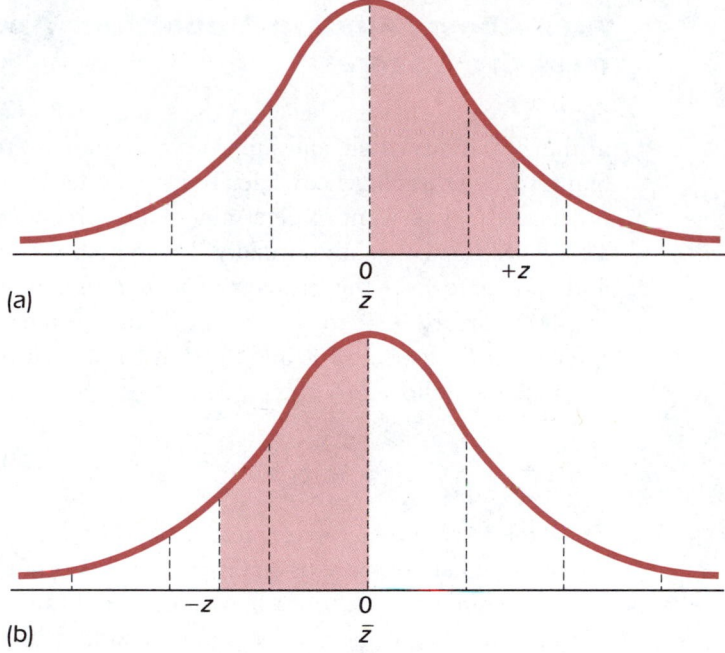

(a)

(b)

Figure 7.4   Areas in column 2 for (a) positive *z* scores and (b) negative *z* scores

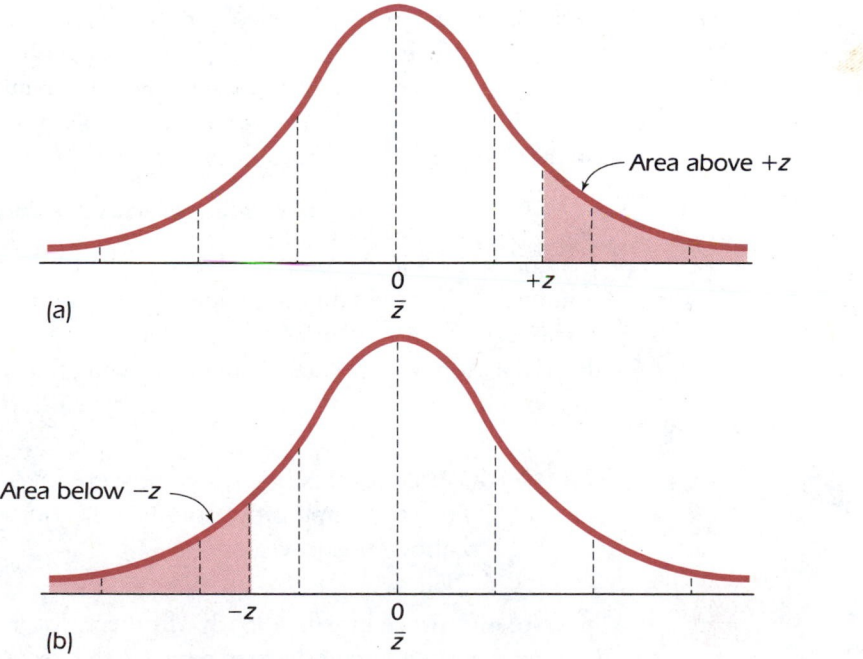

Area above +*z*

(a)

Area below −*z*

(b)

Figure 7.5   Areas in column 3 for (a) positive *z* scores and (b) negative *z* scores

Area Above: Finding Proportions Above Positive and Negative *z* Scores

Suppose you're that teacher with the student who had trouble with reading, arithmetic, and spelling, and suppose you found out that he scored 120 on the Stanford-Binet Intelligence Scale. To get a better idea of how he compares to other people, you want to determine what percentage of people score above 120. Since IQ scores are normally distributed, we can use the normal curve and Table Z to solve this problem. *The first thing you need to do is to convert the IQ score of 120 to a z score.* With the mean of the Stanford-Binet Intelligence Scale being 100 and the standard deviation being 16, the *z* score is computed as follows:

$$z = \frac{X - \mu}{\sigma} = \frac{120 - 100}{16} = \frac{20}{16} = 1.25$$

Thus, the *z* score that corresponds to an IQ of 120 is 1.25. (Remember that you must either compute or be given the mean *and* the standard deviation in order to compute a *z* score.) Next, you should make a rough drawing of a normal curve, marking the mean and standard deviations and shading the portion of the curve that you want to find. This is an invaluable aid to help you estimate your answer and avoid making mistakes. (If you shade approximately 25% of the curve and your answer is 78%, you know that you must have made an error somewhere.) Returning to our IQ problem, we have shaded the area of the curve corresponding to the percentage of scores above a *z* score of 1.25 in the positive tail of Figure 7.6. To find the exact percentage of scores in this area, we need to refer to column 3 in Table Z because it corresponds to the area beyond the *z* score:

$$\text{Area above positive } z \text{ score} = \text{column 3} \qquad (7.1)$$

Locate 1.25 in the partial table shown in Figure 7.3 and read across to column 3. You should find the value .1056. Multiply by 100 to convert it to a percentage; you get 10.56%. Your student is very intelligent if only 10.56% of the population scored better than he. Knowing this will help you make a more responsible recommendation concerning his education.

Question: What if the student's score were low, such as 76? Would I use the same procedure to find the percentage of scores above this low score?

No; the procedure is slightly different for a score below the mean because you need to find the area between the *z* score and the mean and then add it to the entire area above the mean, which is .50 (half of the total distribution):

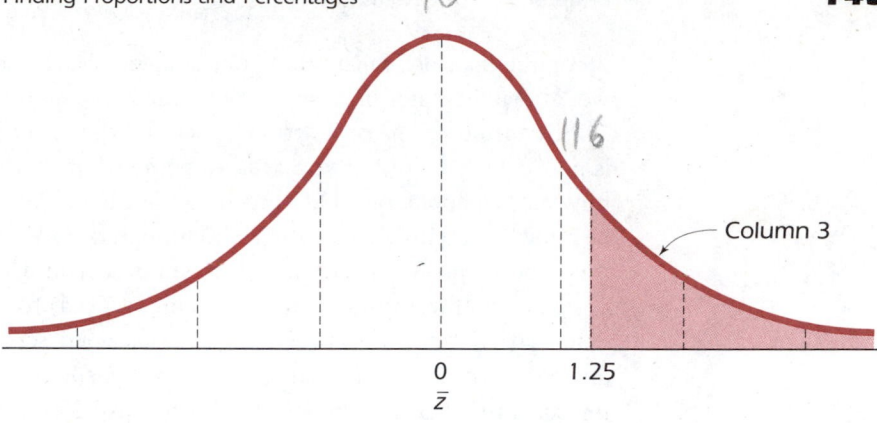

100

116

Figure 7.6 Area above a *z* score of +1.25

$$\text{Area above negative } z \text{ score} = \text{column 2} + .50 \qquad (7.2)$$

As with all procedures involving a normal curve, the first step is to convert the IQ score to a *z* score:

$$z = \frac{76 - 100}{16} = \frac{-24}{16} = -1.5$$

Next, sketch a normal curve and shade the portion you're trying to determine (this is done in Figure 7.7). Then refer to Table Z in Appendix A. Because Table Z does not list negative *z* scores, ignore the minus sign for the moment and look up a *z* score of 1.5 in column 1. Now look across to column 2, which lists the area between the *z* score and the mean. Add this value, .4332, to .50 and you will find that the area above the low score of 76 is .9332:

$$\text{Area above} -1.5 = .4332 + .50 = .9332$$

Converting to a percentage, you find that 93.32% of the population scored above

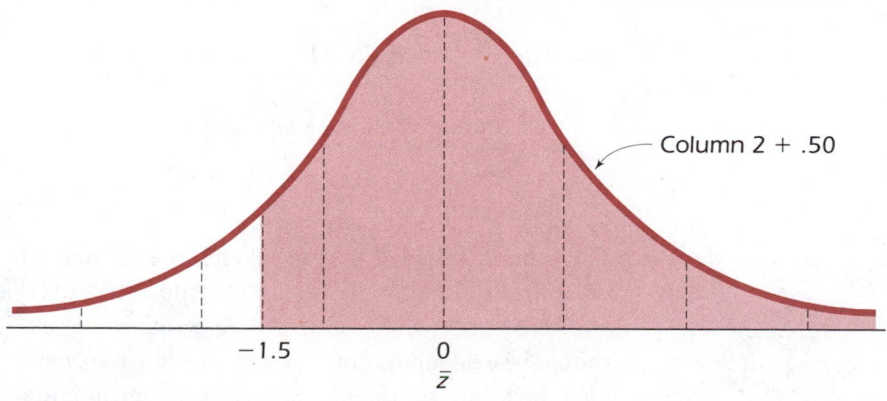

Figure 7.7 Area above a *z* score of −1.5

76 on the Stanford-Binet. Had your student actually scored 76, the test results would definitely not have supported your impression of him as a bright child.

Determining the proportion of people who score above a particular value is particularly helpful if you need to set a cutoff score and you want to know how many people, or what percentage of the people in your population, will be above your cutoff. Researchers in human factors are often confronted with this type of problem. For instance, suppose you are part of a team that is designing a new automatic teller machine (ATM) for banks, and you need to determine the appropriate height for the video screen. The screen is to be angled down to prevent glare; consequently, customers who are shorter than midscreen will be able to see the image easily, but those who are taller will have to stoop to see it. Assuming that height is normally distributed, knowing the mean height and standard deviation of the population, and knowing how to use Table Z, you should be able to determine what percentage of the population is too tall to use the machine comfortably at any set height.

Area Below: Finding Proportions Below Positive and Negative *z* Scores

Question: Is finding the area below the *z* score the same as finding the area above?

Yes and no. The procedures are similar: You must convert the original score to a *z* score and then find the area. But finding the area below a *z* score is the reverse of finding the area above it. Suppose you live in Tyrannia, a totalitarian state where the government has decreed that all graduating eighth-graders who have an IQ score of less than 108 must enter a blue-collar training program. Your job is to find out what percentage of the children this involves. In short, you need to find the area below the IQ score of 108. What do you do first?

Question: Convert the IQ score to a *z* score?

Certainly. This is done as follows:

$$z = \frac{108 - 100}{16} = \frac{8}{16} = 0.5$$

Then (don't forget this step!) sketch the normal curve to be sure you know what area to look up in Table Z in Appendix A. Try doing this yourself first, and then check what you did by referring to Figure 7.8. From your sketch, it should be evident that in order to calculate the area below a *z* score of 0.5, you must first look up the area between the mean and *z*, listed in column 2, and then add .50, which is the area below the mean:

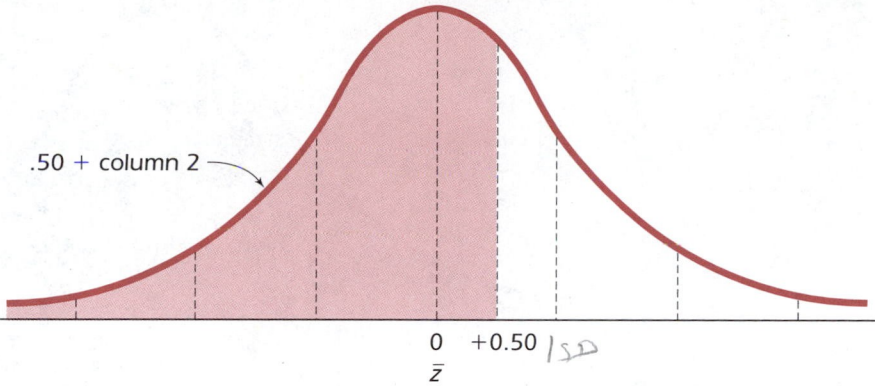

Figure 7.8 Area below a z score of +0.5

$$\text{Area below positive } z \text{ score} = \text{column } 2 + .50 \qquad (7.3)$$

Thus,

$$\text{Area below } 0.5 = .1915 + .50 = .6915$$

Therefore, .6915, or nearly 70%, of the eighth-graders score below 108 and are required to enter Tyrannia's training program.

By inspection, it is evident that the procedure for finding the area above a negative z score is the same as the one for finding the area below a positive z score. Correspondingly, finding the area below a negative z score is similar to finding the area above a positive z score. Suppose the minister of Tyrannia's Department of Education confers with the Secretary of the Treasury and finds that there are not enough funds to train 70% of the people. The Minister of Education arbitrarily lowers the cutoff score to 96 and asks you to determine the percentage of eighth-graders who score below 96. You first convert the IQ score to a z score:

$$z = \frac{96 - 100}{16} = \frac{-4}{16} = -0.25$$

You then make your sketch of the area below −0.25, as in Figure 7.9, and find the area below (beyond z) in Table Z by locating −0.25 (ignore the minus sign) and referring to column 3:

Area below negative z score = column 3   (7.4)
Area below −0.25 = .4013

Because there are ample funds for training 40.13% of the people, the Minister of Education signals a go-ahead for the program.

For an example of how this procedure can be used for measures other than IQ scores, remember our human factors project to determine the optimum height for the ATM video screen. Pretend that after reviewing the report, your superior stated that it was too negative because it emphasized the

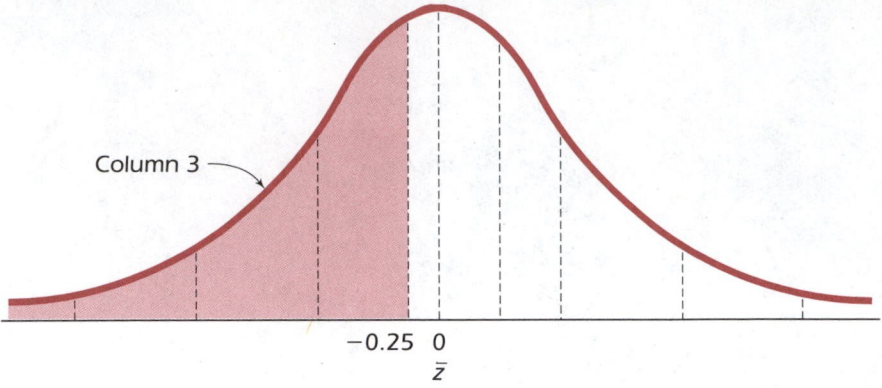

Figure 7.9   Area below a *z* score of −0.25

percentage of people above a certain height who *could not* use the machine comfortably. Your solution: Report the percentage of people who *could* use the machine comfortably by finding the area *below* a particular height. This area is calculated in Table 7.1.

Table 7.1   Computation of the Area Below the Height of the ATM

Mean height of ATM users = $\bar{X}$ = 68 inches

Standard deviation of ATM users = S = 4 inches

Midscreen height of ATM = X = 70 inches

z score for 70 inches = $z = \dfrac{X - \bar{X}}{S} = \dfrac{70 - 68}{4} = \dfrac{2}{4} = 0.5$

Area between mean and z of 0.5 (from Table Z) = .1915

Area below 70 inches = .1915 + .5 = .6915

C O N C E P T   Q U I Z

1. When you want to find the proportion or percentage of scores lying above or below a score, you have to use Table _____ .
2. Table Z in Appendix A is divided into three columns: Column 1 lists the _____ , column 2 lists the area _____ , and column 3 lists the area _____ .
3. To convert the areas in Table Z to percentages, you must multiply the values by _____ .
4. The first thing you must do before you can use Table Z is to convert the raw score to a _____ .

5. To find the area above a positive z score, you must first find the z score in Table Z; then find the area above by _____ .

6. To find the area above a negative z score, you must first find the z score in Table Z; then find the area above by _____ .

7. To find the area below a positive z score, you must first find the z score in Table Z; then find the area below by _____ .

8. To find the area below a negative z score, find the z score in Table Z; then find the area below by _____ .

Answers

1. Z

2. z score; between the mean and z; beyond z

3. 100

4. z score

5. reading the area in column 3

6. adding .5 to the value in column 2

7. adding .5 to the value in column 2

8. reading the area in column 3

Area Between: Finding Proportions Lying Between Two z Scores

Question: Suppose I want to know something more complicated, like what percentage of people score between 92 and 120 on the Stanford-Binet IQ test. How can I do that?

Finding the area between two scores is just as easy as finding the area above or below a single score. What do you think you do first? Convert them both to z scores:

$$z_{92} = \frac{92 - 100}{16} = \frac{-8}{16} = -0.5$$

$$z_{120} = \frac{120 - 100}{16} = \frac{20}{16} = 1.25$$

Now sketch the problem. Our sketch is shown in Figure 7.10. It is easy to see that the area between the two z scores is simply the area between the mean and -0.50 plus the area between the mean and 1.25. You need only look up the column-2 values for the two z scores and add them:

$$\text{Area between } -z \text{ and } +z = (\text{column 2})_{-z} + (\text{column 2})_{+z} \qquad (7.5)$$

Now refer to Table Z and look up the z scores just computed to find their corresponding column-2 values:

$$\text{Column-2 value of } -0.50 \, z \text{ score} = .1915$$
$$\text{Column-2 value of } 1.25 \, z \text{ score} = .3944$$

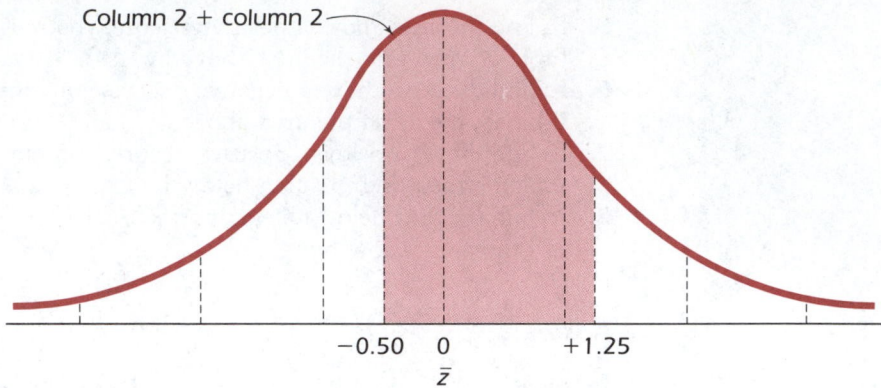

Figure 7.10   Area between *z* scores of −0.5 and +1.25. (One *z* score is negative and one *z* score is positive.)

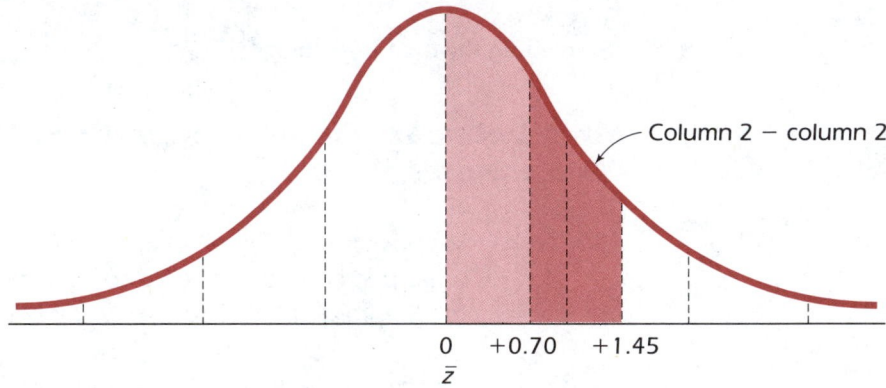

Figure 7.11   Area between *z* scores of +0.70 and +1.45. (Both *z* scores are positive.)

The sum of these column-2 values is

$$.1915 + .3944 = .5859$$

Multiplying this result by 100 to express the percentage indicates that 58.59% of the people who take the Stanford-Binet IQ test score between 92 and 120.

Question: Is the procedure the same if both *z* scores have the same sign—both negative or both positive?

To find the area between two *z* scores that have the same sign, you must still find the column-2 value for each score, but you subtract—rather than add—the column-2 values. Figure 7.11 illustrates this clearly: To find the area between the *z* scores of 0.70 and 1.45, you need to subtract the area between the mean and 0.70 from the area between the mean and 1.45. The column-2 area for a *z* score of 0.70 is .2580, and the column-2 area for a *z* score of 1.45

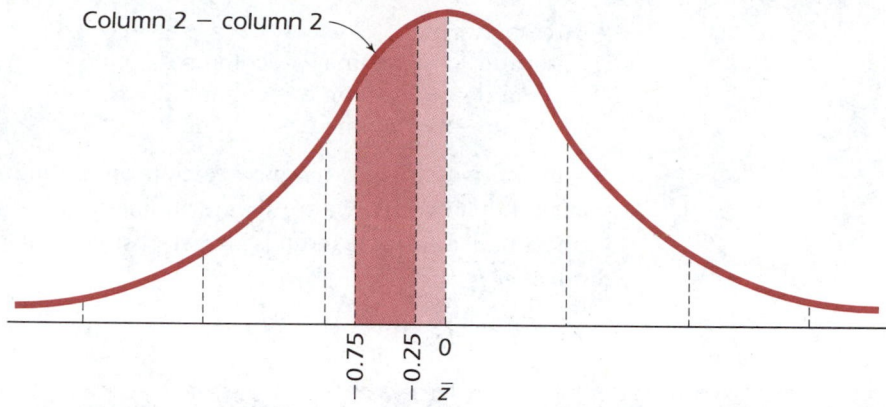

Figure 7.12 Area between z scores of −0.75 and −0.25. (Both z scores are negative.)

is .4265. The difference between the two areas is .1685, or 16.85%. The general formula for computing the area between two z scores that have the same sign is as follows:

$$\text{Area between } (+z_1 \text{ and } +z_2) \text{ or } (-z_1 \text{ and } -z_2) = (\text{col } 2)_{z_2} - (\text{col } 2)_{z_1} \qquad (7.6)$$

where z_2 is the score farther from the mean than z_1.

To illustrate how to calculate the area between two negative z scores, let's find the percentage of people who score between 88 and 96 on the Stanford-Binet test. First, we convert each score to a z score:

$$z_{96} = \frac{96 - 100}{16} = \frac{-4}{16} = -0.25$$

$$z_{88} = \frac{88 - 100}{16} = \frac{-12}{16} = -0.75$$

Sketch the z scores on a normal curve graph, as in Figure 7.12. Find the column-2 values for each of these z scores:

Column-2 value for a z of −0.25 = .0987
Column-2 value for a z of −0.75 = .2734

Finally, find the difference between these two areas, which is .1747. Consequently, 17.47% of the people who take this IQ test are expected to score between 88 and 96.

To summarize this part of the chapter, we present these formulas:

- Area above:
    +z = column 3
    −z = column 2 + .5
- Area below:
    +z = column 2 + .5
    −z = column 3

- Area between:
  +z and −z = column 2 + column 2
  +z and +z = column 2 − column 2
  −z and −z = column 2 − column 2

Before we move to the next section on finding percentiles, we want to point out that because we are always adding areas, or subtracting a larger area from a smaller area, the result is always positive. *You never get a normal curve result that is negative.*

C O N C E P T   Q U I Z

1. The first thing to do when you want to use Table Z to find the area between two scores is to _____ .

2. To find the area between a positive z score and a negative z score, you must first find the column-2 values that correspond to the z scores and then _____ .

3. To find the area between two positive z scores, you must first find the column-2 values that correspond to the z scores and then _____ .

4. To find the area between two negative z scores, you must first find the column-2 values that correspond to the z scores and then _____ .

5. The area between any two z scores is always a positive value. True or false?

Answers

1. convert the raw scores to z scores

2. add the areas

3. subtract the smaller area from the larger area

4. subtract the smaller area from the larger area

5. true

FINDING PERCENTILES

So far in this chapter we have described ways to use a normal curve to determine proportions or percentages. These procedures involve knowing a particular score or scores and then finding the area above, below, or between those scores. But what if the situation is reversed? What if you know the area in the curve below a certain score and you want to find that score? For example, suppose the Tyrannian Minister of Education decrees that only the

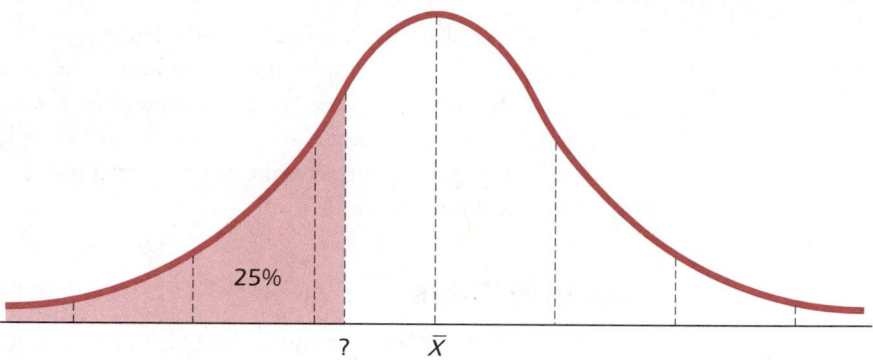

Figure 7.13 Diagram of the known area below a score equal to 25% but an unknown z score

lower 25% of the graduating eighth-graders are required to enter the training program and wants you to calculate which score will be the cutoff. This situation, which is shown in Figure 7.13, involves a known area but unknown raw and z scores. The score you want to find is referred to as the *percentile*.

A **percentile** is a score that has a certain percentage of scores below it. For instance, if you score at the 25th percentile, 25% of the scores fall below your score; if you score at the 75th percentile, 75% of the scores fall below it. Finding the percentile, then, is the exact opposite of finding the area below a score because rather than knowing a score and trying to find the area, you know the area and are trying to find the score. To find the raw score that corresponds to the 25th percentile for the Tyrannian government, look at Figure 7.13 again. The figure shows that the 25th percentile has an area below the score equal to .2500, an area that is obviously in the left tail of the distribution. What should you do with this information?

Question: Shouldn't I try to find .2500 in column 3 of Table Z?

Well, try it. Column 3 gives the area in the tail beyond the z score listed in column 1. Consequently, if you find an area in column 3, you find its corresponding z score in column 1 at the same time. The only problem with this approach is that Table Z was originally designed to be entered from column 1 instead of from column 2 or 3. Therefore, there is no guarantee that the area you are looking up will be listed in column 3. If you have already looked at the table, you have found that .2500 is in fact not listed. The closest figure is .2514.

Question: Can't I just use the figures that are listed on either side of .2500 to estimate its z score?

There is quite a problem with estimating areas and z scores accurately in

Table *Z* because the frequency for adjacent *z* scores on the normal curve is not uniform. Thus, just a slight movement in one direction or another can mean a large difference in respect to the frequency of scores. The solution to this difficulty is not to estimate using Table *Z* but to use Table *P*, which is designed so you can look up an area above or an area below a score in order to find a corresponding *z* score.

Using Table *P*: Finding Distinct Scores

To use Table *P* in Appendix A, first convert a known percentage into a proportion (an area); then find the known area in either column 1 or column 3 and read the *z* score from column 2. Your new assignment for the Tyrannian minister is to find the score, the 25th percentile, below which 25% of the eighth-graders scored. To do this, convert 25% to the area .250. Find .250 in column 3; then find the corresponding *z* score in column 2, which is 0.6745. You need to convert this *z* score to −0.6745. It is negative because all percentiles less than 50 are below the mean, so the *z* scores that represent them are negative. On the contrary, *z* scores that correspond to percentiles greater than 50 are positive. For example, the 90th percentile corresponds to a *z* score of +1.2816, and the 33rd percentile corresponds to a *z* score of −0.4399.

Question: Now that I know how to find a *z* score, how do I convert a
          z score back into an IQ score?

That's easy. Just plug the values of the *z* score, the mean, and the standard deviation into Formula 7.7, which is derived from the *z*-score formula via a little algebraic maneuvering:

$$X = \overline{X} + (z \cdot S) \qquad (7.7)$$

So to find the raw IQ score that represents the 25th percentile, substitute the known values into Formula 7.7:

$$X = 100 + (-0.6745 \cdot 16)$$
$$= 100 - 10.792$$
$$= 89.208$$

Thus, the IQ score of 89.208 is the raw score that represents the 25th percentile.

A note of caution is necessary here: Always remember to make sure that you assign the proper sign to the *z* score after you find it in Table *P*. To repeat, a *z* score is negative when the percentile is less than 50 and positive when the percentile is greater than 50.

Before we end this section on percentiles, let's work one more example. Find the IQ score that represents the 90th percentile. This is illustrated in Figure 7.14. The first step is to determine the *z* score. Locate the area .900 in

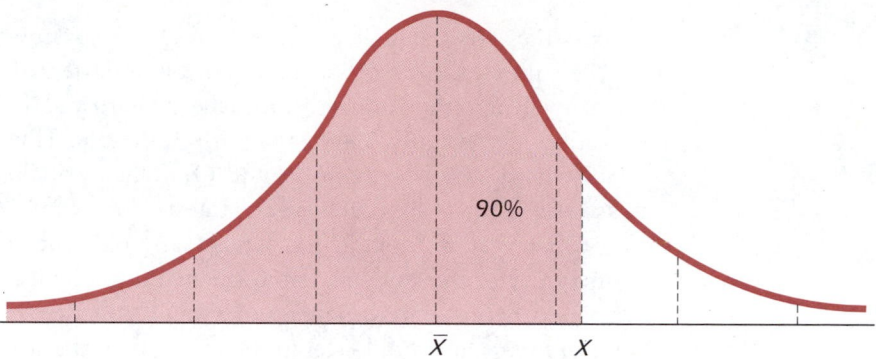

Figure 7.14 Diagram of the known area below a score equal to 90% but an unknown *z* score

Table *P*. It's found in column 1. The corresponding *z* score is 1.2816. Then substitute the known factors into Formula 7.7:

$$X = 100 + (1.2816 \cdot 16) = 100 + 20.5056 = 120.5056$$

An IQ score of just over 120 represents the 90th percentile; this means that 90% of the people who take this IQ test will score below 120.5056.

Question: School principals sometimes talk about a proportion of their students scoring in certain quartiles—the first quartile, the third quartile, and so on. What is the difference between a percentile and a quartile?

   Percentiles and quartiles are quite similar. A percentile is the raw score that has a certain percentage of scores falling below it. Normally, percentiles are stated as whole integers. If you find out that you scored in the 83rd percentile on a standardized test, that means that you scored higher than 83% of the people who take the test. **Quartiles** are the three raw scores that divide the distribution into four equal parts, as shown in Figure 7.15. Normally the

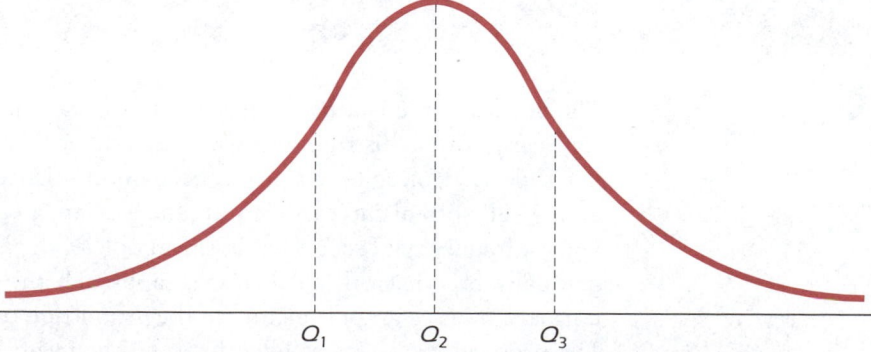

Figure 7.15 Quartiles (Q_1, Q_2, and Q_3) for the normal curve

quartiles are designated Q_1, Q_2, and Q_3. Q_1 is equivalent to the 25th percentile and is the cutoff for the bottom quarter of the distribution. Q_2 is equivalent to the 50th percentile (the median) and divides the distribution into halves. Q_3 is equivalent to the 75th percentile. Thus, 50% of the scores in a distribution fall between Q_1 and Q_3. When principals receive their schools' scores from a state achievement test, they would feel quite dejected and probably start looking for funds to implement remedial programs if the majority of the students fell in the first and second quartiles. However, they would be absolutely elated and would tout their staff's superior efforts to everyone who would listen if the majority of the students fell in the third and fourth quartiles.

C O N C E P T   Q U I Z

1. The 30th percentile is the score with 30% of the scores _____ it.
2. The z score for the 45th percentile is _____ ; the z score for the 73rd percentile is _____ .
3. A percentile must be converted to a(n) _____ before you can look up the z score in _____ .
4. What is the formula for converting a z score to a raw score?

Answers

1. below
2. negative 0.1257; positive 0.6128

3. proportion, or area; Table P
4. $X = \overline{X} + (z \cdot S)$

S U M M A R Y

The normal curve is a bell-shaped, symmetrical curve that graphically illustrates any normal distribution. We often assume that most scientific data, and particularly data collected in the behavioral sciences, are normally distributed. In all normal curves, the mean, the median, and the mode are equal. The highest frequency of scores lies in the middle of the curve, with the frequency gradually tapering off as the scores approach the ends of the curve. The normal curve is a graphic picture of the proportion of scores in a distribution. The proportions of scores lying between the mean and one, two, and three standard deviations, as well as in the area beyond three standard deviations, are shown in Figure 7.2.

The normal curve can be used to answer such questions as what proportion or percentage of the total scores lie above or below a particular score, what proportion of the scores lie between two particular scores, or what proportion of people will receive a specific score. We can also use the normal curve to find a specific score if we know the proportion of scores lying above or below it.

Table Z in Appendix A is used when we know a particular score and want to find the area, or proportion of scores, above or below the score. The first step in this procedure is to convert the raw score to a z score. To compute the area above a z score, note the sign of the z score. If it is positive, find the column-3 value that corresponds to the z score. If it is negative, add .50 to the column-2 value that corresponds to the z score.

Finding the area below a z score is the opposite of finding the area above it. If the z score is positive, look up the column-2 value of the z score in Table Z and add .50. If it is negative, find its corresponding value in column 3.

The computation of the area between two z scores depends on their signs. If they have the same sign (both negative or both positive), look up the column-2 values for each score and subtract the smaller value from the larger value. If one z score is negative and the other is positive, then merely look up the corresponding column-2 values and add them.

Table P is used to find percentiles. A percentile is a score that has a certain percentage of scores falling below it. When using Table P, we know the percentage or the proportion of scores and we need to determine a particular score. To find the raw score that represents a percentile, convert the percentage to a proportion and find the proportion in either column 1 or column 3. Then read across to the corresponding z score. Now convert this z score to a raw score by multiplying it by the standard deviation of the original distribution and adding the mean of the original distribution. Remember that percentiles less than 50 result in negative z scores, whereas percentiles greater than 50 result in positive z scores. Quartiles are the three raw scores that represent the 25th, 50th, and 75th percentiles. Quartiles thereby divide a distribution of scores into four equal parts.

KEY TERMS

normal curve

percentile

normal distribution

quartile

F O R M U L A S

$$\text{Area above positive } z \text{ score} = \text{column 3} \tag{7.1}$$

$$\text{Area above negative } z \text{ score} = \text{column 2} + .50 \tag{7.2}$$

$$\text{Area below positive } z \text{ score} = \text{column 2} + .50 \tag{7.3}$$

$$\text{Area below negative } z \text{ score} = \text{column 3} \tag{7.4}$$

$$\text{Area between } -z \text{ and } +z = (\text{column 2})_{-z} + (\text{column 2})_{+z} \tag{7.5}$$

$$\text{Area between } (+z_1 \text{ and } +z_2) \text{ or } (-z_1 \text{ and } -z_2) = \\ (\text{col 2})_{z_2} - (\text{col 2})_{z_1} \tag{7.6}$$

$$X = \overline{X} + (z \cdot S) \tag{7.7}$$

P R O B L E M S

1. Find the areas beyond the following z scores:

3.0
1.0
0.5
0.0
−0.25
−1.33
−2.75

2. Find the z score that represents each of the following percentiles:

75th
66th
54th
50th
43rd
29th
15th

You have administered a reaction time test to thousands of people and have found that the mean is 150 milliseconds and the standard devi-

ation is 25 milliseconds. Use this information to do Problems 3–10.

3. What proportion of the people who take this test have a reaction time longer than 140 milliseconds?

4. What proportion of the people have a reaction time shorter than 174 milliseconds?

5. What proportion of the people will have a reaction time longer than 162 milliseconds?

6. What proportion of the people will have a reaction time shorter than 130 milliseconds?

7. What proportion of the people will have a reaction time between 120 and 145 milliseconds?

8. What proportion of the people will have a reaction time between 145 and 160 milliseconds?

9. What reaction time represents the 75th percentile?

10. What reaction time represents the 15th percentile?

Suppose you are a designer for the world's largest manufacturer of toy dinosaur cars. You have just designed a toy intended for 3- to 6-year-olds that will safely accommodate a child who is no shorter than 36 inches and no taller than 48 inches. The mean height for children of this age group is 42 inches, and the standard deviation is 5 inches. Use these data in Problems 11–13.

11. What proportion of the target sales population can safely use your product?

12. What proportion of the target sales population is too tall to safely use your product?

13. What proportion is too short?

For Problems 14–21, the mean family income in Uppiton is $68,000 per year, with a standard deviation of $17,000.

14. What proportion of the families in Uppiton earns more than $100,000 per year?

15. What proportion of Uppiton's families earns more than $50,000 per year?

16. What proportion earns less than $75,000 per year?

17. What proportion earns less than $35,000 per year?

18. What proportion earns between $50,000 and $100,000 per year?

19. What proportion earns between $80,000 and $90,000 per year?

20. What would your minimum income have to be in order for you to be in the upper 10% of the families in Uppiton?

21. What would your income be if you were at exactly the 43rd percentile?

Suppose you have just completed a traffic survey to find out how long it takes each student who drives to your college to find a parking place after he or she enters the student parking lot. Your survey indicates that the mean search time is 9 minutes, with a standard deviation of 2.5 minutes. Use this information to do Problems 22–26.

22. What proportion of the students takes more than 15 minutes to find a parking place?

23. What proportion of the students takes less than 5 minutes to find a parking place?

24. What proportion of the students takes between 7 and 10 minutes to find a parking place?

25. How many minutes represent the 90th percentile?

26. How many minutes represent the 45th percentile?

Correlation

Daily life is full of hassles. The car needs gas, the rent is due, your boss wants you to work overtime for the next couple of weeks, there is a statistics test tomorrow, you need to make some kind of dinner out of the stuff that is beginning to smell in your refrigerator (maybe it's too late already), and on top of this you are starting to get a cold. These are all sources of stress. Health psychologists have long been interested in stress and especially in the relationship between stress and illness. Thomas Holmes and Richard Rahe (1967) conjectured that exposure within a short time to several stressful major life events, such as the death of a spouse or a change in residence, may have a detrimental effect on health. More recently, researchers have studied the relationship between minor events, or hassles, and health.

One of these studies, conducted by Rod Martin and James Dobbin (1988), measured the relationship between the number of daily hassles and the amount of immunoglobulin A in a person's system. Whereas high levels of immunoglobulin A indicate a strong immune system and consequent high resistance to illness, low levels indicate a weak immune system. Martin and Dobbin found a significant relationship between the number of daily hassles and the levels of immunoglobulin A in their subjects' saliva. The more hassles a subject reported, the lower the level of immunoglobulin A in his or her saliva. Through awareness of this relationship, health care professionals can target which people are at risk for illness and can work with them to develop strategies for coping with their hassles and the resultant stress.

You have probably noticed that a great variety of other factors are related in one way or another, such as mood swings related to the weather and height related to weight. We have devised a game that illustrates how, once a relationship between two factors has been established, that relationship can be used to make predictions. The setting for the game: the college union or cafeteria. The object of the game: guess the height of the next man to walk through the entrance. The winner: the person whose guess is within an inch of the man's true height three times in a row. The loser has to buy lunch. It is now your turn. What height should you guess? You can use a variety of strategies: Choose the height of a male friend, the height of your favorite actor, or the height of the last man to walk into the cafeteria. Of course, the best strategy is to choose the mean height of the men on campus.

By some stroke of luck, you just happen to have a list of the heights for all the men who attend your school. Hurriedly, you enter the heights into your calculator and compute the mean: 70 inches. Guessing 70 inches each time may not be as much fun as making random guesses, but you will probably be more accurate and more likely to win.

Suppose a friend changes the game slightly and asks another friend to stand outside the cafeteria with a scale. She is to weigh each man before he enters the cafeteria, and then stick her head inside and tell you the person's weight. You're still supposed to guess the person's height, but now you have the advantage of knowing his weight. Let's imagine that your friend outside opens the door and shouts, "120 pounds." What should you guess? Should you guess the mean height, 70 inches? Well, we wouldn't. We would guess a height quite a bit lower, and no doubt you would do the same.

Our guess would be lower because over the years we have learned that height and weight are related to each other. In most instances, taller people weigh more than shorter people. Of course there are exceptions: Some people are like beanpoles—tall and thin—and others resemble bowling balls. But in general, as height goes up, so does weight. Several other variables are related as well: grades and amount of time spent studying, athletic success and practice time, ice cream sales and temperature, calories consumed and weight gained, dog food consumed by your pet and trips made by you to the backyard with shovel in hand, and as previously noted, level of immunoglobulin A and number of daily hassles. When factors are related in some *systematic* way, we say they are *correlated*. A **correlation** is a relationship between variables whereby a change in one variable is associated with a concurrent change in the other. In statistics, we not only establish the existence of certain correlations but also measure the direction and the degree of correlation.

THE NATURE OF CORRELATIONS

Types of Correlation: How Are Variables Related?

Variables can be correlated in any one of three ways. If both factors vary in the same direction—as one goes up, the other goes up—the relationship is described as *positive*. For instance, salary and years of education are positively correlated because the people who make the highest salaries tend to be the ones who have gone to school the longest. Conversely, if two factors vary in the opposite direction—as one goes up, the other goes down—the relationship is *negative*. For example, the number of daily hassles and the amount of immunoglobulin A in a person's system are negatively correlated because as the number of hassles goes up, the amount of immunoglobulin A tends to go down. Finally, variables that are not at all related have a *zero correlation*. The relationship between personality fluctuations and the movement of distant stars has a zero correlation. Contrary to strong beliefs in astrology held by a surprising number of people, bona fide studies have found that there is absolutely no correlation between the position of stars at the time you are born and the true nature of your personality.

Degree of Correlation: How Strongly Are Variables Related?

Question: Aren't some things more closely related than others?

Absolutely; some things are closely correlated, whereas others are only loosely related. One way to visualize the degree of correlation between two variables is to generate a **scatterplot,** which is a graph with plotted values for two variables that are being compared, such as height and weight or grade point average and IQ. Look at the five scatterplots in Figures 8.1(a)–(e). In each one,

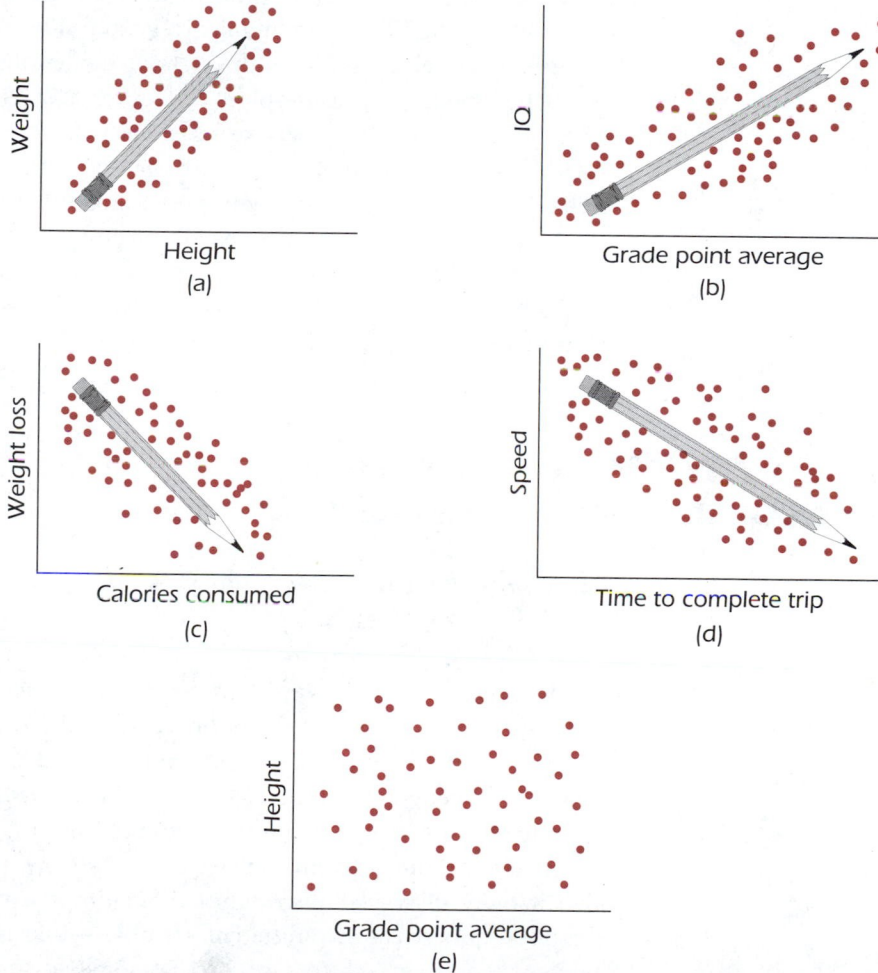

Figure 8.1 Five scatterplots indicating (a) a positive correlation between weight and height; (b) a positive correlation between IQ and grade point average; (c) a negative correlation between weight loss and calories consumed; (d) a negative correlation between speed and time to complete a trip; and (e) a zero correlation between height and grade point average

two sets of data are displayed, one (such as height) along the abscissa and the other (such as weight) along the ordinate. The points are plotted where corresponding X- and Y-values intersect (for example, you would plot a single point where your weight value intersects with your height value).

By merely glancing at the scatterplots, you can often see correlational trends. These trends can be illustrated by laying a pencil, with its tip pointing away from the ordinate, along the imaginary line running lengthwise through the center of the points, as in Figure 8.1(a). The more closely the two variables in the scatterplot are related, the more tightly the points will be bunched around the pencil. Thus, because weight is highly correlated to height [see Figure 8.1(a)], the points are bunched close together along that imaginary line, but because GPA is not at all correlated to height [see Figure 8.1(e)], the points are scattered randomly throughout the graph.

By examining the scatterplots in Figures 8.1(a)–(e), you should also be able to see positive and negative relationships. Variables that are positively correlated show a positive slope, with the tip of the pencil pointing up to the right, away from the abscissa, whereas variables that are negatively correlated show a negative slope, with the pencil's tip pointing down to the right, toward the abscissa. Variables that are not correlated (with a zero correlation) show no discernible slope at all; the points are scattered randomly throughout the scatterplot.

THE CORRELATION COEFFICIENT

Question: Is there a way to measure how closely related two different variables are?

The most common way to measure the relationship between two variables is to compute the **correlation coefficient.** Although there are several measures of correlation, the most common and useful one is the Pearson product moment correlation coefficient, which we represent by the lowercase italic letter r. Before we begin the computation of r, we want to remind you that in the two previous chapters we discussed how to use z scores to compare two initially dissimilar distributions. Since r is a number that describes a relationship between two different variables—that is, two different distributions—converting each to a z score has some advantages.

For example, if we ask five men their height and weight, we might get the responses listed in Table 8.1. For clarity, we have labeled the height variable X and the weight variable Y. Note that we have two scores, a height score and a weight score, for each man. If you scrutinize the data, you may be able to tell

Table 8.1 Men's Heights and Weights

Man	Height (in inches) X	Weight (in pounds) Y
M. P.	72	190
T. D.	66	135
C. Q.	69	155
C. Y.	72	165
D. P.	71	155
	$\bar{X} = 70$	$\bar{Y} = 160$
	$S_X = 2.280$	$S_Y = 17.889$

that there is a positive relationship between height and weight. In general, the taller men are heavier and the shorter men are lighter. However, this relationship is much easier to see when both the heights and weights are converted to z scores, as in Table 8.2.

By comparing the z score for height to the z score for weight, you can see that in four of the five pairs of z scores, both have the same sign—both are either positive or negative. In a distribution that has a positive correlation, this is what we expect. If the pairs of scores tended to have opposite signs, then we would expect a negative correlation. Table 8.3 demonstrates the negative correlation between the number of daily hassles and the amount of immuno-globulin A in the saliva of ten different subjects. The table shows that, in general, the higher the number of hassles, the lower the immunoglobulin A count.

Table 8.2 Men's Heights and Weights Converted to z Scores

Man	Height X	z_X	Weight Y	z_Y
M. P.	72	0.877	190	1.677
T. D.	66	−1.754	135	−1.398
C. Q.	69	−0.439	155	−0.280
C. Y.	72	0.877	165	0.280
D. P.	71	0.439	155	−0.280
	$\bar{X} = 70$		$\bar{Y} = 160$	
	$S_X = 2.280$		$S_Y = 17.889$	

Table 8.3   Number of Hassles and Immunoglobulin A Counts for Ten Subjects

Subject	Daily hassles X	z_X	Immunoglobulin A count Y	z_Y
C. D.	12	−0.896	1.72	0.732
P. M.	15	0.064	1.15	0.070
R. R.	20	1.664	0.15	−1.479
M. D.	12	−0.896	2.00	1.127
J. L.	17	0.704	0.25	−1.388
M. F.	16	0.384	1.33	0.183
J. P.	10	−1.536	2.10	1.268
H. S.	12	−0.896	1.75	0.775
M. H.	15	0.064	1.35	0.211
M. V.	19	1.344	0.20	−1.408
	$\bar{X} = 14.8$		$\bar{Y} = 1.20$	
	$S_X = 3.12$		$S_Y = 0.71$	

z-Score Formula: Convert to z Scores; Then It's Easy

The computation of the correlation coefficient is relatively simple if all the scores have first been converted to z scores. The formula follows:

$$r = \frac{\Sigma(z_X \cdot z_Y)}{n} \tag{8.1}$$

Remember, the correlation coefficient is a way to measure the relationship between two scores. The formula reflects this by treating each pair of scores as just that: a pair. Until this point, we have used n as the symbol for the number of scores in a sample. Because *pairs* of scores are used in computing the correlation coefficient, in this case we use n to designate the number of pairs. As you can see in Formula 8.1, to compute the correlation coefficient for each pair of scores, you need to multiply each z score for X by the corresponding z score for Y before summing the products. In Table 8.4 we compute r for the men's height and weight data given earlier.

Question: Because this is a positive correlation, shouldn't both z scores in each pair always have the same sign?

In general, they should. In a positive correlation, most of the pairs of z scores should have the same sign, but it is not absolutely necessary that *all*

M. 7   P.

Table 8.4 Computation of *r* for Men's Heights and Weights

Man	Height X	z_X	Weight Y	z_Y	$z_X \cdot z_Y$
M. P.	72	0.877	190	1.677	1.471
T. D.	66	−1.754	135	−1.398	2.452
C. Q.	69	−0.439	155	−0.280	0.123
C. Y.	72	0.877	165	0.280	0.246
D. P.	71	0.439	155	−0.280	−0.123

$$\Sigma(z_X \cdot z_Y) = 4.169$$

$$r = \frac{\Sigma(z_X \cdot z_Y)}{n} = \frac{4.169}{5} = .83$$

pairs follow this pattern. You have to remember that in all human populations there is some variation. If one member of a pair has a high positive z score, we expect that the corresponding member will also have a positive z score, with the same being true for high negative z scores. But when scores are near the mean, when they are low positive or low negative, corresponding pairs may have z scores with opposite signs. Both of these z scores will probably be small, so their product will have less of an effect on the total than the products of larger z scores. Take a look at the last pair in the height/weight distribution in Table 8.4. D. P.'s z score for height is +0.439, while his z score for weight is −0.280. These scores are both relatively close to the mean. Their product subtracts only 0.123 from the total, and the result is still a relatively high correlation coefficient of +.83.

Question: Did you say +.83 is *high*? It seems awfully small to me. Shouldn't it be larger, like 100 or 1000?

Correlation coefficients are never more than +1.00 or less than −1.00. So the answer to your question is no, a correlation coefficient of +.83 is not small. In fact, a correlation coefficient of +.83 is relatively high. You need to remember that the sign of the correlation coefficient, minus or plus, indicates the direction of the relationship and the number represents the size of the relationship. A positive correlation represents the situation where both X and Y vary in the same direction, whereas a negative correlation indicates a situation where X and Y vary in opposite directions. Therefore, a correlation coefficient near +1.00 or −1.00 is a large correlation, whereas a correlation close to 0 is small. Table 8.5 illustrates the computation of the correlation coefficient for the data on hassles and immunoglobulin A in Table 8.3.

Table 8.5 Computation of the Correlation Coefficient for Number of Hassles and Immunoglobulin A Counts for Ten Subjects

Subject	Daily hassles X	z_X	Immunoglobulin A count Y	z_Y	$z_X \cdot z_Y$
C. D.	12	−0.896	1.72	0.732	−0.655
P. M.	15	0.064	1.15	0.070	−0.004
R. R.	20	1.664	0.15	−1.479	−2.455
M. D.	12	−0.896	2.00	1.127	−1.007
J. L.	17	0.704	0.25	−1.338	−0.942
M. F.	16	0.384	1.33	0.183	0.070
J. P.	10	−1.536	2.10	1.268	−1.942
H. S.	12	−0.896	1.75	0.775	−0.692
M. H.	15	0.064	1.35	0.211	0.013
M. V.	19	1.344	0.20	−1.408	−1.888

$$\bar{X} = 14.8 \qquad \bar{Y} = 1.20 \qquad \qquad -9.502$$

$$S_X = 3.12 \qquad S_Y = 0.71$$

$$r = \frac{\Sigma(z_X \cdot z_Y)}{n} = \frac{-9.502}{10} = -.95$$

C O N C E P T   Q U I Z

1. A relationship between two variables, whereby a change in one is associated with a concurrent change in the other, is called a _____ .
2. When two variables vary in the same direction, they are said to be _____ ; when two variables vary in the opposite direction, they are said to be _____ .
3. When two variables are not at all related, they have a _____ correlation.
4. The most common way to measure the relationship between two variables is to compute the _____ , which is represented by the letter _____ .
5. When we compute the correlation coefficient, n represents the number of _____ .
6. Correlation coefficients are never more than _____ and never less than _____ .
7. Which of the following are valid correlation coefficients: +.37, +100, +10, −105, −1000, −.95, +.08? Which is the smallest? Which is the largest?

Answers

1. correlation
2. positively correlated; negatively correlated
3. zero
4. correlation coefficient; r
5. pairs
6. +1.00; −1.00
7. +.37, −.95, +.08; +.08 is the smallest; −.95 is the largest

Raw-Score Formula: Beware of Large Numbers

Question: Computing the correlation coefficient when you have to convert all the scores to z scores is a lot of work, especially if there are a lot of scores. Isn't there a simpler way to do this?

That really depends on your sense of humor. Several alternative formulas for computing the correlation coefficient may save you some time, but none is simple. The alternative formula presented next is called a raw-score formula because it does not require the computation of means, standard deviations, or z scores. But as you can see, it is not simple:

$$r = \frac{(n \cdot \Sigma XY) - (\Sigma X \cdot \Sigma Y)}{\sqrt{[(n \cdot \Sigma X^2) - (\Sigma X)^2] \cdot [(n \cdot \Sigma Y^2) - (\Sigma Y)^2]}} \tag{8.2}$$

The only value in Formula 8.2 that we have not discussed is ΣXY. To compute ΣXY, you need to multiply each X by its paired Y and then sum the products. Note that this value is different from $\Sigma X \cdot \Sigma Y$, where we add up all the X's and then multiply that total by the sum of all the Y's. The computation of the correlation coefficient for the height/weight data using Formula 8.2 is presented in Table 8.6.

So you see, the raw-score formula is not a shortcut; the numbers involved can be many digits long. However, it is not really difficult. You need only multiply, divide, subtract, and find square roots to compute the correlation coefficient. If you have a calculator, try using Formula 8.2 to compute the correlation coefficient for the data in Table 8.3, and then check your work with Table 8.7.

The z-score and the raw-score formulas are algebraically equivalent; you can use either one to accurately compute the correlation coefficient. Each has its advantages and disadvantages. The z-score formula is easy to memorize and results in relatively small numerical values. However, it involves several separate computations, and because of this it is subject to errors made by rounding off after each step. The raw-score formula, on the other hand, is quite difficult to memorize and can result in large numerical values in the numerator and denominator, but it involves fewer calculations and is less likely to be affected by roundoff errors. But remember, both formulas will give the same value for the correlation coefficient.

Table 8.6 Computation of the Correlation Coefficient Using the Raw-Score Formula for Men's Heights and Weights

Man	Height X	X²	Weight Y	Y²	XY
M. P.	72	5,184	190	36,100	13,680
T. D.	66	4,356	135	18,225	8,910
C. Q.	69	4,761	155	24,025	10,695
C. Y.	72	5,184	165	27,225	11,880
D. P.	71	5,041	155	24,025	11,005

$$\Sigma X = 350 \quad \Sigma X^2 = 24{,}526 \quad \Sigma Y = 800 \quad \Sigma Y^2 = 129{,}600 \quad \Sigma XY = 56{,}170$$

$$r = \frac{(n \cdot \Sigma XY) - (\Sigma X \cdot \Sigma Y)}{\sqrt{[(n \cdot \Sigma X^2) - (\Sigma X)^2] \cdot [(n \cdot \Sigma Y^2) - (\Sigma Y)^2]}}$$

$$= \frac{(5 \cdot 56{,}170) - (350 \cdot 800)}{\sqrt{[(5 \cdot 24{,}526) - 350^2] \cdot [(5 \cdot 129{,}600) - 800^2]}}$$

$$= \frac{280{,}850 - 280{,}000}{\sqrt{(122{,}630 - 122{,}500) \cdot (648{,}000 - 640{,}000)}}$$

$$= \frac{850}{\sqrt{130 \cdot 8{,}000}} = \frac{850}{\sqrt{1{,}040{,}000}} = \frac{850}{1{,}019.804} = .83$$

Interpreting the Correlation Coefficient: What Do the Numbers Mean?

Question: Obviously, a correlation coefficient of .25 is not the same as a correlation coefficient of .90. But how are they different? What do they mean?

As we mentioned, some variables are related more closely than others, and the more closely they are related, the closer the correlation will be to +1.00 or −1.00. A correlation coefficient of 0 indicates no relationship at all between two variables. The relationship between height and weight ($r = +.83$) results in a much higher correlation coefficient (closer to +1.00) than the relationship between the IQs of a sample of married couples ($r = +.45$). And the correlation between the number of hassles and the level of immunoglobulin A (−.95) is higher than the correlation between grade point average and the amount of time spent watching television (−.68). Using the preceding formulas, you can compute a correlation coefficient between any two interval or ratio variables. You can compute the correlation coefficient between scores on two different tests, temperature and the number of people at a beach, manual dexterity and typing speed, and so on.

Table 8.7 Computation of the Correlation Coefficient Using the Raw-Score Formula for Number of Hassles and Immunoglobulin A Counts for Ten Subjects

Subject	Daily hassles X	X^2	Immunoglobulin A count Y	Y^2	XY
C. D.	12	144	1.72	2.958	20.64
P. M.	15	225	1.15	1.322	17.25
R. R.	20	400	0.15	0.023	3.00
M. D.	12	144	2.00	4.000	24.00
J. L.	17	289	0.25	0.063	4.25
M. F.	16	256	1.33	1.769	21.28
J. P.	10	100	2.10	4.410	21.00
H. S.	12	144	1.75	3.063	21.00
M. H.	15	225	1.35	1.823	20.25
M. V.	19	361	0.20	0.040	3.80

$$\Sigma X = 148 \quad \Sigma X^2 = 2288 \qquad \Sigma Y = 12.00 \qquad \Sigma Y^2 = 19.470 \quad \Sigma XY = 156.47$$

$$r = \frac{(n \cdot \Sigma XY) - (\Sigma X \cdot \Sigma Y)}{\sqrt{[(n \cdot \Sigma X^2) - (\Sigma X)^2] \cdot [(n \cdot \Sigma Y^2) - (\Sigma Y)^2]}}$$

$$= \frac{(10 \cdot 156.47) \cdot (148 \cdot 12)}{\sqrt{[(10 \cdot 2288) - 148^2] \cdot [(10 \cdot 19.470) - 12^2]}}$$

$$= \frac{1564.7 - 1776}{\sqrt{(22,880 - 21,904) \cdot (194.70 - 144)}}$$

$$= \frac{-211.3}{\sqrt{976 \cdot 50.7}} = \frac{-211.3}{\sqrt{49,483.2}} = \frac{-211.3}{222.448} = -.95$$

Question: You say that some things are correlated and some things are not. Isn't it possible to get a high correlation coefficient just by chance? How do you know when a correlation is real and not just due to coincidence?

Detecting whether a correlation is real or is just due to chance can present quite a problem. Even if you are sampling from two populations that have absolutely no relationship, it is possible that you can obtain a group of scores that will return a large correlation coefficient. Let's look at the correlation between two very important human variables: shoe size and number of friends. There is no psychological theory or commonsense reason to suggest

Table 8.8 Correlation Coefficient for Shoe Size and Number of Friends for Five Students

Student	Shoe size X	X²	Number of friends Y	Y²	XY
B. D.	12	144	3	9	36
J. C.	10	100	1	1	10
B. W.	9	81	2	4	18
K. T.	7	49	1	1	7
K. H.	6	36	3	9	18
	$\Sigma X = 44$	$\Sigma X^2 = 410$	$\Sigma Y = 10$	$\Sigma Y^2 = 24$	$\Sigma XY = 89$

$$r = \frac{(n \cdot \Sigma XY) - (\Sigma X \cdot \Sigma Y)}{\sqrt{[(n \cdot \Sigma X^2) - (\Sigma X)^2] \cdot [(n \cdot \Sigma Y^2) - (\Sigma Y)^2]}}$$

$$= \frac{(5 \cdot 89) - (44 \cdot 10)}{\sqrt{[(5 \cdot 410) - 44^2] \cdot [(5 \cdot 24) - 10^2]}}$$

$$= \frac{445 - 440}{\sqrt{(2050 - 1936) \cdot (120 - 100)}} = \frac{5}{\sqrt{114 \cdot 20}} = \frac{5}{\sqrt{2280}}$$

$$= \frac{5}{\sqrt{47.749}} = .105$$

that there is any relationship at all between these two variables. If we sampled the entire population of college students and computed the correlation coefficient, we would expect it to be 0. But if we sampled only a small number of students, it is possible that, just by chance, we could end up with a sample in which big-footed people have the most friends. Consider Table 8.8. The correlation coefficient is positive and small (near 0), but it is not 0. However, it is still close to 0 and the difference is probably due to chance.

Question: But how can you tell when it is just a chance deviation from 0 and when it is a true correlation?

The answer to this question involves a discussion of the concepts of statistical significance, statistical inference, and degrees of freedom. These topics are discussed in detail in Chapters 10, 11, and 12, so we want to reserve a detailed explanation until then. But, as a general rule, large samples and populations require smaller correlations and small samples require larger correlations in order for us to be reasonably sure that a correlation does not occur by chance.

Question: When you find a high correlation between two variables, does that mean that one thing *causes* the other?

NO! The correlation coefficient is merely a measure of whether or not two variables are related. It does *not* indicate whether one variable causes the other. Consider the following example. There is a positive correlation between the number of migrating whales passing Point Loma (in San Diego) and the number of migrating birds passing the same point. But even if this correlation were very high, no rational person would claim that the whale migration is *caused* by the bird migration or, conversely, that the bird migration is caused by the whale migration. (Can you envision a whale breaching and calling to a group of birds nesting nearby, "Yo, birds. Better get a move on; it's time to migrate.") Often, two variables are correlated with each other because they are both caused by a third variable. In the case of the migrations, this variable might be a seasonal change in temperature that in turn affects the availability of food or nesting opportunities. But whatever the cause, it cannot be determined with correlational studies. The only way to determine the cause of any phenomenon is through experimental procedures.

Another important thing to note in this context is that both of the variables of interest (height and weight, number of whales and number of birds, etc.) are measured by the researcher. However, neither is manipulated or controlled by the researcher, as is done in a true experiment. This lack of manipulation or control is the reason no determination of causation can be made using the correlational statistical method. Only by conducting an experiment can a researcher determine that one variable *causes* a change in another.

THE COEFFICIENT OF DETERMINATION

Although correlations cannot be used to explain whether or not one variable causes another, they can be used for predictive purposes. For instance, if the correlation were quite high in the preceding case, we might predict that because the birds were 2 weeks late in their migration, the whales might also be late. But how accurate is such a prediction? Should the companies that organize whale-watching trips postpone the trips for 2 weeks? There is a statistical tool to measure the accuracy of correlational predictions. Known as the **coefficient of determination,** it is the part of the variance of one variable that can be explained by or attributed to the variance of a related variable.

This is a difficult concept to grasp; more explanation might help. There is always some variability in any group of scores. For example, we know that the scores for height and the scores for weight are distributed around their means.

The variability of each of these sets of scores about its mean is measured by the variance. When two variables are correlated, a part of the variance of one factor is attributable or explained solely by another factor; for instance, part of the variance in weight can be directly attributed to height. But the rest of the variance is attributable to other factors. In the weight/height example, the variance in weight can also be related to genes, motivational factors, and environmental factors. By using the coefficient of determination, we can determine how much of the variance of one factor (weight) can be explained by the variability of a factor with which it is correlated (height). Easy to calculate, the coefficient of determination is the square of the correlation coefficient:

$$\text{Coefficient of determination} = r^2 \qquad (8.3)$$

To illustrate, let's suppose that the bird and whale migrations are correlated with an r of .50. This means that .25 ($.50^2$) of the variance in the time of whale migrations can be explained by the variance in the time of bird migrations. Seventy-five percent of the variance could be explained by other variables. Therefore, even if the birds were 2 weeks late in their migration, we would not necessarily expect the whales to be 2 weeks late because 75% of the variation in whale migration is explained by factors other than bird migration.

Question: Considering the formula for the coefficient of determination, I assume that a correlation coefficient of +.40 is not actually half as good as a correlation coefficient of +.80. Is that correct?

That is exactly right. With a correlation coefficient of +.40, only +.16 or 16% of the variance of one variable is predictable from the other variable. A correlation coefficient of +.80 indicates that +.64 or 64% of the variance of one variable is predictable from the variance of the other. Actually, through comparison it is evident that a correlation coefficient of +.80 explains *four times more* of the variance than a correlation coefficient of +.40. Correlation cannot explain causation—only an experiment can do that—but correlation is the basis of most *predictions* that are made using behavioral science data. The use of the correlation coefficient to make predictions is called *regression analysis*, which is the topic of Chapter 9.

C O N C E P T   Q U I Z

1. The computational or raw-score formula allows you to compute r without using _____.
2. The term ΣXY means _____.

3. A high correlation coefficient implies a causal relationship between the two correlated variables. True or false?

4. The coefficient of determination is equal to _____ .

5. With a correlation coefficient of .5, approximately _____ % of the variance of one variable is predictable from the other variable.

Answers

1. means, standard deviations, or z scores

2. to multiply each X by its paired Y value and then sum those products

3. false

4. r^2

5. 25

S U M M A R Y

The correlation coefficient is a measure of the relationship between two variables. Variables can be related in three general ways: They can be positively correlated, they can be negatively correlated, and they can have zero correlation. A positive correlation between two variables means that the two variables covary in the same direction—as one variable increases, the other increases; as one decreases, the other decreases. A negative correlation indicates that the two variables vary in different directions—as one variable increases, the other decreases; and vice versa. A zero correlation indicates that there is no relationship between the two variables; the two variables vary independently.

Two formulas are given for the computation of the correlation coefficient. One formula uses z scores; the other uses raw scores. To compute the correlation coefficient using either score, you must have not only two separate distributions but also pairs of scores. For each score in distribution X there must be a corresponding score in distribution Y.

To compute the correlation coefficient using the z-score formula, first convert each score in distribution X to a z score, and then convert each score in distribution Y to a z score. Next, multiply each z score by its corresponding z score in the other distribution. Then add these z-score products and divide the sum by the total number of pairs of scores.

To compute the correlation coefficient using the raw-score formula, you must calculate several different sums, as shown in Formula 8.2. They include the sum of the X's, the sum of the Y's, the sum of the X^2's, the sum of the Y^2's, and the sum of the XY's. Formula 8.2 can be used to compute the correlation coefficient once all these sums have been computed.

There are advantages and disadvantages to using either of the two formulas presented for computing the correlation coefficient. The z-score formula is easy to memorize and uses relatively small numerical values, but it requires several separate computations and is sometimes affected by roundoff errors. The raw-score formula, on the other hand, is more difficult to memorize and uses relatively large numerical values, but it requires fewer calculations and is less likely to be affected by roundoff errors. Unless directed otherwise, you should use the formula with which you feel most comfortable.

No matter which formula you use, the value of the correlation coefficient will never be greater than +1.00 or less than −1.00. A value close to +1.00 indicates a high positive correlation, whereas a value close to −1.00 indicates a high negative correlation. A correlation of 0 indicates no correlation at all.

Although the correlation coefficient does not imply causation, it can be used for prediction. The accuracy of the prediction can be assessed by using the coefficient of determination, which is the amount of the variance of one variable explained by a related variable. The coefficient of determination is the square of the correlation coefficient.

KEY TERMS

correlation   correlation coefficient

scatterplot   coefficient of determination

FORMULAS

$$r = \frac{\Sigma(z_X \cdot z_Y)}{n} \tag{8.1}$$

$$r = \frac{(n \cdot \Sigma XY) - (\Sigma X \cdot \Sigma Y)}{\sqrt{[(n \cdot \Sigma X^2) - (\Sigma X)^2] \cdot [(n \cdot \Sigma Y^2) - (\Sigma Y)^2]}} \tag{8.2}$$

Coefficient of determination = r^2 (8.3)

PROBLEMS

1. Past research has suggested a correlation between a person's verbal score on the SAT and his or her birth order. Birth order is a measure of the order in which you are born into a family. If you are the first child, your birth order equals 1; if you're the second child, your birth order equals 2; and so on. You want to see whether this trend has changed in recent years, so you ask ten of your friends their birth orders and their verbal SAT scores. Using the data in the table, draw a scatterplot and decide whether the correlation between birth order and verbal SAT scores appears to be positive, negative, or zero.

Subject	Birth order	Verbal SAT score
1	1	650
2	2	550
3	4	450
4	1	500
5	3	475
6	4	425
7	2	565
8	2	525
9	6	400
10	3	480

2. Create a scatterplot for the data in the table; tell whether the correlation appears to be positive, negative, or zero; and tell whether the degree of the correlation appears to be strong or weak. Then compute the correlation coefficient to confirm the results of your scatterplot.

Subject	Number of term papers typed	Typing speed
Chris	12	73
Mary	3	42
Paul	6	38
Juan	8	66
Marcel	10	55
Olga	9	79
Mi	4	34
Nima	7	50
Sari	2	35
Jarrod	10	89

3. Compute the correlation coefficient of the given test data using both the z-score and the raw-score formulas.

Subject	Test A	Test B
T. K.	700	35
D. M.	772	38
S. T.	605	36
B. P.	721	39
S. M.	695	34

4. The following table shows the blood alcohol levels of drivers in single-car accidents and the amount of damage (in dollars) that the accidents caused. Using this table, compute the correlation coefficient between blood alcohol level and monetary damage.

Blood alcohol level	Damage (in dollars)
.001	35
.012	254
.020	2300
.021	2100
.030	6000

5. Given the correlation coefficient you computed in Problem 4, what percentage of the variance in monetary damage can be explained by the blood alcohol level of the driver?

6. An industrial psychologist at XYZZZ, Inc., has collected data consisting of on-the-job aptitude scores and the numbers of assembly line errors for five of his workers. The data are listed in the table. Compute the correlation coefficient between the two variables. What conclusions about job aptitude scores and numbers of assembly line errors can be drawn from these data?

Worker	Aptitude test score	Errors
P. K.	13	22
M. D.	7	48
L. S.	24	5
T. D.	19	12
M. P.	25	6

7. A survey was conducted by a human sexuality research laboratory on the use of birth control by newly married couples. One of their striking findings was that couples who had the most electrical appliances were the ones most likely to use birth control. The data for seven couples are given here. Compute the correlation coefficient between birth control use and number of electrical appliances.

Birth control use	Number of electrical appliances
85	9
80	7
66	7
50	4
40	3
20	1
0	2

8. How do you explain the results of the research depicted in Problem 7? Would you suggest that young couples who want to have children sell their toasters?

9. Using the data in the table gathered from seven students, compute the correlation coefficient between the average number of hours spent studying each day and grade point average (GPA).

Student	Hours spent studying	GPA
P. J.	0.5	2.3
C. D.	3.4	3.3
M. J.	6.0	4.0
V. T.	4.6	3.2
K. T.	2.5	2.5
T. V.	0.8	1.9
B. M.	1.6	2.5

10. What is the coefficient of determination for the scores in Problem 9? What does this coefficient of determination tell about these two variables?

11. Compute the correlation coefficient between the number of statistics courses completed and the number of publications for the following six psychology professors.

Professor	Number of statistics courses	Number of publications
M. K.	3	25
D. D.	2	18
M. V.	3	28
G. B.	1	18
D. O.	2	34
K. H.	1	5

12. What is the coefficient of determination for the variables represented in Problem 11? Does this mean that the larger number of publications is the result of taking more statistics courses?

13. Compute the correlation coefficient between the number of hours spent in job training and the number of errors made on the first day of actual work for the five airline ticket agents listed here.

Agent	Job training hours	Number of errors
B. P.	3	23
C. J.	12	10
B. B.	16	8
C. C.	8	12
D. F.	8	9

14. Compute the correlation between personality test scores for this group of ten pairs of male/female fraternal twins.

Male twin	Female twin
88	86
76	65
96	84
36	47
54	48
66	66
73	65
85	92
90	99
23	18

15. Compute the coefficient of determination for the following correlation coefficients:

a. $r = .07$
b. $r = .35$

c. $r = .77$
d. $r = -.64$
e. $r = -.36$

Use the following values to do Problems 16–18.

.73   1.77   −77   106   −23   −.23   −.75   .45

16. Which scores are possible correlation coefficients?

17. Which score is the highest of the possible correlation coefficients?

18. Which score is the lowest of the possible correlation coefficients?

19. If we know that the correlation between two tests is .79, we expect a person who gets a high score on one of the tests to get a _____ score on the other test.

20. If we know that the correlation between two tests is −.79, we expect a person who gets a high score on one of the tests to get a _____ score on the other test.

21. Explain why a high correlation between two variables does not mean that one variable *causes* the other.

22. Give an example, not used in this book or in your class lectures, of two variables that are correlated but are not causally related.

23. A researcher is interested in knowing whether there is a correlation between the amount of motor activity exhibited by an infant and the number of fears the infant has developed. During a 30-minute observation period, the researcher measures the number of minutes each infant spends walking or crawling and then measures the number of objects in the experimental room that elicit a fear response from the child. The motor activity scores and the number of fears for 12 infants are listed in the table. Compute the correlation between movements and number of fears.

Child	Movements	Fears
R. J.	10	2
M. P.	20	6
J. D.	15	5
T. V.	5	1
B. G.	18	5
V. C.	22	3
D. J.	7	2
C. D.	13	5
W. F.	9	3
B. R.	15	6
J. T.	3	0
P. H.	8	3

24. What is the coefficient of determination for the data in Problem 23? Given this coefficient of determination, explain why you can state that movement is a good or bad predictor of the number of fears a child will acquire.

REFERENCES

Holmes, T. H., & Rahe, R. H. (1967). The social readjustment rating scale. *Journal of Psychosomatic Research, 11,* 213–218.

Martin, R. A., & Dobbin, J. P. (1988). Sense of humor, hassles, and immunoglobulin A: Evidence of a stress-moderating effect of humor. *International Journal of Psychiatry in Medicine, 18*(2), 93–105.

Regression

You are back in the cafeteria playing the same guessing game we described at the beginning of Chapter 8. Once again you are trying to guess the height of the next man who enters the cafeteria, and your friend is still outside weighing each man before he comes through the door. However, this time you have more information. Now you know not only the mean height of all the men who attend your school but also the mean weight and the standard deviations for both height and weight:

Height X	Weight Y
$\overline{X}$ = 70 inches	$\overline{Y}$ = 160 pounds
S_X = 2.28 inches	S_Y = 17.89 pounds

This time, when your friend outside sticks her head in the door and shouts "120 pounds," what will you do? You know from Chapter 8 (only too well!) that height and weight are correlated. You also know that because 120 pounds is well below the mean, you should guess a height that is proportionally as far from the mean as the weight. But how far below the mean should you guess? See if you can figure out a way to use this new information to calculate a guess that will be a realistic estimate based on what you know. Compute your new guess and then continue reading.

Question: Can I just convert the weight to a *z* score and then find the corresponding *z* score for height?

This sounds like a good idea, and it will work if height and weight are perfectly correlated. Let's take a look at this suggestion. Suppose that height and weight *are* perfectly correlated, with r = +1.00. Assuming this, you can predict that the man's height should lie proportionally the same distance from the mean as his weight. Consequently, each pair of height/weight scores should have the same *z* values. Because you know the means and the standard deviations, you can find a specific *z* score for weight, use this to find a *z* score for height, and then convert the *z* score to a raw score.

First you compute the *z* score for a weight of 120 pounds:

$$z_Y = \frac{Y - \overline{Y}}{S} = \frac{120 - 160}{17.89} = \frac{-40}{17.89} = -2.236$$

Then, because of your assumption that height and weight are perfectly correlated, the *z* score for X should equal the *z* score for Y. So z_X = −2.236 because

$$z_X = z_Y$$

for any pair of z scores. By using Formula 7.7, you can convert this z score to a raw score:

$$X = \overline{X} + (z_X \cdot S_X)$$

$$= 70 + (-2.236 \cdot 2.28) = 70 - 5.098 = 64.902 \text{ inches}$$

You can thereby predict that the man who weighs 120 pounds is probably about 65 inches tall.

As we hinted earlier, there is one distinctive flaw in this approach: Behavioral science variables are never perfectly correlated. It's true that taller people tend to weigh more than shorter people; students who spend a lot of time studying tend to get higher grades than those who don't; drivers who receive more speeding tickets are likely to pay more attention to speed limits in the future. But when it comes to human and animal behavior, there are always so many fluctuations and irregularities that there is little chance of a *perfect* correlation ever occurring between two behavioral variables. For instance, have you ever been on a diet and actually *gained* weight? If you doubt that it can happen, attend a couple of Weight Watchers meetings. In our experience we have never run across a study involving two behavioral variables where the correlation was equal to +1.00 or −1.00, and only rarely have we seen a correlation coefficient above +.90 or below −.90. In fact, the preceding example explaining how to predict height based on a z score of weight is *completely invalid* because we assumed a perfect correlation between height and weight. Such a correlation is nonexistent. (Look around in a room full of people and count how many exceptions there are to the "perfect" figure or physique.)

Question: Well, how do you make predictions when the relationship is not perfect?

MAKING PREDICTIONS VIA LINEAR REGRESSION

The simplest way to make predictions is to use linear regression, and making accurate predictions through linear regression is what the rest of this chapter is all about. In using this type of prediction, we make a vital assumption: that the variables used to make the prediction are linearly related. Linear relationships are illustrated in Figures 9.1(a) and (b), where the line that best fits the set of data points is a straight line. Data distributed in a *non*linear fashion, such as those in Figures 9.1(c) and (d), do not satisfy this assumption and cannot be used in linear regression.

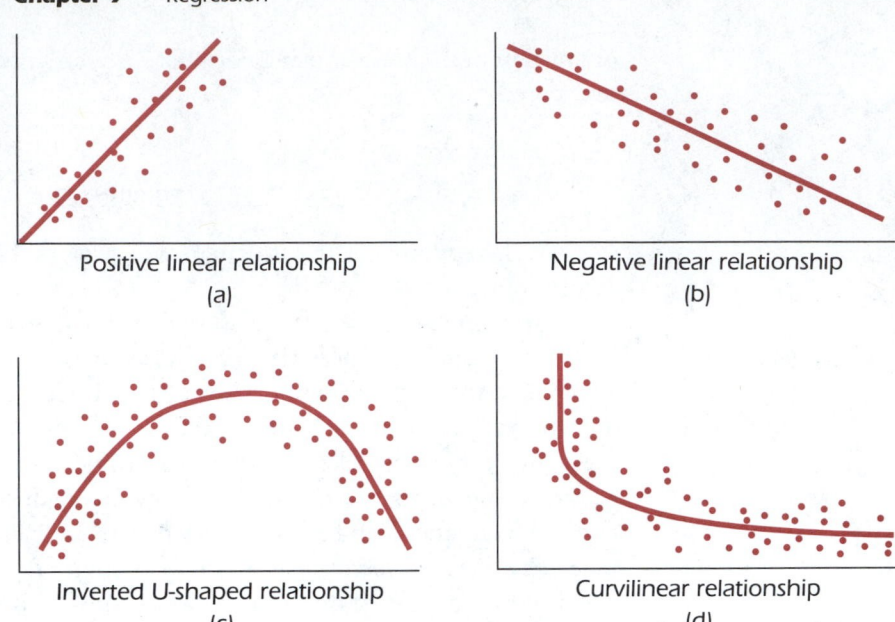

Positive linear relationship
(a)

Negative linear relationship
(b)

Inverted U-shaped relationship
(c)

Curvilinear relationship
(d)

Figure 9.1   Examples of types of relationships: (a) and (b) are linear relationships, whereas (c) and (d) are curvilinear relationships

The *z*-Score Method: Using *Y* to Predict *X*

Height and weight are related in a linear fashion, so we can use linear regression to make height/weight predictions. In the preceding example, we used z scores to predict a man's height when his weight was known. To make such a prediction valid, we must take into consideration the *value of the correlation* between the two variables. The correlation between the two variables is used to adjust our prediction and make it more accurate. If the variables were perfectly correlated, with r equal to +1.00, the preceding method would be acceptable; because they are not perfectly correlated, this fact must be reflected in the prediction. To make a more accurate prediction of one factor (X) from another factor (Y) when there is a known correlation between the two, we need only multiply the z score of the known factor by the correlation coefficient (r_{XY}):

$$z'_X = z_Y \cdot r_{XY} \tag{9.1}$$

[*Note:* The symbol z'_X is used to designate the *predicted* value of the z score of X. The predicted value of a variable or a z score is indicated by ', called "prime," after the symbol (e.g., Y' and z' are called "Y prime" and "z prime").]

For the height/weight data used in Chapter 8, we have the following information:

Height X	Weight Y
$\bar{X}$ = 70 inches	$\bar{Y}$ = 160 pounds
S_X = 2.28 inches	S_Y = 17.89 pounds
r_{XY} = .83	

We can make a valid prediction of the height of a 120-pound man by first computing the z score of his weight:

$$z_Y = \frac{Y - \bar{Y}}{S_Y} = \frac{120 - 160}{17.89} = \frac{-40}{17.89} = -2.236$$

Then we can use Formula 9.1 to predict the z score of his height:

$$z_X' = z_Y \cdot r_{XY}$$
$$= -2.236 \cdot .83$$
$$= -1.856$$

Finally, we can use Formula 7.7 to convert the z score of his height into the raw score, in inches:

$$X' = \bar{X} + (z_X' \cdot S_X)$$
$$= 70 + (-1.856 \cdot 2.28) = 70 - 4.232$$
$$= 65.768 \text{ inches}$$

So we can predict that a man who weighs 120 pounds will be about 65¾ inches tall.

As you may have noticed, 65.768 inches is slightly taller and slightly closer to the mean (70 inches) than the height predicted using z scores alone, which was 64.902 inches. When making predictions, we find that predicted values are always a little closer to the mean than the known values. Consider the task of predicting the height of the son of a 7-foot 5-inch giant woman. Even though tallness may tend to run in families, we have to admit that the giant's height is abnormal and that her son's height will almost certainly be somewhere between the mean and her incredible height. And so it is when we predict any unknown variable from one that is known. The predicted value always *regresses,* or goes back, toward the mean. The term *regression* indicates a movement back toward something. Psychoanalysts use the term *regression* to indicate a backward personality shift toward a more infantile coping strategy. Statisticians use the term **regression** to indicate a backward shift toward the mean when they are predicting an unknown value from a known value when the two values are correlated.

The amount of regression toward the mean depends on the value of the correlation coefficient, r. If r is equal to 0, if there is no correlation, the predicted value will always be a z score of 0, which is the mean; if r is equal to +1.00, the predicted value will be equal to the value of the known variable (remember, $z'_X = r \cdot z_Y$). So if r is low, or close to 0, the predicted value will be closer to the value of the mean than it would be if r were high, in which case it would be close to the z score of the known value. One way to think of this is to consider the coefficient of determination (r^2). A high r will have a high coefficient of determination, and more of the variance of one variable will be explained by the variance in the other variable, thus allowing a prediction farther from the mean and resulting in a more accurate overall prediction.

The *z*-Score Method: Using *X* to Predict *Y*

Question: What if our cafeteria game is once again changed so that now I am told the men's heights but I have to predict their weights. Can I use the same formula?

No; you can't use the *same* formula because you can't plug in a known *X*-value and solve backward to predict *Y*. But there is a similar formula for predicting *Y*-values. The two regression equations are shown here. One is used for predicting *X*, the other for predicting *Y*:

$$z'_X = z_Y \cdot r_{XY} \tag{9.1}$$

$$z'_Y = z_X \cdot r_{XY} \tag{9.2}$$

In your guessing game, you know that the next man who will enter the room is 72 inches tall. His known height is the *X*-value; what you want to predict is the *Y*-value, his weight. So you can use Formula 9.2 to predict the man's weight. The first step is to convert the height of 72 inches to a z score:

$$z_X = \frac{X - \bar{X}}{S_X} = \frac{72 - 70}{2.28} = \frac{2}{2.28} = 0.877$$

Next, predict the z score of *Y* using Formula 9.2:

$$z'_Y = z_X \cdot r_{XY} = 0.877 \cdot .83 = 0.728$$

Now, convert the predicted z score into a raw score by using the equivalent of Formula 7.7:

$$Y' = \bar{Y} + (z'_Y \cdot S_Y) = 160 + (0.728 \cdot 17.89) = 160 + 13.024$$
$$= 173.024 \text{ pounds}$$

Let's apply prediction via linear regression to a more productive situation. Step into the future a few years and imagine yourself as an industrial psychologist who needs to predict job performance from a job aptitude test. You give several current employees the aptitude test and correlate their aptitude scores with their monthly job performance scores. The results of your research are shown in Table 9.1 and are summarized as follows:

Job aptitude test X	Job performance score Y
$\bar{X} = 54$	$\bar{Y} = 77$
$S_X = 7.694$	$S_Y = 11.393$
$r_{XY} = .792$	

Table 9.1 Computation of Mean, Standard Deviation, and Correlation Coefficient for Job Aptitude Test (X) and Job Performance (Y) Data

Employee	X	X^2	Y	Y^2	XY
J.D.	65	4,225	90	8,100	5,850
M.P.	60	3,600	95	9,025	5,700
Q.R.	62	3,844	82	6,724	5,084
N.N.	59	3,481	87	7,569	5,133
M.O.	58	3,364	80	6,400	4,640
T.Y.	53	2,809	75	5,625	3,975
H.F.	50	2,500	60	3,600	3,000
P.C.	48	2,304	69	4,761	3,312
B.C.	45	2,025	60	3,600	2,700
D.B.	40	1,600	72	5,184	2,880
	$\Sigma X = 540$	$\Sigma X^2 = 29,752$	$\Sigma Y = 770$	$\Sigma Y^2 = 60,588$	$\Sigma XY = 42,274$
	$\bar{X} = 54$		$\bar{Y} = 77$		
	$S_X = 7.694$		$S_Y = 11.393$		

$$r_{XY} = \frac{(n \cdot \Sigma XY) - (\Sigma X \cdot \Sigma Y)}{\sqrt{[(n \cdot \Sigma X^2) - (\Sigma X)^2] \cdot [(n \cdot \Sigma Y^2) - (\Sigma Y)^2]}}$$

$$= \frac{(10 \cdot 42,274) - (540 \cdot 770)}{\sqrt{[(10 \cdot 29,752) - 540^2] \cdot [(10 \cdot 60,588) - 770^2]}}$$

$$= \frac{422,740 - 415,800}{\sqrt{(297,520 - 291,600) \cdot (605,880 - 592,900)}}$$

$$= \frac{6,940}{\sqrt{5,920 \cdot 12,980}} = \frac{6,940}{\sqrt{76,841,600}} = \frac{6,940}{8,765.934} = .792$$

A correlation coefficient of +.79 indicates that the aptitude test is a pretty good predictor of job performance, so you decide to use it for screening job applicants. The first applicant who takes the test scores 57. From this, you want to predict her job performance. What do you do first? Convert the test score to a z score:

$$z_X = \frac{X - \overline{X}}{S_X} = \frac{57 - 54}{7.694} = \frac{3}{7.694} = 0.390$$

Next, use Formula 9.2 to compute the predicted z score for job performance:

$$z_Y' = z_X \cdot r_{XY} = 0.390 \cdot .792 = 0.309$$

Then use Formula 7.7 to find the predicted raw score for job performance:

$$Y' = \overline{Y} + (z_Y' \cdot S_Y) = 77 + (0.309 \cdot 11.393) = 77 + 3.520$$
$$= 80.52$$

Should you recommend hiring this applicant? Because her predicted job performance is very high, you would certainly want to hire her if you are basing your decision solely on the outcome of this job aptitude test.

C O N C E P T   Q U I Z

1. The simplest way to make accurate predictions is to use _____ .
2. Linear regression requires a _____ line relationship between the variables involved in the prediction.
3. To use the z-score method of linear regression for predicting an X-value from a Y-value, we must first convert the _____ value to a _____ .
4. The predicted z score of X is equal to the _____ times the _____ .
5. The predicted z score value always _____ toward the _____ .
6. The smaller the correlation coefficient, the _____ the predicted value will be to the mean.

Answers

1. linear regression
2. straight
3. Y; z score
4. z score of Y; correlation coefficient between X and Y
5. regresses; mean
6. closer

Raw-Score Formulas: Input Raw Scores → Output Raw Scores

Question: Do you always have to use three separate formulas to make a prediction?

No; it is possible to convert Formulas 9.1 and 9.2 into formulas that require raw scores as input for X and Y and result in raw scores for X and Y as output. These formulas are slightly more complicated, but in the long run they are more efficient. To illustrate their evolution, we'll start with Formula 9.1:

$$z'_X = z_Y \cdot r_{XY}$$

Because the z score for X and the z score for Y can be obtained by the following formulas,

$$z'_X = \frac{X' - \overline{X}}{S_X}$$

$$z_Y = \frac{Y - \overline{Y}}{S_Y}$$

we can substitute these values for z_X and z_Y into Formula 9.1, and the result is

$$\frac{X' - \overline{X}}{S_X} = \frac{Y - \overline{Y}}{S_Y} \cdot r_{XY}$$

Multiplying each side of the equation by S_X, we get

$$X' - \overline{X} = \frac{Y - \overline{Y}}{S_Y} \cdot r_{XY} \cdot S_X$$

Now we need only add $\overline{X}$ to each side of the equation:

$$X' = \left[\frac{Y - \overline{Y}}{S_Y} \cdot r_{XY} \cdot S_X \right] + \overline{X}$$

By rearranging the terms slightly, we get Formula 9.3:

$$X' = \left[\frac{r_{XY} \cdot S_X}{S_Y} \cdot (Y - \overline{Y}) \right] + \overline{X} \qquad (9.3)$$

There is a similar formula for predicting Y:

$$Y' = \left[\frac{r_{XY} \cdot S_Y}{S_X} \cdot (X - \overline{X}) \right] + \overline{Y} \qquad (9.4)$$

Formulas 9.3 and 9.4 do not require z scores at all. For example, if we want to predict the weight of a man whose height is 73 inches when the correlation between height and weight is +.83, we can use Formula 9.4:

$$Y' = \left[\frac{r_{XY} \cdot S_Y}{S_X} \cdot (X - \bar{X}) \right] + \bar{Y}$$

$$= \left[\frac{.83 \cdot 17.89}{2.28} \cdot (73 - 70) \right] + 160$$

$$= \left[\frac{14.849}{2.28} \cdot 3 \right] + 160 = [6.511 \cdot 3] + 160$$

$$= 19.533 + 160 = 179.533 \text{ pounds}$$

Similarly, if you want to predict the job aptitude test score of a person who got a job performance score of 69, you can use Formula 9.3 (the data for this are in Table 9.1):

$$X' = \left[\frac{r_{XY} \cdot S_X}{S_Y} \cdot (Y - \bar{Y}) \right] + \bar{X}$$

$$= \left[\frac{.792 \cdot 7.694}{11.393} \cdot (69 - 77) \right] + 54$$

$$= \left[\frac{6.094}{11.393} \cdot (-8) \right] + 54 = [0.535 \cdot (-8)] + 54$$

$$= -4.28 + 54 = 49.72$$

Therefore, we can predict that a person who had a job performance rating of 69 would score 49.72, or about 50, on the job aptitude test.

MAKING MULTIPLE PREDICTIONS

Question: Returning to the school cafeteria, what if I were using Formulas 9.3 and 9.4 in my predictions, but it was taking too long. A line of impatient people was forming outside the door. Is there a faster way to make lots of predictions?

Yes. When you need to make multiple predictions from a single set of two correlated variables, such as predicting the heights of many people when their weights are known or predicting the job performances of many applicants when their test scores are known, it can take quite a while if you have to solve the preceding equations for each prediction. Two other methods are quite a bit quicker. The faster way is to graph the regression equations and then read the results from the graph. The other way is to further simplify Formulas 9.3 and 9.4 by substituting known values for means, standard deviations, and the correlation coefficient. Although the graph is faster, the substitution method is more accurate. Let's first take a look at the graph method.

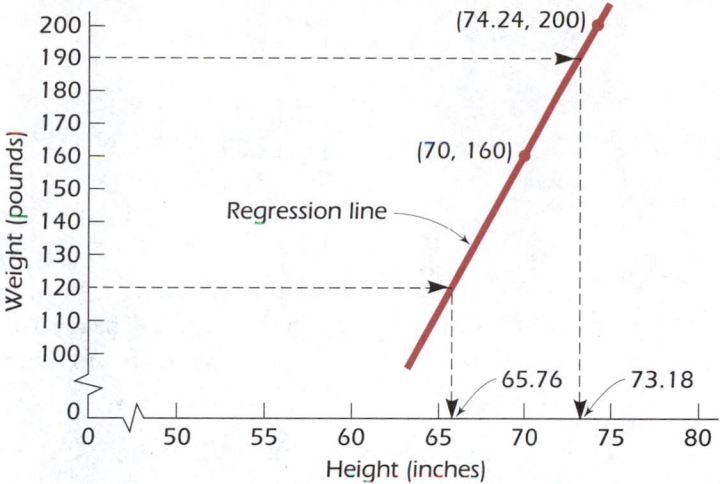

Figure 9.2   A regression line for predicting height from weight

Graphing Linear Regression Equations: Predicting from a Graph

Take a look at Figure 9.2. You see a graph with a diagonal line on it. This line is known as a *regression line*. It can be used to predict any X- or Y-value for any set of correlated variables (height and weight, study time and grades, and so on). For each pair of correlated variables, there are two separate regression lines, one for predicting X and one for predicting Y.

As you may remember from your algebra course, a line can be drawn on a graph by plotting two points on the graph and then connecting the points. The points are determined by using a linear equation, such as Formula 9.3 or 9.4, to compute the value of an unknown variable when the value of a correlated variable is already known. It is the resulting (X, Y)-values that are plotted on the graph and connected with a line to form a regression line.

How can you predict the heights of many people when their weights are known? By looking at a regression line, you can find the weight on the ordinate, read across to the regression line, and then go straight down to the abscissa to find the corresponding height. Of course, in real life the majority of the men whose heights you are guessing will not weigh precisely what the graph says they should weigh, but odds are that the graph will provide you with the best estimate. So how do you generate a regression line for predicting height?

First, as we said earlier, you need two points to plot a straight line. The Y-values (weight) are available, so you need to solve Formula 9.3 to find two X-values. You decide to select 160 pounds, the mean for Y, for one of your points and 200 pounds, the weight of the last man to enter the cafeteria, for the other point. Now solve the formula using 160. If you look closely at Formula 9.3, you will see that when Y is equal to the mean for Y, the predicted X is always the mean for X:

$$X' = \left[\frac{r_{XY} \cdot S_X}{S_Y} \cdot (Y - \overline{Y}) \right] + \overline{X} \qquad (9.3)$$

$$= \left[\frac{.83 \cdot 2.28}{17.89} \cdot (160 - 160) \right] + 70$$

$$= \left[\frac{1.892}{17.89} \cdot 0 \right] + 70 = 0 + 70 = 70$$

Therefore, one of your points is $(\overline{X}, \overline{Y})$ or (70, 160), and you have seen that the mean of Y always predicts the mean of X. The reverse is also true: The mean of X always predicts the mean of Y. Next, you need to compute the other point, where $Y = 200$:

$$X' = \left[\frac{r_{XY} \cdot S_X}{S_Y} \cdot (Y - \overline{Y}) \right] + \overline{X}$$

$$= \left[\frac{.83 \cdot 2.28}{17.89} \cdot (200 - 160) \right] + 70$$

$$= \left[\frac{1.892}{17.89} \cdot 40 \right] + 70 = [0.106 \cdot 40] + 70$$

$$= 4.24 + 70 = 74.24$$

Your second point, then, is (74.24, 200).

Now you are ready to plot the two points and draw the regression line through them. Your graph should look just like the one in Figure 9.2, which you can use to speedily predict as many heights as you need to win your game. But take note that because Formula 9.3 was used to generate this graph, *the graph is accurate only for predicting height (X) from weight (Y)*. Therefore, to use Figure 9.2 you first need a known weight. For instance, the next man's weight is 120 pounds. Find 120 along the ordinate, move horizontally across the graph to the regression line, and then drop vertically to the X-axis where you can read the height of the person, which is about 65¾ inches. If you do the same thing for a person who weighs 190 pounds, you should predict that he is about 73 inches tall.

Question: Can I assume that if we were playing a variation of our game and predicting the man's weight when we knew his height, I would go through the same procedure but use Formula 9.4 instead of Formula 9.3?

Right. If you want to predict weight from height, you need to plot the regression line corresponding to Formula 9.4. Again, one of the points you choose can be the mean for X and the mean for Y, but you will have to compute a second point to plot the regression line. As an example, let's say

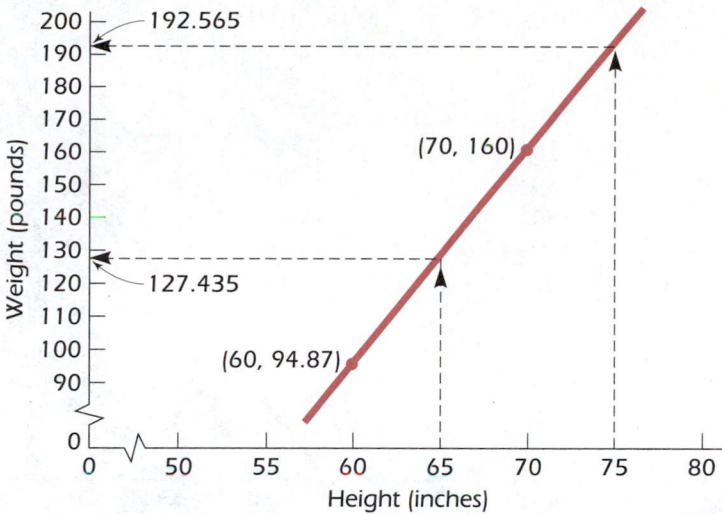

Figure 9.3 A regression line for predicting weight from height

you need to predict the weight of a man who is 60 inches tall. Remember, you need to use Formula 9.4 this time:

$$Y' = \left[\frac{r_{XY} \cdot S_Y}{S_X} \cdot (X - \overline{X}) \right] + \overline{Y} \tag{9.4}$$

$$= \left[\frac{.83 \cdot 17.89}{2.28} \cdot (60 - 70) \right] + 160$$

$$= \left[\frac{14.849}{2.28} \cdot (-10) \right] + 160 = [6.513 \cdot (-10)] + 160$$

$$= -65.13 + 160 = 94.87 \text{ pounds}$$

The point given by the means is the same as in the previous example (70, 160), and your other point is (60, 94.87). The regression line for predicting weight from height is plotted in Figure 9.3, which you can use to predict the weight of the man from his height. For example, you can predict that the weight of a man who is 65 inches tall will be 127 or 128 pounds, and the weight of a man who is 75 inches tall will be 192 or 193 pounds.

Earlier in this chapter we mentioned that each regression equation can be used for predicting either X or Y but cannot be used for both. The difference between the two equations can readily be seen if both equations are plotted on the same graph. Figure 9.4 shows both regression lines from the height and weight data plotted on the same axes. As you can see, the two regression lines cross at the means of height and weight, but they have slightly different slopes.

To plot regression lines for the data from the job aptitude test and job performance scores in Table 9.1, you use the identical procedure. You may

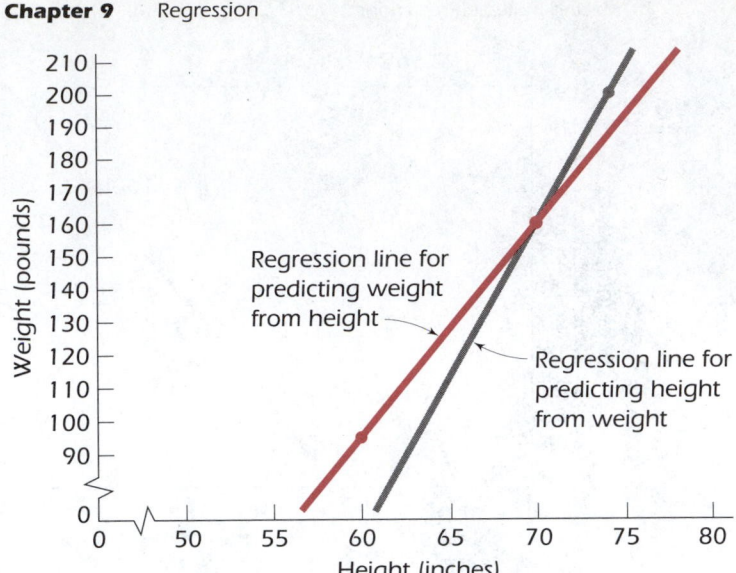

Figure 9.4   Regression lines for predicting height and for predicting weight plotted on the same axes

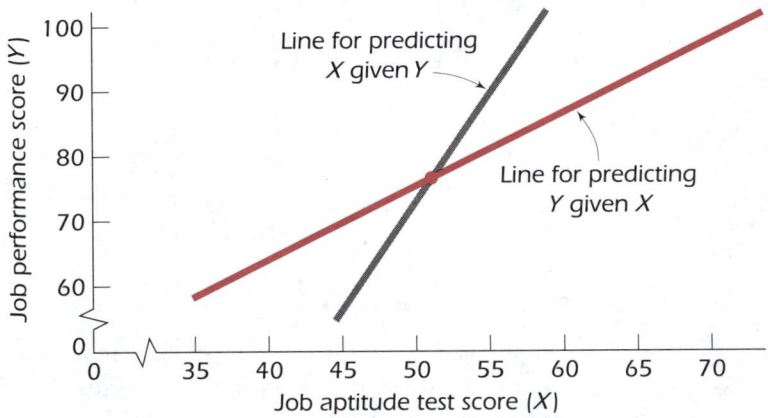

Figure 9.5   Regression lines for predicting job aptitude test scores and for predicting job performance plotted on the same axes

want to construct your own regression lines for practice, one for predicting aptitude test scores from job performance and another for predicting job performance scores from the aptitude test, and compare yours with the ones plotted in Figure 9.5. Note that the lines cross at the mean for X and the mean for Y, and the lines have slightly different slopes. Figure 9.6 illustrates that as the correlation coefficient between two variables grows smaller, or closer to 0, the two regression lines tend to diverge more and more.

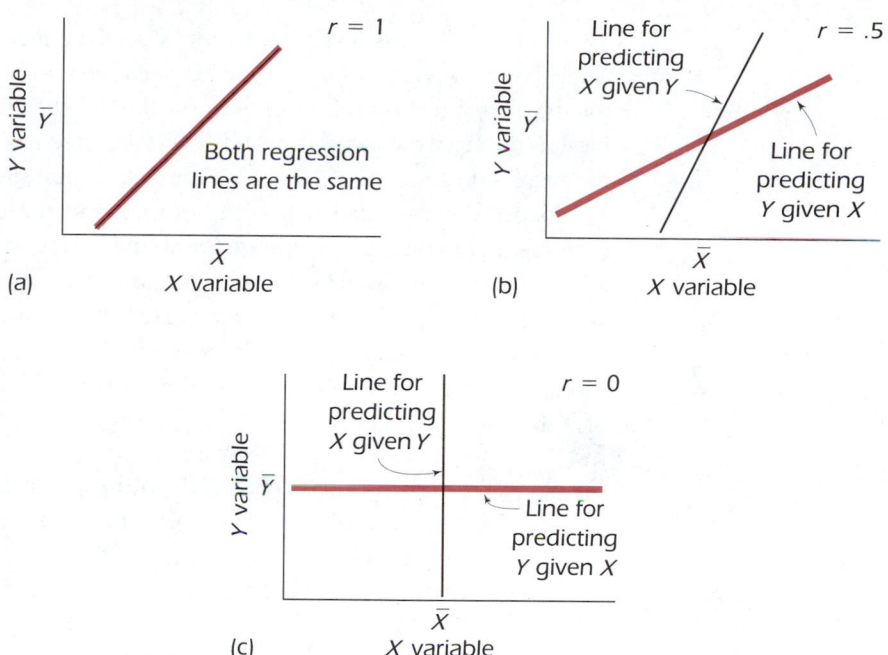

Figure 9.6   The relationship between the two regression lines when: (a) $r = 1$, (b) $r = .5$, and (c) $r = 0$

Question: Why have we plotted two regression lines? Why not just draw the best-fitting straight line through the points and use that to make the predictions?

The easiest way to answer this question is to refer to Figure 9.6. This figure shows regression lines for three hypothetical situations, where the means and standard deviations remain constant for X and Y and the correlation coefficient changes from +1.00 to .5 to 0. Let us assume that we have two types of psychological tests, Test X and Test Y, and we would like to be able to predict scores on one test based on scores from the other. If we know that there is no measurable relationship between the two tests, $r = 0$, then no matter what a person scores on Test Y, our best estimate of that person's score on Test X will always be the mean for X, $\overline{X}$. This particular prediction is represented by the black line in Figure 9.6(c). Conversely, if we wish to predict a person's score on Test Y, it doesn't matter what score he or she receives on Test X, we would still predict the mean for Y, $\overline{Y}$. This situation is represented by the colored line in Figure 9.6(c). It should be obvious that two different lines are necessary when there is no correlation.

In Figure 9.6(b), the correlation is .5. The black line, the one for predicting X, has rotated away from the mean in light of the correlational information. The colored line, the one for predicting Y, has likewise rotated away from the mean.

These lines still cross at the mean for X and the mean for Y. The best-fitting single line for Figure 9.6(b) is a line between the two lines, but it cannot be used reliably for prediction purposes—as you can see, the lines still diverge by quite a bit. It is not until the correlation is 1.00, as depicted in Figure 9.6(a), that both of the regression lines are the same as the line of best fit.

Figure 9.6 can also help you comprehend patterns of predicting from regression lines on a graph. Figure 9.6(a) makes it clear that when both factors are perfectly correlated, you can make an exact prediction of Y when you know the value of X, and vice versa. In Figure 9.6(c), it is plain to see that when there is no relationship whatsoever between the variables, the best you can do is to predict the mean of Y no matter what the value of X, and the mean of X from any value of Y.

Question: These graphs *do* speed up the prediction process, but they aren't very accurate. On the other hand, solving the regression equations is accurate but takes forever. Is there a way to make predictions that is both fast *and* accurate?

Simplified Regression Equations: Shortcut Predictions

There *is* a way that involves solving a regression equation for each prediction. You already know how tedious this can be; but when making multiple predictions, you can save a great deal of time if you take a few minutes at the beginning to substitute all the known values (mean of X, mean of Y, standard deviation of X, standard deviation of Y, and the correlation coefficient) into the regression equation and then simplify the equation. To show you what we mean, let's say that you need to predict men's heights (X'). Thus, you need to start with Formula 9.3, but before you plug in any Y (weight) values, substitute in the known values of the means, the standard deviations, and the correlation coefficient for the height and weight data:

$$X' = \left[\frac{r_{XY} \cdot S_X}{S_Y} \cdot (Y - \overline{Y}) \right] + \overline{X} \qquad (9.3)$$

Height X	Weight Y
$\overline{X} = 70$ inches	$\overline{Y} = 160$ pounds
$S_X = 2.28$ inches	$S_Y = 17.89$ pounds
$r_{XY} = .83$	

$$X' = \left[\frac{.83 \cdot 2.28}{17.89} \cdot (Y - 160) \right] + 70$$

Now, still before inserting any Y-values, simplify this equation:

$$X' = \left[\frac{1.892}{17.89} \cdot (Y - 160) \right] + 70 = [0.106 \cdot (Y - 160)] + 70$$

$$= 0.106 \cdot Y - 16.96 + 70$$

$$= 0.106 \cdot Y + 53.04$$

This is the simplified regression equation you'll use to make each separate prediction. You have to agree that it's quite a handy shortcut: Multiple predictions are a lot speedier when you simplify the original equation in this way. Using the simplified version, you can substitute in any value of Y (weight) and swiftly compute an accurate value for X' (height). Of course, if you are making only one prediction, there is no need to go through the step of simplifying, but if you are going to make several predictions from the same data, this procedure will save you lots of unnecessary time and work.

To illustrate how much faster the simplified equation can be, let's use an example we used to illustrate Formula 9.3. We supposed that you needed to find the height of a man who weighs 120 pounds. Using the simplified equation, we get

$$X' = 0.106 \cdot Y + 53.04 = (0.106 \cdot 120) + 53.04 = 12.72 + 53.04$$

$$= 65.76 \text{ inches}$$

This is the same height we predicted earlier. Thus, if by this time you are still making predictions in your cafeteria game, you can go through a one-time procedure of simplifying Formula 9.3 and then predict all your heights promptly and accurately. If you were an industrial psychologist in charge of hiring at the company where the data in Table 9.1 were compiled, you could easily generate a formula that would similarly enable you to make quick and accurate predictions about job performance from scores on the job aptitude test.

THE STANDARD ERROR OF ESTIMATE

Using the regression equations paid off in your cafeteria game: Your friend treated you to lunch. In fact, you felt so assured of your predictive proficiency that the next day you proposed playing the same game with another friend, but with higher stakes. This time, the loser would take the winner out to dinner at a fancy restaurant. You used the same formulas that won you a lunch the day before but, instead of winning a dinner, you ended up buying one for your friend.

Question: What went wrong? Isn't it more accurate to use regression equations than to guess?

Yes, regression equations are more accurate than just guessing. But even if you are using a regression equation, you should not fall into the trap of thinking that these equations will give you predictions that are 100% accurate. As long as the correlation coefficients you're using are not perfect, your predictions will not be perfect. Remember what we mentioned in our discussion about the correlation between height and weight: Some people are tall and thin, and some are short and stout. In all psychological and biological populations some unexplained variance will cause inaccuracies in predictions made using regression equations. As you may recall, the coefficient of determination expresses the amount of variance in one variable that is explained by the other variable. Whenever the correlation coefficient is not +1.00 or −1.00, an unexplained variance will always cause some error in prediction. This error of prediction is called the *standard error of estimate*.

The **standard error of estimate** is the standard deviation of the actual values of a variable from the predicted values. For example, suppose we had a sample of 100 men who all weighed 150 pounds. We would not expect all these men to be exactly the same height. If we used the simplified formula for predicting height from weight, $X' = 0.106 \cdot Y + 53.04$, we would predict that a man who weighs 150 pounds will be 68.94 inches tall. But of course not all, perhaps even none, of the 100 men in our sample would be exactly that height. The heights of these 150-pound men would form a normal distribution around the mean height of 68.94 inches, and the standard deviation of this distribution would be the standard error of estimate. The smaller the standard error of estimate, the closer the actual scores are to the predicted value.

Just as there are two separate regression equations, there are also two equations for the standard error of estimate, one for the prediction of X from Y:

$$S_{XY} = S_X \sqrt{1 - r^2} \tag{9.5}$$

and one for the prediction of Y from X:

$$S_{YX} = S_Y \sqrt{1 - r^2} \tag{9.6}$$

To determine the standard error of estimate for the height prediction made above, we would use Formula 9.5:

$$S_{XY} = S_X \sqrt{1 - r^2}$$
$$= 2.28 \sqrt{1 - .83^2} = 2.28 \sqrt{1 - .689}$$
$$= 2.28 \sqrt{.311} = 2.28 \cdot .558$$
$$= 1.272 \text{ inches}$$

Because the standard error of estimate is the standard deviation of the actual scores from the predicted regression line, we can use the logic discussed in Chapter 6 (on the normal curve) to predict the proportion of people who fall within a certain distance of the regression line. In the preceding example, we can think of 1.272, which is the standard error of estimate for the height/weight data, as a standard deviation. Thus, we can say that approximately 68%, or two-thirds, of the people in the sample population who all weighed 150 pounds will have heights between 70.212 and 67.668 inches (68.94 inches ± 1.272 inches). This type of analysis is valid only if the standard deviation of the Y-values is the same at every value of X. This assumption of equal standard deviations is referred to as **homoscedasticity.**

In this chapter we demonstrated how to make predictions about one variable from another known variable. The formulas in this chapter will allow you to make accurate predictions if the correlation between the two factors is high and their relationship is linear. If the variables are not linearly related, or if it might be more accurate to make predictions based on several variables rather than just one, other types of regression analysis need to be used. A discussion of these procedures is beyond the scope of this book. If you need to perform more complicated regression analysis, you will need to consult a more advanced statistics textbook.

In closing this chapter, we want to remind you that correlation and regression are helpful in measuring the relationship between variables and in making predictions. However, keep in mind that the correlation coefficient you compute and the predictions you make are only as good as the data you use to make those measurements. In addition, all predictions are subject to some error. You must always state the standard error of estimate along with your prediction. Whenever you hear of a new prediction—an earthquake will destroy half of California sometime during July, the Yankees will win the pennant, or maze-bright rats will learn a maze faster than maze-dull rats—try to look for the data used in making those predictions. Remember that anyone can make a prediction or hold an opinion, but accurate predictions come from accurate data collection and analysis, not ESP, horoscopes, or guesswork. Also remember that correlation will never pinpoint the causal relationships between variables; only an experiment can do that.

CONCEPT QUIZ

1. For each pair of correlated variables, there is (are) _____ regressions line(s).

2. The regression line for predicting X from Y cannot be used to predict Y from X. True or false?

3. Whenever the correlation coefficient is different from +1.00 or −1.00, some unexplained variance will cause error in prediction. This error of prediction is called the _____ .

4. The standard error of estimate for the prediction of X from Y is equal to the _____ times _____ .

5. The assumption that the standard deviation of all Y-values is the same at every value of X is referred to as _____ .

Answers

1. two

2. true

3. standard error of estimate

4. standard deviation of X; $\sqrt{1 - r^2}$

5. homoscedasticity

S U M M A R Y

When the correlation between two variables is known, we can predict, to a certain degree of accuracy, the value of an unknown variable from a known variable based on their means and standard deviations and the correlation coefficient between the two variables. In this chapter we presented two ways to generate regression equations that can be used to make these predictions. The first method is the z-score approach. The predicted z score of X is equal to the correlation coefficient times the z score of Y. Conversely, the predicted z score of Y is equal to the correlation coefficient times the z score of X. These formulas are easy to memorize, but they are time-consuming because raw scores must be converted to z scores and z scores must then be converted back to raw scores.

The raw-score method eliminates the need to convert to z scores, but the formula is much more difficult to memorize (see Formulas 9.3 and 9.4). If multiple predictions need to be made from the same set of data, two methods can be used. One is to graph the regression equations. Two separate regression lines can be drawn from the equations, one for predicting X and another for predicting Y. From these regression lines, any unknown value can be predicted by finding the value of the known variable along the ordinate or the abscissa and then using the regression line to locate the corresponding value for the unknown variable.

The second method for making multiple predictions using the same set of data is to simplify the regression equation by substituting the means, the standard deviations, and the correlation coefficient into the regression equations. The simplified equation can then be solved for unknown variables by substituting multiple values of the known variable.

The standard error of estimate is the standard deviation of actual values from the value estimated from the regression equation. The smaller the standard error of estimate, the closer to the actual real-world values the prediction is likely to be. Since there are two regression equations, there are also two standard errors of estimate, one for the prediction of Y from a known X and another for the prediction of X from a known Y.

K E Y   T E R M S

regression   homoscedasticity
standard error of estimate

F O R M U L A S

$$z'_X = z_Y \cdot r_{XY} \tag{9.1}$$

$$z'_Y = z_X \cdot r_{XY} \tag{9.2}$$

$$X' = \left[\frac{r_{XY} \cdot S_X}{S_Y} \cdot (Y - \overline{Y}) \right] + \overline{X} \tag{9.3}$$

$$Y' = \left[\frac{r_{XY} \cdot S_Y}{S_X} \cdot (X - \overline{X}) \right] + \overline{Y} \tag{9.4}$$

$$S_{XY} = S_X \sqrt{1 - r^2} \tag{9.5}$$

$$S_{YX} = S_Y \sqrt{1 - r^2} \tag{9.6}$$

P R O B L E M S

Each year millions of babies are born in the United States. Some are firstborns, some are the second born, and so on. Using census data, we can compute the average birth order of all children born in any one year. A researcher is interested in seeing whether there is a relationship between the birth order average and SAT scores for high school seniors. The data for national birth order averages and the mean SAT scores for ten years are listed in the table. Use them in Problems 1–3.

Birth order average	Mean SAT score
2.5	485
2.6	480
2.6	480
2.6	475
2.7	475
2.7	470
2.8	470
2.8	465
2.8	460
2.9	455

1. Compute the means, standard deviations, and correlation coefficient.

2. Using the z-score regression equations, predict the average SAT score for a year that has a corresponding birth order average of 2.4.

3. Using the raw-score regression equations, predict the average birth order for a year that has a corresponding SAT score of 440.

Twenty-five mothers along with their daughters were asked to participate in a test of manual dexterity. The means, the standard deviations for each group, and the correlation coefficient for the mothers' and daughters' scores are listed here. Make the predictions in Problems 4–11.

	Mothers	Daughters
Mean	45	52
Standard deviation	4.5	6.5
Correlation coefficient	+.55	

4. Mother's score when a daughter's score is 50

5. Mother's score when a daughter's score is 47

6. Mother's score when a daughter's score is 40

7. Mother's score when a daughter's score is 60

8. Mother's score when a daughter's score is 52

9. Daughter's score when a mother's score is 44

10. Daughter's score when a mother's score is 49

11. Daughter's score when a mother's score is 45

12. A graduate school selection committee has filled all but one of its openings for next year's psychology class. The committee is having difficulty deciding between two applicants, Sigmund F., who attended Psychoanalytic U., and Carl R., who attended Client-Centered U.

    The committee decides that both are equally desirable, so they will pick the student whose undergraduate grade point average predicts the highest grade point average in graduate school. Sigmund F. graduated with a 3.9 GPA from Psychoanalytic U., and Carl R. graduated with a 3.6 GPA from Client-Centered U.

    Using the data in the table, predict the graduate school GPA for each applicant. Also compute the standard error of estimate for each of those predictions.

School	Mean	Standard deviation	Correlation with grad school grades
Grad school	3.5	0.3	—
Psychoanalytic U.	3.7	0.2	.5
Client-Centered U.	3.4	0.1	.9

Suppose a physiological psychologist, using a sample of 25 pairs of mothers and their children with mental retardation, has found that a relationship exists between the level of alcohol in the mother's bloodstream during the first trimester of pregnancy and the IQ of the child. These data follow:

Correlation between blood alcohol level and
  IQ = −.65
Standard deviation of blood alcohol level =
  0.003
Mean of blood alcohol level = 0.010
Standard deviation of child's IQ = 10
Mean of child's IQ = 75

Using the preceding data, predict the child's IQ for each mother's blood alcohol level in Problems 13–18.

13. 0.001

14. 0.007

15. 0.012

16. 0.020

17. 0.000

18. 0.010

19. Using the preceding means and standard deviations, compute the standard error of estimate for predicting the IQ score of a child from the blood alcohol level of the mother.

The data in the table, gathered from ten students, are the average number of hours they spent studying each day and their grade point averages (GPA).

Student	Hours spent studying	GPA
P. J.	0.5	2.3
C. D.	3.4	3.3
M. J.	6.0	4.0
V. T.	4.6	3.2
K. T.	2.5	2.5
T. V.	0.8	1.9
B. M.	1.6	2.5
T. J.	5.6	3.3
M. V.	1.6	3.0
P. Q.	2.9	2.9

After computing the means, the standard deviations, and the correlation coefficient for the data, do Problems 20–26.

20. Given that a student has a GPA of 2.8, predict how many hours she spends studying each day.

21. Given that a student has a GPA of 1.7, predict how many hours he spends studying each day.

22. Given that a student has a GPA of 4.0, predict how many hours she spends studying each day.

23. Predict the GPA for a student who spends 2.7 hours studying each day.

24. Predict the GPA for a student who spends 4.5 hours studying each day.

25. Predict the GPA for a student who spends 1.6 hours studying each day.

26. Predict the GPA for a student who never studies.

Probability Theory and Sampling

Have you seen the movie *Ghostbusters*? Bill Murray plays the unorthodox psychologist, Dr. Peter Venkman, who in one of the opening scenes is showing a set of "Zener" cards to two subjects in his ESP experiment. Zener cards are used in real-life experiments to investigate extrasensory perception (ESP). A Zener deck consists of 100 cards, each showing one of five symbols—a circle, a square, a star, a set of wavy lines, or a plus. In the movie, we see Dr. Venkman holding up the cards one by one, with the symbols facing away from the subjects, and asking the subjects to guess which symbol is on each card. Whenever the man responds, Dr. Venkman invariably shocks him, whether or not he answers correctly; whenever the beautiful woman responds, the good doctor smiles, congratulates her, and administers no shock, whether or not she is correct. It is obvious that the unethical Venkman is more concerned with courting the woman's favors than with obtaining objective, scientific data.

Let's suppose that we are more serious about investigating ESP, and we set up a research project to determine whether people actually possess clairvoyance. Our materials consist solely of a Zener deck of 100 cards, 20 of each of the 5 types. Like Dr. Venkman, we shuffle the deck, hold up each card, and ask subjects to guess what symbol is on it. Now comes the critical question: How many cards must they guess correctly before we can legitimately declare them clairvoyant? 50? 75? All 100? The answer is: They must consistently score higher than a person who does not have ESP and is just guessing.

Question: How many cards out of 100 will people guess correctly if they do *not* have ESP?

To compute the answer, we need to know something about probability. Nearly all psychological research is reported in terms of probabilities, as are many of its "facts" and "laws." Thus, studying or working with psychological research requires at least a basic understanding of probability theory.

PROBABILITY THEORY

Question: What do you mean by "probability"? How are psychological results reported as probabilities?

Probability is a measure of how likely it is that a given event or behavior will happen. Stop to think a moment. Isn't probability what psychological research is all about? What psychologists want to determine in their studies is how probable it is that the behavior they are studying is actually the one that is typical of most people under the same circumstances. In one experiment they may determine the probability of an enriched environment producing brighter children than a deprived one. In another, they may determine the probability of a behavior therapy program increasing the life span of high-risk patients who have cancer.

Probability is measured in terms of numbers. If the probability of an event occurring is 0, it means that the event will never happen. If the probability is 1, it means that the event will definitely happen. If the probability is somewhere between 0 and 1, it means that the event *may* happen, and the closer it is to 1, the stronger is the probability that the event will occur. Let's illustrate this with an example.

Suppose you are taking your Introduction to Psychology midterm test. What is the probability of getting question 10 correct? Well, you say, that depends on the question. Here it is:

10. Which of the following men is generally known as the "father of psychology"?
   a. Herman Ebbinghaus
   b. Wilhelm Wundt
   c. Sigmund Freud
   d. B. F. Skinner

Now that you know the question, it is easier to determine the probability of getting it correct. If you are absolutely sure of the answer, the probability is 1.00. If you don't have a clue and must make a wild guess, the probability of your getting the correct answer is 1 out of 4, or .25. If you are certain the answer is *not* B. F. Skinner but are not sure of the other three, the probability is 1 out of 3, or .33, and so on. (By the way, for those of you who have repressed it, the answer is Wilhelm Wundt.)

Sometimes it is easy to tell the probability of an event occurring. The probability of getting heads when tossing an evenly balanced coin is .5. The probability of drawing any spade from a normal deck of playing cards is .25. In short, the probability of any one event occurring is the number of possible ways it can occur divided by the total number of all possible events relating to that one event:

$$\text{Probability of event A} = \frac{\text{number of events in A}}{\text{total number of all events}} \text{ or } p(A) = \frac{n(A)}{n} \quad (10.1)$$

Using this formula, we can test the accuracy of the probabilities just mentioned. Every fair coin has two sides, one head and one tail. Thus, the probability of getting a head on a single toss of a coin is the number of possible heads, which is 1, divided by the number of possible outcomes, a head or a tail, which is 2:

$$p(\text{head}) = \frac{1}{2} = .5$$

The probability of drawing a spade from a deck of 52 cards is the number of spades, 13, divided by the number of cards, 52:

$$p(\text{spade}) = \frac{13}{52} = .25$$

We can do the same thing with the deck of ESP cards discussed previously. Suppose we want to know the probability of the next card drawn being a plus. We know there are 20 pluses in the deck and there are 100 total cards. Therefore, the probability of drawing a plus from that deck is

$$p(\text{plus}) = \frac{20}{100} = .20$$

If a subject in our ESP experiment guesses that a card shows a plus, he or she has a .20 chance of being correct. Extending this formula to every guess, each subject has a .20 chance of being correct. Because there are 100 cards in the deck, the subjects should guess correctly 20 times out of 100, just by chance.

Question: It's easy to figure out probabilities when you're just choosing cards or tossing coins, but how about figuring out the probability that someone will develop schizophrenia or that someone is color-blind?

Finding these probabilities is not as easy as finding the probability of getting heads or a spade, but it *may be* possible if you collect the appropriate data for estimating these probabilities. Let's figure out the probability that any one individual will develop schizophrenia. How should we proceed? One way is to interview several thousand people—say, 10,000—and create a frequency distribution. Let's say that we did this and came up with the following data:

Label	Frequency	Relative frequency
Schizophrenia	108	.0108
No disorder	9,027	.9027
Other psychological or psychiatric disorders	865	.0865
Total	10,000	1.0000

Using Formula 10.1 and the preceding data, we can compute the probability of a person having schizophrenia. (Remember, these are not real-life data.)

$$p(\text{schizophrenia}) = \frac{\text{number of occurrences of schizophrenia}}{\text{total number of people}}$$

$$= \frac{108}{10,000} = .0108$$

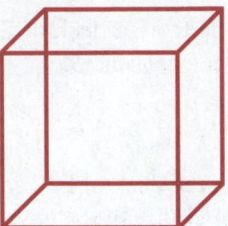

Figure 10.1   The Necker cube is an ambiguous figure that can be seen as a cube with its front square face either toward the top right of the page or toward the bottom left of the page.

Thus, the probability of a person having schizophrenia, given the preceding sample, is .0108, or about 1 out of every 100. Take another look at the frequency distribution. Do you notice that the relative frequency for schizophrenia in the table is the same as the computed probability? Another way to think of the probability of a behavior or event happening is to think of the relative frequency of that same behavior or event occurring in the population. Any time the data of an event can be displayed in a frequency distribution, we can estimate the probability of that event by computing its relative frequency. To carry this idea further, once we know the probabilities of single events, we can compute the probabilities of multiple events.

Take a look at the Necker cube in Figure 10.1. Which square forms its front face? Close your eyes, look at it again, and this time try to make yourself see the other square as being the one in front. Since the Necker cube ignores perspective, people are normally able to perceive either the right square or the left square as being the front of the cube. Now let's ask a probability question: What is the probability that either the square on the right or the square on the left is seen in front? The answer is 1.00. There are only two perceptual organizations possible, either the right square in front or the left square in front, and the possibility of seeing at least one of them is 1.00.

Question: Does this mean that when figuring out the probability of one event *or* another event, we need only sum the probabilities of the two?

Yes, *if* the two events are **mutually exclusive**—that is, if the two events cannot occur simultaneously. This is an important point. In the Necker cube example, you perceive either the right square or the left square in front; you never see a combination of the two. Similarly, the probability of the next animal you see being a dog *or* a cat is merely the sum of the individual probabilities because no animal can be both a dog and a cat. This relationship is often called the **addition rule of probability,** or the **addition theorem of probability,** and it is expressed by the following formula:

$$p(\text{A or B}) = p(\text{A}) + p(\text{B}) \tag{10.2}$$

Remember that Formula 10.2 holds true only if the two events are mutually exclusive. Of course, many events are not mutually exclusive. For instance, you might ask the question, What is the probability of drawing a jack or a heart from a deck of cards? or What is the probability that the next person I meet will be a man or someone who has schizophrenia? The answers to these are a bit more complicated because a card can be both a jack and a heart, and a person can be both a man and have schizophrenia.

To answer these probability questions, let's first focus on the card problem. We know that 4 of the cards in the deck are jacks. We also know that 13 of the cards are hearts, but we need to keep in mind that 1 of those 13 hearts is also a jack. So rather than 17 cards (4 jacks + 13 hearts) being either a jack or a heart, there are only 16—the 4 jacks plus the 12 hearts that are not jacks. From Formula 10.1, the probability of drawing a jack or a heart is the number of cards that are either jacks or hearts divided by the total number of cards in the deck:

$$p(\text{jack or heart}) = \frac{16}{52} = .308$$

Often we know the probabilities associated with individual events rather than the number of events themselves. For example, we might know that the probability of drawing a heart is .25 without knowing how many hearts there actually are. If this is the case, there is a general probability formula we can use to compute the probability of event A or event B:

$$p(\text{A or B}) = p(\text{A}) + p(\text{B}) - p(\text{A and B}) \qquad (10.3)$$

This formula can be used whether or not events A and B are mutually exclusive: If they are mutually exclusive, the probability of A and B—$p(\text{A and B})$—equals 0, and Formula 10.3 will lead to the same result as Formula 10.2.

We can apply Formula 10.3 to determine the probability of drawing a jack or a heart. To do this, we use Formula 10.1 to compute the separate entities of Formula 10.3:

$$p(\text{jack}) = \frac{4}{52} = .077$$

$$p(\text{heart}) = \frac{13}{52} = .25$$

$$p(\text{jack and heart}) = \frac{1}{52} = .019$$

Now we plug all these values into Formula 10.3:

$$p(\text{heart or jack}) = p(\text{heart}) + p(\text{jack}) - p(\text{heart and jack})$$
$$= .25 + .077 - .019 = .308$$

If you remember, this value is identical to the one we computed earlier for the same problem.

We can do a similar analysis to determine the probability of the next person you meet being a man or someone who has schizophrenia. Here we must make some assumptions: (1) that the population is half men and half women; (2) that 1% of the population has schizophrenia; and (3) that men and women are equally likely to have schizophrenia. If these assumptions are true, then the probability of meeting a man is .5, the probability of meeting a person who has schizophrenia is .01, and the probability of meeting a man who has schizophrenia is .005. From Formula 10.3:

$$p(\text{man or schizophrenia}) = .5 + .01 - .005 = .505$$

Question: I'm stumped. How did you figure the probability of being a man *and* a person who has schizophrenia?

If two events are independent, the probability of both of them occurring together is the product of their separate probabilities:

$$p(A \text{ and } B) = p(A) \cdot p(B) \tag{10.4}$$

This is often called the **multiplication rule of probability,** or the **multiplication theorem of probability.** So if the probability of being a man is .5 and the probability of being a person who has schizophrenia is .01, then the probability of being a man who also has schizophrenia is

$$p(\text{man and schizophrenia}) = p(\text{man}) \cdot p(\text{schizophrenia})$$
$$= .5 \cdot .01 = .005$$

Similarly, if the probability of a card being a heart is .25 and the probability of a card being a jack is .077, then the probability of a card being a heart that is a jack is the product of their probabilities:

$$p(\text{heart and jack}) = p(\text{heart}) \cdot p(\text{jack})$$
$$= .25 \cdot .077 = .019$$

In Chapter 7, we discussed another means of computing probability, the normal curve. If a population variable is normally distributed and if we know the mean and the standard deviation of the population, we can readily make probability computations using the normal curve tables. For example, the probability of getting a score of 130 (X) or higher on the Wechsler Adult Intelligence Scale is equal to the area under the normal curve above 130. To compute the probability of your getting a score of 130 or higher, you convert the test score to a z score and then look up the probability in Table Z. If the population mean (μ) for this test is 100 and the population standard deviation (σ) is 15, then the z score equals

$$z = \frac{X - \mu}{\sigma} = \frac{130 - 100}{15} = \frac{30}{15} = 2$$

Now look up the area above a z score of 2 in Table Z. It equals .0228. Therefore, the probability of getting a test score equal to or higher than 130 is .0228.

As illustrated in the preceding example, the normal curve can be helpful for making probability statements about populations, which is the primary goal of psychological research. Unfortunately, population means and population standard deviations are not always available for various reasons. Sometimes populations are so large that it is financially impossible to gather data from every member of the population. At other times, it may be too difficult or too dangerous (collecting data from every ice cream parlor in the country could be detrimental to your weight). Due to such problems, researchers frequently sample a small portion of the population and then estimate population values from their sample.

C O N C E P T   Q U I Z

1. The _____ of an event occurring is the number of possible ways the event can occur divided by the total number of all possible events relating to that one event.
2. Any time data can be displayed in a frequency distribution, you can estimate the probability of any particular event by computing the _____ frequency of that event.
3. If two events are mutually exclusive, the probability that one or the other will occur is the _____ of the probabilities for each event.
4. When two events are not mutually exclusive, the probability that one or the other will occur is the _____ of the probabilities for each event _____ the probability of both occurring at the same time.
5. For two independent events, the probability of both of them occurring at the same time is the _____ of their separate probabilities.
6. We can also determine probabilities by computing _____ and then finding the corresponding area under the normal curve.

Answers

1. probability
2. relative
3. sum
4. sum; minus
5. product
6. a *z* score

SAMPLING

There are several ways to collect a sample from a population, but no matter what method you use, one consideration is paramount. *The sample collected must be as representative of the target population as possible.* Obtaining a

representative sample means that all significant subgroups of the population must be represented in the sample. If you were hired to assess how people would vote on a critical national issue, you would certainly not restrict your sample to college sophomores because opinions and voting patterns are too influenced by such factors as age, years of schooling, and geographic location to assume that college students would be representative of the entire voting population. On the other hand, if you were studying how people perceive depth in motion pictures, a sample of college sophomores might be quite representative of the general population because no research indicates any difference between college sophomores and the general population in perceiving depth. Therefore, it is critically important to be aware of all relevant population characteristics before taking a sample. Unfortunately this is often difficult, if not impossible, so researchers frequently resort to **random sampling** to increase the chances of obtaining a representative sample.

Random sampling is much like picking a name from a hat. It assumes that everyone in the population of interest is equally likely to be chosen as a subject, and that all subjects are chosen by some completely random process.

Question: If I want to estimate the grade point average of my entire college student body, how should I go about collecting a random sample of 25 students?

There are many ways to collect a random sample. One of the easiest is to find a list of all the students who attend your college and then randomly select 25 names from the list. You could put the name of each student on a card, place the cards in a box, mix them up, and then draw out 25 cards. Of course, this could be quite time-consuming if the list were long, and you would have to take great care to mix the cards thoroughly before your drawing. Even with a lot of mixing, the sample might not be very random; if you put the cards in the box alphabetically, the A's through G's would probably tend to remain toward the bottom, with the T's through Z's tending to stay at the top.

A more efficient and accurate way of generating a random sample is to assign each member of the student body a number and then select numbers at random. For a number to be totally random, it must have the same probability of occurring as any other number. Because people are almost never completely impartial, the best generator of totally unrelated, random numbers is a computer. A computer-generated **random number table** can be found in most statistics books. To illustrate their use, let's suppose that 1000 students are enrolled in your college. You assign each of the 1000 students a three-digit number (from 000 to 999) and then refer to a random number table like Table N in Appendix A (N for *number*), which contains 2000 random digits. Turn to this table, choose a starting place—anywhere—and read the three-digit number you fix your eyes on. If the number is the same as one you have

Table 10.1 Grade Point Averages for 25 Randomly Selected Students

3.95	2.13	3.24	1.67	2.10	3.44
3.33	2.01	1.11	2.00	2.75	2.98
3.33	2.25	1.90	0.87	2.18	2.82
3.45	3.77	1.88	2.84	1.92	3.86
3.25					

$n = 25$

$\Sigma X = 65.03$

$\Sigma X^2 = 186.5605$

$\overline{X} = 2.601$

$S = 0.834$

assigned to a student, that student will be part of your sample. Continue reading down the table and choose all 25 students in this way. In modern-day laboratories, random assignment is more likely to be done by a random number generator in a computer than by an experimenter using a random number table. But the procedure is similar and the results are the same.

After selecting a random sample, you can collect whatever information you need (in this case, GPAs) and reasonably assume that this information can safely be used to make inferences about your general population (the college student body). Table 10.1 lists the grade point average data for the 25 students in your sample. From these data, we can compute a mean and a standard deviation for the sample: The mean GPA is 2.601 and the standard deviation is 0.834.

Question: But this information pertains to the sample only. How do I know that the mean and the standard deviation of the sample are the same as the mean and the standard deviation for the population?

If the sample is completely random, then the sample mean should be a good estimate of the population mean. This follows from the fact that random sampling, if it is truly random, should produce scores that are above, below, and close to the actual population mean. The larger the sample, the greater the chance that the sample mean will approximate the population mean. When the sample is small, it may happen that, just by coincidence, most or even all of the scores may fall at one end of the scale; they may all be high or all be low.

Such a case results in an especially high or low sample mean. When the sample is large, this is much less likely to happen. For instance, suppose that in the previous example we sampled only 5 students out of the 1000 who attend the school, rather than 25. The 5 we sampled may be friends who are all on academic probation (birds of a feather . . .), or they may all be on the dean's list. By enlarging the sample, we increase the likelihood that some of our students will be on probation, some will be at the top of their class, and most will be somewhere in between. Thus, the larger the sample, if it is random, the more likely it will be representative of the population. However, whether the sample is large or small, the mean of the sample is the best estimate of the population mean.

Question: How big does a sample have to be in order to be representative of the population?

The general rule is: The bigger, the better. Researchers should try to collect samples that are as large as possible, given their resources of time and money. This concept may be even clearer if we examine estimates of the variance and standard deviation rather than the mean.

Chapter 5 describes the standard deviation as a standard of measurement that indicates how much the scores in a distribution deviate from the mean. With this in mind, let's compare the standard deviation of a sample with that of a population. The standard deviation of a population is calculated using all the scores in the population, including the most extreme scores. Because a sample is smaller than the population, it is not likely that the sample will include all the extreme scores. For example, it is unlikely that our sample of 25 students will contain the student with the highest GPA as well as the student with the lowest. It's possible, but highly unlikely.

Because samples rarely contain all the extreme scores of a population, their standard deviations are generally smaller than those of the population. In other words, the scores in the sample are likely to be more closely packed around the mean. Therefore, the standard deviation of a sample cannot be considered a good estimate of the standard deviation of the population. The usual correction for this underestimation is to divide by $n - 1$ rather than n when estimating the population value (est. σ). Formulas 5.4 and 5.6 for the variance and the standard deviation of a sample are repeated here:

$$S^2 = \frac{\Sigma(X - \overline{X})^2}{n} = \frac{\Sigma X^2 - (n \cdot \overline{X}^2)}{n} \qquad (5.4)$$

$$S = \sqrt{\frac{\Sigma(X - \overline{X})^2}{n}} = \sqrt{\frac{\Sigma X^2 - (n \cdot \overline{X}^2)}{n}} \qquad (5.6)$$

By substituting $n - 1$ for n in the denominators, we get Formulas 10.5 and

10.6, which are formulas for the estimates of the variance and the standard deviation of the population:

$$\text{est. } \sigma^2 = \frac{\Sigma(X - \overline{X})^2}{n - 1} = \frac{\Sigma X^2 - (n \cdot \overline{X}^2)}{n - 1} \tag{10.5}$$

$$\text{est. } \sigma = \sqrt{\frac{\Sigma(X - \overline{X})^2}{n - 1}} = \sqrt{\frac{\Sigma X^2 - (n \cdot \overline{X}^2)}{n - 1}} \tag{10.6}$$

The effect of this change from n to $n - 1$ varies depending on the size of n. If n is small, subtracting 1 may make a large difference in the computed value of the variance; if n is large, subtracting 1 may make no noticeable difference. For example, if $n = 5$, then dividing by 4 ($n - 1$) rather than by 5 (n) will create a 25% increase in the size of the estimated variance. On the other hand, if $n = 100$, then dividing by 99 ($n - 1$) rather than by 100 (n) will create only a 1% increase. The change in the standard deviation will be even smaller than that, as you can see in the following example.

Suppose we have two samples, both having the same variance and standard deviation but differing in number. Sample 1 has an n_1 of 5, whereas sample 2 has an n_2 of 100:

$$S_1^2 = \frac{500}{5} = 100 \qquad S_2^2 = \frac{10,000}{100} = 100$$

$$S_1 = \sqrt{100} = 10 \qquad S_2 = \sqrt{100} = 10$$

Now let's compute the estimated variance of the population and the estimated standard deviation of the population from these two samples:

$$\text{est. } \sigma_1^2 = \frac{500}{5 - 1} = 125 \qquad \text{est. } \sigma_2^2 = \frac{10,000}{100 - 1} = 101.010$$

$$\text{est. } \sigma_1 = \sqrt{125} = 11.180 \qquad \text{est. } \sigma_2 = \sqrt{101.010} = 10.050$$

So you see, subtracting 1 made a noticeable difference when the sample was small, as in sample 1; the standard deviation changed from 10 for the sample to 11.18 for the population estimate. However, there was little difference— from 10 to 10.05—when the sample was large, as in sample 2. Because this distinction between sample values and population estimates is important when we compare separate samples to one another, we will return to this topic in Chapter 12.

Any time we take a sample from a population, that sample is only one of the many, sometimes countless, samples we *could* take from that same population. Therefore, if we take several samples, all the same size, from one particular population, it is quite possible that each sample will be different from all of the others. Some samples may have means similar to the mean of the population, most will have means a little different from the population mean, and a few may have means far below or above the population mean.

Question: Can't you average these sample means and come up with a mean that's pretty close to the population mean?

Yes. In fact, from any population, we can create a distribution made up of an unlimited number of sample means from that population. This is known as the **distribution of sample means.** In such a distribution, if all samples are the same size, the mean of the sample means ($\mu_{\bar{x}}$) will equal the population mean (μ):

$$\mu_{\bar{x}} = \mu \tag{10.7}$$

How about the standard deviation of this distribution? For a distribution of sample means with an n greater than 1, will its standard deviation be the same as that of the population? Take a few minutes to puzzle this out. The answer is that it will be smaller than the standard deviation for the population.

THE STANDARD ERROR OF THE MEAN

The standard deviation of the distribution of sample means is known as the **standard error of the mean** ($\sigma_{\bar{x}}$). The standard error of the mean is always equal to the standard deviation of the population divided by the square root of the sample size:

$$\sigma_{\bar{x}} = \frac{\sigma}{\sqrt{n}} \tag{10.8}$$

As Formula 10.8 reflects, the standard error of the mean decreases as n increases. You can see this graphically in Figure 10.2.

Figure 10.2 shows the frequency polygons of four sampling distributions involving 1000 samples that were taken from the same population ($\mu = 50.5$ and $\sigma = 28.866$). The only difference in the sampling distributions is the sizes of the samples, which are 2, 10, 25, and 100. Notice in the figure that when the sample is small, the polygon is flat because the means of the samples are spread apart. When the sample is large, the polygon has a definite peak near the population mean because the means of the samples are concentrated toward the center. These patterns occur because with small samples it is more likely that the scores will be extreme and will tend to lie in the same direction (they may be greater than or less than the population mean), but with large samples extreme scores in one direction tend to be offset by extreme scores in the other. Consequently, the standard deviation of the distribution of sample means (the standard error of the mean) grows smaller as the sample grows

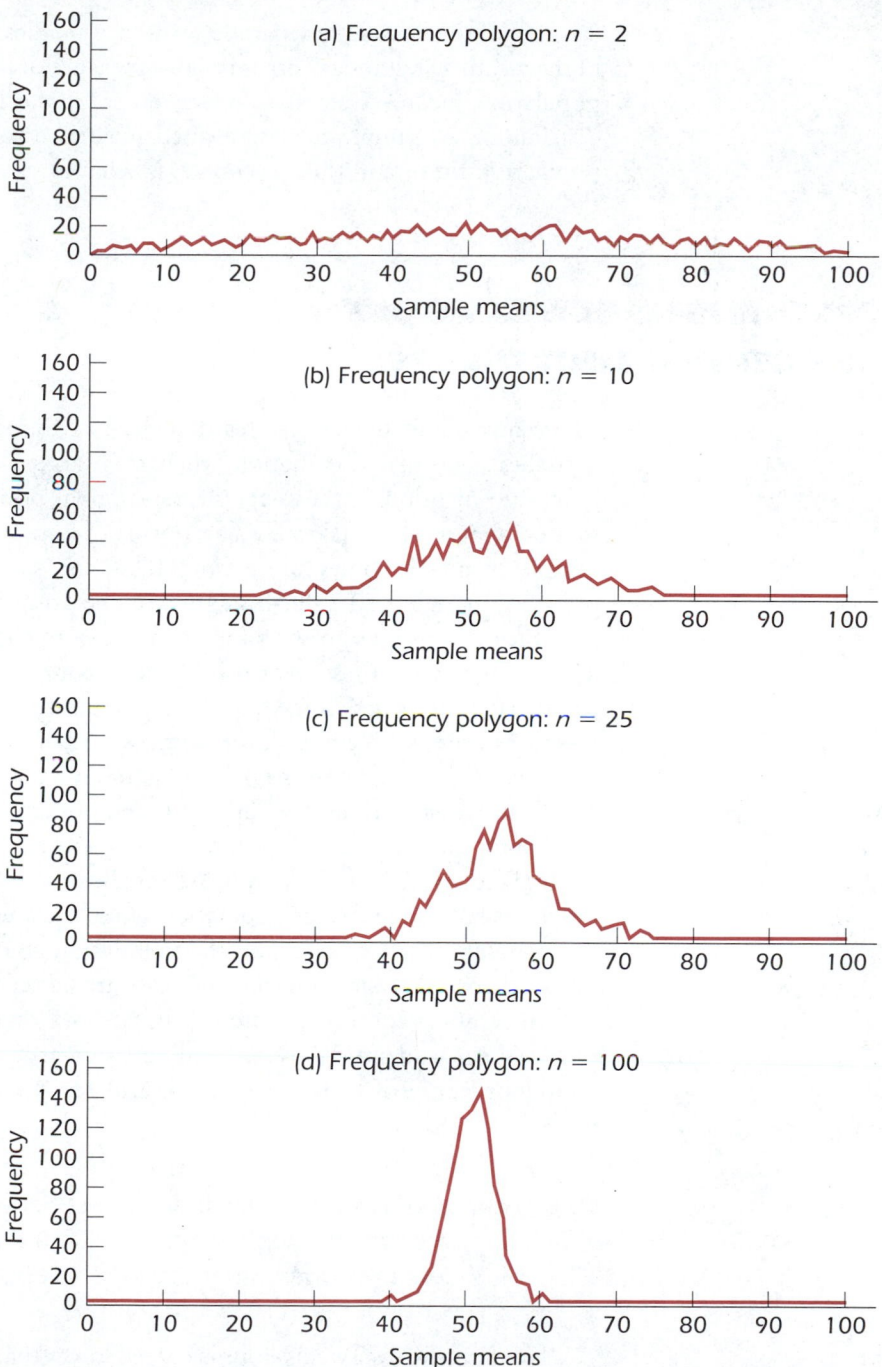

Figure 10.2 Frequency polygons of four distributions of 1000 sample means. Each distribution differs only in the number of subjects (*n*) used to generate each sample: (a) *n* = 2, (b) *n* = 10, (c) *n* = 25, and (d) *n* = 100.

larger, and this is exactly what we want: the smallest possible standard error of the mean. The standard error is like a measure of the error in estimating the population mean. A small standard error of the mean indicates that the distribution of sample means resulted in little error in estimating the true population mean and this, of course, is what all research strives for.

THE CENTRAL LIMIT THEOREM

The **central limit theorem** states that the distribution of sample means approaches a normal distribution when *n* is large. Notice that this theorem makes no mention of the shape of the original population distribution. No matter what its shape (skewed, flat, normal, or any other), the distribution of sample means becomes more normal as the sample size increases. The polygons in Figure 10.2 illustrate this: As the sample sizes increase from 2 to 100, the distributions grow to approximate more and more the normal curve. This is important for statistical inference because when the sample is sufficiently large, we can assume that the distribution of sample means is normal. It is therefore easy to compare the samples we have collected to the theoretical distribution of sample means. Let's illustrate this with an experiment using a test of stress (something we hope you aren't overly experiencing right now).

Suppose we have developed, over a period of years, the Stress Battery for College Students, 1st edition (SBCS-1 for short). We have previously administered this battery to a large population of college students, and we know that the population mean is 25 and the population standard deviation is 5. We have a theory that intercollegiate athletes are better able to handle stress and will thereby have a lower score on the SBCS-1 than will the population of other college students. We run a small research project and give the SBCS-1 to a random sample of 100 intercollegiate athletes. We find that their mean score is 24.

Question: Your hypothesis must be correct because the mean score for the athletes was less than 25, so the athletes *do* experience less stress than other college students. Right?

Not necessarily. Twenty-four is indeed lower than the population mean of 25, but it is possible that this difference is due entirely to sampling error or to chance. To confirm our hypothesis, we must establish that there is a true difference between the population mean and the sample mean—that the athletes actually scored significantly lower on the stress battery than the population of other students. We must show, using the normal curve, that our sample mean of 24 is extremely unlikely to have occurred strictly by chance.

What we need to do is to compare the mean of our sample to the mean of a theoretical distribution of sample means that has an *n* of 100. The mean of the sample means, as you may remember from Formula 10.7, is equal to the mean of the original population. The standard deviation of the distribution of sample means—the standard error of the mean—is equal to the population standard deviation divided by the square root of *n* (Formula 10.8). By now, you know that the distribution of sample means approaches a normal distribution when the sample is large. Our sample size of 100 is fairly large, so we can use the sample mean as well as the mean and the standard deviation of the sampling distribution to determine how likely it is that a sample drawn from the general college population will have a mean of 24. To do this, we need only compute a *z* test.

THE *z* TEST

A *z* **test** is used to compare the mean of a particular sample to the mean of a population. To do this, you determine the *z* score for the sample mean and then find the area beyond the *z* score to see how it compares to the mean of the population. To compute a *z* test on the preceding example, we first compute a *z* score for a raw score of 24 (the mean of the sample) and then find the area beyond the *z* score.

The formula for a *z* score is

$$z = \frac{X - \mu}{\sigma}$$

where X normally equals the score that is being converted to a *z* score, μ equals the population mean, and σ equals the standard deviation of the population. So in the distribution of sample means, $\overline{X}$ represents each of the sample means that make up the distribution, $\mu_{\overline{X}}$ equals the mean of the distribution of sample means, and $\sigma_{\overline{X}}$ equals the standard error of the mean. The formula for converting a sample mean to a *z* score, then, is

$$z = \frac{\overline{X} - \mu_{\overline{X}}}{\sigma_{\overline{X}}} \qquad (10.9)$$

Before computing the *z* score for our sample value, we need to compute the value for the standard error of the mean. We also need to compute the mean of the distribution of sample means. Knowing that the standard deviation of the population is 5 and the sample size is 100, we can use Formula 10.8 to calculate the standard error of the mean:

$$\sigma_{\bar{X}} = \frac{\sigma}{\sqrt{n}} = \frac{5}{\sqrt{100}} = \frac{5}{10} = 0.5$$

And we can use Formula 10.7 to compute the mean of the distribution of sample means:

$$\mu_{\bar{X}} = \mu = 25$$

Therefore, the z score for a sample mean of 24 from this population is

$$z = \frac{\bar{X} - \mu_{\bar{X}}}{\sigma_{\bar{X}}} = \frac{24 - 25}{0.5} = \frac{-1}{0.5} = -2.00$$

Now that we have a z score, what do we do with it? We use the procedures developed in Chapter 6 to look up the z score of −2.00 in Table Z to find out how extreme the score actually is. From Table Z, we see that the area below a score of −2.00 is .0228, or 2.28%, of all the possible samples. This means that, out of all the samples with a size of 100 that were drawn from the college student population, we expect that only 2.28 out of 100 samples (2.28% of the samples) will have a mean of 24 or less. Our sample of athletes is among this 2.28% because its mean is 24. If we refer to a normal curve of the population's scores on this stress test, we find that a score of 24 is out in the tail and is not representative of the average college student in this population. So our sample of athletes *may* come from this population, but it is highly unlikely.

Question: So can we conclude that intercollegiate athletes score lower on this stress test than other college students and that they therefore experience less stress?

The answer to this question is discussed in great detail in the next chapter. But briefly, most psychologists agree that if a sample mean has a probability of less than .05 (5%) of coming from a particular population, then the sample is probably not a part of that population but is from another population. Applying this to the preceding example, the probability is 2.28% that the sample of athletes is from the population of general college students and, because 2.28% is less than 5%, most psychologists would agree that the athlete sample probably does not belong to this general college student population. The athlete sample more likely belongs to a different population, a population of people who score lower than 25 on the stress test. So in answer to the question, yes, athletes probably do experience less stress than other college students.

Before ending this chapter, let's work through one more example of a z test. You are probably aware of the use of hypnosis as an aid to memory in certain legal cases. The theory behind this is that witnesses will remember more under hypnosis than they would otherwise. Have you wondered whether this premise is true? Does hypnosis really help people remember? Suppose we conduct a research project to determine whether people can remember a list of objects better when they are hypnotized than when they are not.

To begin our research, we ask a large population of people (several thousand) to attempt to remember a list of 100 items. Five days later, we ask them to write down all the items they remember. We find that the mean number of items remembered by this population is 17, and the population's standard deviation is 7. Next, we recruit a random sample of 144 people and have them do the same thing, except that they are hypnotized before they are instructed to recall the list. The mean number of items recalled by this hypnotized sample is 17.75. This mean is higher than the population mean, but is it high enough that we can confidently state that memory under hypnosis is better than memory without it?

To make that determination, we conduct a *z* test. First, we compute the standard error of the mean:

$$\sigma_{\bar{X}} = \frac{\sigma}{\sqrt{n}} = \frac{7}{\sqrt{144}} = \frac{7}{12} = 0.583$$

Knowing the standard error of the mean, we can now complete the *z* test:

$$z = \frac{\bar{X} - \mu_{\bar{X}}}{\sigma_{\bar{X}}} = \frac{17.75 - 17}{0.583} = \frac{0.75}{0.583} = 1.29$$

By using Table Z, we find the area of the normal curve that falls beyond a *z* score of 1.29. The area beyond is .0985, or 9.85%. Few, if any, psychologists would state, based on this memory recall task, that recall under hypnosis is any better than with no hypnosis. It is certainly not clear from this research whether hypnosis has any effect on memory.

C O N C E P T   Q U I Z

1. For a sample to be useful, it must be _____ of the population you wish to describe.

2. _____ sampling is the most common method used to create a representative sample.

3. To create formulas for estimating a population's variance and standard deviation from a sample, it is necessary to substitute _____ for _____ in the formulas for the variance and the standard deviation of the samples.

4. The standard deviation of the distribution of sample means is called the _____ and is computed by dividing the population's standard deviation by the _____ .

5. The central limit theorem states that the distribution of sample means approaches a _____ distribution when the sample size (n) is _____ .

6. To compare the mean of a sample to the mean of a population, you can use a _____ test.

Answers

1. representative

2. Random

3. $n - 1$; n

4. standard error of the mean; square root of the sample size

5. normal; large

6. z

S U M M A R Y

Results of psychological research are reported in terms of probabilities. As illustrated by the heads-or-tails example, the probability of any one event occurring can be computed by dividing the number of possible ways it can occur by the total number of all possible ways that related events can occur. The probability of an event occurring is also equal to the relative frequency of that event in the population. The probability of one or the other of two *mutually exclusive* events occurring is equal to the sum of their individual probabilities. Similarly, the probability of one or the other of any two events occurring, whether or not they are mutually exclusive, is the sum of their probabilities, minus the probability that both events will occur at the same time. If the events are mutually exclusive, then the probability that both will occur at the same time is 0. Finally, the probability of two events occurring at the same time is equal to the product of their separate probabilities. It is possible to compute probabilities associated with populations by using the normal curve formulas discussed in Chapter 7.

Often we do not have direct access to population information, and we must use a sample as an estimate of the population values. The most important thing to remember when taking a sample is that the sample must be as representative of the population as possible. You can do this either by very careful selection of the sample or by random sampling. Once the sample is collected, it is possible to use it to estimate the mean, the variance, and the standard deviation of the population. The mean of the sample is the best estimate of the population's mean, but the sample variance and the standard deviation are normally smaller than those of the population. This is particularly true for small samples. The correction for this is to use Formulas 10.5 and 10.6, which substitute $n - 1$ for n in the denominators of Formulas 5.4 and 5.6.

Whenever we take many samples of the same size from a population and calculate their means, we get a distribution of sample means. This distribution has a mean equal to the population's mean and a standard deviation equal to the population's standard deviation, divided by the square root of the size of the samples used to form the distribution. The standard deviation of the distribution of sample means is called the standard error of the mean. It is possible to use the mean and the standard error to conduct a z test to determine whether a sample is part of a particular population or whether it belongs to some other population.

KEY TERMS

probability
mutually exclusive
addition rule of probability, or
    addition theorem of
    probability
multiplication rule of probability,
    or multiplication theorem of
    probability

representative sample
random sampling
random number table
distribution of sample means
standard error of the mean
central limit theorem
z test

FORMULAS

$$\text{Probability of event A} = \frac{\text{number of events in A}}{\text{total number of all events}} \text{ or } p(A) = \frac{n(A)}{n} \quad (10.1)$$

$$p(A \text{ or } B) = p(A) + p(B) \quad (10.2)$$

$$p(A \text{ or } B) = p(A) + p(B) - p(A \text{ and } B) \quad (10.3)$$

$$p(A \text{ and } B) = p(A) \cdot p(B) \quad (10.4)$$

$$\text{est. } \sigma^2 = \frac{\Sigma(X - \overline{X})^2}{n - 1} = \frac{\Sigma X^2 - (n \cdot \overline{X}^2)}{n - 1} \quad (10.5)$$

$$\text{est. } \sigma = \sqrt{\frac{\Sigma(X - \overline{X})^2}{n - 1}} = \sqrt{\frac{\Sigma X^2 - (n \cdot \overline{X}^2)}{n - 1}} \quad (10.6)$$

$$\mu_{\overline{X}} = \mu \quad (10.7)$$

$$\sigma_{\overline{X}} = \frac{\sigma}{\sqrt{n}} \tag{10.8}$$

$$z = \frac{\overline{X} - \mu_{\overline{X}}}{\sigma_{\overline{X}}} \tag{10.9}$$

P R O B L E M S

1. If there are 900 psychology majors at a university with 12,000 students, what is the probability that the next person who comes through the library door will be a psychology major?

Using the frequency data in the table and assuming that these events are mutually exclusive, compute the probabilities in Problems 2–5.

Label	Frequency
Highly introverted	106
Average	798
Highly extroverted	213

2. The probability of being highly introverted

3. The probability of being either highly introverted or average

4. The probability of being either average or highly extroverted

5. The probability of being either highly introverted or highly extroverted

Use the following probabilities to do Problems 6–12.

Probability of having schizophrenia = .01
Probability of being extroverted = .10
Probability of being employed by the government = .25

Probability of being employed in the private sector = .65
Probability of being unemployed = .10
Probability of being a high sensation seeker = .20
Probability of being a low sensation seeker = .35

6. What is the probability of being either employed by the government or unemployed?

7. What is the probability of being unemployed and having schizophrenia?

8. What is the probability of both being employed by the government and having schizophrenia?

9. What is the probability of being an unemployed high sensation seeker?

10. What is the probability of being employed by the government and being a low sensation seeker?

11. What is the probability of being employed by the private sector and being a high sensation seeker who has schizophrenia?

12. What is the probability of being either unemployed or employed by the private sector?

13. Ideally, any sample created must be as _____ of the target population as possible.

14. When we pick names from a hat, we are using a form of _____ sampling.

15. Estimate the population's standard deviation and variance, given the following sample scores:

| 21 | 20 | 19 | 25 | 26 |

16. Estimate the population's variance and standard deviation using the reaction times from the following sample:

Reaction times (in milliseconds)			
1120	1221	1361	1106
1147	1242	1246	
1189	1139	1324	

For Problems 17–23, estimate the population variance and the population standard deviation using the data sets gathered from small samples.

17. The number of times that patients at a community mental health clinic have used the defense mechanism of projection during their last month of therapy sessions:

| 18 | 23 | 8 | 3 | 4 | 5 |
| 8 | 3 | 23 | 2 | 8 | 9 |

18. The number of items from a list of 25 words that are remembered 3 hours after the list was learned:

| 5 | 6 | 7 | 12 | 4 | 5 | 7 |
| 9 | 15 | 3 | 4 | 6 | 7 | 3 |

19. The scores of eight students with learning disabilities on the last Introduction to Psychology exam:

| 69 | 88 | 80 | 92 | 75 | 77 | 82 | 72 |

20. The number of psychology graduate students receiving their Ph.D. from a major university over the past 10 years:

| 8 | 3 | 12 | 5 | 1 | 4 | 5 | 6 | 7 | 0 |

21. The number of different drugs used by each of eight recent drug offenders during the last 6 months:

| 3 | 1 | 2 | 4 | 5 | 3 | 3 | 5 |

22. The number of journal articles published each year for the last 15 years by the head of the psychology department at a small college:

| 5 | 3 | 2 | 1 | 1 | 1 | 0 | 2 |
| 3 | 3 | 2 | 1 | 3 | 4 | 5 | |

23. The IQ scores of children who completed a preschool readiness program:

| 123 | 89 | 90 | 106 | 111 | 98 | 96 |
| 84 | 77 | 105 | 103 | 89 | 94 | |

Using the frequency data in the table and assuming that these events are mutually exclusive, compute the answers for Problems 24–30.

Behavioral type	Frequency
Type A	123
Type B	177
Average (not A or B)	200

24. The probability of being Type A

25. The probability of being Type B

26. The probability of being average

27. The probability of being either Type A or Type B

28. The probability of being either Type A or average

29. The probability of being either Type B or average

30. The probability of being Type A or Type B or average

Experimental Design

Put yourself in the following situation. You spent the last 2 weeks finishing up the semester and working overtime. When not attending classes or working, you were completing term papers or cramming for finals until long into the night. The last day of finals was the worst, with three exams back to back. The day after finals, instead of winding down and relaxing like the rest of your friends, you had to report for jury duty. What a way to spend your break!

At first, jury duty was so boring it almost made you long for the History of Civilization lectures you slept through during your freshman year. But after the first few days, that changed. Now you're hearing a criminal case that is turning out to be quite intriguing.

The defendant is accused of robbing a convenience store at gunpoint. He maintains his innocence, but the store clerk has positively identified him as the person who robbed her. Although the gun and the money were never recovered and several people claim they were with the defendant at the time of the robbery, the prosecution insists that this is the person who robbed the store. Who are you to believe?

The prosecution's case relies solely on the eyewitness testimony of the store clerk. But how dependable is her memory? How reliable in general are eyewitnesses? Should this man be sent to jail solely on the clerk's testimony?

Several researchers have examined these questions and, on the whole, have found that eyewitness testimony is not reliable. (For a detailed discussion of eyewitness testimony, see Brown, 1986; Loftus, 1979; or Penrod, Loftus, & Winkler, 1982.) As a juror, however, you know nothing of this research. Consequently, you spend much of your time agonizing over whether or not you should trust the store clerk or the defendant and his friends.

It is now a few months later, and you are reflecting on the course of the trial, particularly the problems the jury had in deciding whether to trust the clerk's testimony. In a flash of insight, you realize that the area of eyewitness testimony would be a fascinating research topic for your senior thesis. You want to begin working on your thesis, but how do you start? You know what you want to study, but how do you go about studying it? The best way is to conduct an experiment, which involves formulating a hypothesis (a possible explanation for some behavior) and testing it by following standardized procedures.

Question: But I don't even know where to start. What do I do first?

First you need to survey the research literature to find out what previous researchers have discovered and how they have gone about obtaining their results. This literature search can be done in many different ways using a variety of sources available to you as a student and as a researcher. In the area of eyewitness testimony and memory, some of the possible sources are textbooks or chapters in books on memory and cognition, current journals such as *Memory and Cognition*, literature reviews such as *Psychological Bulletin* or the *Annual Review of Psychology* that cover certain topic areas in psychology, journals of abstracts such as *Psychological Abstracts* and *Sociological Abstracts,* and of course electronic databases such as *PsycInfo* and *ERIC,* which can be searched by computers. In addition to literature searches, you should attempt to make personal contact with other researchers who are currently working in the area by using the telephone, mail, fax, or more probably e-mail on the Internet.

Next, based on your research and personal observations and knowledge, you can formulate a hypothesis, a prediction concerning the behavior you are studying, which in this case is memory for faces. Once you have identified the relevant factors, you can get down to actually designing your experiment by establishing various experimental conditions and controls, deciding how to assign subjects to the conditions, and so on. Keep in mind that the basic idea behind an experiment is to investigate the validity of a hypothesis by manipulating critical variables under rigidly controlled conditions. The purpose of this chapter is to teach you how to do this.

DEVELOPING A HYPOTHESIS

To reiterate, the first step in developing a research project is to survey previous research relating to that field, not only to uncover any pertinent information but also to learn how other researchers have investigated similar topics. The next step is to define your hypothesis. A scientific research **hypothesis** is a prediction based predominantly on a scientific theory or body of knowledge. As first proposed by Karl Popper in 1959, there is only one criterion it must meet: The hypothesis must be falsifiable; that is, it must be logically possible to show the hypothesis false. The following two statements are examples of hypotheses you might consider in your research on eyewitness testimony. Only one is a true scientific hypothesis. Which is it?

HYPOTHESIS 1: Memory for new faces declines rapidly with time.

HYPOTHESIS 2: We remember every face we see, but often we are unable to retrieve that information from long-term memory.

To test Hypothesis 1, you could set up an experiment that requires subjects to identify previously shown faces after a set period of time. Results of such an experiment would show either that subjects do remember new faces after a set period of time or that they do not remember faces after a set period of time. Thus, Hypothesis 1 could be either supported or falsified by research findings. Hypothesis 2, on the other hand, is stated in such a way that it is impossible to collect data showing it false. However unlikely, we *could* obtain data showing support for the proposition that recall for faces is always perfect. But there is no way we can reach into people's brains to determine whether memories of faces actually perish after a short time or whether memories remain, present but unattainable. Thus, Hypothesis 2 is not a scientific hypothesis because it cannot be falsified.

IDENTIFYING VARIABLES

After you have generated a hypothesis, the next step is to identify the relevant variables. Based on your research and with your hypothesis in mind, you need to determine what factors—what variables, such as scores on a visual memory task—will best help you test your hypothesis and measure your results. There are basically three types of variables: independent variables, dependent variables, and subject variables.

Independent variables are those that are manipulated by the experimenter and applied to the subject in order to determine what effect they may have. These are the factors that the experimenter *varies* from one condition to another, such as the items in memory lists or the dosages of an experimental drug. In an experiment, a researcher may want to compare the effects of two different independent variables or the effects of varying *amounts* (such as different dosages of drugs) or *levels* (such as low imagery or high imagery in a memory experiment) of one particular independent variable.

Dependent variables are those that are used to assess or measure the effects of the independent variables. In psychology, dependent variables are measures of the behavior being studied. Examples are scores on an interest survey, the number of visual images identified correctly, and the amount of time it takes to push a button. An easy way to remember the difference between an independent and a dependent variable is that the dependent variable *depends on* the independent variable; if the variables are causally related, the dependent variable will vary, or change, as the independent variable changes. Thus, dependent variables are measured by the experimenter to determine whether the experimental procedures result in any behavioral change.

Subject variables are those that describe subjects' characteristics or attributes, factors that cannot be manipulated by the experimenter. Examples of subject variables are gender, IQ, ethnicity, and age.

Question: Aren't subject variables just other kinds of independent variables?

No, they aren't. Subject variables are determined *before* subjects enter into a research project, so the experimenter cannot control these qualities and certainly cannot randomly assign the subjects to the various conditions. Control of the independent variable enables the researcher to determine whether or not that variable is the factor responsible for any change in a subject's behavior. Without this control, as when the factor is a subject variable rather than a true independent variable, the researcher cannot know whether the change is actually due to the subject variable or to some alternative explanation. An example will illustrate this point.

Suppose your research on eyewitness testimony leads you to believe that women are better at remembering faces than men (remember, gender is a subject variable), and you set up an experiment to test your hypothesis. Unfortunately, you cannot randomly assign subjects—they are already either men or women—although you do keep other variables constant, such as stimulus materials and the room environment. Let's say your hypothesis is supported, that the female subjects do indeed remember more faces than the male subjects. Does this mean that being female causes a person to remember faces? Or can there be alternative explanations? Perhaps women learn to notice facial details when applying makeup, or perhaps our society encourages women more than men to pay attention to bodily appearance. Your study may enable you to document a discrepancy between men and women, but this discrepancy is not necessarily due to an inborn gender difference. It may be due solely to social or learned factors. And so it is with all subject variables. Because they allow the researcher no control, the researcher cannot tell whether subject variables actually cause the behavior being studied or whether the behavior is caused by related but alternative factors.

Question: Does this mean, then, that good research never involves subject variables?

No, not at all. Experimental research requires the use of independent variables, but much of the research in the behavioral sciences is *non*experimental and uses subject variables. For example, correlational research techniques do not require a manipulated independent variable and therefore often involve subject variables. Gender research often does not have a true independent variable. Nonexperimental research techniques are valuable because they allow us to identify relationships between variables, including subject variables. They do not, however, lead to scientific explanations for *causes* of behavior as do experimental research techniques. The major difference between experimental and nonexperimental research is that in a nonexperimental research situation we lack a true independent variable that can be controlled by the experimenter. Experimental research requires an independent variable that the experimenter can control. Because subject variables are frequently analyzed as if they were independent variables, just looking at the statistical test that is used to analyze the collected data can be misleading. Always remember that you need to be careful when you make generalizations regarding subject variables.

CONCEPT QUIZ

1. A prediction based predominantly on a scientific theory or body of knowledge is called a scientific _____ .
2. Variables that are manipulated by the experimenter and applied to the subject in order to determine their effect on the behavior of the subject are called _____ variables.
3. Variables that are used to measure the effects of experimenter-manipulated variables are called _____ variables.
4. Variables such as gender, IQ, ethnicity, and age are _____ variables.
5. A hypothesis must be stated in such a way that it can be shown to be _____ .

Answers

1. hypothesis
2. independent
3. dependent

4. subject
5. false

FACTORS IN EXPERIMENTAL DESIGN

You have identified the variables in your project, taking care that your independent variable is not a subject variable. The next step is to design an experiment that effectively tests the validity of your hypothesis. Your experimental design depends on the number of independent variables investigated, the number of levels or manipulations of each independent variable, and the way in which you assign subjects to the various experimental conditions. It is the experimental design that determines exactly how you will analyze the data collected in the experiment.

Between-Subjects Designs, Within-Subjects Designs, and Mixed Designs

One of the primary decisions to make when designing an experiment is how to assign subjects to the various experimental conditions. The assignment depends on several factors; most important are the number of independent variables and the number of levels within each independent variable. Remember that the independent variable is manipulated by the experimenter. The levels are the different ways that you manipulate that variable. For example, if you are studying the effects of differing amounts of alcohol on driving performance, the independent variable is the amount of alcohol. The levels of this independent variable might be the one-beer level, the two-beer level, the three-beer level, and the no-beer level. Each level is a separate group within the independent variable.

There are basically three ways of assigning subjects to experimental conditions: a between-subjects design, a within-subjects design, and a mixed design. A **between-subjects design** (sometimes called an independent-group design) requires that each level of each independent variable has different subjects; thus, there is a distinct difference *between* each level of the experiment because each subject participates in one and only one level. A **within-subjects design** (also called a repeated-measures design) requires that each subject participates in all levels of all independent variables; thus, each subject stays *within* the experiment for its entire run. A **mixed design** most often occurs when there are at least two independent variables and each subject participates in all levels of one variable but not all levels of at least one of the other variables.

Let's use a sports psychology example to illustrate these design differences. Suppose we know a judge who plays golf. She's not a particularly good golfer, but she relishes the game nonetheless. The judge offers us a grant to investigate possible techniques to improve her golf swing. After a review of the sports literature, we hit upon two techniques worth studying: mental imagery (visualizing each golf shot) and relaxation techniques (specifically, deep breathing). The general design of our experiment is shown in Figure 11.1. There are two independent variables, mental imagery and relaxation, and each of the independent variables has two levels: no imagery or imagery and no relaxation or relaxation. Thus, there are four possible conditions: no-

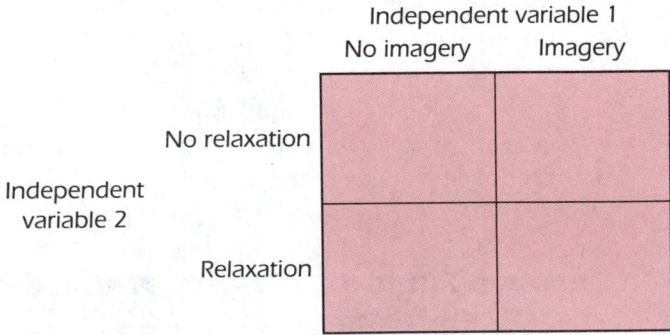

Figure 11.1 The general experimental design for the experiment to improve golf swings

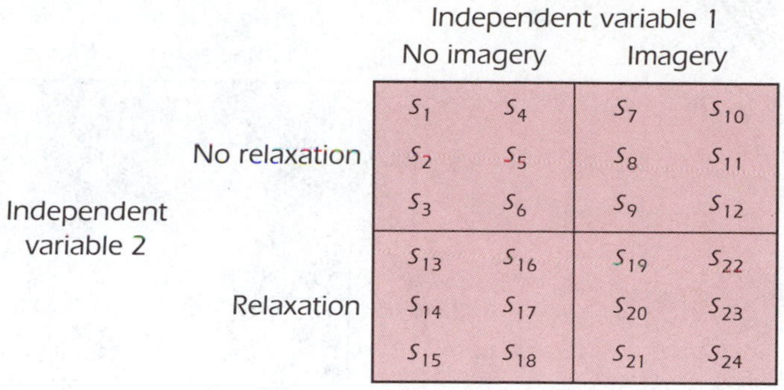

Independent variable 1

	No imagery		Imagery	
	S_1	S_4	S_7	S_{10}
No relaxation	S_2	S_5	S_8	S_{11}
	S_3	S_6	S_9	S_{12}
	S_{13}	S_{16}	S_{19}	S_{22}
Relaxation	S_{14}	S_{17}	S_{20}	S_{23}
	S_{15}	S_{18}	S_{21}	S_{24}

Independent variable 2

Figure 11.2 *The subject assignment for a between-subjects design. Each subject participates in only one experimental condition.*

imagery/no-relaxation, no-imagery/relaxation, imagery/no-relaxation, and imagery/relaxation. Depending on how we assign subjects to groups, we can use one of the three experimental designs just discussed.

As we mentioned before, in a *between-subjects design,* each subject participates in only one of the experimental conditions and is independent of the other groups (see Figure 11.2). The subjects in the no-imagery/no-relaxation condition are different from the subjects in the imagery/relaxation condition, and so forth. In this way, subject effects such as innate athletic ability are randomized throughout all conditions. A major advantage of the between-subjects design is that it is not affected by order effects where, as subjects participate in several conditions, they tend to improve with practice until they are considerably more adept in the final condition than they were in the initial condition. Another advantage is that the between-subjects design is statistically the simplest and is therefore easier to analyze. The major drawback of this design is that it requires more subjects. If you want to use six subjects in each condition, you need 24 subjects to complete your design.

At the other extreme is the *within-subjects design,* where each subject participates in every condition (see Figure 11.3). Thus, in order to have six subjects in each condition, you need a total of only six subjects in the entire experiment. You can appreciate the merit in this if you've ever had to recruit subjects without an Introductory Psychology pool available. Another advantage is that subject effects, at least theoretically, may be eliminated or subtracted out. Still another advantage is that experiments using this design tend to be more sensitive to differences between experimental conditions. For example, in the golf improvement study, the same subject participates in each of the relaxation/imagery conditions, so each group, or cell, will have subjects of equally good or equally poor ability. The major problem with the within-subjects design is the difficulty in controlling learning factors. Thus, the within-subjects design should not be used when the subject's behavior is likely to change with the practice or knowledge gained through previous conditions.

Independent variable 1

	No imagery		Imagery	
No relaxation	S_1	S_4	S_1	S_4
	S_2	S_5	S_2	S_5
	S_3	S_6	S_3	S_6
Relaxation	S_1	S_4	S_1	S_4
	S_2	S_5	S_2	S_5
	S_3	S_6	S_3	S_6

Independent variable 2

Figure 11.3 The subject assignment for a within-subjects design. Each subject participates in all experimental conditions.

For instance, by the time the subjects participate in the fourth condition, they may all score higher than they did in the first condition, merely because of practice effects. Another disadvantage is that after participating in a couple of conditions, subjects may figure out the purpose of the experiment and change their responses accordingly. This is sometimes a problem, especially in experiments that, by their nature, require a certain amount of deception.

Finally, a *mixed design* is used when it is necessary to have each subject participate in all levels of one independent variable, while participating in only one level of another independent variable. For example, if we were to use a mixed design in the golfing study, we could assign a particular subject (S_1) to only the no-relaxation conditions, as shown in Figure 11.4(a). Then this subject participates solely in the no-relaxation/no-imagery and the no-relaxation/imagery conditions. Or we could assign the subject to only the two no-imagery conditions, as shown in Figure 11.4(b). Mixed designs use fewer subjects than between-subjects designs, but they are the most difficult to analyze statistically.

In the following chapters, these designs are discussed where appropriate. Most often, however, we use between-subjects designs as examples because they are the most common simple designs and the statistics needed to analyze them are easier to compute and therefore more appropriate to an introductory statistics course.

One-Group Experimental Designs

Another consideration in designing experiments is the number of samples you need to collect. The simplest experimental design, known as the **one-group experimental design,** involves comparing a single sample mean to the mean of a known population. Suppose you want to know whether convenience store clerks have better memories than people in the general population. If you have access to population data for a memory task, you can give that memory task to a sample of convenience store clerks and compare its mean to the mean of

(a)

	Independent variable 1	
Independent variable 2	No imagery	Imagery
No relaxation	S_1 S_4 S_2 S_5 S_3 S_6	S_1 S_4 S_2 S_5 S_3 S_6
Relaxation	S_7 S_{10} S_8 S_{11} S_9 S_{12}	S_7 S_{10} S_8 S_{11} S_9 S_{12}

OR

(b)

	Independent variable 1	
Independent variable 2	No imagery	Imagery
No relaxation	S_1 S_4 S_2 S_5 S_3 S_6	S_7 S_{10} S_8 S_{11} S_9 S_{12}
Relaxation	S_1 S_4 S_2 S_5 S_3 S_6	S_7 S_{10} S_8 S_{11} S_9 S_{12}

Figure 11.4 Two possible subject assignments for a mixed design. Each subject participates in all levels of one independent variable but in only one level of the other independent variable.

the population. Do you remember the z test discussed in Chapter 10, where we compared intercollegiate athletes' scores on a stress test with those of the general population of college students? That is an example of a single-sample test with a one-group design.

Completely Randomized Designs

One of the simplest ways to compare more than one sample is to use the **completely randomized experimental design.** In this design there is one independent variable with at least two different levels, and subjects are selected and assigned to one of the groups in a completely random fashion. Let's illustrate this design by placing you in the role of a human factors psychologist who has just been employed by a large computer manufacturer. If you have ever used more than one type of computer, you are probably aware that computers come equipped with a variety of keyboards, each with its own distinctive touch and key positions. You have been hired by the computer firm to determine which of two keyboards is more efficient.

Independent variable

Keyboard 1		Keyboard 2	
S_1	S_4	S_7	S_{10}
S_2	S_5	S_8	S_{11}
S_3	S_6	S_9	S_{12}

Figure 11.5   A two-group completely randomized design having one independent variable

The easiest way to do this it to conduct an experiment comparing one keyboard to another by using a completely randomized design. First, you need to devise or acquire a typing test that will provide a fair assessment of the two keyboards. Scores on this test will be the dependent variable. The type of keyboard used during the typing test will be the independent variable. All other variables—room illumination, noise level, computer and monitor used, word-processing program, and so on—should remain constant. You select subjects randomly from a population of possible computer users, and then randomly assign them to one of the two groups (see Figure 11.5). This two-group design will enable you to determine which of two keyboards is the more efficient. Analysis of this type of experiment is discussed in Chapter 12.

Question: What if I want to test more than two keyboards? Does that increase the number of independent variables?

No, it doesn't. You can certainly test more than two keyboards by adding more groups—by randomly selecting more subjects and assigning them in a random fashion to the additional groups. But adding more keyboards simply extends the completely randomized design; it does not increase the number of independent variables. There is still only one, the type of keyboard (see Figure 11.6). You have merely increased the number of *levels* (number of different keyboards) of the independent variable. If you decide to test an additional factor, such as various word-processing programs, you are adding another independent variable and need to use a factorial design.

In the **completely randomized factorial experimental design,** there are at

Independent variable

Keyboard 1		Keyboard 2		Keyboard 3	
S_1	S_4	S_7	S_{10}	S_{13}	S_{16}
S_2	S_5	S_8	S_{11}	S_{14}	S_{17}
S_3	S_6	S_9	S_{12}	S_{15}	S_{18}

Figure 11.6   A completely randomized design with three levels of one independent variable

least two independent variables—each having at least two levels—and subjects are randomly assigned to the experimental conditions. If, as suggested earlier, you want to add two word-processing programs to your experiment on two keyboards, your study will have two independent variables, each having two levels. This is known as a 2×2 (read "two by two") factorial design. If you add still another keyboard and another word-processing program, you will have created a 3×3 factorial design.

CONCEPT QUIZ

1. An experimental design in which each subject participates in only one of the experimental conditions is called a _____ design.
2. When each subject participates in all experimental conditions, the design is a _____ design.
3. Experiments in which subjects participate in only one level of one independent variable, while participating in all levels of the other independent variable, are called _____ designs.
4. Experimental designs that compare a single sample mean to the population mean are called _____ designs.
5. In the _____ design, there is one independent variable with at least two different levels, and the subjects are selected and assigned to one of the groups in a completely random fashion.
6. In the _____ design, there are at least two independent variables, each having at least two levels, and the subjects are randomly assigned to the experimental conditions.

Answers

1. between-subjects
2. within-subjects
3. mixed
4. one-group

5. completely randomized
6. completely randomized factorial

IMPORTANT ASPECTS OF EXPERIMENTAL DESIGN

Question: Where do statistics come in? What does experimental design have to do with statistics?

The type of statistics used in any experiment depends on the design of that experiment. The chapters immediately following explain the statistical procedures necessary to analyze experiments using the various experimental designs. The purpose of *this* chapter is to introduce you to these designs and discuss their critical aspects. One of the most important aspects is the very crucial need for control.

The Necessity for Control

A fact of life about science in general and psychology in particular is that it pays to be skeptical. A scientific skeptic is a person who does not accept a hypothesis as true until there is proof that alternative hypotheses are extremely unlikely. The scientific technique used to rule out alternative hypotheses is **experimental control.** Not only must experimenters ensure objective selection and assignment of subjects but they must also exercise stringent control over the design of the experiment and the experimental situation in general. They need to make sure that each independent variable consists of one single factor. Furthermore, they must ensure that subjects in all conditions receive identical treatment under identical circumstances. If a relevant factor, an extraneous variable, is introduced to one group but not to another, and if a behavior change is recorded for that group, then the experimenter cannot determine whether the change in behavior is due to the independent variable or to the extraneous variable. Thus, the experimental results will not be altogether valid.

The need for strict control is illustrated in the following example, which is derived from a craving of one of the authors for chocolate. Suppose, from your personal experience, you develop the hypothesis that eating chocolate improves memory for new faces. (If found to be true, the prosecution from our convenience store trial could use the results to argue for the good memory of the store clerk!) You design an experiment to test your hypothesis. You find 30 people who eat chocolate, who in fact eat an average of one chocolate bar per day. You find another 30 people who never eat chocolate. You give both groups a test of memory for new faces and find that the chocolate eaters are much better at remembering faces than the non-chocolate eaters. Does this prove that eating chocolate improves memory for faces? Not really. It may be that the elevated blood sugar level influences the metabolism of the brain and increases memory. It may be that the caffeine in the chocolate results in heightened alertness. It may be that for some reason, chocolate candy commercials particularly appeal to people who have good memories. As you may have gathered, this chocolate study is not a true experiment. The various groups are based on a subject variable: whether or not the subject regularly eats chocolate. No independent variable is manipulated by the experimenter, and the experimenter cannot randomly or otherwise assign subjects to groups; the subjects have already assigned themselves based on whether or not they regularly eat chocolate.

Question: So how can you design an experiment that will determine whether eating chocolate improves people's memories?

You design your experiment so that subjects can be assigned to groups randomly and so that you can manipulate the independent variable. And you must control any relevant **extraneous variables** (those "extra" variables that may affect subjects' responses but are not the ones being examined). Basically, your revised experiment should be as described here.

First, you randomly select 60 people and randomly assign them to one of two conditions, chocolate eating or non-chocolate eating. This eliminates the objection made earlier that perhaps it is merely people with good memories who like to eat chocolate. You require the chocolate-eating group to eat, every day, six tollhouse cookies, each with a half ounce of chocolate chips. You require the non-chocolate-eating group to eat six identical cookies minus the chocolate chips, but with the same amounts of sugar, caffeine, and other ingredients as the chocolate chip cookies. In this way you, like all competent experimenters, maintain control through the random selection and assignment of subjects and through the control of extraneous variables. Any difference between the two groups will be due solely to the manipulation of the independent variable.

Experimenter Bias and Demand Characteristics

Experimenters are people, and people make mistakes. When researchers make mistakes, the mistakes tend toward favoring the experimental hypothesis. Occasionally, there are cases in which experimenters make conscious attempts to influence their subjects. This is outright fraud and, fortunately, it is relatively rare in psychological research. More common are cases of unintentional error, anything from simple mistakes in recording data to subtle, unintentional hints made to subjects by experimenters. This latter error, known as **experimenter bias,** is a noteworthy problem. Because they know the research hypothesis and wish to prove it true, experimenters may inadvertently behave in a way that influences their results. For instance, suppose that in studying the recognition of new faces, you design an experiment in which you present subjects with photographs of people's faces and ask them to memorize the faces. When the subjects return 2 weeks later, you show them several groups of photos, and you ask them to point to the faces in each group that they remember having seen before. It is highly likely that you will exhibit some kind of experimenter bias. Because you know the correct responses, you may without knowing it give your subjects subtle cues as to which pictures are correct by making offhand comments, stressing certain words in the instructions, using facial expressions or body language, and so on. Thus, you may convey crucial information to your subjects that increases, or perhaps even decreases, their accuracy in the task.

The best way to control experimenter bias is to somehow distance the subjects from experimenters who know the hypothesis. This can be done in several ways, the most effective being (1) to hire assistants who are unaware of the hypothesis to conduct the experiment and (2) to completely automate the experiment. In many cases, researchers do both: They hire undergraduate or graduate research assistants to do such tasks as read instructions and answer questions, and they use computers to control the actual experimental procedures.

Closely associated with the problem of experimenter bias is the problem of demand characteristics. If experimenters, by knowing their research hypothesis, can unintentionally influence their subjects' behavior, then it follows that subjects, by figuring out the research hypothesis, may alter their behavior to meet the predictions of the hypothesis. **Demand characteristics** occur when subjects change their responses based on knowledge of the experimental hypothesis. Subjects tend to find even the most mundane research interesting, and they want to help in whatever way they can. If a subject can figure out the research hypothesis via the design of the experiment or via comments made by the experimenter, he or she may try to give the "correct" response whenever possible. This, of course, can work to support or not to support the research hypothesis, depending on whether the subject's guessed hypothesis is the same as the experimenter's actual hypothesis.

It is difficult to avoid demand characteristics. The most effective way to do so is to use deception, where experimenters tell their subjects they are investigating one particular factor or behavior, but in reality they are studying another. An alternative is to discuss the experiment with subjects after collecting the necessary data and then discard the data from those who discovered the hypothesis. Be aware, however, that extreme deception and the discarding of data for no apparent reason are unethical. If you do discard data, be sure to report that fact, as well as the reason why, in your experimental write-up. The best way to control demand characteristics is to run a pilot study and watch for indications of them. If such indications are detected, analyze the design of the experiment and redesign it so that subjects will have a more difficult time figuring out the hypothesis.

In a nutshell, for an experiment to have merit, the experimenter must exert rigorous and thorough control over every aspect. He or she must maintain such rigid control over all extraneous variables that the only difference between experimental groups is the manipulation of the independent variable. Furthermore, the researcher must take special care to eliminate any experimenter bias and to minimize demand characteristics.

C O N C E P T   Q U I Z

1. The scientific technique used to rule out alternative hypotheses is _____ .

2. _____ variables make it difficult to rule out alternative hypotheses.

3. Unintentional errors in the direction of the research hypothesis made by experimenters are called _____ .

4. _____ arise when subjects change their behavior based on their knowledge of the research hypothesis.

Answers

1. experimental control

2. Extraneous

3. experimenter bias

4. Demand characteristics

STATISTICAL SIGNIFICANCE

Question: So if I run a well-controlled and well-designed experiment and if I observe a notable difference in behavior between the groups, then I should be able to generalize my findings to the entire population, right?

Wrong. You need to take one more step before generalizing, and that is to test your results for statistical significance. Any time you observe a difference in behavior between your groups, as indicated by the difference in the sample means, it may exist for one of two reasons: (1) there is no actual difference between the groups because both samples were taken from the same population—the observed difference is just a chance occurrence due to the error involved in sampling; or (2) a difference actually exists because each sample came from a different population and the difference is therefore real. Thus, in any experiment there are two distinct, mutually exclusive hypotheses regarding the data collected: the **null hypothesis** (H_0), which states that there is no real difference between the sample means or between the sample mean and the population mean, and the actual hypothesis, called the **research hypothesis** (H_1) or *alternative hypothesis,* which states that the difference between the sample means or between the sample mean and the population mean is real. The difference between these mutually exclusive hypotheses is illustrated next, using the example of a facial memory study.

RESEARCH HYPOTHESIS (H_1): When shown faces and given a test of facial memory 8 hours later, subjects who rehearse the faces once an hour via mental imagery *score higher* than subjects who do not rehearse. There is a real difference between subjects who use mental imagery and those who do not.

NULL HYPOTHESIS (H_0): When shown faces and given a test of facial memory 8 hours later, subjects who rehearse the faces once an hour via mental imagery *score the same* as subjects who do not rehearse. There is *no* real difference between subjects who use mental imagery and those who do not. Any observed difference is due to *chance*—to the fact that subjects in each group were not identically matched.

Statistical tests are formulated in such a way that they test the null hypothesis. They are set up to test whether the difference between the groups' performances (the difference between the sample means) is significantly large enough for researchers to rule out the possibility that the difference occurred by chance. If the results of the tests indicate that the difference is real—that it is significant—then researchers can *reject the null hypothesis* and accept the research hypothesis. On the other hand, if the results indicate that the difference between the groups is not significant, researchers say that they *fail to reject the null hypothesis*. They cannot accept the null hypothesis; they can only fail to reject it because there's always a chance, however small, that the difference is real but your experiment was not sensitive enough to confirm your research hypothesis.

Question: So how can we determine whether the difference between samples is real or chance?

This determination is based on several important factors, such as the number of samples, the variances of the population and the sample, and the size of the risk taken by experimenters that their conclusion will be wrong. Remember the preceding example involving mental imagery as an aid to remembering faces? H_0 stated that there is no difference between the sample mean of memory scores and the population mean; H_1 stated that there *is* an actual difference between the sample and population means. Suppose you are a researcher who has just conducted an experiment investigating these hypotheses, and you need to decide which one is actually true. As you make this decision, there are two ways you can be correct and two ways you can be wrong (see Figure 11.7). Obviously, you will be correct if you reject the null hypothesis when it is in reality false or if you fail to reject it when it is in reality true. However, if you decide to reject the null hypothesis when it is actually true (you accept a false research hypothesis), you will have committed a **Type I error.** If you fail to reject the null hypothesis when it is actually false (you fail to accept a true research hypothesis), you will have committed a **Type II error.**

It is imperative that researchers take great pains to avoid making these errors, particularly Type I errors. When researchers accept research hypotheses that are in truth false, they can mislead not only themselves and other researchers but also people who apply the research results to the real world. If Type I errors are committed in a series of learning studies and if the results are applied to the classroom, countless hours of learning time may be wasted. Thus, Type I errors are considered to be much more serious than Type II

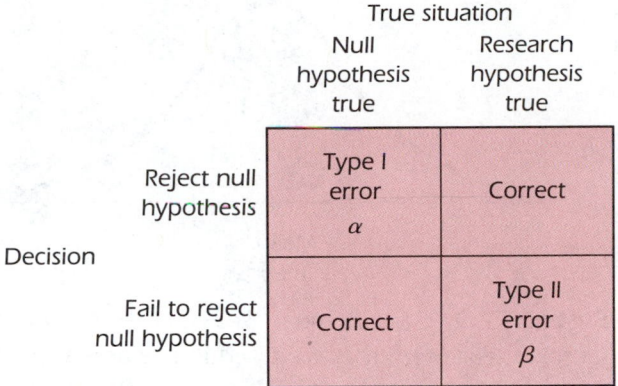

True situation

	Null hypothesis true	Research hypothesis true
Reject null hypothesis	Type I error α	Correct
Fail to reject null hypothesis	Correct	Type II error β

Decision

Figure 11.7   *The four possible outcomes of a statistical decision*

errors. When a Type II error is made because a researcher fails to reject the null hypothesis when the research hypothesis is actually true, the researcher or some other researcher may have to repeat the experiment, for a variation of it, sometime in the future. This may result in lost time, but it will not result in fallacious theories being implemented in the real world. Type II errors may slow down the progress of science, but they don't lead it down blind alleys.

Actually, if researchers select the appropriate statistical tests (the most widely used tests are explained in the following chapters) and apply their results to the tests correctly, the chance of committing a Type I error is very small (about .05 or 5 out of 100). The purpose of these tests is to determine whether the statistical differences recorded among the sample groups are significant. Figures 11.8 and 11.9 will help you understand the rationale underlying the success of the tests in determining significance.

Figure 11.8 shows a distribution of all possible sample means; any one particular sample mean will fall somewhere within this distribution. If that sample mean is near the population mean, as is $\overline{X}_1$ in Figure 11.9, it is likely that H_0 is true, and that any difference between the experimental group receiving the independent variable and the rest of the population not receiving it is negligible and is due merely to a sampling error. In such a case, the

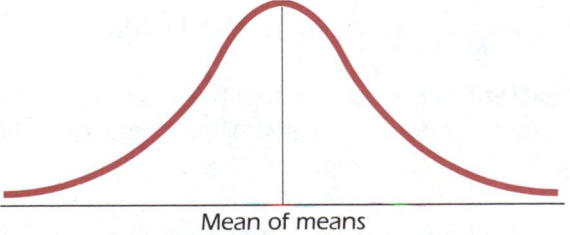

Mean of means

Figure 11.8   *The distribution of sample means*

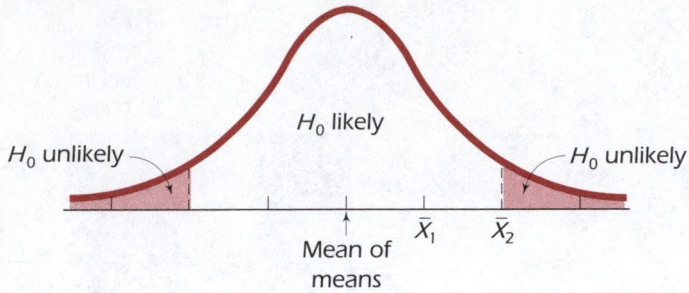

Figure 11.9 is labeled with: H_0 likely, H_0 unlikely (left), H_0 unlikely (right), $\bar{X}_1$, $\bar{X}_2$, Mean of means.

Figure 11.9 *Sample mean 1 is near the mean of the distribution of sample means and therefore within the area where the null hypothesis is likely, whereas sample mean 2 is out in the tail of the distribution where the null hypothesis is unlikely.*

researcher should accept the sample as being part of the greater population. On the other hand, if the sample mean lies in one of the tails of the distribution, as does $\bar{X}_2$ in Figure 11.9, it is quite unlikely that H_0 is true. In this case, the researcher should reject the null hypothesis and accept the research hypothesis. In other words, the experimental group receiving the independent variable is different enough from the population not receiving it that the researcher should consider the experimental group as part of a separate population that behaves in a distinct manner because of the effects of the independent variable.

Question: How far out in the tail should the sample mean lie before H_0 can be rejected?

The answer to this question is based on another question: How much of a chance do researchers want to take that they will not commit a Type I error? The probability of committing a Type I error is designated by alpha (α). Most psychologists agree that an alpha level of .05 is reasonable, which means that the null hypothesis can reasonably be rejected if there is less than .05 probability of committing a Type I error. Therefore, the alpha levels should be set at the points in the tails where only 5% (.05) of the distribution will yield more extreme scores. If a particular sample mean falls within these areas of the curve, we can reject H_0 (see Figure 11.10).

Question: Since each sample has only one mean, it can lie on only one side of the curve. Why does Figure 11.10 show alpha areas in both tails?

The decision to spread the alpha areas between the two tails of the distribution or to concentrate all of the alpha area in only one tail of the

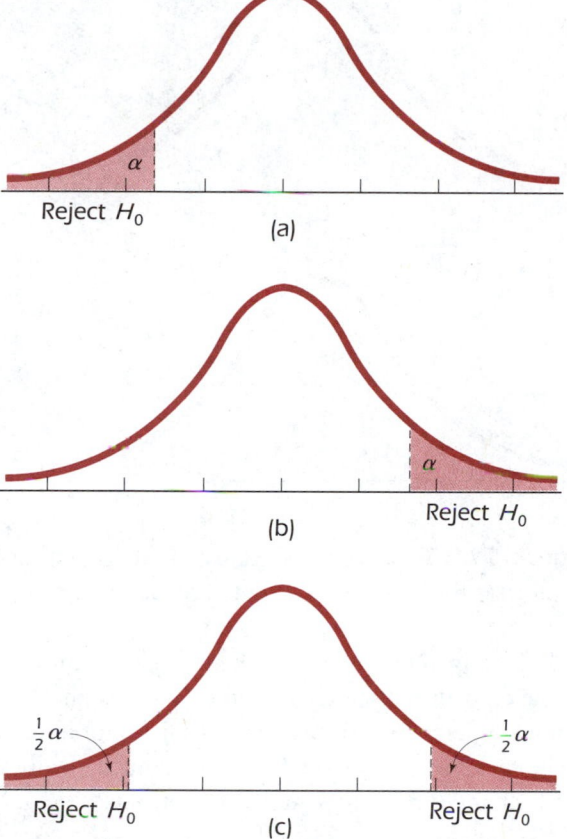

Figure 11.10 The placement of alpha areas for (a and b) a one-tailed test and (c) a two-tailed test. If a sample mean falls within the alpha area, we can reject the null hypothesis.

distribution depends on the research hypothesis. If the research hypothesis specifies that the sample mean will definitely be above or definitely be below the population mean, it is of course reasonable to look in only one tail of the theoretical sampling distribution to see whether the sample mean is significant. For example, if our research hypothesis states that eating chocolate will *improve* memory, then we only need to look in the tail above the population mean for significance. Research hypotheses that specify the direction of the experimental effect are called *one-tailed hypotheses* because we need to look in only the one specified tail for significance. Tests of hypotheses such as these are called **one-tailed tests** (see Figure 11.11).

Many research hypotheses suggest merely that the sample mean will be different from the population mean without specifying the direction of the difference. Because the direction is not specified, it is necessary to look in both tails of the theoretical sampling distribution for significance (see Figure

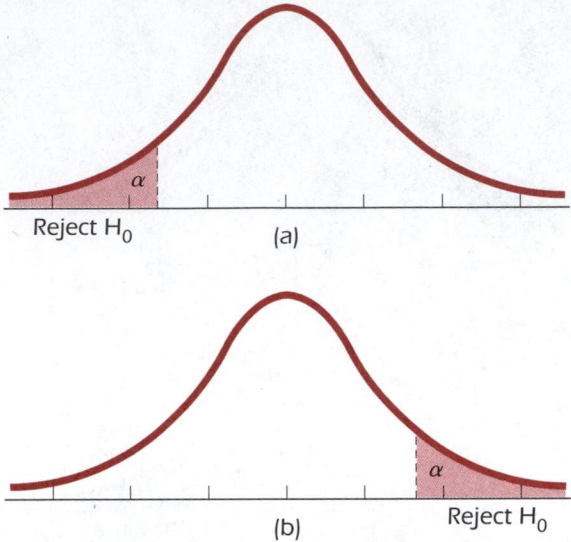

Reject H_0

(a)

α

(b)

α

Reject H_0

Figure 11.11   One-tailed statistical tests put all alpha (a) in the tail below the mean *or* (b) in the tail above the mean.

11.12). Tests of hypotheses such as these are known as **two-tailed tests**. As an example, if our research hypothesis states that a diet including chocolate changes a person's memory for faces, it is not clear whether this change is for the better or for the worse. Since the hypothesis does not specify the direction of the change, it is a two-tailed hypothesis.

Question: How do we know when to use a one-tailed test and when to use a two-tailed test?

The decision to use a one-tailed test or a two-tailed test begins with your literature search and the statement of your research hypothesis. If your knowledge of previous research leads you to believe that your experiment will result in the mean of one group or one level of the independent variable being greater than the mean of the other, then your research hypothesis should state this

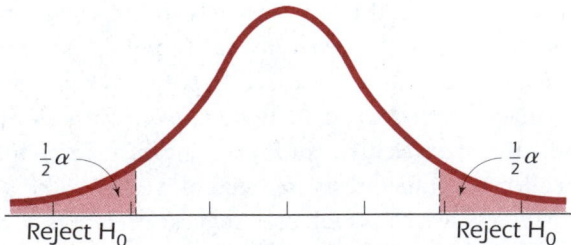

$\frac{1}{2}\alpha$

$\frac{1}{2}\alpha$

Reject H_0

Reject H_0

Figure 11.12   Two-tailed statistical tests split alpha and put half of alpha in the tail below the mean and the other half of alpha in the tail above the mean.

prediction and you will run a one-tailed test. If, on the other hand, it is not clear from your knowledge of previous research which group or level will have the larger mean, then your hypothesis will reflect this uncertainty and you will do a two-tailed test. Remember, in order to determine which type of test to conduct, you need only look at the research hypothesis. When it predicts a direction, do a one-tailed test; if it does not predict a direction, then do a two-tailed test. For example, if I know that caffeine aids memory, I can hypothesize that people who use caffeine before taking a memory test will perform better than people who do not use caffeine. This hypothesis leads to a one-tailed test because the prediction is that one group will perform better than the other group. In the real world of research, most researchers take the conservative approach and use the two-tailed test more often than the one-tailed.

Whenever you begin any research project, you are faced with many choices: whether to conduct an experiment, how many independent variables to investigate, how many subjects to use and how to assign them to the various groups, and what controls to implement. Each of these choices has an impact on the experimental design and subsequently on the statistical analysis of the data you collect. Because of this close interrelationship between experimental design and statistics, it is to your advantage as a researcher to be knowledgeable about both. Often experimenters, especially those who are inexperienced, conduct research without considering the eventual analysis of the data. Mere possession of data does not mean that the data are useful or that the data will answer the questions you have posed. It is best to design all research projects with the statistical analyses of the data in mind.

POWER

Another factor researchers need to consider is the power of the statistical test they will use to analyze their experiment. The more powerful the statistical test, the more likely it is that the test will yield a positive result for the experiment. In other words, the more powerful the test, the more likely the test will reject the null hypothesis and allow the researcher to accept the research hypothesis. More technically, the **power** of a statistical test is the probability that the test will *reject* the null hypothesis when the null hypothesis is in fact false. Because the probability of making a Type II error, beta (β), is the probability of *failing* to reject the null hypothesis when the null hypothesis is in fact false, the power of any statistical test is equal to 1 minus the probability of a Type II error, or $1 - \beta$ (see Figure 11.13):

$$\text{Power} = 1 - \beta$$

Several factors can affect the power of a statistical test: (1) the size of alpha,

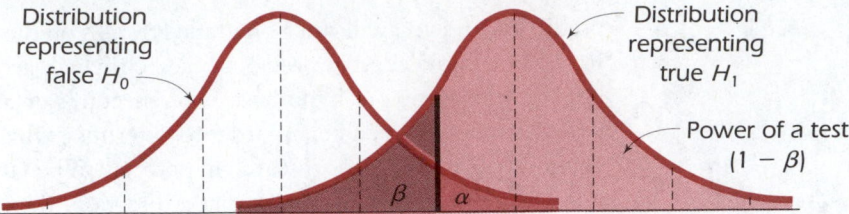

Figure 11.13   The probability of a Type I error, α, and the probability of a Type II error, β. The power of a statistical test is the shaded area, 1 − β.

(2) the sample size, (3) the difference between the means of the two populations that the samples come from ($\mu_1 - \mu_2$), and (4) the type of statistical test used in the analysis.

As previously mentioned, when doing research you should try to choose an alpha (α) level that minimizes the chance of Type I errors. This naturally leads to relatively small values for α. However, the smaller the α level, the more likely there will be a Type II error, β. This relationship between the size of α and the size of β is illustrated in Figure 11.14. Figure 11.14(a) shows that a small α will produce a relatively larger β, which results in lower power. An increase in the size of α, as shown in Figure 11.14(b), produces a smaller β and therefore results in higher power. Because the power of a test is equal to 1 − β, you can increase the power of your test by choosing a larger value for α. For example, the power of the test increases if you change the α level from .01 to .05.

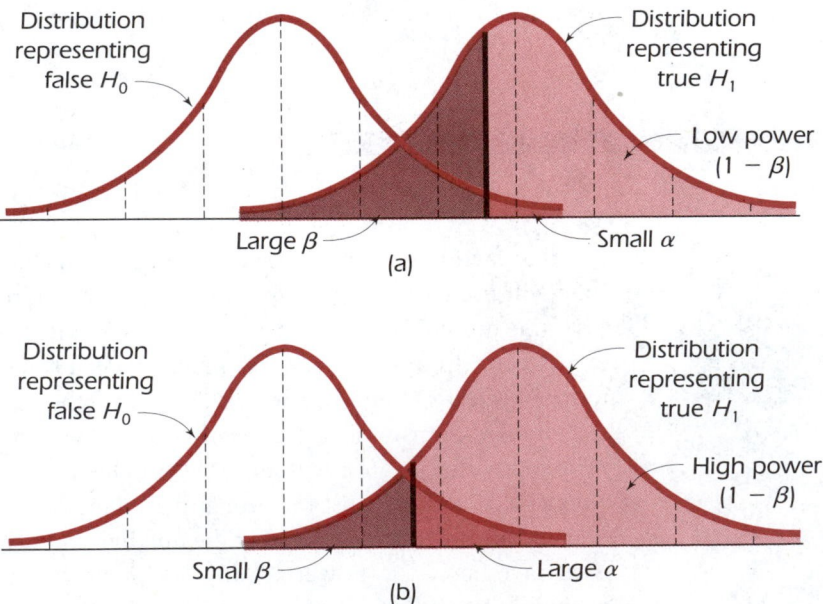

Figure 11.14   (a) A small α causes a large β, which decreases the power of the test. (b) A large α causes a small β, which increases the power of the test.

The power of a test also increases as you enlarge the size of your sample. An increase in the sample size decreases the standard deviation of the sampling distributions, which reduces the overlap between the two distributions and decreases β. Therefore, going to the trouble of recruiting lots of subjects can pay off because a large sample increases the power of your statistical test. Given the same statistical test, you will more likely be correct in rejecting the null hypothesis when your sample size is 50 than when your sample size is 10.

It also follows that the power of the test increases as the means of the two populations that represent H_0 and H_1 move farther apart. As the distance between the means increases, there is less overlap and therefore a smaller β. Figure 11.15 illustrates the decrease in β as the means of the two populations move apart. Remember that any decrease in β increases the power of a test.

Finally, some statistical tests are just more powerful than others. Tests that use interval or ratio data and require you to estimate population standard deviations and population means are more powerful than tests without these features. Tests that involve accurate estimates of population parameters are called *parametric* tests; statistical tests that do not require the estimation of population parameters are called *nonparametric* tests. Parametric tests are generally more powerful than nonparametric tests. Chapters 12–14 describe the uses of the major parametric statistical tests. Nonparametric tests are covered in Chapter 15.

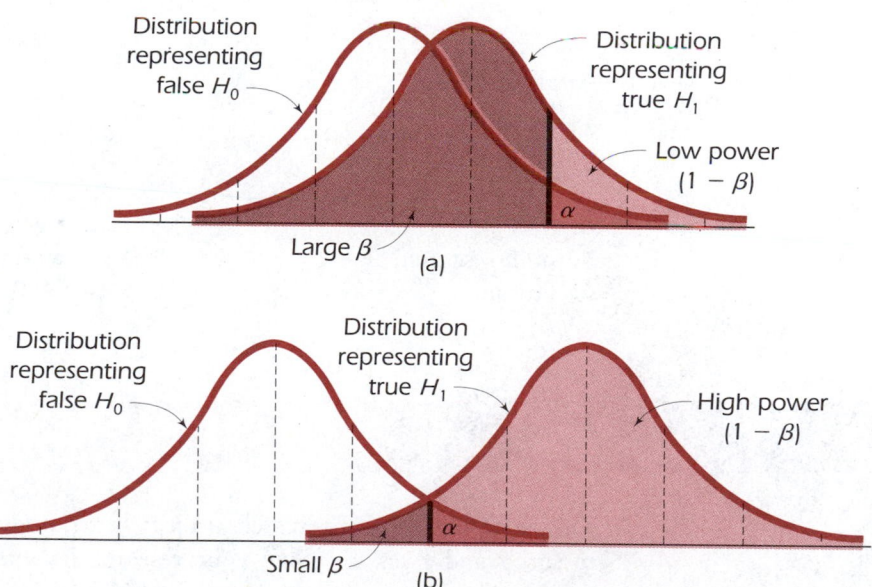

Figure 11.15 (a) If the means of the two populations are close together, β is large and the power is low. (b) If the means of the two populations are far apart, β is small and the power is high.

CONCEPT QUIZ

1. In any experiment there are two distinct, mutually exclusive hypotheses regarding the data collected; the _____ hypothesis and the _____ hypothesis.
2. The hypothesis claiming that there is no real difference between groups in your experiment is called the _____ hypothesis.
3. The hypothesis that claims there is a real difference between groups in your experiment is called the _____ hypothesis.
4. Statistical tests are formulated to test the _____ hypothesis.
5. If the difference in your experiment is real, or significant, you can then reject the _____ hypothesis and accept the _____ hypothesis.
6. If the difference in your experiment is not significant, then you _____ to reject the _____ hypothesis.
7. Failing to reject a false null hypothesis results in a Type _____ error.
8. Rejecting a true null hypothesis results in a Type _____ error.
9. The probability of committing a Type I error is called _____ .
10. Tests of research hypotheses that predict the direction of the experimental effect are called _____ tests.
11. Tests of research hypotheses that do not specify the direction of the experimental effect are called _____ tests.
12. Power is equal to _____ .

Answers

1. null; research	7. II
2. null	8. I
3. research	9. alpha (α)
4. null	10. one-tailed
5. null; research	11. two-tailed
6. fail; null	12. $1 - \beta$

SUMMARY

The first step in any research project is to study any available previous research and then to define your research hypotheses. Scientific research hypotheses are predictions based on scientific theories or on a body of research knowledge. All research hypotheses must be falsifiable.

The three major classifications of variables are independent variables, dependent variables, and subject variables. The independent variable is the variable that is manipulated by the experimenter. The variable that is used to measure behavior, such as a test score or reaction time, is the dependent variable. The value of the dependent variable depends on the experimental manipulations of the independent variable. Subject variables are those that describe subjects' characteristics or attributes that cannot be manipulated by the experimenter. For instance, the experimenter cannot change the race, height, or IQ of the subject; therefore, these characteristics are subject variables.

The basic idea behind conducting experiments is to explain the causes of behavior by manipulating relevant independent variables. To eliminate possible rival explanations for the data collected, the researcher must control all relevant variables that are not manipulated in the experiment. The two major types of experimental control are (1) randomly assigning subjects to groups and (2) identifying relevant extraneous variables and holding them constant. Experimental designs are described by both the number and the type of independent variables, as well as by the way subjects are assigned to the various conditions in the experiments. There are one-group, completely randomized, and factorial experimental designs. In a one-group design, the mean of a single experimental group is compared to a population's mean. In a completely randomized design, the experiment has only one independent variable, but that independent variable has two or more levels. The factorial design has at least two different independent variables, and each of the independent variables has at least two different levels.

Experiments can also be classified by the procedures used to assign subjects to the experimental conditions. In a between-subjects design, each subject is randomly assigned to only one of the experimental conditions. In a within-subjects design, each randomly selected subject participates in all experimental conditions for all independent variables. A mixed design occurs in factorial experiments when a subject participates in all levels of one independent variable but participates in only one level of the other independent variables.

All experiments have two mutually exclusive hypotheses. The first, called the null hypothesis (H_0), states that the experimental manipulation has no effect. The second, called the research hypothesis (H_1), states that the experimental manipulations have a significant effect on the experimental data that are collected. Using statistical tests of the data collected in the experiment, the experimenter decides whether to reject one hypothesis in favor of the other. Rejecting the null hypothesis when it is true is called a Type I error. Failing to reject the null hypothesis when the research hypothesis is true is called a Type II error. Because the Type I error, rejecting the null hypothesis when it is actually true, is the more serious error, psychologists try to reject the null hypothesis only when the probability of a Type I error is .05 or less.

The power of a statistical test is the probability the test will reject the null hypothesis when the null hypothesis is in fact false. Power is equal to 1 minus beta. Power can be increased by using a larger value for alpha, by increasing the sample size, by increasing the difference between the means of the populations being tested, or by using a parametric statistical test.

KEY TERMS

hypothesis
independent variables
dependent variables
subject variables
between-subjects design
within-subjects design
mixed design
one-group experimental design
completely randomized
    experimental design
completely randomized factorial
    experimental design

experimental control
extraneous variable
experimenter bias
demand characteristics
null hypothesis (H_0)
research hypothesis (H_1)
Type I error
Type II error
one-tailed test
two-tailed test
power

PROBLEMS

1. A _____ is a statement, based on a body of research knowledge or on a scientific theory, that is in the form of a prediction.

2. Alyson's adviser told her to revise her research proposal because he said her hypothesis was not _____ .

3. Variables that are manipulated by the experimenter are called _____ .

4. _____ variables are those that are measures of the subjects' behavior.

5. Reaction time, test scores, and heart rate are all examples of _____ variables.

6. Attributes or characteristics of subjects that cannot be manipulated by the experimenter, such as hair color and athletic ability, are known as _____ variables.

7. Juan worked with people who had strokes and subsequent language impairment. They often became frustrated because they were unable to communicate their wants and needs. Some of the journal articles he was reading led him to believe that using sign language might be the answer. For his senior project, Juan decided to see whether these people might learn to communicate through sign language faster than through oral speech.

Juan divided his subjects randomly into two groups, and each group received the following treatment on three separate days: A picture was projected onto a screen; a spoken word or a gestured sign, depending on the condition, accompanied the picture; the subject was asked to repeat the spoken word or the sign. On the fourth day, Juan showed each subject the same pictures and asked: "What is this?" He recorded their answers and then counted the number of responses for each group. In Juan's study, identify these:

a. Research hypothesis
b. Independent variable
c. Dependent variable

8. Dr. Peña is conducting research to see whether the severity of the chronic headaches suffered by her patients will be lessened through the use of biofeedback. Based on what she has read in medical journals and on her own observations, Dr. Peña has determined that the headaches are caused by muscle tension, so she feels that patients who learn to relax will have fewer or less severe headaches. To test her theory, she attaches electrodes to the skin of the patients in her experimental group. These tiny wires measure electrical activity in the surrounding skin. When patients relax sufficiently so that the electrical activity in their skin falls below a certain level, they receive feedback in the form of soothing music. Dr. Peña finds that, compared to a separate control group of people to whom electrodes are attached but who receive no feedback, the experimental group reports fewer and less severe headaches during the week following the biofeedback session. In this study, identify the following:

a. Research hypothesis
b. Independent variable
c. Dependent variable

9. Dr. Hilo developed a theory that tall people are more self-assured than short people. To test this theory, he recruited subjects and placed them into three groups—tall, medium, and short—according to their height. Dr. Hilo then asked the subjects to answer questions on the standardized Self-Assurance Rating Scale. What is wrong with Dr. Hilo's design?

10. In Problem 8, Dr. Peña used a _____ - _____ design in assigning subjects to her two groups.

11. In a within-subjects design, each subject participates in _____ level(s) of the experiment.

12. In a between-subjects design, each subject participates in _____ level(s) of the experiment.

13. If Juan, in his study in Problem 7, required that each subject participate in both conditions, it would be a _____ - _____ design.

14. Ima Researcher is conducting an experiment with three independent variables, where each independent variable has two levels. Her subjects participate in both levels of one of the independent variables but in only one level of the other two. What kind of research design is this?

15. Between-subjects designs have many advantages; the major drawback is that they require _____ .

16. Suppose you are interested in studying hearing loss caused by frequent exposure to loud noises. You have access to a group of jackhammer operators, and you want to see whether their hearing is more impaired than that of the general population. You administer a hearing test to this group and compare the mean score of this group to the population mean score. The test you conduct is known as a _____ - _____ test.

17. Dr. Bambino is doing research on pattern recognition in babies. He randomly selects and randomly assigns infants to two experimental groups. One group is presented with a card showing lines arranged in a random fashion; the second group is presented with a card showing horizontal lines arranged in a regular pattern. Dr. Bambino wants to see whether the infants spend more time looking at the organized array. Identify the following:

    a. Type of design
    b. Research hypothesis
    c. Independent variable
    d. Dependent variable
    e. Some of the variables that need to be held constant

18. In a multilevel completely randomized design, the number of _____ of the independent variable is increased, as opposed to the number of independent variables.

19. In another study, Dr. Bambino is investigating whether, in addition to organization, familiarity is a factor in the time infants attend to a stimulus. He randomly selects and randomly assigns infants to four groups. Group 1 is presented with a card showing a random arrangement of lines; group 2 is presented with a card showing an organized arrangement of horizontal lines; group 3 is presented with a card showing a drawing of a human face; group 4 is presented with a card showing the same facial features as those on group 3's card but with the features arranged in a helter-skelter fashion. Dr. Bambino's design is a _____ experimental design, and it is in the form of a _____ × _____ factorial design.

20. A true scientist is unwilling to accept a hypothesis until all other alternative hypotheses are ruled out. The way to rule out other possible hypotheses is through effective use of _____ .

21. Whenever possible, all _____ should be held constant so that they don't interfere with the identification of the variables that are the true cause of a behavior.

22. Remember Juan's study from Problem 7? He himself elicited and recorded subjects' responses. By so doing, he failed to control for the effect of _____ . To prevent this, what could he have done?

23. _____ occur when subjects figure out the hypothesis and try to "help" by providing responses that they think support that hypothesis.

24. What should you do if you find that demand characteristics are cropping up in your experiment?

25. To determine whether observed differences in experimental samples are real or are just due to chance, researchers need to test their results for _____ .

26. The _____ states that there is no real difference between the sample means or between the sample mean and the population mean. The

_____ states that there *is* a real difference between the sample means or the sample mean and the population mean.

27. What is the null hypothesis in Dr. Peña's experiment on the use of biofeedback to reduce headaches in Problem 8?

28. Suppose that biofeedback really does have some effect on reducing headache pain but, because of experimental error, Dr. Peña's results led her to the conclusion that it has no significant effect. This is a _____ error.

29. What is the null hypothesis in Juan's experiment from Problem 7 involving learning sign language versus oral speech?

30. Suppose there is no actual difference between people who have had strokes learning to communicate through sign language and their learning to communicate through speech. However, because of ex-perimenter bias, Juan's results led him to believe that learning sign language was a definite help. Juan committed a _____ error.

31. _____ errors are more serious than _____ errors.

32. It is generally agreed that _____ is an acceptable alpha level.

33. When the hypothesis states that there should be a difference between two samples but the direction of the difference is not stated, the hypothesis is _____ -tailed.

34. Dr. Bambino's study on infant pattern recognition is a _____ -tailed test because he specifies that familiar, organized stimuli will hold infants' attention longer than unfamiliar, random stimuli.

R E F E R E N C E S

Brown, R. (1986). *Social psychology* (2nd ed.). New York: Free Press.

Loftus, E. (1979). *Eyewitness testimony.* Cambridge, MA: Harvard University Press.

Penrod, S., Loftus, E., & Winkler, J. (1982). The reliability of eyewitness testimony: A psychological perspective. In N. L. Kerr & R. M. Bray (Eds.), *The psychology of the courtroom* (pp. 119–168). New York: Academic Press.

Popper, K. (1959). *The logic of scientific discovery.* New York: Basic Books.

t Tests

Get out your stopwatch. If you don't have one, find a watch or a clock that measures time in seconds. Now, take a look at the following 30 shapes and time how long it takes you to read the entire list out loud as fast as you can, from left to right, top to bottom.

That was easy, wasn't it? You were probably pretty fast—about 20 seconds, plus or minus a little? Now try again, but this time see how long it takes you to say aloud the shapes in the list on the next page. Remember to read from left to right and top to bottom.

It took longer, didn't it? It might have taken even twice as long, and it was probably more than a little frustrating. This is a modified version of the "Stroop effect." It has fascinated psychologists since 1935 when J. R. Stroop first described it after using a list of color words as the stimulus in a learning experiment.

Question: *Why is it so hard to read the shapes when the words above them are different from the shapes?*

For most of us, reading words is automatic by the time we become adults. We read every word presented to us without thinking about it. Consequently, *not* reading words that are put in front of us is extremely difficult, if not impossible. So when you look at a stimulus that contains printed words plus another attribute, you automatically read the words first, even if you are asked to attend to the other attribute. If a word and an attribute conflict with each other (as when the word *spade* is written above a diamond shape), naming the attribute usually takes longer because the brain processes the

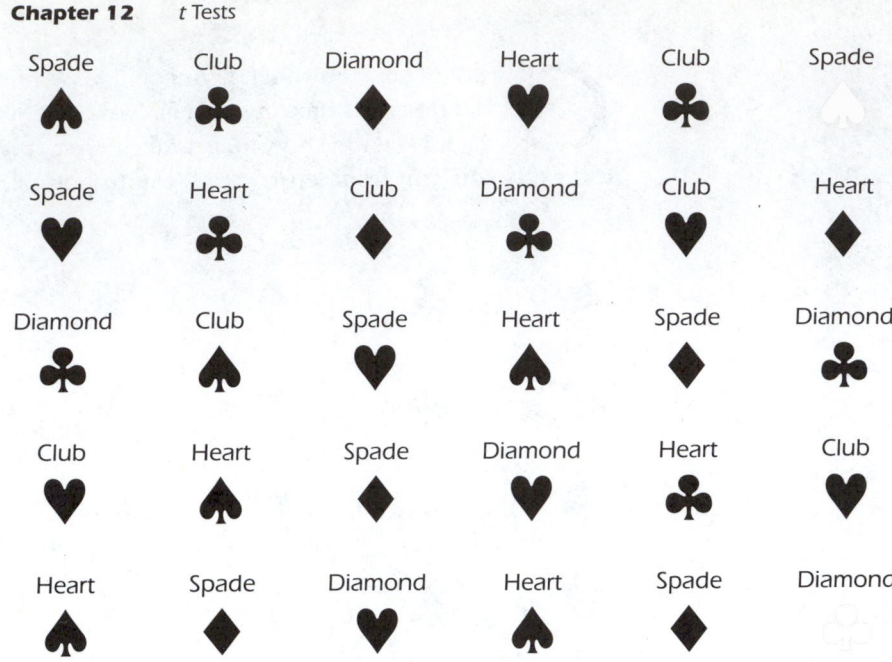

word before it processes the shape. Thus, the automaticity of reading the word interferes with the processing of the shape.

Many researchers have studied the Stroop effect and variations of it using various research designs. Let's say we ran an experiment using the preceding lists as our stimuli. We had one group of people name the symbols from one list, and we compared the results to a second group who named the symbols from the other list. We observed a difference in speed similar to your difference in speed when you read the lists. As you have learned from the preceding two chapters, however, merely observing a difference between two groups is not sufficient; you must test the difference via statistical methods to determine whether the difference is statistically significant. The difference must be large enough to be considered unlikely to have happened by chance. The way to test for statistical significance is to conduct a statistical test on the data. The test you use depends on a number of factors, such as the availability of population data, the size of the sample, the number of independent variables, and whether the samples are correlated, to name just a few. We devote the bulk of this chapter to examining *t* tests—one of the most widely used tests of significance in the behavioral sciences. You will learn when to use *t* tests, how to use them, and which one to use on what type of data. Before explaining *t* tests, we review *z* tests, not only because you might benefit from a review but also because understanding the rationale behind *t* tests is based on understanding *z* tests.

z TESTS (A REVIEW)

Suppose that by an amazing stroke of luck we came across some population data indicating that, on the average, it takes people in the general population 15 seconds to name all the shapes from the shapes-alone list at the beginning of this chapter. (Realistically, of course, it is probably impossible to find such population data because to obtain a true population mean, one must obtain a measurement from every member of that population and no one is willing to expend such effort for such trivial data.) For our experiment, therefore, we need to round up only one sample group and compare its mean to the population mean. Our research hypothesis (H_1) states: People will take longer to name the shapes when reading from a list of combined shapes and words than when reading from a list of shapes alone. To test the hypothesis, we ask a single group of 25 people to name only the shapes from a combined list of conflicting words and shapes. Given what we know about the speed of the general population on the shapes-alone list, we can compare the mean from our single sample to the population mean. Our results are as follows:

Population mean (μ) = 15
Sample mean ($\overline{X}$) = 18
Sample standard deviation (S) = 5
Number of subjects (n) = 25

Our sample mean of 18 seconds is indeed longer than the population mean of 15 seconds, but is this a true difference or just a chance variation from the population mean? We can conduct a *z* test to determine the probability of the difference occurring just by chance. Formula 10.9 states that

$$z = \frac{\overline{X} - \mu_{\overline{X}}}{\sigma_{\overline{X}}} \tag{10.9}$$

Because we know the sample mean and the population mean, we need only compute the standard error of the mean ($\sigma_{\overline{X}}$) to compute the *z*.

Question: How can we compute the standard error of the mean if we don't know the standard deviation of the population?

If we know the standard deviation of the population, we should use it. If we do not, as is the case this time, we must estimate it. We can do this in two ways. The first is to use Formula 10.6 to obtain the estimated standard deviation of the population and then use Formula 12.1, which follows, to compute the standard error of the mean:

$$\text{est. } \sigma = \sqrt{\frac{\Sigma(X - \overline{X})^2}{n - 1}} = \sqrt{\frac{\Sigma X^2 - (n \cdot \overline{X}^2)}{n - 1}} \tag{10.6}$$

$$\text{est. } \sigma_{\overline{X}} = \frac{\text{est. } \sigma}{\sqrt{n}} \tag{12.1}$$

This method works well if we have access to the raw data from the sample; then we can compute the sums. If we do not have access to the raw data, we must use another method, which involves Formula 12.2:

$$\text{est. } \sigma_{\overline{X}} = \frac{S}{\sqrt{n-1}} \tag{12.2}$$

Both of the preceding methods generate the same estimate of the standard error of the mean. We can use Formulas 10.6 and 12.1 when we have the raw data; we can use Formula 12.2 when we know the sample standard deviation.

In our experiment testing people's speed in naming playing card symbols, we know only the sample standard deviation. Thus, we should use Formula 12.2 to compute the estimate of the standard error of the mean and subsequently the *z* score:

$$\text{est. } \sigma_{\overline{X}} = \frac{S}{\sqrt{n-1}} = \frac{5}{\sqrt{25-1}} = \frac{5}{4.899} = 1.021$$

Now, using Formula 10.9, we can compute the *z* score:

$$z = \frac{\overline{X} - \mu_{\overline{X}}}{\sigma_{\overline{X}}} = \frac{18 - 15}{1.021} = \frac{3}{1.021} = 2.938$$

Question: A *z* score of 2.938 is pretty large, but refresh my memory: How do we know that it is large enough not to have happened by chance?

As we stated in Chapter 11, most psychologists agree that an alpha level of .05 is sufficient grounds for rejecting the null hypothesis. In our experiment on naming the symbols, the null hypothesis can be stated as: There is no difference between the time it takes to name a single list of only playing card symbols and the time it takes to name a combined list of symbols and words. To test this hypothesis, we compute the *z* score as shown here and then look up in the appropriate table the probability of getting a score as extreme as the one obtained in our experiment. By looking up the *z* score of 2.94 in Table Z in Appendix A, we find that the probability of getting a *z* score as large as or larger than 2.94 is .0016, or much less than 1 out of 100. When we use an alpha level of .05, any *z* score that results in a probability of less than .05 allows us to reject the null hypothesis and accept the research hypothesis. Our probability, .0016, is less than .05. Therefore, we can reject the null hypothesis and accept the research hypothesis. The difference between the sample mean and the population mean is significant, so we can assert that people do take longer to say the names of shapes when reading from a combined list of conflicting words and shapes than when reading from a list of shapes alone.

It is relatively simple to conduct a *z* test. You need only compute the *z* score and then use Table Z to read the probability beyond the *z* score. If your research hypothesis is one-tailed, the area beyond the *z* score must be less than .05 (see Figure 12.1). If the research hypothesis is two-tailed, you must split the .05 probability between the two tails, with .025 in one tail and .025 in the other (see Figure 12.2). Thus, as explained in Chapter 11, a *z* score must be farther out in the tail in order for you to reject the null hypothesis when you use a two-tailed test.

People who do a lot of research and run a lot of *z* tests don't continually refer to Table Z. They memorize two *z* scores that correspond with the level of significance required for their experiments. For one-tailed tests, they know

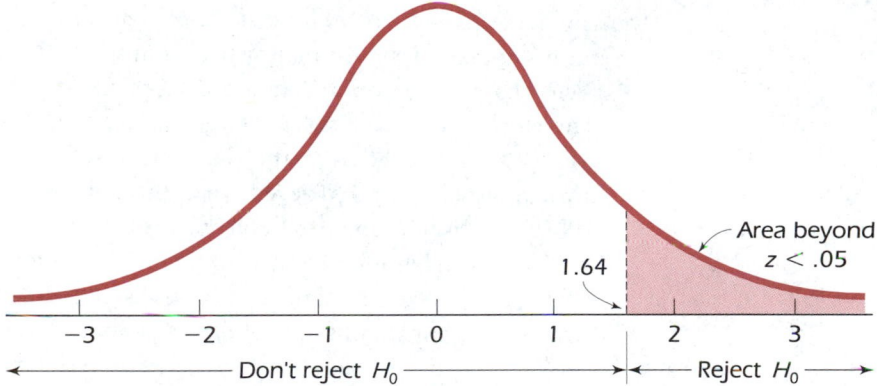

Figure 12.1 For a one-tailed *z* test, the area beyond the *z* score must be less than .05.

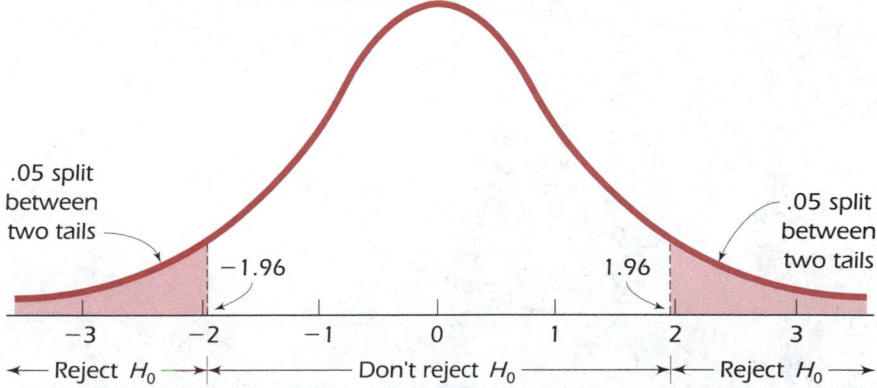

Figure 12.2 The *z* score must be farther out in the tail in order for us to reject the null hypothesis when we use a two-tailed test.

that the z score necessary for a .05 level of probability is 1.645 or −1.645 (found in column 3, *Area beyond z*, in Table Z). For two-tailed tests, they know that the z score necessary for a .025 level of probability is 1.96, which means that the computed z score must be −1.96 or less, or +1.96 or greater in order to reject the null hypothesis. Thus, if you compute several z scores and need to determine their significance, you don't have to keep referring to the table. All you need to know is the minimum z score necessary for significance.

t TESTS

The central limit theorem provides the justification for using sample data to run a z test. The *central limit theorem* states that any distribution of sample means approaches a normal distribution when the sample is infinitely large. (See Chapter 10 for a detailed discussion of the central limit theorem.) Therefore, when a sample is large (more than 1000), it is appropriate to conduct a z test because the distribution of sample means approaches a normal distribution. However, when the sample is relatively small (less than 1000), the distribution of sample means is best matched by the **t distribution**.

The t distribution is similar to the z distribution in that both are symmetrical, bell-shaped sampling distributions. However, there is a noteworthy difference: The overall shape of the t distribution is influenced strongly by the size of the samples used to generate it. For very large samples, the t distribution approaches the z distribution, but for smaller samples, the t distribution is flatter. Figure 12.3 illustrates the differences between the two.

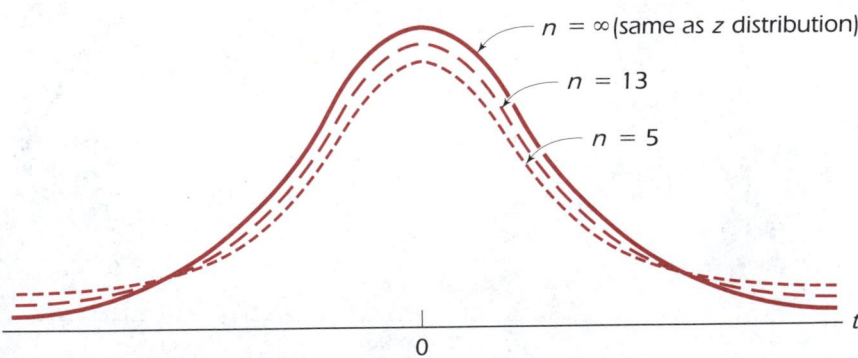

Figure 12.3 The t distribution for small samples is flatter than the z distribution, but as the sample size increases, the t distribution approaches the shape of the z distribution.

Question: But in your example for the *z* test, the sample size was only 25. Why?

We hoped you would notice this. We used a small sample intentionally to call your attention to this fact: When the sample is large, you should use a *z* test; when the sample is small, you should use a *t* **test**. So instead of using a *z* test on our data, we should have used a *t* test.

SINGLE-SAMPLE *t* TESTS

Question: Is the *t* test anything like the *z* test?

You bet! That's why we spent so much time reviewing the *z* test—because the *z* test and the *t* test are not much different. Both involve comparing the sample mean to the population mean. The formula for computing the *t* score is essentially the same as that for computing the *z* score:

$$t = \frac{\overline{X} - \mu_{\overline{X}}}{\text{est. } \sigma_{\overline{X}}} \tag{12.3}$$

Not only is the formula similar, but the procedure for computing a *t* score is identical to that for computing a *z* score. The sample mean, the population mean, and the standard error of the mean are needed for the *t* score. If the standard deviation of the population is not available for computing the standard error of the mean, we use the standard deviation of the sample to estimate the standard error of the mean, just as we do in computing a *z* score. In fact, the only difference between conducting a *z* test and conducting a *t* test is that after computing the *z* score, you look it up in Table *Z*, and after computing the *t* score, you look it up in Table *T*.

We will illustrate how to conduct the single-sample *t* test with the following example. Dr. Tee has developed a language-training system that, she claims, significantly increases the number of new words acquired by infants. Average children in this part of the world begin to speak a few basic words by the time they are 1 year old; by the time they are 2, average toddlers have a vocabulary of 210 words. To test her system, Dr. Tee randomly selects 12 sets of parents who are willing to use her language-training system with their newborn infants for 2 years. At the end of the 2-year test period, she tabulates the number of words in each toddler's vocabulary. The results are displayed in Table 12.1.

Table 12.1   Number of Words in Vocabulary for 12 Toddlers Using the Language-Training System

Child	Number of words in vocabulary X	X^2
C. W.	197	38,809
D. J.	223	49,729
P. V.	241	58,081
J. I.	183	33,489
T. B.	222	49,284
B. C.	231	53,361
R. A.	297	88,209
B. B.	220	48,400
D. T.	188	35,344
P. P.	231	53,361
C. D.	210	44,100
M. L.	234	54,756

$$\Sigma X = 2677 \qquad \Sigma X^2 = 606,923$$

$$\overline{X} = 223.083$$

$$S = 28.474$$

The mean number of words in the vocabularies of the infants in the experimental group is 223.083. This is obviously greater than the population mean of 210 words, but Dr. Tee wants to be certain that this difference is not due merely to chance. Since her sample was small, $n = 12$, she needs to conduct a *t* test, as opposed to a *z* test, to determine whether the observed difference between the means is significant. Because her statistics skills are rusty, she engages our help to determine whether her results are significant. Before we begin, let's consider Dr. Tee's research and null hypotheses. The research hypothesis is: The language-training system will increase the size of a child's vocabulary as measured at age 2 years. The null hypothesis is: The language-training system will make no difference in the size of a child's vocabulary as measured at age 2 years.

To run a *t* test, we need to compute the *t* score using Formula 12.3. We already know the sample mean (223.083 words) and the population mean (210 words), but we still need to compute the standard error of the mean. We do not have access to the standard deviation of the population, so we are forced to estimate the standard error of the mean by using one of the two methods described previously in our review of the *z* test. To show that we can obtain the same result by using either method, we estimate the standard error of the mean using both. First, we use Formula 10.6 to estimate the population standard deviation and Formula 12.1 to compute the estimate of the standard error of the mean. Following this, we use the standard deviation of the sample in Formula 12.2 to compute the estimate of the standard error of the mean. Using Formulas 10.6 and 12.1:

$$\text{est. } \sigma = \sqrt{\frac{\Sigma X^2 - (n \cdot \overline{X}^2)}{n - 1}} \tag{10.6}$$

$$= \sqrt{\frac{606{,}923 - (12 \cdot 223.083^2)}{12 - 1}} = \sqrt{\frac{606{,}923 - (12 \cdot 49{,}766.025)}{11}}$$

$$= \sqrt{\frac{606{,}923 - 597{,}192.299}{11}} = \sqrt{\frac{9730.78}{11}}$$

$$= \sqrt{884.616} = 29.742$$

$$\text{est. } \sigma_{\overline{X}} = \frac{\text{est. } \sigma}{\sqrt{n}} \tag{12.1}$$

$$= \frac{29.742}{\sqrt{12}} = \frac{29.742}{3.464} = 8.586$$

Using Formula 12.2:

$$\text{est. } \sigma_{\overline{X}} = \frac{S}{\sqrt{n - 1}} \tag{12.2}$$

$$= \frac{28.474}{\sqrt{12 - 1}} = \frac{28.474}{\sqrt{11}} = \frac{28.474}{3.317} = 8.584$$

(The difference between the two estimates, .002 word, is due merely to roundoff error.)

Now we can use Formula 12.3 to compute the *t* score for the group of toddlers:

$$t = \frac{\overline{X} - \mu_{\overline{X}}}{\text{est. } \sigma_{\overline{X}}} \tag{12.3}$$

$$= \frac{223.083 - 210}{8.584} = \frac{13.083}{8.584} = 1.524$$

If this *t* score were a *z* score, Dr. Tee would need a *z* of 1.645 or larger to reject the null hypothesis because her research hypothesis is one-tailed, so a score of 1.524 would fail to reject the null hypothesis. Because this is a *t* score instead of a *z* score, however, we need to look in a different table. The critical values for *t* are listed in Table *T* in Appendix A.

To find the critical value in this table for any particular *t*, you need know only what we call the "degrees of freedom" for your particular sample. The degrees of freedom (*df*) vary with different types of *t* tests, but when used with the single-sample *t* test, the number of **degrees of freedom** equals the total number of scores in the sample minus 1:

$$df = n - 1 \qquad\qquad (12.4)$$

Because there are 12 scores in Dr. Tee's sample, the degrees of freedom are 11:

$$df = 12 - 1 = 11$$

As indicated before, the *t* distribution changes with the sample size. This fact is taken into account in Table *T* because when entering (starting to use) the table, we must have already computed the degrees of freedom.

To find the *t* for Dr. Tee's sample, we use the one-tailed section of the table and look down the *df* column until we find the row headed by the number 11. This row lists the critical values for the *t* statistic at the .05, .01, and .001 levels of statistical significance. In this book we always use the .05 level, which, for a one-tailed test, is the first *shaded* column to the right of the *df* column. (The column for testing a two-tailed hypothesis is the second shaded column to the right of the *df* column.) We read from the table that the critical value of *t* at the .05 level of statistical significance for a one-tailed test is 1.796. This means that the computed *t* must be greater than or equal to 1.796 for us to reject the null hypothesis and accept the research hypothesis. In this case, the computed value for *t* equals 1.524, which is less than the table value of 1.796. We therefore fail to reject the null hypothesis, so we can conclude that Dr. Tee's language-training system will make no difference in the size of a child's vocabulary. Even though the mean of the sample was larger than the population mean, this difference could have occurred by chance.

Question: Before you move on, will you please explain in more detail what you mean by "degrees of freedom"?

Degrees of freedom (*df*) is a statistical term used to denote the number of scores within any distribution that are free to vary without restriction. Every distribution has a mean and so does every sample. If you remember back to Chapter 5, the sum of all the deviations from the mean, $\Sigma(X - \overline{X})$, is always equal to zero. Thus, in any sample with a fixed mean, the sum of the deviations from the mean is equal to zero. For example, suppose we have a sample of five student grades that has a mean of 87. Let's call these grades X_1, X_2, X_3, X_4, and X_5. Within reason, the first four of these scores can be anything; they are free to vary. Let's say, for example, that $X_1 = 89$, $X_2 = 84$, $X_3 = 100$, $X_4 = 96$, and we are not sure what X_5 equals. Because we know that the mean of this sample equals 87 and we know that the sum of the mean deviations must be zero, we can do the following calculations to compute the correct value for X_5:

$$(X_1 - 87) + (X_2 - 87) + (X_3 - 87) + (X_4 - 87) + (X_5 - 87) = 0$$

Substituting the known values for X_1 through X_4, we get:

$$(89 - 87) + (84 - 87) + (100 - 87) + (96 - 87) + (X_5 - 87) = 0$$
$$2 - 3 + 13 + 9 + (X_5 - 87) = 0$$
$$X_5 - 66 = 0$$
$$X_5 = 66$$

Given the first four scores, X_5 *must* be equal to 66. This last score is not free to vary. It is predetermined by the first four scores. Thus, the number of degrees of freedom of this sample is 4 because only four ($n - 1$) scores are free to vary. The concept of degrees of freedom appears again and again throughout the last several chapters of this book, but it is based on the fact that normally $n - 1$ scores in any sample are free to vary.

CONCEPT QUIZ

1. To estimate the standard error of the mean, you can either divide the _____ by the square root of $n - 1$ or divide the _____ by the square root of n.

2. For a one-tailed z test to be significant with an alpha level of .05, the absolute value of z must exceed _____ .

3. For a two-tailed z test to be significant with an alpha level of .05, the absolute value of z must exceed _____ .

4. When your sample is relatively small, the distribution of sample means is best matched by the _____ .

5. If we do not know the population standard deviation, the formula for a single-sample z test and the formula for a single-sample t test are _____ .

6. Critical values of t are found in Appendix A in _____ .

7. The number of degrees of freedom for a single-sample t test is equal to _____ .

Answers

1. sample standard deviation; estimate of the standard deviation of the population

2. 1.645

3. 1.96

4. t distribution

5. identical

6. Table T

7. $n - 1$

t TESTS BETWEEN TWO INDEPENDENT SAMPLE MEANS

Now that you know how to conduct single-sample *z* tests and *t* tests, we have to tell you that most psychological research is not designed in such a way that the mean of one sample is compared to the population mean. Although there are several reasons for this, the two main ones are that (1) the mean of the population is often not known and (2) most experimenters like to use control groups in their research. Often control groups are used as substitutes for population values. For example, in Dr. Tee's vocabulary-learning experiment, we could have compared the 12 infants in the experimental group to a similar control group that did not go through the language-training program. Then, instead of comparing the mean of the research sample to the mean of the population, we could have compared the mean of the research sample to the mean of the control sample. This is normally done by computing the difference between the two means and then comparing this difference to the mean of the **sampling distribution of differences between means**.

Yes, as you may have feared, there is yet another distribution that you need to become familiar with: the distribution of differences between means, which is generated by taking two random samples and computing the difference between their means. By doing this a great number of times, a distribution is formed. If all the samples are selected from the same population or from populations with equal means, the mean of this distribution should be zero because the sum of all the differences between the sample means should be zero. On the other hand, if there are two independent samples from populations that have different means, with population 1 being the control population and population 2 being the research population, then the distribution of differences between the sample means should have a mean equal to the difference between the two population means: $\mu_1 - \mu_2$. Thus, when we are comparing two independent samples, the null hypothesis states: The two samples derive from populations with equal means ($\mu_1 - \mu_2 = 0$). The two-tailed research hypothesis states: The two samples derive from populations with different means ($\mu_1 - \mu_2 \neq 0$).

We can use a *t* test to test these hypotheses. Note that in this case, the score we are testing is the *difference* between the two sample means. We then compare this difference to the difference between the means of the two population distributions used to create the independent samples. The following formula shows how to compute a *t* test for independent sample means:

$$t = \frac{(\overline{X}_1 - \overline{X}_2) - (\mu_1 - \mu_2)}{\sigma_{\text{diff}}} \tag{12.5}$$

Question: How do we know the means of these two different populations? And what is σ_{diff}?

Well, we really have no way of knowing these means, but luckily we don't need to know the actual means of the two different populations. Because the *t* test is used to test the null hypothesis, we need to know merely the value of $\mu_1 - \mu_2$ as predicted by the null hypothesis. As previously stated, the null hypothesis predicts that $\mu_1 - \mu_2 = 0$. So we can substitute 0 for $\mu_1 - \mu_2$ in Formula 12.5:

$$t = \frac{(\overline{X}_1 - \overline{X}_2) - (\mu_1 - \mu_2)}{\sigma_{\text{diff}}} = \frac{(\overline{X}_1 - \overline{X}_2) - 0}{\sigma_{\text{diff}}}$$

$$t = \frac{\overline{X}_1 - \overline{X}_2}{\text{est. } \sigma_{\text{diff}}} \tag{12.6}$$

The standard deviation of the distribution of differences between sample means, which is drawn from two different independent populations (population 1 and population 2), is called the **standard error of the difference between independent sample means** (σ_{diff}). It is given by the following formula:

$$\sigma_{\text{diff}} = \sqrt{\sigma^2_{\overline{x}_1} + \sigma^2_{\overline{x}_2}} \tag{12.7}$$

The standard error of the difference between independent sample means is equal to the square root of the sum of the standard error of the mean for population 1, squared, and the standard error of the mean for population 2, squared. In most cases, the standard error of the mean must be estimated from the sample standard deviations, rather than computed directly from the population values. This means that the standard error of the difference between independent sample means can be estimated by the following equivalent formulas:

$$\text{est. } \sigma_{\text{diff}} = \sqrt{(\text{est. } \sigma_{\overline{x}_1})^2 + (\text{est. } \sigma_{\overline{x}_2})^2} \tag{12.8}$$

$$\text{est. } \sigma_{\text{diff}} = \sqrt{\frac{S_1^2}{(n_1 - 1)} + \frac{S_2^2}{(n_2 - 1)}} \tag{12.9}$$

Are you thoroughly bogged down with verbiage and formulas? Let's take time to work an example; we return to the analysis of Dr. Tee's language-training experiment. Suppose that instead of having us compare the sample mean to the population mean, Dr. Tee asks us to compare her experimental group to a control group of 12 similar children who did not receive language training. The data for both groups are listed in Table 12.2. Because we will compare the mean of the control sample to the mean of the research sample, we need to change the research hypothesis to: The mean number of vocabulary words for the research sample is greater than the mean number of vocabulary words for the control sample. This implies that the research and control samples come from different populations with means of μ_1 and μ_2, respectively, and that $\mu_1 > \mu_2$. The null hypothesis states that there is no difference between the means of the research and the control populations and that $\mu_1 - \mu_2 = 0$. Knowing this, we can now compute the *t* score. We use Formulas 12.6 and 12.9, starting with Formula 12.9 to compute the estimate

Table 12.2   Number of Words in Vocabulary for Research Group of 12 Toddlers Using the Language-Training System and Control Group of 12 Toddlers Without the Language-Training System

Research group Number of words in vocabulary			Control group Number of words in vocabulary		
Child	X_1	X_1^2	Child	X_2	X_2^2
C. W.	197	38,809	P. J.	206	42,436
D. J.	223	49,729	D. M.	199	39,601
P. V.	241	58,081	Q. C.	205	42,025
J. I.	183	33,489	M. V.	203	41,209
T. B.	222	49,284	B. T.	223	49,729
B. C.	231	53,361	Z. S.	189	35,721
R. A.	297	88,209	K. H.	221	48,841
B. B.	220	48,400	B. S.	195	38,025
D. T.	188	35,344	G. S.	218	47,524
P. P.	231	53,361	A. G.	177	31,329
C. D.	210	44,100	H. D.	203	41,209
M. L.	234	54,756	K. T.	174	30,276

$\Sigma X_1 = 2677$ $\Sigma X_1^2 = 606,923$ $\Sigma X_2 = 2413$ $\Sigma X_2^2 = 487,925$

$\overline{X}_1 = 223.083$ $\overline{X}_2 = 201.083$

$S_1 = 28.474$ $S_2 = 15.030$

of the standard error of the difference between means and then using Formula 12.6 to compute the *t* score:

$$\text{est. } \sigma_{\text{diff}} = \sqrt{\frac{S_1^2}{(n_1 - 1)} + \frac{S_2^2}{(n_2 - 1)}} \tag{12.9}$$

$$= \sqrt{\frac{28.474^2}{12 - 1} + \frac{15.030^2}{12 - 1}} = \sqrt{\frac{810.769}{11} + \frac{225.901}{11}}$$

$$= \sqrt{73.706 + 20.536} = \sqrt{94.242} = 9.708$$

Substituting the appropriate values in Formula 12.6, we get

$$t = \frac{(\overline{X}_1 - \overline{X}_2)}{\text{est. } \sigma_{\text{diff}}} = \frac{(223.083 - 201.083)}{9.708} \tag{12.6}$$

$$= \frac{22.000}{9.708} = 2.266$$

So we computed the *t* score. Now we need to calculate the degrees of freedom and then refer to Table *T* to determine whether the score is significant.

Question: When we look up the critical value of *t* in Table *T*, which $n - 1$ do we use for the degrees of freedom?

When you conduct a *t* test between two independent samples, the total number of degrees of freedom is equal to the degrees of freedom in sample 1 plus the degrees of freedom in sample 2:

$$df = (n_1 - 1) + (n_2 - 1) \tag{12.10}$$

In the preceding example, the total number of degrees of freedom is

$$
\begin{aligned}
df &= (n_1 - 1) + (n_2 - 1) \\
&= (12 - 1) + (12 - 1) \\
&= 11 + 11 = 22
\end{aligned}
$$

By looking in Table *T*, we find that for a one-tailed research hypothesis with 22 degrees of freedom, the critical value of *t* equals 1.717. Our computed *t* score of 2.266 is greater than the table value, so we can reject the null hypothesis and accept the research hypothesis. This means that the language-training method does indeed lead to a more expanded vocabulary for 2-year-olds who participated in the program than for those in the control group who did not participate.

t TESTS FOR CORRELATED SAMPLES

Not all *t* tests are conducted between independent sample means. Frequently, the two samples are positively correlated with each other, as in a within-subjects design where each subject participates in each of the experimental conditions. A case in point is the opening exercise for this chapter, where we asked you to time how long it takes you to name the shapes from the shapes-alone list, and then to time how long it takes you to name the shapes from the combined words-and-shapes list. If this were an experiment, you as a subject would have participated in each condition, and you would have been a member of two correlated samples. If you asked several friends to participate in the same experiment, you might obtain results similar to those in Table 12.3. From this table you can see that it takes longer, on the average, for most people to name the shapes on the words-and-shapes list than on the shapes-alone list.

Let's analyze the results to be sure that the observed difference is not due

Table 12.3 The Time (in seconds) Needed for Ten Subjects to Name the Shapes from Two Different Lists

Subject	List 1 (shapes only)	List 2 (words and shapes)
H. J.	22	27
T. B.	27	25
J. J.	23	32
M. V.	29	32
D. J.	32	51
P. T.	24	33
N. Z.	33	30
A. H.	23	29
K. L.	15	24
S. E.	12	20
	$\Sigma X_1 = 240$	$\Sigma X_2 = 303$
	$\bar{X}_1 = 24.0$	$\bar{X}_2 = 30.3$
	$S_1 = 6.403$	$S_2 = 7.925$
	est. $\sigma_{\bar{x}_1} = 2.134$	est. $\sigma_{\bar{x}_2} = 2.642$
	$r = .674$	

to mere chance. To do so, we need to conduct a *t* test. This *t* test, however, must be different from those previously described; these two samples are not independent because the same subjects participated in both conditions. Therefore, we must conduct a *t* test for *correlated samples*.

The major difference between a *t* test for *independent samples* and a *t* test for *correlated samples* is that in the latter, the correlation between the samples can be used to reduce the size of the standard error of the difference between the sample means. Reducing the standard error of the difference can be a real advantage because the smaller the standard error of the difference, the larger the *t*. Because each subject is used twice, we can compute the amount of error that is due to the variability of each subject and use this to reduce the standard error of the difference, thereby increasing the size of *t*. To illustrate this reduction, we present the formulas for computing the standard error of the difference for both independent and correlated samples. The formula for the standard error of the difference between *independent* sample means is

$$\sigma_{\text{diff}} = \sqrt{\sigma^2_{\bar{x}_1} + \sigma^2_{\bar{x}_2}} \tag{12.7}$$

Now, compare this to the formula for the **standard error of the difference between correlated sample means:**

$$\sigma_{\text{diff}} = \sqrt{\sigma^2_{\bar{x}_1} + \sigma^2_{\bar{x}_2} - (2 \cdot r \cdot \sigma_{\bar{x}_1} \cdot \sigma_{\bar{x}_2})} \tag{12.11}$$

Did you notice that the standard error of the difference between means is made smaller by subtracting a factor of the correlation between the two samples?

By examining Formula 12.11 closely, you can see that if $r = 0$, the entire expression within the parentheses equals zero, and Formula 12.11 reduces to Formula 12.7. This is logical because, as you may remember from our discussion of correlation in Chapter 8, samples that are totally independent of each other have a zero correlation.

Unfortunately, Formula 12.11 is practical only when the population standard deviations of distribution 1 and distribution 2 are known. When they aren't, as is most often the case, we must estimate these values and use Formula 12.12 to estimate the standard error of the difference:

$$\text{est. } \sigma_{\text{diff}} = \sqrt{(\text{est. } \sigma_{\bar{x}_1})^2 + (\text{est. } \sigma_{\bar{x}_2})^2 - (2 \cdot r \cdot \text{est. } \sigma_{\bar{x}_1} \cdot \text{est. } \sigma_{\bar{x}_2})} \tag{12.12}$$

Now we're ready to run a *t* test on the data in Table 12.3. First, we compute the standard error of the difference. We need to use Formula 12.12 because we have no population data and the samples are correlated:

$$\begin{aligned}
\text{est. } \sigma_{\text{diff}} &= \sqrt{(\text{est. } \sigma_{\bar{x}_1})^2 + (\text{est. } \sigma_{\bar{x}_2})^2 - (2 \cdot r \cdot \text{est. } \sigma_{\bar{x}_1} \cdot \text{est. } \sigma_{\bar{x}_2})} \\
&= \sqrt{2.134^2 + 2.642^2 - (2 \cdot .674 \cdot 2.134 \cdot 2.642)} \\
&= \sqrt{4.554 + 6.980 - 7.600} = \sqrt{3.934} \\
&= 1.983
\end{aligned}$$

The formula for *t* remains the same as that for independent samples. Using the value just computed for the estimate of the standard error of the difference as well as the mean for 1 and the mean for 2 from Table 12.3, we can now compute the *t*:

$$t = \frac{\bar{X}_1 - \bar{X}_2}{\text{est. } \sigma_{\text{diff}}} = \frac{24 - 30.3}{1.983} = \frac{-6.3}{1.983} = -3.177 \tag{12.6}$$

Again, we need to compute the degrees of freedom before looking up the *t* score in Table *T* to tell whether it is significant. The number of degrees of freedom for a *t* test between two correlated means is equal to the number of pairs of scores minus 1:

$$df_{\text{correlated samples}} = \text{number of pairs} - 1 \tag{12.13}$$

We have ten pairs of scores in our sample, so

$$df = 10 - 1 = 9$$

Because our research hypothesis is one-tailed (we predicted that it would take longer to name the shapes when the words are present), we can look up the critical value of *t* in Table *T* for a one-tailed test with 9 degrees of freedom. That value is 1.833.

Question: Do we fail to reject the null hypothesis because our computed value for *t*, −3.177, is less than the critical value in Table *T*, 1.833?

No, not in this case. If, as is true in this example, your hypothesis is one-tailed and it predicts that the second mean (naming the symbols with the words) will be greater than the first mean (naming the symbols alone), then your computed value *should* be negative. Before you even look up the *t* value in the table, you need to analyze what your hypothesis predicts. If it predicts that the second mean will be greater than the first mean, you should expect a negative *t*-value because the formula requires that you subtract the second mean from the first. If, on the other hand, your hypothesis predicts that the first mean will be greater than the second, you should expect a positive *t*-value. Remember, *when the research hypothesis predicts a negative* t *value and your computed* t*-value is negative, or when the research hypothesis predicts a positive* t*-value and your computed* t*-value is positive, you can ignore the sign when looking up the value in Table* T *and compare the absolute value of* t *to the critical value listed in the table.* On the other hand, if the research hypothesis predicts a value in the opposite direction of your computed value (for instance, if it predicts a positive value and you compute a negative value), you don't even need to bother looking it up because you know it is not significant, and you must fail to reject the null hypothesis. In our example, because the hypothesis predicts that the second mean will be greater than the first and should therefore be negative, we ignore the minus sign and look up the absolute value of our computed *t* in Table *T*. We find that the computed value is greater than the critical value in the table, so we can reject the null hypothesis and accept the research hypothesis. It does take longer to name the shapes when the conflicting words are present.

The above holds true for one-tailed hypotheses. With two-tailed, non-directional hypotheses, it doesn't matter whether the computed *t*-value is positive or negative. If the absolute value of the computed *t* is larger than the value in Table *T*, then it is significant because the hypothesis doesn't specify the direction of significance; it just specifies that there is a difference, no matter the direction.

Before we move off this topic, we want to emphasize that one-tailed hypotheses and one-tailed tests are a bit tricky. A computed value for *t* is significant *only* if: (1) the difference between the means is in the same direction as that predicted by the research hypothesis *and* (2) the absolute value of *t* is greater than the critical value found in Table *T*. You do not even need to compute a *t* or look up a critical value when the difference between the means for the two samples lies in the wrong direction (if one is positive and the other negative).

Question: Life is too short to have to compute a correlation coefficient each time I need to do a *t* test between correlated sample means. Isn't there a faster way?

Yes. When you don't already know the correlation coefficient and the standard deviation for each sample, an alternative we call the **difference method** can save you considerable time. This method for computing *t* relies on the differences between the paired scores rather than on the standard deviations and the correlation coefficient to calculate the estimate of the standard error of the difference between means. The formula for the estimated standard error of the difference between means using difference scores is:

$$\text{est. } \sigma_{\text{diff}} = \sqrt{\frac{\frac{\Sigma D^2}{n} - \overline{D}^2}{n-1}} \tag{12.14}$$

where $\overline{D}$ is the mean of the difference scores and ΣD^2 is the sum of the squared differences.

In Table 12.4, the difference scores and the sum of their squares have been calculated for the data in the shape task analyzed here. We obtained the differences by substracting the X_2-value from the X_1-value in each pair. We then added these differences and computed the mean of the differences. (The mean of the differences, in this case −6.3 seconds, is equal to the difference between the means of the two correlated samples, 24 seconds minus 30.3 seconds.) Next, we squared each of the difference scores and then added the squares of the differences. With the data from Table 12.4, we can compute the standard error of the difference between the means:

$$\text{est. } \sigma_{\text{diff}} = \sqrt{\frac{\frac{\Sigma D^2}{n} - \overline{D}^2}{n-1}} \tag{12.14}$$

$$= \sqrt{\frac{\frac{751}{10} - (-6.3)^2}{10-1}} = \sqrt{\frac{75.1 - 39.69}{9}}$$

$$= \sqrt{\frac{35.41}{9}} = \sqrt{3.934} = 1.983$$

This value is identical to the one we computed for the standard error of the difference between the means when we used the formula with the correlation coefficient.

Table 12.4 The Data Listed in Table 12.3, Plus Differences (D) and Differences Squared (D^2) Between Time (in seconds) Needed to Name Shapes from Two Different Lists

Subject	List 1 (shapes only)	List 2 (words and shapes)	D	D^2
H. J.	22	27	−5	25
T. B.	27	25	2	4
J. J.	23	32	−9	81
M. V.	29	32	−3	9
D. J.	32	51	−19	361
P. T.	24	33	−9	81
N. Z.	33	30	3	9
A. H.	23	29	−6	36
K. L.	15	24	−9	81
S. E.	12	20	−8	64
			$\Sigma D = -63$	$\Sigma D^2 = 751$
			$\overline{D} = -6.3$	

Because the mean of the difference scores is always equal to the difference between the means of the two samples, we can use the following formula to compute the *t* score:

$$t = \frac{\overline{D} - (\mu_1 - \mu_2)}{\text{est. } \sigma_{\text{diff}}} \tag{12.15}$$

The null hypothesis states that there is no difference between the two populations; therefore, $\mu_1 - \mu_2 = 0$. Knowing this, we can simplify Formula 12.15 as

$$t = \frac{\overline{D}}{\text{est. } \sigma_{\text{diff}}} \tag{12.16}$$

Now we can compute the *t* score using the mean of the differences and the standard error of the difference between the means just computed:

$$t = \frac{\overline{D}}{\text{est. } \sigma_{\text{diff}}} = \frac{-6.3}{1.983} = -3.177$$

This value is exactly the same as the *t* score previously computed for the same data using the correlation coefficient. As you have seen, the difference method can be much easier and faster than the method first described, which involved computing the standard deviations and standard error of the means, in addition to calculating the correlation coefficient.

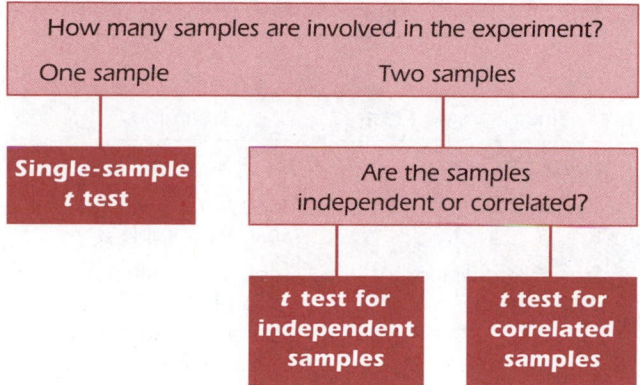

Figure 12.4 This flowchart can help you determine which of the three *t* tests to use.

Question: I'm really confused. It sounds as if there are a lot of different kinds of *t* tests. How do I know which one to use?

When you have one or two samples, there are only three possible *t* tests to choose from. Knowing which one to use is really not at all confusing if you just take the time to examine your research design and ask yourself the questions in the flowchart in Figure 12.4.

Question: That sounds easy enough, but it would help if you would review the steps that are involved in each type of *t* test.

Table 12.5 summarizes the factors you need to compute each *t* test. It is arranged in a way that makes it easy to compare the *t* tests with one another.

The statistical analyses described in this chapter apply to experiments that have only one independent variable and one or two samples. Obviously, many psychological experiments are not limited to this basic design. Experiments often involve more than one independent variable and three or more samples. To analyze these more complicated experimental designs, we might use different statistical tests such as the one- or two-way analysis of variance. These analyses are described in the next two chapters.

C O N C E P T   Q U I Z

1. In a *t* test between two independent sample means, the difference between the two means is divided by the _____ .

2. The standard error of the difference between two independent sample means is equal to the square root of the _____ .

Table 12.5   Factors Needed to Compute the Different *t* Tests

Single-sample *t* test	*t* test for independent samples	*t* test for correlated samples (difference method)
Population mean		
Sample mean	Mean for sample 1 Mean for sample 2	Mean of the differences
Standard deviation of the sample	Standard deviation of sample 1 Standard deviation of sample 2	
Estimate of standard error of the mean	Estimate of standard error of the mean for sample 1 Estimate of standard error of the mean for sample 2	
	Estimate of standard error of the difference	Estimate of standard error of the difference

3. The number of degrees of freedom in a *t* test between independent sample means is equal to _____ .

4. If the two samples are positively correlated, we can still conduct a *t* test, but the _____ must take into account the _____ .

5. The degrees of freedom for a *t* test for correlated samples is equal to _____ .

6. The mean of the differences between two samples is _____ the difference between the means of the two samples.

7. The difference formula for computing the standard error of the difference between two correlated means can save time and effort because it does not require the computation of _____ .

Answers

1. standard error of the difference between two independent sample means

2. standard error of the mean for sample 1, squared, plus the standard error of the mean for sample 2, squared

3. the degrees of freedom in sample 1 ($n_1 - 1$) plus the degrees of freedom in sample 2 ($n_2 - 1$)

4. standard error of the difference between the means; correlation coefficient

5. the number of pairs minus 1

6. equal to

7. the sample means, the sample standard deviations, or the correlation coefficient

S U M M A R Y

The three major types of *t* tests are: single-sample *t* tests, *t* tests for independent samples, and *t* tests for correlated samples. A single-sample *t* test is similar to a *z* test, where a single sample mean is compared to the mean of the population. In the single-sample *t* test, the population mean is subtracted from the sample mean and then divided by the standard error of the mean. However, instead of looking up the resulting value in the normal curve table, the researcher refers to Table *T*, which lists critical values of the *t* statistic. In order to enter this table, it is necessary not only to compute the value of *t* but also to calculate the number of degrees of freedom in the research sample. The number of degrees of freedom for a single-sample *t* test is equal to the number of subjects in the sample minus 1.

When you want to compare the means of two independent samples, you can also conduct a *t* test. A *t* test for independent sample means is calculated by subtracting the mean of the second sample from the mean of the first sample and then dividing the result by the standard error of the difference between the means. The number of degrees of freedom for a *t* test for independent sample means is equal to the degrees of freedom in the first sample, $n_1 - 1$, plus the degrees of freedom in the second sample, $n_2 - 1$. Or it is equal to the number of subjects in the first sample plus the number of subjects in the second sample, minus 2.

The means of two correlated samples can be compared using the *t* test for correlated samples. When two samples are correlated, the correlation can be used to reduce the size of the standard error of the difference between means, thereby increasing the size of *t*. Two separate methods were discussed for computing a *t* score from two correlated samples. One method uses the correlation coefficient to compute the standard error of the difference between the means, whereas the other method uses the differences between the paired scores. No matter which procedure is used to compute the *t* score for correlated samples, the number of degrees of freedom is equal to the number of pairs minus 1.

K E Y   T E R M S

t distribution
t test
degrees of freedom
sampling distribution of
    differences between means

standard error of the difference
    between independent sample
    means
standard error of the difference
    between correlated sample
    means
difference method

F O R M U L A S

$$\text{est. } \sigma_{\bar{x}} = \frac{\text{est. } \sigma}{\sqrt{n}} \tag{12.1}$$

$$\text{est. } \sigma_{\bar{x}} = \frac{S}{\sqrt{n-1}} \tag{12.2}$$

$$t = \frac{\bar{X} - \mu_{\bar{x}}}{\text{est. } \sigma_{\bar{x}}} \tag{12.3}$$

$$df = n - 1 \tag{12.4}$$

$$t = \frac{(\bar{X}_1 - \bar{X}_2) - (\mu_1 - \mu_2)}{\sigma_{\text{diff}}} \tag{12.5}$$

$$t = \frac{\bar{X}_1 - \bar{X}_2}{\text{est. } \sigma_{\text{diff}}} \tag{12.6}$$

$$\sigma_{\text{diff}} = \sqrt{\sigma^2_{\bar{x}_1} + \sigma^2_{\bar{x}_2}} \tag{12.7}$$

$$\text{est. } \sigma_{\text{diff}} = \sqrt{(\text{est. } \sigma_{\bar{x}_1})^2 + (\text{est. } \sigma_{\bar{x}_2})^2} \tag{12.8}$$

$$\text{est. } \sigma_{\text{diff}} = \sqrt{\frac{S_1^2}{(n_1 - 1)} + \frac{S_2^2}{(n_2 - 1)}} \tag{12.9}$$

$$df = (n_1 - 1) + (n_2 - 1) \tag{12.10}$$

$$\sigma_{\text{diff}} = \sqrt{\sigma^2_{\bar{x}_1} + \sigma^2_{\bar{x}_2} - (2 \cdot r \cdot \sigma_{\bar{x}_1} \cdot \sigma_{\bar{x}_2})} \tag{12.11}$$

$$\text{est. } \sigma_{\text{diff}} = \sqrt{(\text{est. } \sigma_{\bar{x}_1})^2 + (\text{est. } \sigma_{\bar{x}_2})^2 - (2 \cdot r \cdot \text{est. } \sigma_{\bar{x}_1} \cdot \text{est. } \sigma_{\bar{x}_2})} \tag{12.12}$$

$$df_{\text{correlated samples}} = \text{number of pairs} - 1 \tag{12.13}$$

$$\text{est. } \sigma_{\text{diff}} = \sqrt{\frac{\frac{\Sigma D^2}{n} - \bar{D}^2}{n - 1}} \tag{12.14}$$

$$t = \frac{\bar{D} - (\mu_1 - \mu_2)}{\text{est. } \sigma_{\text{diff}}} \tag{12.15}$$

$$t = \frac{\bar{D}}{\text{est. } \sigma_{\text{diff}}} \tag{12.16}$$

P R O B L E M S

1. Suppose that as a military psychologist, you know that the population of sonar operators has a mean identification rate of 82 targets out of 100, with a population standard deviation of 12 targets. You have just developed a new sonar training system that, you claim, will increase the number of targets correctly identified. Using the data from the 15 trainees listed here, conduct a t test to determine whether they perform significantly better than the population trained in the traditional manner.

Number of targets correctly identified out of 100				
88	79	92	87	82
86	91	80	77	83
91	85	82	89	94

2. Mrs. Yonrev thinks that her class of fourth-grade students is exceptionally bright. In order to test this hypothesis, she decides to compare her students' IQ scores to a population mean of 100 and a population standard deviation of 16. Using school records, she computes the mean IQ of her 25 students and finds that it is 110. From these data, compute t and state whether the hypothesis suggested by Mrs. Yonrev can be accepted.

3. Conduct a t test to see whether for a sample of 65 people, a mean of 83 with a standard deviation of 5.4 is significantly greater than a population mean of 80.

4. A psychologist studying the human factors of computer keyboards sets up an experiment to compare two different keyboard designs. He determines the number of words per minute typed by one group on keyboard A and the number typed by another group on keyboard B. Use the results listed in the table to compute t, and determine whether the mean typing speeds on the two keyboards are significantly different.

Words per minute	
Keyboard A	Keyboard B
54	47
62	51
75	54
59	62
78	44
64	51
69	48
72	65
50	42
73	44
	71
	68

5. Herman Boncor, the local dog catcher, thinks that the dogs at the pound tend to bark less when they are fed expensive brand-name dog food as opposed to a cheaper generic brand of dog food. To test his theory, he feeds one group of dogs the expensive brand for 1 week and records the number of barks during the 1-hour period following each feeding. The next week, he feeds an entirely different group the inexpensive dog food and records the number of barks during 1 hour after each feeding. The means, standard deviations, and number of dogs in each sample are

listed in the table. Conduct a *t* test to see whether the type of food made a significant difference in the barking behavior of the dogs.

Barks per hour	
Expensive food	Inexpensive food
$\bar{X}_1 = 135$	$\bar{X}_2 = 142$
$S_1 = 23.5$	$S_2 = 32.4$
$n_1 = 26$	$n_2 = 17$

6. A researcher studying the effects of alcohol asks 25 people to take a reaction time task before and after drinking 1 ounce of alcohol per 50 pounds of body weight. The results for the pretest and posttest, as well as the correlation between the two tests, are listed. Use these results to compute the appropriate *t* test to tell whether there is a significant difference between the pretest and posttest results.

Pretest	Posttest
$\bar{X}_1 = 235$ msec	$\bar{X}_2 = 342$ msec
$S_1 = 52$ msec	$S_2 = 85$ msec
Correlation = .77	

7. An eyeglass manufacturer is interested in finding out whether people can read a computer screen faster using glasses with specially coated lenses as opposed to regular uncoated lenses. Seventeen people are asked to read a computer screen for 20 minutes with the coated lenses; on a separate day, the same people are asked to read a computer screen for 20 minutes using lenses without the coating. Using the summary of results, compute a *t* test to determine whether the coating significantly improves the reading speed of these 17 people.

Number of pages read	
With coating	Without coating
$\bar{X}_1 = 13.4$	$\bar{X}_2 = 12.7$
$S_1 = 2.6$	$S_2 = 2.1$
Correlation = .64	

8. A human factors psychologist who works for an automobile manufacturer believes that it is possible to decrease the number of brake pedal errors by changing the location of the brake pedal in relation to the gas pedal in the best-selling model, the Zoomer Special. He asks ten subjects to drive in a driving simulator with the old pedal arrangement. Later he asks the same ten subjects to drive in a simulator using the new pedal arrangement. The number of errors for each subject in both conditions is listed. Using these data, test the preceding hypothesis by computing *t*.

Subject	New	Old
H. J.	3	5
G. M.	5	7
C. M.	3	4
J. P.	7	9
F. C.	10	14
M. G.	3	3
T. D.	7	9
H. A.	13	11
C. A.	4	6
T. C.	2	4

9. Twelve subjects underwent an assertiveness training program. Before and after completing the program, they were asked to check off on a list adjectives that describe their personality. The number of adjectives describing positive attributes were compiled in the "before" condition and in the "after" condition. Using the data in the table, compute t.

Subject	Before	After
1	14	21
2	21	22
3	24	21
4	16	19
5	18	18
6	20	25
7	15	17
8	20	18
9	17	21
10	16	24
11	19	21
12	12	15

10. In your Introduction to Psychology classes, you probably learned that short-term memory has a capacity of seven items, plus or minus two. But is this capacity the same for different categories of items? Might it not be possible to store more words than letters or numbers in short-term memory? The data in the table are from an experiment comparing the short-term memory capacity of 24 subjects who were randomly assigned to one of two conditions. In the first condition, the subjects were asked to remember a list of words; in the other condition, the subjects were asked to remember a list of numbers. Generate a null hypothesis and a research hypothesis for this experiment. Then compute t and tell whether it is significant.

Words	Numbers
5	4
7	6
5	6
4	3
3	7
8	5
3	8
7	9
8	7
8	7
5	4
7	9

11. Given the computed t value and the significance level, what conclusions can you reach about the experiment described in Problem 10?

12. A psychologist who is an expert on proofreading has developed two ten-page manuscripts for an experiment. One manuscript has no errors on the first seven pages and then 20 errors on the last three pages. The other manuscript has an average of 5 errors per page on the first seven pages and the identical 20 errors on the last three pages. The dependent variable in this experiment is the number of errors subjects find on the last three pages of the manuscript they are assigned. The psychologist predicts that subjects who are assigned the manuscript with the errors throughout will catch more errors on the last three pages. Using the data in the table, compute t and determine whether it is significant.

Errors in first 7 pages	No errors in first 7 pages
13	10
18	12
7	6
15	10
14	6
12	8
17	3
19	9
15	10

13. State the null hypothesis and the research hypothesis for the experiment described in Problem 12. Given the *t*-value that you computed, what conclusions can you draw about these hypotheses?

14. A physiological psychologist has reason to expect that the blood level of a particular hormone will increase when an animal is under stress. To induce this stress, he places 25 rats in an ice water bath and allows each rat to swim in the bath for 30 seconds. After the swim, the psychologist takes a blood sample and measures the hormone level. The population value for normal, nonstressed rats is 250 micrograms of this hormone per milliliter of blood. The mean for the sample of stressed rats is 267 micrograms of this hormone per milliliter of blood, with the standard deviation of the sample being 25 micrograms. Using the appropriate *t* test, determine whether stressed rats do indeed have significantly increased hormone levels.

15. Is computer-synthesized speech as easy to understand as speech that is spoken by a human? To find an answer to that question, we randomly assigned 20 people to one of two different groups. One group was asked to transcribe a 100-word statement "spoken" by a computer, and the other group was asked to transcribe the same 100-word statement spoken by a human. The mean number of errors made in the synthesized condition was 10, with a standard deviation of 4. The mean number of errors made in the human condition was 8, with a standard deviation of 2. Use the appropriate *t* to determine whether the difference between these two conditions is significant.

For Problems 16–25, given the information presented, compute an appropriate *t* and tell whether it is significant.

16.

Control group	Experimental group
$\bar{X}_1 = 124$	$\bar{X}_2 = 130$
$S_1 = 23$	$S_2 = 32$
$n_1 = 37$	$n_2 = 26$

17.

Experimental group	Population
$\bar{X} = 87$	$\mu = 92$
$S = 10$	$\sigma = 3$
$n = 36$	

18.

Pretest	Posttest
$\bar{X}_1 = 12$	$\bar{X}_2 = 13$
$S_1 = 2$	$S_2 = 3$
$n_1 = 50$	$n_2 = 50$
$r = .67$	

19.

Pretest	Posttest
$\bar{X}_1 = 88$	$\bar{X}_2 = 97$
$S_1 = 23$	$S_2 = 41$
$n_1 = 65$	$n_2 = 65$
	$r = .38$

20.

Experimental group	Population
$\bar{X} = 45$	$\mu = 49$
$S = 24$	
$n = 101$	

21.

Control group	Experimental group
$\bar{X}_1 = 227$	$\bar{X}_2 = 245$
$S_1 = 29$	$S_2 = 42$
$n_1 = 10$	$n_2 = 17$

22.

Control group	Experimental group
$\bar{X}_1 = 64$	$\bar{X}_2 = 45$
$S_1 = 42$	$S_2 = 34$
$n_1 = 5$	$n_2 = 5$

23.

Experimental group	Population
$\bar{X} = 123$	$\mu = 122$
$S = 4$	
$n = 101$	

24.

Pretest	Posttest
$\bar{X}_1 = 38$	$\bar{X}_2 = 45$
$S_1 = 16$	$S_2 = 18$
$n_1 = 50$	$n_2 = 50$
	$r = .28$

25.

Experimental group	Population
$\bar{X} = 3$	$\mu = 0$
$S = 22$	$\sigma = 30$
$n = 144$	

One-Way Analysis of Variance

I
magine yourself as an affluent professional sitting in the front seat of your brand-new Mercedes. You close the door, fasten the seat belt, insert the key in the ignition, and start the motor. After shifting into reverse, you turn around and look behind you as you back your car out of the garage. Suddenly the car begins to speed up. You jam your foot on the brake pedal but instead of stopping, the car accelerates to more than 40 miles per hour before smashing into your neighbor's car on the other side of the street. Luckily, you are not seriously hurt. But your Mercedes and your neighbor's BMW are both a total loss. After hearing your explanation, both your insurance company and that of your neighbor insist that you have a mechanic inspect your car's brakes, engine, and throttle control linkage. Your mechanic, as well as a couple of other ones, is unable to detect any mechanical malfunction that might be responsible for your accident.

The phenomenon just described has become known as "unintended acceleration." Automobiles accelerate out of control while their drivers press as hard as they can on what they think is the brake pedal, but the cars stop only when they hit something or when the ignition is turned off. Fortunately, this kind of accident is relatively rare. Nevertheless, several accidents of this type have been the basis of lawsuits against automobile manufacturers for faulty car design. Although unintended acceleration sounds as if it is due to some sort of intermittent mechanical malfunction, most researchers who have studied these accidents believe that they are the result of driver error, not a malfunction of the automobile (Vernoy & Tomerlin, 1990).

Any time a person makes a movement, there is some possibility of making an error. Even a very practiced movement like writing your name, climbing stairs, or eating with a fork is not perfectly accurate *every time*. Sometimes your pen makes an upsweep at the wrong time, occasionally you trip on a step, and sometimes food falls off your fork. In like manner, well-practiced drivers may just happen to hit the accelerator rather than the brake pedal in a panic situation.

Fortunately, driver mistakes are relatively rare, but they do occur and can be measured and documented. Let's say that as a result of your accident, you decide to study unintended acceleration. First, you need to develop some kind of viable hypothesis. After examining the related research and scrutinizing the positions of the pedals in various cars, you come to believe that the distance between the brake and the accelerator pedals may be a contributing factor in driver error. To test this hypothesis, you design an experiment in which subjects use one of three driving simulators, each with a different pedal arrangement. In the close-pedal arrangement, the distance between pedals is only 1 inch; in the moderate-pedal arrangement, it's 2 inches; and in the far-pedal arrangement, 3 inches. You assign ten subjects to each condition and instruct them to drive their simulators for 4 hours. During these 4 hours, the number of errors made by each driver is recorded, as shown in Table 13.1.

Table 13.1 Number of Pedal Errors
with Three Pedal Arrangements in a
Driving Simulator

Pedal arrangement		
Type 1	Type 2	Type 3
3	4	6
2	3	4
4	4	3
1	3	4
0	5	7
2	4	6
3	2	5
2	5	8
1	4	5
2	4	6

Explanation: Pedal
arrangement type 1 has a 1-
inch separation between
brake and accelerator, type 2
has a 2-inch separation, and
type 3 has a 3-inch
separation.

After gathering your data, you are faced with analyzing them. How do you do
this with three groups of subjects?

Question: Can't I just do *t* tests among the different groups?

ANALYSIS OF VARIANCE: ONE TEST IS BETTER THAN MANY

All *t* tests are conducted between only two samples, so if we want to run *t* tests
for this experiment, we have to conduct three separate tests to analyze these
data: one between pedal arrangement types 1 and 2, one between types 1 and
3, and a third between 2 and 3. If there were four groups, we would have to
conduct six *t* tests, and if there were five groups, we would have to conduct
ten. Besides taking a lot of time, doing multiple *t* tests is statistically question-
able because with every *t* test performed on the same data, the probability of
making a Type I error increases. We know that the probability of a Type I
error is equal to α, or .05, for each individual test, so we can use Formula 10.3
(because these two events are not mutually exclusive) to figure out the
probability of either test A or test B being significant just by chance when we
do two tests at the same time:

$$p(A \text{ or } B) = p(A) + p(B) - [p(A) \text{ and } p(B)] \qquad (10.3)$$
$$= .05 + .05 - [.05 \cdot .05] = .10 - .0025$$
$$= .0975$$

Therefore, the probability of getting at least one significant result just by chance when you do two simultaneous t tests is almost one in ten. If we expand this to the situation with three tests, as for Table 13.1, we have:

$$p[(A \text{ or } B) \text{ or } C] = p(A \text{ or } B) + p(C) - [p(A \text{ or } B) \cdot p(C)]$$
$$= .0975 + .05 - [.0975 \cdot .05] = .1475 - .0049$$
$$= .1426$$

The probability is about one in seven that we will get at least one significant result just by chance. As you can see, this error escalates as you do additional t tests. Therefore, conducting multiple t tests is not statistically valid. Fortunately, statisticians have developed a means of comparing multiple samples that *is* statistically valid: analysis of variance.

HYPOTHESIS TESTING AND ANALYSIS OF VARIANCE

Both the t test and the analysis of variance are tests of the null and research hypotheses. The difference between them is that the t test is used when the research design involves a comparison of two samples, whereas the **one-way analysis of variance** is used when the research design involves a comparison of three or more levels of one independent variable. The null hypotheses for the t test and the analysis of variance are similar. In a t test, the null hypothesis states that $\mu_1 = \mu_2$, meaning that the two samples both come from the same population or from populations that have the same means, and there is no difference between them. In an analysis of variance, the null hypothesis states that $\mu_1 = \mu_2 = \mu_3 = \cdots = \mu_k$, where k is the number of levels of the independent variable. This means that there is no difference between the sample means of any of the levels. The research hypotheses for a t test and an analysis of variance are also similar. In a t test, the research hypothesis predicts that the two samples come from distributions that have different population means. In an analysis of variance, the research hypothesis predicts that at least one of the sample means comes from a population different from that of the other sample means. As explained in Chapter 12, the point of running a t test is to determine whether the null hypothesis can be safely rejected. The same is true for an analysis of variance. If the null hypothesis is rejected, then at least part of the research hypothesis is supported because the null hypothesis and the research hypothesis are mutually exclusive. This is the reason for conducting an analysis of variance: to see whether the null hypothesis can be rejected.

CONDUCTING AN ANALYSIS OF VARIANCE

Basically, an analysis of variance is an evaluation of the random differences between scores or subjects. In any research involving three or more groups, with each group containing several subjects, it is possible that any differences between the groups are due either to experimental manipulation or to chance differences between the subjects in the different groups. For example, the means of the three groups shown in Table 13.1 are all different from one another. The type 1 pedal arrangement has a mean of 2 errors, whereas the type 2 pedal arrangement has a mean of 3.8 errors and the type 3 pedal arrangement has a mean of 5.4 errors. These differences may be because increasing the separation between the pedals causes more errors, or because just by chance the people who tend to make more pedal errors were assigned to the type 3 pedal arrangement. If the null hypothesis is true and the independent variable has no real effect, then the differences in the number of errors for the three pedal arrangements are due solely to chance differences in the drivers' abilities.

To test whether differences among sample groups are due merely to chance, we can conduct an analysis of variance. In an analysis of variance, we use the data gathered from the samples to make two separate estimates of the variance in the population. We arrive at these estimates using two very different methods, and then we compare the two estimates to see whether they are similar.

Question: Why do you estimate the variance in the population? How does that tell you whether the differences between the samples are due to chance?

Merely estimating the population variance tells you nothing. The key is in *comparing* two separate estimates that are arrived at using two distinctly different methods. If both estimates are similar or exactly the same, then it stands to reason that the samples are probably from the same population and the null hypothesis is true. Most likely, the manipulation of the independent variable had no effect, and any difference between the groups is due to subject variability. On the other hand, if the estimates are very different, then at least one of the samples probably comes from a population different from the other samples, so the research hypothesis is true. Most likely, the manipulation of the independent variable was the cause of the difference between the sample groups.

Question: What are the two methods used to estimate the population variance?

One of the methods estimates the population variance by using the variance *within* each sample, or group. The other method uses the difference *between* the means of the samples, or groups. We discuss these methods in detail, but first we need to explain the notation we are using.

Thus far we have used the symbol est. σ for the estimate of the population standard deviation and est. σ^2 for the estimate of the population variance. In an analysis of variance we use a different term for the variance estimate: the **mean square,** abbreviated **MS.** The mean square is so called because it is the *mean* (the average) of the *squared* deviation scores used to calculate the variation. Furthermore, until this point in the book, we have used n to represent the number of scores in a sample. But in calculating certain values for an analysis of variance we have three different n-values, so we need to denote each in a different way. We will use lowercase n to indicate the number of subjects or scores in a sample, lowercase k to indicate the number of samples, and N_{total} to indicate the total number of subjects or scores in all the samples combined. Now we examine the two approaches used to estimate the population variance, or the mean square.

Two Methods for Estimating the Population Variance

One approach is to examine the variation of the scores *within* each sample group. Remember, the variance of a sample is the mean of the squared deviation scores of that sample. Formula 10.6 estimates the population standard deviation using data from only one sample:

$$\text{est. } \sigma = \sqrt{\frac{\Sigma(X - \overline{X})^2}{n - 1}} \tag{10.6}$$

The formula for estimating the population variance is the square of this:

$$\text{est. } \sigma^2 = \frac{\Sigma(X - \overline{X})^2}{n - 1} \tag{10.5}$$

When there is more than one group, as in the pedal error experiment, we can generate several estimates of the population variance and then average them to obtain a combined estimate from the several groups. The formula for this combined estimate, if all the groups are the same size, looks like this:

$$\text{MS}_{wg} = \frac{\Sigma(X_1 - \overline{X}_1)^2 + \Sigma(X_2 - \overline{X}_2)^2 + \cdots + \Sigma(X_k - \overline{X}_k)^2}{(n_1 - 1) + (n_2 - 1) + \cdots + (n_k - 1)} \tag{13.1}$$

where n is the number of subjects in each group and k is the total number of different groups. This is called the **mean square within groups,** or the within-groups variance estimate.

Now let's look at the other way to estimate the variance of the population, which involves examining the differences *between* the means of the sample groups. Do you remember the formula for the standard error of the mean? In case you have repressed it, here it is again:

$$\sigma_{\overline{X}} = \frac{\sigma}{\sqrt{n}} \qquad (10.8)$$

Multiplying each side of this equation by the square root of n results in:

$$\sigma = \sqrt{n} \cdot \sigma_{\overline{X}} \qquad (13.2)$$

Thus, the population variance is equal to

$$\sigma^2 = n \cdot \sigma_{\overline{X}}^2 \qquad (13.3)$$

Because the standard error of the mean is the same as the standard deviation of the distribution of sample means, the square of the standard error of the mean can be computed by using the following formula:

$$\sigma_{\overline{X}}^2 = \frac{\Sigma(\overline{X} - \overline{\overline{X}})^2}{k}$$

where k equals the number of samples and $\overline{\overline{X}}$ equals the mean of all the sample means. If we estimate this from only a *few* sample means, then we must divide by $k - 1$ rather than by k, as follows:

$$\text{est. } \sigma_{\overline{X}}^2 = \frac{(\overline{X}_1 - \overline{\overline{X}})^2 + (\overline{X}_2 - \overline{\overline{X}})^2 + \cdots + (\overline{X}_k - \overline{\overline{X}})^2}{k - 1} \qquad (13.4)$$

Substituting Formula 13.4 into Formula 13.3 results in the formula for the **mean square between groups:**

$$\text{MS}_{bg} = \frac{n_1(\overline{X}_1 - \overline{\overline{X}})^2 + n_2(\overline{X}_2 - \overline{\overline{X}})^2 + \cdots + n_k(\overline{X}_k - \overline{\overline{X}})^2}{k - 1} \qquad (13.5)$$

This formula is known as the mean square between groups because the differences between the group means and the mean of the means are used to calculate the variance estimate. The mean square between groups represents the variance that is due to the manipulation of the independent variable. It is a measure of the variance between the group means.

Question: So, again, why do we need to compute these two variance estimates? What can be gained by estimating the same variance twice?

If there is no difference between the samples—if they are all taken from the same population—these two methods of estimating the population variance should return exactly the same values. That is, if the null hypothesis is true, then the mean square between-groups estimate and the mean square within-groups estimate should be the same. And the ratio of the mean square between to the mean square within, which is called the **F ratio,** will equal 1. On the other hand, if the research hypothesis is true, then it is reasonable to expect that the two mean squares will have two different values. And in fact, if the research hypothesis is true, the mean square between groups will be much larger than the mean square within groups. This situation will then result in a ratio of the mean square between to the mean square within that is much greater than 1. This, then, is why we need to compute the two estimates: to determine whether the two values are the same. If their ratio, the F ratio, is significantly greater than 1, we can reject the null hypothesis.

To illustrate the procedure, let's conduct an analysis of variance for the driving simulator experiment using the data from Table 13.1. To do so, we need to compute both the mean square within and the mean square between and then compare them.

C O N C E P T   Q U I Z

1. t tests are used to test the significance of the difference between _____ means, whereas analysis of variance is used to test the significance among _____ means.

2. $\mu_1 = \mu_2 = \mu_3$ is an example of the null hypothesis for _____ .

3. An analysis of variance consists of _____ the population _____ using two very different methods.

4. In an analysis of variance, the _____ is the equivalent of the estimate of the population variance.

5. The mean square _____ groups is calculated by averaging the variance estimates of all groups in the analysis.

6. The differences between the group means and the mean of the means are used to compute the mean square _____ groups.

7. If the research hypothesis is true, then we expect the mean square _____ to be greater than the mean square _____ .

Answers

1. two; three or more
2. an analysis of variance
3. estimating; variance
4. mean square

5. within
6. between
7. between; within

Computation of the Mean Square Between Groups

To compute the mean square between groups, we use Formula 13.5:

$$\text{MS}_{\text{bg}} = \frac{n_1(\overline{X}_1 - \overline{\overline{X}})^2 + n_2(\overline{X}_2 - \overline{\overline{X}})^2 + \cdots + n_k(\overline{X}_k - \overline{\overline{X}})^2}{k - 1} \qquad (13.5)$$

We begin by calculating the mean for each sample as well as the mean of the sample means. Remember that each sample represents a different level of the independent variable. We compute the mean of each sample as we always have: by summing all the scores in the sample and dividing by the number of scores in that sample. Then, because the samples are all the same size and thus have equal n's, we can do one of two things. We can compute the mean of the sample means by summing all the means and dividing by the number of samples:

$$\overline{\overline{X}} = \frac{\Sigma \overline{X}}{k} = \frac{\overline{X}_1 + \overline{X}_2 + \cdots + \overline{X}_k}{k} \tag{13.6}$$

Or we can compute the mean of the means by summing all the scores in all the samples and dividing by the total number of scores:

$$\overline{\overline{X}} = \frac{\Sigma(\Sigma X)}{N_{\text{total}}} = \frac{\Sigma X_1 + \Sigma X_2 + \cdots + \Sigma X_k}{N_{\text{total}}} \tag{13.7}$$

The means for the data in the pedal error experiment are computed in

Table 13.2   Calculation of Sample Means and the Grand Mean for the Number of Pedal Errors with Three Pedal Arrangements

	Pedal arrangement	
Type 1 X_1	Type 2 X_2	Type 3 X_3
3	4	6
2	3	4
4	4	3
1	3	4
0	5	7
2	4	6
3	2	5
2	5	8
1	4	5
2	4	6
$\Sigma X_1 = 20$	$\Sigma X_2 = 38$	$\Sigma X_3 = 54$
$\overline{X}_1 = 2$	$\overline{X}_2 = 3.8$	$\overline{X}_3 = 5.4$

$$\overline{\overline{X}} = \frac{\overline{X}_1 + \overline{X}_2 + \overline{X}_3}{k} = \frac{2 + 3.8 + 5.4}{3} = \frac{11.2}{3} = 3.733$$

or

$$\overline{\overline{X}} = \frac{\Sigma X_1 + \Sigma X_2 + \Sigma X_3}{N_{\text{total}}} = \frac{20 + 38 + 54}{30} = \frac{112}{30} = 3.733$$

Table 13.2. Using the computations in this table, we can compute the mean square between:

$$MS_{bg} = \frac{n_1(\overline{X}_1 - \overline{\overline{X}})^2 + n_2(\overline{X}_2 - \overline{\overline{X}})^2 + n_3(\overline{X}_3 - \overline{\overline{X}})^2}{k - 1} \tag{13.5}$$

$$= \frac{10(2 - 3.733)^2 + 10(3.8 - 3.733)^2 + 10(5.4 - 3.733)^2}{3 - 1}$$

$$= \frac{10(-1.733)^2 + 10(0.067)^2 + 10(1.667)^2}{2}$$

$$= \frac{10 \cdot 3.003 + 10 \cdot 0.004 + 10 \cdot 2.779}{2}$$

$$= \frac{30.03 + 0.04 + 27.79}{2} = \frac{57.86}{2} = 28.93$$

Computation of the Mean Square Within Groups

The computation of the mean square within groups involves the same procedures used in computing the standard deviation for each of the samples. We subtract the mean from each score and square the result. Then we sum these squares for each sample and use Formula 13.1 to compute the mean square within. Table 13.3 has the necessary calculations. Using Formula 13.1, we now substitute the appropriate sums to compute the variance estimate within groups:

$$MS_{wg} = \frac{\Sigma(X_1 - \overline{X}_1)^2 + \Sigma(X_2 - \overline{X}_2)^2 + \Sigma(X_3 - \overline{X}_3)^2}{(n_1 - 1) + (n_2 - 1) + (n_3 - 1)} \tag{13.1}$$

$$= \frac{12 + 7.60 + 20.40}{(10 - 1) + (10 - 1) + (10 - 1)} = \frac{40}{9 + 9 + 9}$$

$$= \frac{40}{27} = 1.481$$

Question: OK. Now we have estimated the population variance in two different ways and have gotten very different results. What does this mean? Can we say that there is a difference among these three samples?

The *F* Test

The way to decide whether to reject the null hypothesis or fail to reject it is to compare the two mean squares by using an **F test.** In a one-way analysis of variance, *F* is the ratio of the mean square between groups to the mean square within groups:

$$F = \frac{MS_{bg}}{MS_{wg}} \tag{13.8}$$

Table 13.3 Calculations of Deviations and Squared Deviations for the Number of Pedal Errors with Three Pedal Arrangements

				Pedal arrangement				
	Type 1			Type 2			Type 3	
X_1	$X_1 - \bar{X}_1$	$(X_1 - \bar{X}_1)^2$	X_2	$X_2 - \bar{X}_2$	$(X_2 - \bar{X}_2)^2$	X_3	$X_3 - \bar{X}_3$	$(X_3 - \bar{X}_3)^2$
3	1	1	4	0.2	0.04	6	0.6	0.36
2	0	0	3	−0.8	0.64	4	−1.4	1.96
4	2	4	4	0.2	0.04	3	−2.4	5.76
1	−1	1	3	−0.8	0.64	4	−1.4	1.96
0	−2	4	5	1.2	1.44	7	1.6	2.56
2	0	0	4	0.2	0.04	6	0.6	0.36
3	1	1	2	−1.8	3.24	5	−0.4	0.16
2	0	0	5	1.2	1.44	8	2.6	6.76
1	−1	1	4	0.2	0.04	5	−0.4	0.16
2	0	0	4	0.2	0.04	6	0.6	0.36
	$\Sigma(X_1 - \bar{X}_1)^2 = 12$			$\Sigma(X_2 - \bar{X}_2)^2 = 7.60$			$\Sigma(X_3 - \bar{X}_3)^2 = 20.40$	

Theoretically, if the null hypothesis is true, then the mean square between and the mean square within will equal each other and the F ratio will equal 1. On the other hand, if the null hypothesis is false and the research hypothesis is true, the mean square between will be significantly larger than the mean square within. This difference in size will result in an F ratio that is significantly greater than 1. Therefore, the next step is to compute the value of F using Formula 13.8:

$$F = \frac{MS_{bg}}{MS_{wg}} = \frac{28.930}{1.481} = 19.534$$

To find out whether the ratio we computed is significant, we need to compare the computed value of F to the critical value of F given in Table F in Appendix A. Just as there are many different t distributions, there are also many F distributions, so we must use the degrees of freedom of both the numerator, mean square between, and the denominator, mean square within, to enter Table F. In a one-way analysis of variance, the number of degrees of freedom for the mean square between is equal to the number of samples in the experiment minus 1:

$$df_{bg} = k - 1 \tag{13.9}$$

To calculate the degrees of freedom for the mean square within groups, we add together the degrees of freedom for all the samples in the experiment:

$$df_{wg} = (n_1 - 1) + (n_2 - 1) + \cdots + (n_k - 1) \qquad (13.10)$$

Thus, in our example, we compute the degrees of freedom between groups as follows:

$$df_{bg} = k - 1 = 3 - 1 = 2$$

and we compute the degrees of freedom within groups in the following way:

$$
\begin{aligned}
df_{wg} &= (n_1 - 1) + (n_2 - 1) + (n_3 - 1) \\
&= (10 - 1) + (10 - 1) + (10 - 1) \\
&= 9 + 9 + 9 = 27
\end{aligned}
$$

Now we can see whether our computed F-value is significant by looking in Table F. This table is arranged so that we look for the computed degrees of freedom between groups (which is 2 in our example) in the row at the top of the table. Then we look down that column until we reach the computed degrees of freedom within groups (which is 27 in our example). If you haven't already, find Table F and do this. You will find that the critical value of F necessary to reject the null hypothesis with $\alpha = .05$ is 3.35. For the computed value of F to be significant, it must be *greater than or equal to* the critical value found in Table F. Because the critical value of F is 3.35 and our computed F is 19.534, we can reject the null hypothesis, which states that there is no difference between the three pedal arrangements, and we can accept the research hypothesis. Thus, we can safely assume that there is a difference between at least two of the pedal arrangements and that difference is significant.

C O N C E P T   Q U I Z

1. The way to decide whether to reject or fail to reject the null hypothesis is to compare the two _____ by using an _____ test.

2. F is the ratio of the _____ to the _____ .

3. Given that the mean square between equals 16 and the mean square within equals 4, what does F equal?

4. Theoretically, if the null hypothesis is true, the F ratio should be _____ .

5. The degrees of freedom for the mean square between are equal to _____ .

6. The degrees of freedom for the mean square within are equal to _____ .

7. Is an F ratio of 5.66 significant at $\alpha = .05$ if the degrees of freedom for the mean square within are 12 and the degrees of freedom for the mean square between are 3?

Answers

1. mean squares; F

2. mean square between; mean square within

3. 4

4. 1

5. the number of samples in the experiment minus 1 $(k - 1)$

6. the sum of the degrees of freedom for all the samples in the experiment

7. yes

Computational Formula for *F*

Question: Is there a faster way to compute *F*?

Yes, there are raw-score equivalent formulas for computing F that are faster than the definitional formulas we just used. But to use these raw-score formulas, it is necessary to break the variance estimates—the mean squares—into two parts: sum of squares and degrees of freedom. The **sum of squares** is similar to the sum of the deviation scores used in Chapter 5 to compute the variance of a sample; the **degrees of freedom** are similar to those used in the calculation of t. The sum of squares is always the numerator in the computation of the mean square, and the degrees of freedom is always the denominator. Consequently, the mean square between groups equals the sum of squares between divided by the degrees of freedom between:

$$MS_{bg} = \frac{SS_{bg}}{df_{bg}}$$

Likewise, the mean square within groups equals the sum of squares within divided by the degrees of freedom within:

$$MS_{wg} = \frac{SS_{wg}}{df_{wg}}$$

We already know how to compute the degrees of freedom both between and within from the discussion of Formulas 13.9 and 13.10. All we need to know is how to compute the sum of squares. The computational formulas for the sum of squares between groups as well as within groups are given next:

$$SS_{bg} = \left[\frac{(\Sigma X_1)^2}{n_1} + \frac{(\Sigma X_2)^2}{n_2} + \cdots + \frac{(\Sigma X_k)^2}{n_k} \right] - \frac{(\Sigma X_1 + \Sigma X_2 + \cdots + \Sigma X_k)^2}{N_{total}} \quad (13.11)$$

$$SS_{wg} = \Sigma X_1^2 + \Sigma X_2^2 + \cdots + \Sigma X_k^2 - \left[\frac{(\Sigma X_1)^2}{n_1} + \frac{(\Sigma X_2)^2}{n_2} + \cdots + \frac{(\Sigma X_k)^2}{n_k} \right] \quad (13.12)$$

Table 13.4 Calculation of Sums Needed to Use Computational Formulas for Sum of Squares in One-Way Analysis of Variance

Type 1		Type 2		Type 3	
X_1	X_1^2	X_2	X_2^2	X_3	X_3^2
3	9	4	16	6	36
2	4	3	9	4	16
4	16	4	16	3	9
1	1	3	9	4	16
0	0	5	25	7	49
2	4	4	16	6	36
3	9	2	4	5	25
2	4	5	25	8	64
1	1	4	16	5	25
2	4	4	16	6	36
$\Sigma X_1 = 20$	$\Sigma X_1^2 = 52$	$\Sigma X_2 = 38$	$\Sigma X_2^2 = 152$	$\Sigma X_3 = 54$	$\Sigma X_3^2 = 312$

Pedal arrangement (header spanning Type 1, Type 2, Type 3)

If you want to check your work, you can compute the **sum of squares total,** which is equal to the sum of squares between plus the sum of squares within. Formula 13.13 is the computational formula for the sum of squares total. You can compute this and then check to see whether it equals the sum of the other two computed sums of squares:

$$\text{SS}_{\text{total}} = \Sigma X_1^2 + \Sigma X_2^2 + \cdots + \Sigma X_k^2 - \frac{(\Sigma X_1 + \Sigma X_2 + \cdots + \Sigma X_k)^2}{N_{\text{total}}} \quad (13.13)$$

Let's apply this formula to our unintentional acceleration example. We have calculated the necessary sums in Table 13.4. Now we can use Formula 13.11 to compute the sum of squares between groups:

$$\text{SS}_{\text{bg}} = \left[\frac{(\Sigma X_1)^2}{n_1} + \frac{(\Sigma X_2)^2}{n_2} + \frac{(\Sigma X_3)^2}{n_3} \right] - \frac{(\Sigma X_1 + \Sigma X_2 + \Sigma X_3)^2}{N_{\text{total}}} \quad (13.11)$$

$$= \left[\frac{20^2}{10} + \frac{38^2}{10} + \frac{54^2}{10} \right] - \frac{(20 + 38 + 54)^2}{30}$$

$$= \left[\frac{400}{10} + \frac{1444}{10} + \frac{2916}{10} \right] - \frac{(112)^2}{30}$$

$$= [40 + 144.4 + 291.6] - \frac{12,544}{30} = 476 - 418.133$$

$$= 57.867$$

This value is the same as we computed for the numerator in Formula 13.5 on page 292. The slight difference is due entirely to roundoff error.

Having computed the sum of squares between, we can proceed to the computation of the sum of squares within groups using Formula 13.12:

$$SS_{wg} = \Sigma X_1^2 + \Sigma X_2^2 + \Sigma X_3^2 - \left[\frac{(\Sigma X_1)^2}{n_1} + \frac{(\Sigma X_2)^2}{n_2} + \frac{(\Sigma X_3)^2}{n_3} \right] \tag{13.12}$$

$$= 52 + 152 + 312 - \left[\frac{20^2}{10} + \frac{38^2}{10} + \frac{54^2}{10} \right]$$

$$= 516 - \left[\frac{400}{10} + \frac{1444}{10} + \frac{2916}{10} \right]$$

$$= 516 - [40 + 144.4 + 291.6] = 516 - 476$$

$$= 40$$

Again, this value is the same as the numerator computed using Formula 13.1 on page 292.

The sum of squares within and the sum of squares between are the only sums of squares we need to complete the F test. But because, when added together, the sums of squares between and within equal the sum of squares total, it is often a good idea to use Formula 13.13 to compute the sum of squares total as a final check. This computation is relatively simple because we already computed the major terms of Formula 13.13 when we computed the sums of squares between and within:

$$SS_{total} = \Sigma X_1^2 + \Sigma X_2^2 + \Sigma X_3^2 - \frac{(\Sigma X_1 + \Sigma X_2 + \Sigma X_3)^2}{N_{total}} \tag{13.13}$$

$$= 52 + 152 + 312 - \frac{(20 + 38 + 54)^2}{30}$$

$$= 516 - \frac{(112)^2}{30} = 516 - \frac{12,544}{30} = 516 - 418.133$$

$$= 97.867$$

Because the sum of squares total should equal the sum of squares between plus the sum of squares within, we can check to see whether the previously computed values add to 97.867:

$$SS_{total} = SS_{bg} + SS_{wg} \tag{13.14}$$
$$= 57.867 + 40 = 97.867$$

This checks out. Now we can finish the analysis of variance by computing the mean squares and F.

The computation of the mean squares and F is usually done with the aid of a **source table,** which displays the source of variation as well as the sums of

Table 13.5 Source Table for Analysis of Variance of Pedal Error Data

Source	Sum of squares	df	Mean square	F	p
Between	57.867	2	28.934	19.537	<.05
Within	40.000	27	1.481		
Total	97.867	29			

squares, the degrees of freedom, the mean squares, the F ratio, and the p-value. Table 13.5 is the source table for the pedal error data. Here the number of degrees of freedom is computed using Formulas 13.9 and 13.10. The degrees of freedom between are equal to 2, and the degrees of freedom within are equal to 27. The result is a total number of degrees of freedom equal to 29. The sums of squares for between, within, and total are also calculated. The mean square is the sum of squares divided by the degrees of freedom. Let's compute these values and enter them in the mean square column:

$$MS_{bg} = \frac{SS_{bg}}{df_{bg}} = \frac{57.867}{2} = 28.934$$

$$MS_{wg} = \frac{SS_{wg}}{df_{wg}} = \frac{40}{27} = 1.481$$

F is the mean square between divided by mean square within:

$$F = \frac{MS_{bg}}{MS_{wg}} = \frac{28.934}{1.481} = 19.537$$

Again, we have an F-value that is significant, and we are able to reject the null hypothesis. We can find the p-value, which is less than .05, in Table F in Appendix A.

Question: We have a significant F. This tells us that there is a significant difference among the groups in our experiment, but does this mean that all groups are significantly different from one another, or does it mean that just two groups are different, or what?

The F test tells us that we can reject the null hypothesis. It indicates that there is some difference between at least two and possibly more of the groups, but it does not reveal where that difference lies. However, there are several tests that can do so. These are called **post hoc tests.** *Post hoc* is Latin for *after the fact*. These tests are only conducted *after* you have determined that you have an F ratio that is significant.

The one we discuss next is called the **HSD,** which stands for *honestly significant difference.* The HSD is used to compare sample means when an analysis of variance leads to a significant F; it cannot be used when the F ratio is not significantly large. It reveals how far apart the sample means must be in order for them to be significantly different. We can compute the HSD by using the following formula:

$$\text{HSD} = q\sqrt{\frac{\text{MS}_{\text{wg}}}{n}} \qquad (13.15)$$

This formula contains two values that we have already used, MS_{wg} and n, and one value that we have not yet used: q. The mean square within groups, MS_{wg}, is 1.481, and n is the number of subjects in each sample, 10. The value for q is the studentized range statistic, which can be found in Table Q in Appendix A. To find the value of q, you must enter Table Q with the number of samples in the analysis of variance (k) and the number of degrees of freedom within (df_{wg}). This is sometimes a problem because the table does not list all possible degrees of freedom. Thus, if your number of degrees of freedom is not listed, you must find the value in the table that is closest to yours without going over it. Try to find the q-value using the data from the pedal error experiment. Turn to Table Q if you haven't done so already. In the pedal error problem, $k = 3$, so find the column for three groups. Now you need to look for the number of degrees of freedom, which is 27, but there is no listing for 27 degrees of freedom within groups. Therefore, you must find the value for the next lower number of degrees of freedom, which is 24. Look across to find q at an alpha level of .05, equal to 3.53. Having all the values we need, we can now compute the HSD:

$$\text{HSD} = q\sqrt{\frac{\text{MS}_{\text{wg}}}{n}} = 3.53\sqrt{\frac{1.481}{10}} = 3.53\sqrt{0.1481}$$

$$= 3.53 \cdot 0.385 = 1.359$$

This HSD value tells us that any difference between means of 1.359 pedal errors or greater is significant. Let's examine the differences between the means of the various pedal arrangement types. The means for types 1, 2, and 3, respectively, are 2 errors, 3.8 errors, and 5.4 errors. The difference between the means for types 1 and 2 is 1.8 errors, which is greater than the required 1.359. The difference between the means for types 1 and 3 is 3.4 errors, and the difference between types 2 and 3 is 1.6 errors, both of which are also greater than the HSD of 1.359. Thus, in this experiment all three pedal arrangements are significantly different from one another. Based on these results, automobile designers should choose pedal arrangement 1 because drivers who used it made significantly fewer errors.

So you see, an analysis of variance consists of three basic steps: (1) Compute the mean square between-groups variance estimate and the mean square within-groups variance estimate. (2) Determine whether they are significantly different by computing the F ratio, which is the ratio of the mean square between to the mean square within. (3) If this ratio is significant, determine which sample(s) is significantly different from the others by conducting one more test, such as the honestly significant difference (HSD) test.

C O N C E P T   Q U I Z

1. The mean square has two parts; the _____ and the _____ .
2. Sum of squares total (SS_{total}) equals _____ plus _____ .
3. The score that reveals how far apart the sample means must be in order for them to be significantly different is the _____ .
4. In computing the HSD, what value do you need to look up in a table?

Answers

1. sum of squares; degrees of freedom
2. sum of squares between groups (SS_{bg}); sum of squares within groups (SS_{wg})
3. HSD, honestly significant difference
4. q

S U M M A R Y

One-way analysis of variance is used when the research design involves one independent variable with three or more levels. The one-way analysis of variance tests the null hypothesis, which proposes that all the independent samples come from the same population. The rationale for using the one-way analysis of variance is relatively straightforward. Because there are two different methods, within groups and between groups, to estimate the population variance, both variance estimates should be equal if all the samples are from the same population. If the samples are from different populations, the between-groups variance estimate should be larger than the within-groups variance estimate. One-way analysis of variance involves computing these two variance estimates, called the mean square between groups and the mean square within groups, and then comparing them using an F ratio.

The mean square between is equal to the sum of squares between groups divided by the degrees of freedom between groups. The mean square within groups is equal to the sum of squares within groups divided by the degrees of freedom within groups. The F ratio equals the mean square between divided by the mean square within. If the samples come from different populations and are therefore significantly different from one another, then the value of the F ratio will be significantly greater than 1. The critical value for the F ratio can be found by entering Table F in Appendix A using the degrees of freedom between groups and the degrees of freedom within groups. Once it has been determined that the computed F ratio is significant, it is necessary to compare the group means to one another.

The HSD statistic is used for comparing the means after obtaining a significant F ratio. The HSD is q, the studentized range statistic, times the square root of the mean square within divided by the number of samples in the analysis of variance. Any pair of means with a difference greater than the HSD can be said to come from different populations.

KEY TERMS

one-way analysis of variance
mean square (MS)
mean square within groups (MS_{wg})
mean square between groups
   (MS_{bg})
F ratio
F test

sum of squares
degrees of freedom
sum of squares total (SS_{total})
source table
post hoc tests
HSD

FORMULAS

$$MS_{wg} = \frac{\Sigma(X_1 - \overline{X}_1)^2 + \Sigma(X_2 - \overline{X}_2)^2 + \cdots + \Sigma(X_k - \overline{X}_k)^2}{(n_1 - 1) + (n_2 - 1) + \cdots + (n_k - 1)} \tag{13.1}$$

$$\sigma = \sqrt{n} \cdot \sigma_{\overline{X}} \tag{13.2}$$

$$\sigma^2 = n \cdot \sigma_{\overline{X}}^2 \tag{13.3}$$

$$\text{est. } \sigma_{\overline{X}}^2 = \frac{(\overline{X}_1 - \overline{\overline{X}})^2 + (\overline{X}_2 - \overline{\overline{X}})^2 + \cdots + (\overline{X}_k - \overline{\overline{X}})^2}{k - 1} \tag{13.4}$$

$$MS_{bg} = \frac{n_1(\overline{X}_1 - \overline{\overline{X}})^2 + n_2(\overline{X}_2 - \overline{\overline{X}})^2 + \cdots + n_k(\overline{X}_k - \overline{\overline{X}})^2}{k - 1} \tag{13.5}$$

$$\overline{\overline{X}} = \frac{\Sigma\overline{X}}{k} = \frac{\overline{X}_1 + \overline{X}_2 + \cdots + \overline{X}_k}{k} \tag{13.6}$$

$$\overline{\overline{X}} = \frac{\Sigma(\Sigma X)}{N_{total}} = \frac{\Sigma X_1 + \Sigma X_2 + \cdots + \Sigma X_k}{N_{total}} \tag{13.7}$$

$$F = \frac{MS_{bg}}{MS_{wg}} \tag{13.8}$$

$$df_{bg} = k - 1 \tag{13.9}$$

$$df_{wg} = (n_1 - 1) + (n_2 - 1) + \cdots + (n_k - 1) \tag{13.10}$$

$$SS_{bg} = \left[\frac{(\Sigma X_1)^2}{n_1} + \frac{(\Sigma X_2)^2}{n_2} + \cdots + \frac{(\Sigma X_k)^2}{n_k} \right] - \frac{(\Sigma X_1 + \Sigma X_2 + \cdots + \Sigma X_k)^2}{N_{total}} \tag{13.11}$$

$$SS_{wg} = \Sigma X_1^2 + \Sigma X_2^2 + \cdots + \Sigma X_k^2 - \left[\frac{(\Sigma X_1)^2}{n_1} + \frac{(\Sigma X_2)^2}{n_2} + \cdots + \frac{(\Sigma X_k)^2}{n_k} \right] \tag{13.12}$$

$$SS_{total} = \Sigma X_1^2 + \Sigma X_2^2 + \cdots + \Sigma X_k^2 - \frac{(\Sigma X_1 + \Sigma X_2 + \cdots + \Sigma X_k)^2}{N_{total}} \tag{13.13}$$

$$SS_{total} = SS_{bg} + SS_{wg} \tag{13.14}$$

$$HSD = q\sqrt{\frac{MS_{wg}}{n}} \tag{13.15}$$

P R O B L E M S

Problems 1–9 are hypothetical experiments that must be analyzed using the one-way analysis of variance. For each problem, generate a null hypothesis and a research hypothesis and then create a source table that includes the following:

Source	SS	df	MS	F	p
Between groups	SS_{bg}	df_{bg}	MS_{bg}	F < or > .05	
Within groups	SS_{wg}	df_{wg}	MS_{wg}		
Total	SS_{total}	df_{total}			

Once you have created the source table, refer to Table F in Appendix A and determine whether the F ratio is significant. If the F ratio is significantly large for you to reject the null hypothesis, then compute an HSD to determine which levels of the independent variable are significantly different from one another.

1. Much of an academic psychologist's professional success is based on his or her ability to conduct consequential research and to publish that research. Suppose you, as a new assistant professor, have noticed that papers submitted with multiple authors are more likely to be accepted for publication than papers with only one author. You are also aware that one indicator of whether a paper will be published is the number of negative comments received when the paper is reviewed. So you decide to conduct a small experiment. Changing only the number of authors on the paper, you submit the same paper for publication to several journals. Your independent variable, then, is the number of authors, and your dependent variable is the number of negative comments received. The number of negative comments are listed in the table. (To solve this problem, follow the instructions preceding Problem 1.)

	Number of authors		
1	2	3	4
16	24	13	15
23	20	9	5
28	16	17	19
23	14	19	17

2. The human nervous system is extremely sensitive to changes in the environment. Stimuli that remain the same do not demand the same amount of attention as those that are novel. Pretend you are a human factors psychologist working for a large automobile manufacturer. You have been assigned the task of determining what type of hot-engine warning system will be used on the next generation of small pickup trucks. The designers have given you three alternative systems: (a) a traditional temperature gauge that reads cold to the left, normal in the middle, and hot to the right; (b) a hot-engine warning light that flashes when the engine is about to overheat; and (c) a temperature gauge similar to (a), except that the entire gauge flashes on and off when the engine is about to overheat. You decide to test these three designs by having three separate groups of subjects use the various warning systems in a driving simulator. The independent variable in this experiment is the type of warning system, whereas the dependent variable is the number of seconds it takes a driver to respond to the warning that the engine is about to overheat. The reaction times are given in the table.

Gauge	Flashing light	Flashing gauge
30	10	5
22	15	10
26	10	15
23	20	5

3. Scrooge McDuck has turned philanthropist and is itching to award scholarship money to deserving students. He feels that students who have full scholarships should get higher grades because they need to work only a minimum number of hours to support themselves and should therefore have abundant time to study. He has some doubts about his theory, however, and he doesn't want to part with his hard-earned money if his hypothesis is incorrect, so he hires you to study it. You randomly assign 15 scholarship applicants to one of the following conditions: full scholarship, partial scholarship, and no scholarship. At the end of 1 year you compute the grade point average for each student. Using the grade point averages in the table, determine whether there is a difference between the grade point averages of students getting full scholarships, partial scholarships, or no scholarships at all.

Full scholarship	Partial scholarship	No scholarship
2.9	3.0	3.2
3.7	3.3	2.9
1.7	2.2	3.4
2.5	3.8	2.0
2.9	2.2	1.8

4. As a psychologist who works with people who have Down's syndrome, you design a study intended to determine which rewards are most effective for use in training your patients. You select four different groups of patients and record the number of days it takes to teach them a particular task, with each group receiving one of four types of rewards: Reward A, Reward B, Reward C, or Reward D. The numbers of days are given in the table.

Reward A	Reward B	Reward C	Reward D
3	6	9	12
5	7	10	13
6	9	15	15
2	7	12	18
1	11	11	15
2	6	10	13

5. A good friend of yours is a teacher of medical doctors. Through her experience, she has come to feel that doctors in various specialties differ in their moral and ethical standards. She decides to test this hypothesis using some of her interns as subjects. She gives them a test that measures moral development on a 100-point interval scale, where a high score represents high moral development and a low score represents low moral development. The interns are specialists in three areas, orthopedics (bones and joints), pediatrics (children), and oncology (cancer), and their scores are shown in the accompanying table.

Orthopedics	Pediatrics	Oncology
77	63	54
84	93	97
66	83	76
44	56	65

6. You are interested in the processes involved in solving anagrams. An anagram is a word with the letters *mdlcsarbe* (*scrambled*). You believe that an anagram is easier to solve if the word is familiar to the subject. Because of this, you choose three five-letter words that differ in familiarity and ask three different sets of subjects to solve the anagrams. The dependent variable in this research proj-

ect (with values listed in the table) is the time in seconds for each subject to solve the anagram.

Very familiar	Familiar	Not familiar
37	47	69
30	56	67
10	43	77
21	39	82
17	30	92
25	54	66

7. Everybody has taste preferences. Most of us claim to be able to tell the difference between "our" brand and other nonpreferred brands. Suppose we put your taste buds to the test to see whether you can tell the difference between three brands of beer. Beer is normally priced according to the percentage of imported hops and grains used in production, beers with the higher percentages being priced higher. Suppose we test three different beers, each produced by the same brewery and differing only in the percentage of imported ingredients. One beer has all imported hops and grains, another beer is 50% imported, and the third beer is entirely domestic. We then ask three separate groups of five people to rate the tastes of the beer using an interval rating scale from 1 (bad) to 7 (great).

100% Imported	50% Imported	0% Imported
7	3	5
4	2	7
5	6	3
2	5	5
3	6	2

8. We are trying to determine whether there is a difference between four biofeedback methods for lowering blood pressure. We teach subjects one of the methods and then measure the change in their blood pressure. The table values for decreases in blood pressure are for 20 subjects who used one of the four methods.

Method A	Method B	Method C	Method D
12	22	17	13
5	19	7	0
2	16	4	10
11	23	12	7
13	25	8	9

9. A psychologist interested in studying the effectiveness of subliminal perception (the perception of a stimulus presented below threshold) asked subjects to view a screen and identify a group of five letters flashed on it. Three separate groups were composed of ten subjects each: one that was presented letters flashed at a rate *above* the subjects' threshold, another that was presented letters flashed *at* their threshold, and another that was presented letters flashed *below* their threshold. The dependent variable, given in the table, was the percentage of letters correctly identified.

Above threshold	At threshold	Below threshold
90	50	20
95	55	25
85	55	15
90	45	20
80	40	20
90	45	25
85	50	20
90	55	15
80	50	20
95	45	20

10. The data in the accompanying table were gathered from 24 subjects, divided into three equal groups, who participated in an experiment comparing short-term memory capacity for three different types of items: words, nonwords, and numbers. Generate a null hypothesis and a research hypothesis for this experiment and then, using the data, conduct an analysis of variance and tell whether the F ratio is significant.

Words	Nonwords	Numbers
8	5	6
9	4	6
7	5	5
10	6	7
9	3	5
8	5	6
8	4	7
7	3	7

11. Given the results of the analysis of variance conducted in Problem 10, what do you conclude about the stated hypotheses?

12. Three separate groups of randomly assigned subjects were asked to list the number of words they recognized from a 100-word list spoken by a man, a woman, or a computer. Use the numbers of words listed in the table to conduct an analysis of variance. What is the F ratio? Is it significant?

Man	Woman	Computer
97	99	86
96	94	80
93	92	88
94	97	80
93	92	81
92	94	80
95	96	82
95	96	87
93	94	79

13. If the *F* ratio in Problem 12 is significant, compute an HSD and discuss which of the levels (man, woman, or computer) are significantly different from one another.

14. A physiological psychologist knows that the blood level of a particular hormone increases when an animal is under stress. He decides to use the blood level of this hormone as a measure of stress in four situations: (a) having the animal swim in an ice water bath for 30 seconds, (b) administering a 5-second electric shock to the animal's feet, (c) dropping the animal from a height of 10 feet into a net, or (d) using a control condition where he gives no stressor. Using the blood levels from the table, test the research hypothesis stating that there is a significant difference between at least two of these four conditions by using analysis of variance. Make sure you show the entire source table.

Swimming	Shock	Drop	Control
265	260	265	250
266	271	267	245
267	268	266	250
268	266	265	252
272	269	268	253

15. What can you conclude from the experiment in Problem 14? If the *F* ratio was significant, test the four means for significance using HSD.

R E F E R E N C E

Vernoy, M. W., & Tomerlin, J. (1989). Pedal error and misperceived center line in eight different automobiles. *Human Factors, 31,* 369–375.

Factorial Analysis of Variance: Two-Way

You're late. You miscalculated the time it would take to drive to the university, and now you're going to be late for your final exam. You're going as fast as you dare, but you keep getting stuck behind slow trucks and stopped at traffic lights, and now railroad crossing signals are flashing up ahead. Maybe you can beat the train across the tracks. You look for the train. You see it, but it looks like it's pretty far away and going slowly. Should you chance it? You're late, and you have to take the final in order to pass the course. You go for it! You jam the accelerator to the floor and whiz toward the tracks, but when you look again, you see that *the train is on top of you!* How could you have made such a gross misjudgment?

Such miscalculations have cost people their lives. A researcher named Herschel Leibowitz (1985) studied the perceptual errors people make in depth and motion detection—errors that lead to car/train accidents such as the imminent one we just described. After careful study, Leibowitz found that we perceive large objects like locomotives as moving more slowly than smaller ones and that when we move our heads and eyes to track objects, we tend to perceive these objects as moving more slowly than we do when we keep our heads and eyes still. These factors may be responsible for car/train collisions.

Ever since psychology has been a science, psychologists have been interested in perception—the process of interpreting information sent from the sense organs to the brain. The perception of such things as sound, pain, taste, and smell has been the subject of thousands of psychological experiments. The study of visual perception has been especially alluring, particularly the perception of depth. How well we perceive depth and distance is of extreme importance. As in the preceding example, you have to know how far away approaching vehicles are and how fast they are going so that you can avoid crashing into them. You have to know how close the soda machine lever is or you'll have trouble refilling your cup. You have to know the distance to first base so that you can throw out the batter whose ground ball you've just fielded.

Countless factors affect visual depth perception. One factor is whether you use one eye or both eyes. A second is whether your head is stationary or in motion. Most people guess correctly that depth perception is far better with two eyes open than one. This is because there are depth cues available to us when we use both eyes that are not available when we use only one. But can you estimate distances more accurately when you move your head or when you keep your head still? The obvious answer is that keeping your head stationary allows you to see sharper images and therefore estimate distances more accurately. However, this answer overlooks the fact that the relative motion of objects can be an important cue to their distance. You can observe this phenomenon when you are a passenger in a moving car. As you move, near objects appear to pass you at a faster rate than more distant objects. Therefore, moving your head may add an additional distance cue that can enhance the accuracy of your perception of depth.

Suppose you survived your near-collision with the train and you decide to enlist our aid in studying some of the factors that led to your perceptual error. We design an experiment in depth and motion perception using the two independent variables mentioned earlier: number of eyes open and movement/nonmovement of head. The first independent variable, number of eyes open, has two levels—one or two. The second independent variable, head motion, has three levels—no motion, slow motion, and moderate motion. We measure the accuracy of each subject's depth perception by requiring him or her to align two small rods from a distance of 6 meters. The dependent variable, then, is the distance (in millimeters) between the two rods.

In the previous two chapters we discussed how to analyze data from studies that had multiple levels of one independent variable. In this chapter, we discuss how to analyze data from studies involving two independent variables, each having two or more levels. The study in our example has two independent variables, one with two levels (one eye or two eyes open) and another with three (type of head motion). Now, we *could* separate our problem into two experiments. The first one could investigate the perception of depth using either one eye or two eyes open, and because it would involve one independent variable with only two levels, we could use a *t* test to analyze the data. The second experiment could investigate differences in perceived depth as a result of head motion, and because this would involve one independent variable with three different levels, we could use a one-way analysis of variance to analyze the data. This approach is certainly feasible and reasonable, but it is more intriguing, as well as easier, to investigate the two independent variables in the same experiment. That way we can explore the effects of each independent variable on the dependent variable, as well as any effects that the combination of the two independent variables may have on the dependent variable.

An experiment with two or more independent variables is called a **factorial experiment**. The simplest of these is a two-way factorial in which there are just two independent variables (a three-way factorial design would be used when there are three independent variables, and so on). In this chapter, we discuss only the analysis of two-way factorial experiments.

The design of a factorial experiment is represented in a matrix, with the first independent variable displayed in the columns and the second independent variable displayed in the rows. The matrix for our depth perception experiment is illustrated in Table 14.1. Because there are two levels of the first independent variable and three levels of the second, the design is known as a two-by-three (2×3) factorial. This type of completely randomized factorial design was discussed in Chapter 11. In such an experiment, each subject participates in only one level of the first independent variable and in only one level of the second independent variable. As you can see in Table 14.1, there are six (2×3) separate independent conditions or cells in this experiment.

If we want to have five subjects participate in each cell, we need a total of 30 subjects. Table 14.2 displays the information gathered from our sample experiment. In addition to the data from the individual subjects, it includes the individual cell means, or the mean of all the scores within each cell; the column means, or the mean of each column; and the row means, or the mean of each row. The row and column means give an indication of the effects of the two independent variables (the main effects) as well as the interaction between the two independent variables. To analyze these data, we need to run a two-way analysis of variance.

Table 14.1 The Design of the Depth Perception Experiment

Independent variable 1

	One eye open	Two eyes open
No head movement		
Slow head movement		
Moderate head movement		

Independent variable 2

MAIN EFFECTS

As you may recall, in a one-way analysis of variance, the total variance in the collected data is separated into two different variance estimates, between groups and within groups, which are then compared in the F ratio. In a two-way analysis of variance, the between variance is further partitioned into three separate variance estimates, two of which are known as *main effects* and the other as the *interaction*. The effect of one independent variable on the dependent variable is called a **main effect**. In the depth perception experiment, there are two independent variables and therefore two main effects: (1) the effect of the number of eyes open on the perception of depth (as measured by the distance between the rods) and (2) the effect of the type of head motion on the perception of depth. The main effect for number of eyes open is represented by the columns in Table 14.2. When we compare the mean for the one-eye-open column (5.8 mm error) to the mean for the two-eyes-open column (2.467 mm error), it seems obvious that subjects are more accurate with two eyes open than with one. The other main effect, type of head motion, is represented by the rows in Table 14.2. When we compare the means for no head motion (6 mm error), slow head motion (3.7 mm error), and moderate head motion (2.7 mm error), we notice a systematic difference.

By this point in your study of statistics you should know that even though it *looks* obvious from the data that there are differences among the samples, you don't know whether the differences are due to mere chance or whether each of the samples in each main effect came from a different population. Thus, it is necessary to test one null hypothesis for each of the main effects (the rows and the columns). The null hypothesis for the columns is

$$H_{0_{col}}: \mu_{col_1} = \mu_{col_2} = \cdots = \mu_{col_k}$$

The null hypothesis for the rows is

$$H_{0_{row}}: \mu_{row_1} = \mu_{row_2} = \cdots = \mu_{row_k}$$

Here are the corresponding research hypotheses:

$H_{1_{col}}$: At least one of the samples represented by the columns comes from a different population distribution than the others.

$H_{1_{row}}$: At least one of the samples represented by the rows comes from a different population distribution than the others.

In the depth perception example, the research hypothesis for the columns states that there is a difference in the accuracy of depth perception when a subject views the display with one eye instead of two eyes. The research hypothesis for the rows states that the type of head motion—none, slow, or moderate—affects the subjects' perception of depth. After running an experiment to test these hypotheses, we must conduct an analysis of variance to analyze the results. Before we do so, however, let's find out a little more about the interaction.

Table 14.2 Data from the Depth Perception Experiment

| | | Independent variable 1 | |
		One eye open	Two eyes open	
Independent variable 2	No head movement	X 8 10 8 6 13 $\Sigma X = 45$ $\bar{X}_{\text{cell}} = 9$	X 5 4 1 2 3 $\Sigma X = 15$ $\bar{X}_{\text{cell}} = 3$	$\bar{X}_{\text{row}} = 6$
	Slow head movement	X 4 6 3 5 7 $\Sigma X = 25$ $\bar{X}_{\text{cell}} = 5$	X 4 1 2 3 2 $\Sigma X = 12$ $\bar{X}_{\text{cell}} = 2.4$	$\bar{X}_{\text{row}} = 3.7$
	Moderate head movement	X 2 2 3 4 6 $\Sigma X = 17$ $\bar{X}_{\text{cell}} = 3.4$	X 3 0 3 2 2 $\Sigma X = 10$ $\bar{X}_{\text{cell}} = 2$	$\bar{X}_{\text{row}} = 2.7$
		$\bar{X}_{\text{col}} = 5.8$	$\bar{X}_{\text{col}} = 2.467$	

INTERACTION

In a two-way factorial analysis of variance, the **interaction** is the effect of the *combination* of the two independent variables on the dependent variable. Graphing the cell means from the experiment (see Figure 14.1) will help you understand what we mean by *interaction*. In the graph of an interaction, the dependent variable is always represented along the *y*-axis, and in most cases the independent variable with the greatest number of levels is represented along the *x*-axis; separate lines are used to represent different levels of the other independent variable.

To decipher Figure 14.1, you need some additional explanation. To begin

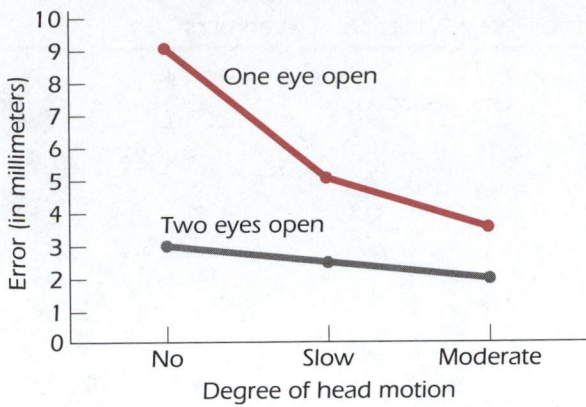

Figure 14.1   A graph of the cell means from the depth perception experiment illustrates the *interaction*.

with, as we just mentioned, the dependent variable (amount of error, in millimeters) is represented along the y-axis, whereas the independent variable with the most levels (degree of motion) is represented along the x-axis. The independent variable with the fewest levels (number of eyes open) is represented by separate lines on the graph. You can see from Figure 14.1 that the two lines have different slopes. Although both lines slope down to the right, the line for one eye open has a much steeper slope than the line for two eyes open. *Whenever there is an interaction,* the lines on this type of graph have different slopes, as in Figure 14.2. The separation between the lines is of no consequence; the only significant factor is the difference in the slopes of the two lines. If there is *no interaction*, as in Figures 14.3 and 14.4, the lines are parallel at all points. (When one line goes up, the other goes up and when one line goes down, the other goes down.)

When an interaction exists, it is often more interesting than any of the

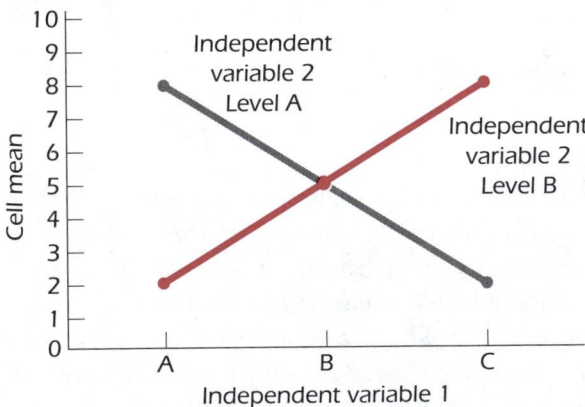

Figure 14.2   The intersecting lines indicate an interaction between the two independent variables.

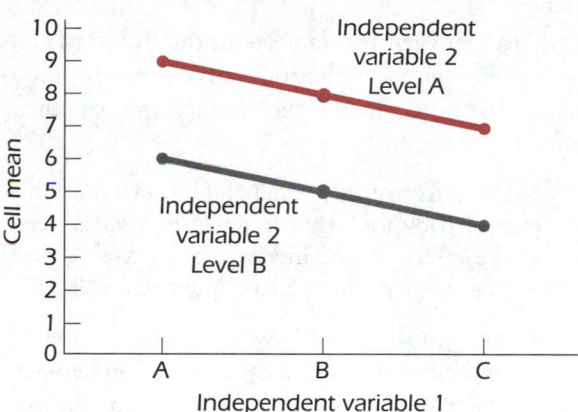

Figure 14.3 The parallel lines indicate that there is no interaction between the two independent variables.

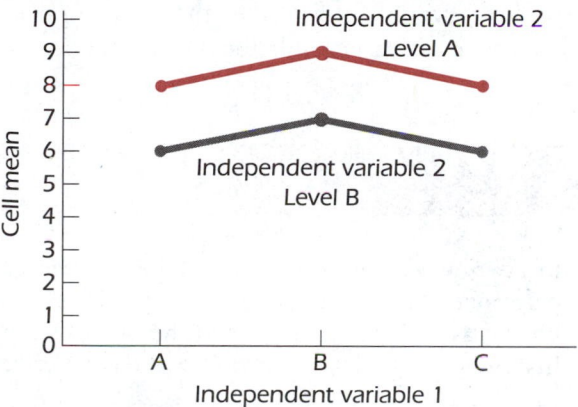

Figure 14.4 The nonintersecting lines indicate that there is no interaction between the two independent variables.

main effects. For instance, look at Figure 14.1. It appears that head motion drastically reduced the error rate in the one-eye-open condition but had very little effect on the errors made when subjects had both eyes open. Thus, even though the main effect of head motion may be significant, the interaction effect indicates that head motion is most effective when people use only one eye. Remember, it is the pattern of the responses that is important when we investigate interaction. Parallel lines indicate no interaction, whereas nonparallel or intersecting lines usually indicate an interaction.

Question: Does that mean, then, that if we graph the cell means and find even a slight difference in the slopes, there is a significant interaction?

Not necessarily. Slight differences in the slopes could be due to chance variability between the subjects in the different conditions. Even though we notice an apparent interaction on the graph, we must conduct an analysis of variance to know whether the interaction is significant. Here are the hypotheses for the interaction:

$H_{0_{r \times c}}$: The effect of one independent variable on the dependent variable is unaffected by the other independent variable(s).

$H_{1_{r \times c}}$: The effect of one independent variable on the dependent variable is affected by the other independent variable(s).

Therefore, in the depth perception experiment, the research hypothesis for the interaction states that the interaction between the number of eyes used to view the display and the type of head motion will affect the subjects' perception of depth. Basically this means that the effect of head motion depends on the number of eyes used to view the display. The rejection of the null hypothesis by the analysis of variance will not *explain* the interaction effects; it will only confirm that the interaction is significant. You, as the experimenter, are responsible for the explanation of any interaction effects.

CONCEPT QUIZ

1. In a two-way analysis of variance, the between-groups variance estimate is partitioned into three separate variance estimates, two of which are known as _____ and the other as the _____ .

2. In a two-way analysis of variance, the main effects are represented by the _____ and the _____ .

3. The research hypothesis for the rows states that at least _____ of the samples represented by the rows comes from a different population distribution.

4. The research hypothesis for the columns states that at least _____ of the samples represented by the columns comes from a different population distribution.

5. In a two-way analysis of variance, the interaction is the effect of the _____ of the two independent variables on the dependent variable.

6. When we graph lines representing a significant interaction, their slopes are _____ .

7. Lines on a graph that represent no interaction are _____ .

Answers

1. main effects; interaction
2. rows; columns
3. one
4. one
5. combination
6. different
7. parallel

COMPUTATION OF SUMS OF SQUARES FOR TWO-WAY ANALYSIS OF VARIANCE

In an analysis of variance, we are testing two main effects and the interaction, so we need to compute four sums of squares—columns, rows, interaction, and within—plus the total sum of squares, along with the corresponding degrees of freedom, mean squares, and F ratios. The values needed for these computations are shown in a source table, Table 14.3. The formulas for the sum of squares within groups (SS_{wg}) and the sum of squares total (SS_{total}) are the same as the computational formulas used in a one-way analysis of variance. They are slightly rewritten because we now have rows (no, slow, or moderate head motion), columns (one or two eyes open), and cells rather than just different samples. Because in two-way analysis of variance the between-group sum of squares (SS_{bg}) has been partitioned into rows, columns, and interaction, the formulas for these sum of squares values are new. These new sums of squares and the resulting mean squares represent the amount of variance that is due only to the manipulation of the two different independent variables as well as the amount of variance that is due only to the interaction of the two independent variables.

Before we discuss the formulas, we will take time out to clarify some new notation. As you can see in Table 14.3, the sum of squares total is still represented by SS_{total}, and the sum of squares within groups by SS_{wg}. The sum of squares rows is represented by SS_r, the sum of squares columns is represented by SS_c, and the sum of squares for the interaction is represented by $SS_{r \times c}$. All the formulas used to compute these values require some sum of scores. The following is a list of the summation notation that is used in those formulas:

$\Sigma\Sigma X^2 =$ the sum of the sums of the X^2 for all the cells in the entire analysis. You square each score, add up the scores in each cell, and then add all the cells together. In the depth perception example, the result is 752.

Table 14.3 Source Table for Two-Way Factorial Analysis of Variance

Source of variation	Sum of squares	Degrees of freedom	Mean square	F
Rows	SS_r	df_r	MS_r	F_r
Columns	SS_c	df_c	MS_c	F_c
Interaction	$SS_{r \times c}$	$df_{r \times c}$	$MS_{r \times c}$	$F_{r \times c}$
Within	SS_{wg}	df_{wg}	MS_{wg}	
Total	SS_{total}	df_{total}		

$\Sigma\Sigma X$ = the sum of the sums of the X-values for all cells in the entire analysis. You add up all the scores in each cell and then add up all the cells in the analysis. In the depth perception example, the result is 124.

$\Sigma(\Sigma X_{cell})^2$ = the sum of the square of the sum of the X-values for each cell. You compute the sum of the scores within each cell, square that value, and then add up these squared values in all cells. In the depth perception example, the values are $45^2 + 15^2 + 25^2 + 12^2 + 17^2 + 10^2$.

$\Sigma(\Sigma X_{row})^2$ = the sum of the square of the sum of the X-values for each row. You compute the sum of the scores within each row, square that value, and then add up these squared values in all rows. In the depth perception example, the values are $60^2 + 37^2 + 27^2$.

$\Sigma(\Sigma X_{col})^2$ = the sum of the square of the sum of the X-values for each column. You compute the sum of the scores within each column, square that value, and then add up these squared values in all columns. In the depth perception example, the values are $87^2 + 37^2$.

There are also several types of N's:

N_{total} = the total number of scores in all the samples. In the depth perception experiment, there is a total of 30 scores.

n_{cell} = the number of scores in an individual cell. In the depth perception experiment, there are 5 scores per cell.

n_{row} = the number of scores in each row. In the depth perception experiment, there are 10 scores in each row.

n_{col} = the number of scores in each column. In the depth perception experiment, there are 15 scores in each column.

Now we can get on with the formulas needed to calculate the various sums of squares. The formula for the sum of squares total for a two-way analysis of variance is

$$SS_{total} = \Sigma\Sigma X^2 - \frac{(\Sigma\Sigma X)^2}{N_{total}} \qquad (14.1)$$

The formula for the sum of squares within is

$$SS_{wg} = \Sigma\Sigma X^2 - \frac{\Sigma(\Sigma X_{cell})^2}{n_{cell}} \qquad (14.2)$$

The formula for the sum of squares rows is

$$SS_r = \frac{\Sigma(\Sigma X_{row})^2}{n_{row}} - \frac{(\Sigma\Sigma X)^2}{N_{total}} \qquad (14.3)$$

The formula for the sum of squares columns is

$$SS_c = \frac{\Sigma(\Sigma X_{col})^2}{n_{col}} - \frac{(\Sigma\Sigma X)^2}{N_{total}} \qquad (14.4)$$

Finally, the sum of squares for the interaction is arrived at by subtraction:

$$SS_{r \times c} = SS_{total} - (SS_{wg} + SS_r + SS_c) \qquad (14.5)$$

Question: If I come up with a negative sum of squares, does that mean my results are opposite to my research hypothesis?

No, it means that you have made a mistake. Sums of squares can *never* be negative. If you look carefully at Formulas 14.1–14.5, you will notice that all of them involve adding or subtracting squared values. All the squared values will, of course, be positive. Also, you will always subtract a smaller value from a larger value; therefore, the result can never be negative. If you do compute a negative value for any sum of squares, you need to go back and find where you made the error.

Computing the sum of squares for the depth perception experiment is just a matter of finding the appropriate values or sums from Table 14.4 and then using Formulas 14.1–14.5. We begin by computing the sum of squares total using Formula 14.1:

$$SS_{total} = \Sigma\Sigma X^2 - \frac{(\Sigma\Sigma X)^2}{N_{total}} = 752 - \frac{124^2}{30}$$

$$= 752 - \frac{15,376}{30} = 752 - 512.533$$

$$= 239.467$$

Next we compute sum of squares within using Formula 14.2:

$$SS_{wg} = \Sigma\Sigma X^2 - \frac{\Sigma(\Sigma X_{cell})^2}{n_{cell}} = 752 - \frac{45^2 + 15^2 + 25^2 + 12^2 + 17^2 + 10^2}{5}$$

$$= 752 - \frac{2025 + 225 + 625 + 144 + 289 + 100}{5}$$

$$= 752 - \frac{3408}{5} = 752 - 681.6$$

$$= 70.4$$

Now we compute the sum of squares for the rows using Formula 14.3. Remember that the rows represent no head motion, slow head motion, and moderate head motion:

$$SS_r = \frac{\Sigma(\Sigma X_{row})^2}{n_{row}} - \frac{(\Sigma\Sigma X)^2}{N_{total}} = \frac{60^2 + 37^2 + 27^2}{10} - \frac{124^2}{30}$$

$$= \frac{3600 + 1369 + 729}{10} - \frac{15,376}{30} = \frac{5698}{10} - 512.533$$

$$= 569.8 - 512.533$$

$$= 57.267$$

Table 14.4 Sums Needed to Compute the Analysis of Variance for the Depth Perception Experiment

| | | Independent variable 1 | | | |
| | | One eye open | | Two eyes open | |

		X	X^2	X	X^2	
		8	64	5	25	
No		10	100	4	16	$\Sigma X_{\text{row}} = 60$
head movement		8	64	1	1	$\bar{X}_{\text{row}} = 6$
		6	36	2	4	$\Sigma X_{\text{row}}^2 = 488$
		13	169	3	9	
		$\Sigma X = 45$	$\Sigma X^2 = 433$	$\Sigma X = 15$	$\Sigma X^2 = 55$	
		$\bar{X}_{\text{cell}} = 9$		$\bar{X}_{\text{cell}} = 3$		
		X	X^2	X	X^2	
		4	16	4	16	
Slow		6	36	1	1	$\Sigma X_{\text{row}} = 37$
head movement		3	9	2	4	$\bar{X}_{\text{row}} = 3.7$
		5	25	3	9	$\Sigma X_{\text{row}}^2 = 169$
		7	49	2	4	
		$\Sigma X = 25$	$\Sigma X^2 = 135$	$\Sigma X = 12$	$\Sigma X^2 = 34$	
		$\bar{X}_{\text{cell}} = 5$		$\bar{X}_{\text{cell}} = 2.4$		
		X	X^2	X	X^2	
		2	4	3	9	
Moderate		2	4	0	0	$\Sigma X_{\text{row}} = 27$
head movement		3	9	3	9	$\bar{X}_{\text{row}} = 2.7$
		4	16	2	4	$\Sigma X_{\text{row}}^2 = 95$
		6	36	2	4	
		$\Sigma X = 17$	$\Sigma X^2 = 69$	$\Sigma X = 10$	$\Sigma X^2 = 26$	
		$\bar{X}_{\text{cell}} = 3.4$		$\bar{X}_{\text{cell}} = 2$		

	$\Sigma X_{\text{col}} = 87$		$\Sigma X_{\text{col}} = 37$		$\Sigma\Sigma X = 124$
	$\bar{X}_{\text{col}} = 5.8$		$\bar{X}_{\text{col}} = 2.467$		
	$\Sigma X_{\text{col}}^2 = 637$		$\Sigma X_{\text{col}}^2 = 115$		$\Sigma\Sigma X^2 = 752$

Independent variable 2 (left vertical label)

We compute the sum of squares for columns with Formula 14.4. Remember that the columns represent the number of eyes used to view the depth perception apparatus:

$$SS_c = \frac{\Sigma(\Sigma X_{\text{col}})^2}{n_{\text{col}}} - \frac{(\Sigma\Sigma X)^2}{N_{\text{total}}} = \frac{87^2 + 37^2}{15} - \frac{124^2}{30}$$

$$= \frac{7569 + 1369}{15} - \frac{15{,}376}{30} = \frac{8938}{15} - 512.533$$

$$= 595.867 - 512.533$$

$$= 83.334$$

Table 14.5   Source Table for Two-Way Factorial Analysis of Variance Showing the Computed Sums of Squares

Source of variation	Sum of squares	Degrees of freedom	Mean square	F
Rows	57.267			
Columns	83.334			
Interaction	28.466			
Within	70.400			
Total	239.467			

Finally, we compute the sum of squares for the interaction by using Formula 14.5 and the preceding results from Formulas 14.1–14.4:

$$SS_{r \times c} = SS_{total} - (SS_{wg} + SS_r + SS_c)$$

$$= 239.467 - (70.4 + 57.267 + 83.334)$$

$$= 239.467 - 211.001$$

$$= 28.466$$

After computing all the sums of squares, we create a *source table* like Table 14.5. We enter the sums in the table. The next step is to compute the degrees of freedom for each term in the analysis.

C O N C E P T   Q U I Z

1. List the sums of squares that must be computed for a two-way analysis of variance.

2. The computational formulas for sum of squares _____ and sum of squares _____ are the same as the computational formulas used in one-way analysis of variance.

3. In a two-way analysis of variance, the sum of squares between is partitioned into what three different sums of squares?

4. Express each of the following in words:
  a. $\Sigma\Sigma X^2$
  b. $\Sigma\Sigma X$
  c. $\Sigma(\Sigma X_{cell})^2$
  d. $\Sigma(\Sigma X_{row})^2$
  e. $\Sigma(\Sigma X_{col})^2$
  f. N_{total}

   g. n_{cell}
   h. n_{row}
   i. n_{col}
5. Which sum of squares is arrived at by subtraction?

Answers

1. sum of squares rows (SS_r); sum of squares columns (SS_c); sum of squares interaction ($SS_{r \times c}$); sum of squares within (SS_{wg}); sum of squares total (SS_{total})

2. within groups; total

3. sum of squares rows; sum of squares columns; sum of squares interaction

4. a. The sum of the sums of the X^2 for all the cells in the entire analysis. You square each score and add them all up.

   b. The sum of the sums of the X-values for all cells in the entire analysis. You add up all the scores from all the cells in the analysis.

   c. The sum of the square of the sum of the X-values for each cell. You compute the sum of the scores within each cell, square that value, and then add up these squared values across all cells.

   d. The sum of the square of the sum of the X-values for each row. You compute the sum of the scores within each row, square that value, and then add up these squared values across all rows.

   e. The sum of the square of the sum of the X-values for each column. You compute the sum of the scores within each column, square that value, and then add up these squared values across all columns.

   f. The total number of scores in all the samples.

   g. The number of scores in an individual cell.

   h. The number of scores in each row.

   i. The number of scores in each column.

5. sum of squares interaction

COMPUTATION OF DEGREES OF FREEDOM FOR TWO-WAY ANALYSIS OF VARIANCE

In referring to the source table, Table 14.5 or Table 14.6, you can see that there are five different types of degrees of freedom in a two-way analysis of variance: rows (df_r), columns (df_c), interaction ($df_{r \times c}$), within groups (df_{wg}), and total (df_{total}). The number of degrees of freedom for the rows is equal to the number of rows minus 1:

$$df_r = \text{number of rows} - 1 \qquad (14.6)$$

Similarly, the number of degrees of freedom for the columns is equal to the number of columns minus 1:

$$df_c = \text{number of columns} - 1 \qquad (14.7)$$

The degrees of freedom for the interaction are equal to the degrees of freedom for the rows times the degrees of freedom for the columns:

$$df_{r \times c} = df_r \cdot df_c$$

$$= (\text{number of rows} - 1) \cdot (\text{number of columns} - 1) \qquad (14.8)$$

The degrees of freedom within are equal to the sum of the separate degrees of freedom for each cell or the total number of scores in all samples minus the number of cells:

$$df_{wg} = (n_{cell1} - 1) + (n_{cellk} - 1) + \cdots + (n_{cellk} - 1)$$

or

$$df_{wg} = N_{total} - \text{number of cells} \qquad (14.9)$$

Last, the number of degrees of freedom total equals the total number of scores minus 1:

$$df_{total} = N_{total} - 1 \qquad (14.10)$$

Let's use what we know to compute the degrees of freedom for the depth perception experiment. We use Formulas 14.6–14.10 for our computations and then enter the results in the source table as shown in Table 14.6. Because three different types of motion are represented by the rows, the number of degrees of freedom for rows is

$$df_r = \text{number of rows} - 1 = 3 - 1 = 2$$

The columns represent two conditions, one eye open and two eyes open; therefore, the number of degrees of freedom for columns is

$$df_c = \text{number of columns} - 1 = 2 - 1 = 1$$

From Formula 14.8, the number of degrees of freedom for the interaction is

$$df_{r \times c} = df_r \cdot df_c = (\text{number of rows} - 1) \cdot (\text{number of columns} - 1)$$

$$= 2 \cdot 1 = 2$$

There are 30 subjects and six different cells in our experiment, so the number of degrees of freedom within is equal to

$$df_{wg} = N_{total} - \text{number of cells} = 30 - 6 = 24$$

Finally, the number of degrees of freedom total is equal to the 30 total subjects minus 1:

$$df_{total} = N_{total} - 1 = 30 - 1 = 29$$

Table 14.6 Source Table for Two-Way Factorial Analysis of Variance Showing the Computed Sums of Squares and Degrees of Freedom

Source of variation	Sum of squares	Degrees of freedom	Mean square	F
Rows	57.267	2		
Columns	83.334	1		
Interaction	28.466	2		
Within	70.400	24		
Total	239.467	29		

COMPUTATION OF THE MEAN SQUARES FOR TWO-WAY ANALYSIS OF VARIANCE

After the sums of squares and the degrees of freedom have been computed, the mean squares can be computed in the same way as in the one-way analysis of variance. The mean square is equal to the sum of squares divided by the degrees of freedom. The computations of all the mean squares are as follows:

$$MS_r = \frac{SS_r}{df_r} = \frac{57.267}{2} = 28.634 \tag{14.11}$$

$$MS_c = \frac{SS_c}{df_c} = \frac{83.334}{1} = 83.334 \tag{14.12}$$

$$MS_{r \times c} = \frac{SS_{r \times c}}{df_{r \times c}} = \frac{28.466}{2} = 14.233 \tag{14.13}$$

$$MS_{wg} = \frac{SS_{wg}}{df_{wg}} = \frac{70.400}{24} = 2.933 \tag{14.14}$$

When we have completed the mean squares computations, we need to plug the values into the source table. Table 14.7 contains all the values we just computed. At long last, we can calculate the F ratios.

Table 14.7 Source Table for Two-Way Factorial Analysis of Variance Showing the Computed Sums of Squares, Degrees of Freedom, and Mean Squares

Source of variation	Sum of squares	Degrees of freedom	Mean square	F
Rows	57.267	2	28.634	
Columns	83.334	1	83.334	
Interaction	28.466	2	14.233	
Within	70.400	24	2.933	
Total	239.467	29		

COMPUTATION OF THE *F* RATIOS FOR TWO-WAY ANALYSIS OF VARIANCE

In two-way analysis of variance, we are testing three sets of null hypotheses; thus, it is necessary to compute three different *F* ratios. We need to compute one *F* ratio to test the rows, one to test the columns, and one to test the interaction. All the *F* ratios are computed in the same way as in the one-way analysis of variance: We divide the mean square for the source of variation being tested by the mean square within. The formulas and computations of each *F* for the depth perception data follow. Keep in mind that the rows represent the main effect of the type of motion on the dependent variable, the columns represent the main effect of the number of eyes open on the dependent variable, and the interaction represents the effect of both independent variables on the dependent variable:

$$F_r = \frac{MS_r}{MS_{wg}} \tag{14.15}$$

$$= \frac{28.634}{2.933} = 9.763$$

$$F_c = \frac{MS_c}{MS_{wg}} \tag{14.16}$$

$$= \frac{83.334}{2.933} = 28.413$$

$$F_{r \times c} = \frac{MS_{r \times c}}{MS_{wg}} \tag{14.17}$$

$$= \frac{14.233}{2.933} = 4.853$$

With the computation of these F ratios, we can now complete the source table (see Table 14.8).

Table 14.8 Source Table for Two-Way Factorial Analysis of Variance Showing the Computed Sums of Squares, Degrees of Freedom, Mean Squares, and F Ratios

Source of variation	Sum of squares	Degrees of freedom	Mean square	F
Rows	57.267	2	28.634	9.763
Columns	83.334	1	83.334	28.413
Interaction	28.466	2	14.233	4.853
Within	70.400	24	2.933	
Total	239.467	29		

SIGNIFICANCE OF THE MAIN EFFECTS

Question: Do we still have to look up these F ratios in Table F to see whether they are significant?

Sure. We still need to compare each computed F ratio to the appropriate value in Table F, and we do this the same way we did it for the one-way analysis of variance. We enter Table F by using the degrees of freedom of the numerator and the denominator in the F ratio. Our first step is to compare the critical value in Table F to our computed F ratio for the main effect of rows (type of motion), which is 9.763. Looking in the table, we find our computed values of 2 degrees of freedom for the numerator and 24 degrees of freedom for the denominator, and we find the critical value to be 3.40. Because our computed value for F is greater than the value in the table, we can reject the null hypothesis and accept the research hypothesis. This means that it is pretty certain that at least one of the samples came from a different population than the other samples, and that head motion makes a difference in the accuracy of depth perception.

When there are more than two levels of an independent variable, as is the case with types of head motion, a significant F tells us that there is a real difference, but we cannot be sure which means are significantly different from one another. Therefore, we must use the HSD (honestly significant difference) test, which is computed the same way it was in the one-way analysis of variance, by using Formula 13.15:

$$\text{HSD} = q\sqrt{\frac{\text{MS}_{wg}}{n}} \tag{13.15}$$

We look up the value of q in Table Q in Appendix A using the number of means to be compared, 3, and the degrees of freedom within, 24, and find the q-value of 3.53. The value for n is equal to the number of subjects in each level being compared; in this case, it is equal to n_{row}, or 10. Thus,

$$\text{HSD} = q\sqrt{\frac{\text{MS}_{wg}}{n}} = 3.53\sqrt{\frac{2.933}{10}} = 3.53 \cdot \sqrt{0.293}$$

$$= 3.53 \cdot 0.541 = 1.910$$

This result tells us that any difference of 1.91 millimeters between means is an honestly significant difference. The means for the three different levels of head motion are:

$$\overline{X}_{no} = 6.0 \text{ millimeters}$$

$$\overline{X}_{slow} = 3.7 \text{ millimeters}$$

$$\overline{X}_{moderate} = 2.7 \text{ millimeters}$$

The differences, then, are

$$\overline{X}_{no} - \overline{X}_{slow} = 6.0 - 3.7 = 2.3 \text{ millimeters}$$

$$\overline{X}_{no} - \overline{X}_{moderate} = 6.0 - 2.7 = 3.3 \text{ millimeters}$$

$$\overline{X}_{slow} - \overline{X}_{moderate} = 3.7 - 2.7 = 1.0 \text{ millimeter}$$

Comparing these three differences to the HSD, we find that the difference between the means for the no-motion and slow-motion conditions are significant, as is the difference between the no-motion and moderate-motion conditions. On the other hand, the difference between the slow- and moderate-motion conditions is not significant. It is clear from these data, then, that the perception of depth is significantly better when subjects move their heads as compared to no movement.

Similar comparisons must be done with the computed F ratio for the columns (number of eyes open). See if you can think this through on your own before reading our procedure. If you're still a little fuzzy, review the procedures we used for the rows. Ready? What do you do first? You look up the F ratio for the columns, with 1 degree of freedom for the numerator and 24 degrees of freedom for the denominator. What do you do with these figures? Use them to look up the critical value of *F* in Table *F*, and compare this critical value, which is 4.26, to our computed value of 28.413. Does this mean that you can reject the null hypothesis? You bet it does! So you can accept the research hypothesis relating to the columns. And what does it state? Try to say it in your own words before reading further. It states that the samples represented by one-eye-open and two-eyes-open viewing come from different populations. Now, do you have to use the HSD test? You don't, because there are only two levels of the independent variable and the *F* ratio is significant. Therefore, the mean error of 5.8 millimeters in the one-eye-open condition is significantly greater than the mean error of 2.6 millimeters in the two-eyes-open condition, which confirms what we all knew to start with, that two eyes are better than one.

SIGNIFICANCE OF THE INTERACTION

The computed *F* ratio for the interaction is tested by comparing it to the value in Table *F* for 2 degrees of freedom in the numerator and 24 degrees of freedom in the denominator. Our computed *F* ratio for the interaction is 4.853, whereas the comparison value in Table *F* is 3.40. Because the computed value is greater than the critical table value, we can reject the null hypothesis for the interaction and accept the research hypothesis, which states that the interaction of the independent variables represented by the columns and rows has an effect on the dependent variable. As we mentioned at the beginning of the chapter, merely knowing that a significant interaction exists does not explain the *reason* for the interaction or its implications. These explanations are up to the researcher, and they are often quite difficult. Graphing the means of the different experimental cells in Figure 14.1 (see page 314) indicates that head motion drastically reduces the error rate in the one-eye-open conditions, whereas it has a minimal effect when subjects use both eyes. By using these data, we can recommend that people who have the use of only one eye should move their head back and forth if they want to determine the distance of a stationary object. This movement will greatly enhance their depth perception and make them almost as accurate as people who have the use of both eyes.

C O N C E P T   Q U I Z

1. List the five different types of degrees of freedom in a two-way analysis of variance and give the general formulas for computing them.
2. In a two-way analysis of variance, as in a one-way analysis of variance, the mean square is equal to the _____ divided by the _____ .

3. The F ratio is computed by dividing the mean square of interest (rows, columns, or interaction) by the mean square _____ .

4. For our computed F ratio to be significant, it must be _____ the value in Table _____ .

5. If the F ratio for a main effect—columns or rows—with more than two levels is significant, you can use the _____ to determine which levels are significantly different from one another.

6. The effects of a significant interaction are usually easiest to see in a _____ .

Answers

1. rows (df_r); columns (df_c); interaction ($df_{r \times c}$); within (df_{wg}); total (df_{total})

df_r = number of rows − 1

df_c = number of columns − 1

$df_{r \times c} = df_r \cdot df_c$ = (number of rows − 1) · (number of columns − 1)

$df_{wg} = (n_{cell1} − 1) + (n_{cell2} − 1) + \cdots + (n_{cellk} − 1)$

or

$df_{wg} = N_{total}$ − number of cells

$df_{total} = N_{total} − 1$

2. sum of squares; degrees of freedom

3. within

4. greater than or equal to; F

5. HSD

6. graph

S U M M A R Y

Experiments that have more than one independent variable are called factorial experiments. Factorial experiments that have two independent variables are analyzed by a two-way analysis of variance. In a two-way analysis of variance, four separate variance estimates are computed. Two of these are called the main effects and are represented by the mean square for rows and the mean square for columns. In addition to the main effects, there is a mean square for the interaction of the two variables being tested as well as a mean square within. Each main effect represents the effect of only one of the independent variables on the dependent variable. The interaction is the effect of the combination of both independent variables on the dependent variable. The easiest way to illustrate an interaction is to graph the two independent variables on the same axes and compare the slopes of the two lines. If the slopes are similar, there is little or no interaction, but if the slopes are very different or opposite, an interaction exists.

The computations for the various sums of squares—total, within, main effects, and interaction—are given in Formulas 14.1–14.5. The number of degrees of freedom for the main effects is merely the number of rows or the number of columns in the analysis minus 1. The number of degrees of freedom for the interaction is the degrees of freedom for the columns times the degrees of freedom for the rows. The number of degrees of freedom for the within term is the total number of subjects minus the number of cells in the analysis.

The mean square for each element in the analysis of variance consists of the sum of squares divided by the corresponding degrees of freedom. F-values for the two main effects and the interaction are then computed by dividing the appropriate mean squares by the mean square within.

KEY TERMS

factorial experiment

main effect

interaction

FORMULAS

$$SS_{total} = \Sigma\Sigma X^2 - \frac{(\Sigma\Sigma X)^2}{N_{total}} \tag{14.1}$$

$$SS_{wg} = \Sigma\Sigma X^2 - \frac{\Sigma(\Sigma X_{cell})^2}{n_{cell}} \tag{14.2}$$

$$SS_r = \frac{\Sigma(\Sigma X_{row})^2}{n_{row}} - \frac{(\Sigma\Sigma X)^2}{N_{total}} \tag{14.3}$$

$$SS_c = \frac{\Sigma(\Sigma X_{col})^2}{n_{col}} - \frac{(\Sigma\Sigma X)^2}{N_{total}} \tag{14.4}$$

$$SS_{r \times c} = SS_{total} - (SS_{wg} + SS_r + SS_c) \tag{14.5}$$

$$df_r = \text{number of rows} - 1 \tag{14.6}$$

$$df_c = \text{number of columns} - 1 \tag{14.7}$$

$$df_{r \times c} = df_r \cdot df_c$$
$$= (\text{number of rows} - 1) \cdot (\text{number of columns} - 1) \tag{14.8}$$

$$df_{wg} = N_{total} - \text{number of cells} \tag{14.9}$$

$$df_{total} = N_{total} - 1 \tag{14.10}$$

$$MS_r = \frac{SS_r}{df_r} \tag{14.11}$$

$$MS_c = \frac{SS_c}{df_c} \tag{14.12}$$

$$MS_{r \times c} = \frac{SS_{r \times c}}{df_{r \times c}} \tag{14.13}$$

$$MS_{wg} = \frac{SS_{wg}}{df_{wg}} \tag{14.14}$$

$$F_r = \frac{MS_r}{MS_{wg}} \tag{14.15}$$

$$F_c = \frac{MS_c}{MS_{wg}} \tag{14.16}$$

$$F_{r \times c} = \frac{MS_{r \times c}}{MS_{wg}} \tag{14.17}$$

P R O B L E M S

All these problems are examples of possible experiments. Do all of the following steps for each problem using the data presented.

a. Write down each research hypothesis being tested in the experiment.

b. Create a two-way analysis of variance source table, including the sources of variation, degrees of freedom, sums of squares, mean squares, and F ratios.

c. Look up each F ratio in Table F in Appendix A and determine whether it is significant.

d. If one of the main effects is significant and it contains more than two levels, compute an HSD and determine which levels are significantly different from one another.

e. Graph the interaction if it is significant and, using your knowledge of the problem, attempt to explain the significant interaction.

f. What can you conclude from this experiment? Discuss the results of this experiment in a few sentences.

1. Your computer company is about to market a new laptop computer, and you are asked to determine which of two screens should be used with the computer. One screen's display has orange letters on a dark background, whereas the other has blue letters on a light background. An adjunct factor you are to explore is which type of lighting, incandescent or fluorescent, should be used with each screen for optimum readability. You design an experiment in which 20 people are divided into four different groups: those seeing the orange screen under incandescent lights, those seeing the orange screen under fluorescent lights, those seeing the blue screen under incandescent lights, and those seeing the blue screen under fluorescent lights. The dependent variable, listed in the table at the top of page 332, is the number of seconds each person takes to read 1000 words displayed on the screen.

	Type of light	
	Fluorescent	Incandescent
Blue	130	132
	129	117
	118	123
	133	129
	125	122
Orange	144	147
	139	143
	145	141
	139	134
	139	140

2. A memory experiment is conducted to determine whether the type of task—recognition or free recall—is affected by the type of word list used—meaningful or nonsense. Both meaningful and nonsense lists are made up of three-letter consonant-vowel-consonant combinations. Subjects are briefly shown a list of "words" and are then asked to remember the list using either recognition (identifying whether the word was on the list) or recall (generating the entire list without prompting). The dependent variable is the number of correct words recognized or recalled from a 50-word list. The numbers are listed in the table.

	Type of word	
	Nonsense	Meaningful
Recall	23	36
	18	39
	20	33
	16	35
Recognition	27	34
	29	37
	28	38
	32	35

3. The Diagnostic and Statistical Manual (DSM) of the American Psychiatric Association is an attempt at the classification of all mental disorders. Unfortunately, or fortunately, depending on your point of view, every few years the DSM must be revised to account for new research on psychopathology. Every change in the DSM requires that all psychologists and psychiatrists learn the new classification system. You are a state government researcher who works with the psychology and psychiatry licensing board. The board has ruled that all clinical psychologists and psychiatrists must complete a continuing education course that teaches the new version of the DSM. In the past, two different kinds of courses have been offered by your office: lecture and television courses. You are asked to determine the relative effectiveness of these two methods of instruction for both psychiatrists and psychologists. Therefore, you design an experiment with two independent variables: type of instruction (lecture or television) and type of license (psychologist or psychiatrist). The dependent variable is the number of correct items on a test called the DSM-KT (the DSM–Knowledge Test) that you have constructed. The test scores for your experiment are given here.

	Psychologist	Psychiatrist
Television	88	65
	93	98
	63	85
Lecture	75	88
	94	71
	81	94

4. As a psychobiologist you are interested in the effect of two new drugs on the electrical charge of a neuron membrane. In addition to observing general differences between the two drugs, you want to see whether their effects vary at different temperatures. Therefore, you design an experiment whereby you inject the drugs into a giant squid's large neurons that have been kept alive in a saline solution. You inject each drug into four separate neurons at 20 degrees Celsius (normal room temperature) and then again at 37 degrees Celsius (normal human body temperature). For each presentation of the drug, you measure the change in the electrical charge (in millivolts) of the neuronal membrane. For a total of 16 neurons, the table lists the results for the four conditions.

	Temperature	
	20 degrees	37 degrees
Drug A	4	3
	−2	7
	1	9
	2	11
Drug B	9	13
	8	12
	7	14
	8	15

5. As a budding psychologist, you wonder whether you can teach old dogs new tricks. So you go to the pound and adopt a bunch of old dogs, as well as a bunch of puppies, and you attempt to teach all the dogs three of the old standards: "sit," "shake," and "roll over." Teaching only one trick to each dog, you keep a record of how many days it takes before they learn the tricks. The results of your experiment are listed in the table.

	Type of trick		
	"Sit"	"Shake"	"Roll over"
	2	4	6
	1	5	9
Young dog	3	4	7
	1	6	8
	2	7	10
	2	9	13
	5	10	12
Old dog	2	11	15
	4	13	17
	3	7	13

6. A psychologist who is an expert on proofreading is interested in the effect of two separate variables on proofreading. He develops two ten-page manuscripts, one having no errors in the first seven pages and then 20 errors over the last three pages, and the other having 5 errors per page in the first seven pages and the same 20 errors over the last three pages. His experiment has two independent variables. One independent variable is the number of errors in the first seven pages; the other is the method of displaying the manuscript, on a computer monitor or on paper. The first independent variable, number of errors, has two levels: no errors in the first seven pages and an average of five errors per page in the first seven pages. The second independent variable also has two levels: paper or computer presentation of the manuscript. The dependent variable is the number of errors detected on the last three pages. Data are given here for this 2×2 factorial experiment.

	Errors on first seven pages	
	Yes	No
	16	5
	14	9
Computer	18	7
	17	6
	14	9
	15	12
Paper	15	11
	14	10

7. Although the vast majority of psychological subjects are human, animal rights have become a major concern for psychology. Because of the importance of animal rights issues, a group of researchers has designed an experiment to determine the effectiveness of various animal rights messages. The researchers want to see whether subjects perceive animal research differently depending on whether they know where the research is being conducted and whether they can form some sort of empathy with the researcher by seeing his or her photograph. Thus, there are two independent variables, the first being whether or not the institution is mentioned and the second being the presence or absence of the experimenter's photo. The dependent variable is the subject's rating of the effectiveness of the message on a ten-point interval scale. The results of this 2×2 factorial experiment are given here.

	Institution mentioned	
	Yes	No
	6	9
	4	9
Photograph	8	7
	7	6
	4	4
	5	2
No photograph	3	1
	4	5

R E F E R E N C E

Leibowitz, H.W. (1985). Grade crossing accidents and human factors engineering. *American Scientist, 73,* 558–562.

Nonparametric Statistics: Chi-Square, Mann-Whitney *U* Test, Wilcoxon *T* Test, and the Kruskal-Wallis Test

O U T L I N E

- Chi-Square
- The Mann-Whitney *U* Test
- The Wilcoxon *T* Test
- The Kruskal-Wallis Test
- Summary
- Key Terms
- Formulas
- Problems
- References

One out of every four Americans can expect to be diagnosed as having some type of cancer during his or her lifetime. One out of every four! How many people are in your immediate family? Two? Four? Five? How many are in your extended family? 20? 30? More? Who of these family members might suffer from cancer sometime during their lives? Your grandma, your uncle, a niece, your dad, *you*? With this in mind, you can appreciate the extreme importance of cancer research, not only in finding cures for the more than 100 different types of cancer but also in exploring ways to minimize our chances of getting cancer. These ways often involve behavioral changes that diminish our exposure to carcinogens, such as moving away from a chemical plant or stopping smoking. Recently, several researchers in health psychology have begun investigating other, less obvious factors related to cancer, such as personality, exercise, and social support networks.

In a study of social connections conducted by Kaplan and Reynolds in 1988, women who reported that they were socially isolated were significantly more likely to die of cancer than their same-age peers who had many social connections. Based on this study, it is logical to propose that the extent of a person's social network may be a factor in the development of terminal cancer. Suppose that we decide to conduct a hypothetical study to try to confirm this research hypothesis. We spend months recruiting women for our study and assign them to three nearly identical groups of 1000 women each, the only difference being that all the women in the first group have a poor social network (they are socially isolated with no close friends or relatives), all the women in the second group have a moderate social network (they have only one or two close friends or relatives), and all the women in the third group have a good social network (they have more than two close friends or relatives). Over the next 5 years, we keep in touch with the people in the three groups and record the number of cancer deaths. Table 15.1 shows what these hypothetical data might look like.

Of the 99 women who died of cancer, 45 had a poor social network, 34 had a moderate social network, and 20 had a good social network. We, of course, would like to know whether the type of social network had a significant effect on the cancer mortality rate. So the question is: How do we analyze these data? There is one variable, type of social network, that has three levels—poor, moderate, and good.

Question: Isn't this a multilevel experimental design that can be analyzed using a one-way analysis of variance?

This does resemble the experimental design requiring a one-way analysis of variance, except that in a one-way analysis of variance there is a separate interval or ratio score for each subject, rather than a table listing merely the

Table 15.1 Number of Deaths Per Thousand Women for Three Types of Social Networks

| | Type of social network | |
Poor	Moderate	Good
45	34	20

number of subjects in each condition. Do you remember reading in Chapter 1 about the different scales of measurement? Well, the analysis of variance analyzes data from interval or ratio scales. The data in Table 15.1 are different. They are **nominal data**; that is, they are reported only as a list of the numbers of people who fit into certain categories. Analysis of variance is not appropriate for such data, but there is an appropriate statistic for analyzing nominal data. It is known as chi-square (χ^2).

CHI-SQUARE

Chi-square (χ^2) is a statistical technique that enables us to compare the observed frequencies in different categories (the actual numbers obtained) with the frequencies expected from some theory or hypothesis. We represent an **observed frequency** with the symbol f_o, and we represent an **expected frequency** with the symbol f_e. The formula for χ^2 is

$$\chi^2 = \Sigma \frac{(f_o - f_e)^2}{f_e} \tag{15.1}$$

Chi-square, then, is computed by subtracting the frequency expected from the frequency observed, squaring this difference and dividing the squared value by the frequency expected for each cell, and then summing these terms over all the cells.

Question: I can see how to get the observed frequency; that's just the data we collect. But how do you come up with the expected frequency?

In our cancer study we would, as before, have two different hypotheses: the null hypothesis that cancer rates are the same for all types of social networks, and the research hypothesis that cancer rates are not the same for all the types. If the null hypothesis were true and cancer death rates were the same for each type, we would expect that the 99 cancer deaths would be spread evenly across all the types, and there would be 33 deaths in each category. Thus, the expected frequency for each category would be 33. Table 15.2 shows the observed frequency as well as the expected frequency for each category. It is obvious from these data that the number of deaths in the poor and good conditions are different from the expected frequency, but the χ^2 test indicates whether the pattern of responses is significantly different from what is expected, given the null hypothesis.

Table 15.2   Frequency Observed and Frequency Expected for the Social Networks Research Project

Type of social network		
Poor	Moderate	Good
$f_o = 45$	$f_o = 34$	$f_o = 20$
$f_e = 33$	$f_e = 33$	$f_e = 33$

Using Formula 15.1 to compute χ^2 from the data in Table 15.2 results in the following:

$$\chi^2 = \Sigma \frac{(f_o - f_e)^2}{f_e} = \frac{(45 - 33)^2}{33} + \frac{(34 - 33)^2}{33} + \frac{(20 - 33)^2}{33}$$

$$= \frac{12^2}{33} + \frac{1^2}{33} + \frac{-13^2}{33} = \frac{144}{33} + \frac{1}{33} + \frac{169}{33}$$

$$= 4.364 + 0.030 + 5.121$$

$$= 9.515$$

Question: Is a χ^2 of 9.515 good or bad?

If by good or bad you mean significant or not significant, then you've just pinpointed the next step: to determine whether the χ^2 is significant. But short of determining significance, we can certainly say that the larger the χ^2, the more likely it will be significant. You can see this by taking a look at Formula 15.1 Because χ^2 is a comparison of the observed frequency to the expected frequency, a larger discrepancy between the observed frequency and the expected frequency results in a larger χ^2. Another interesting point about the χ^2 distribution is that χ^2 is likely to become larger as additional cells are added to the analysis.

Table 15.3 A Portion of Table χ, Critical Values of the χ^2 Statistic

df	.25	.10	.05	.025	.01	.005
1	1.323	2.706	3.841	5.024	6.635	7.879
2	2.773	4.605	5.991	7.378	9.210	10.597
3	4.108	6.251	7.815	9.348	11.345	12.838
4	5.385	7.779	9.488	11.143	13.277	14.860
5	6.626	9.236	11.071	12.833	15.086	16.750

Source: Owen, 1962.

Now, to determine the significance of the χ^2. Just as we would for a computed *t*-value or a computed *F*-value, we compare our computed χ^2 to a table value to see whether it is significant. We use Table χ in Appendix A, the chi-square distribution table, a small portion of which is reproduced in Table 15.3. As with Table *T* and Table *F*, we need to know the degrees of freedom in order to enter Table χ. The degrees of freedom for a chi-square with only one row is the number of cells minus 1. (The computation of the number of degrees of freedom changes slightly when additional rows are added.) Our study of the effects of social networks on cancer rates has only one row and three cells. Therefore, the number of degrees of freedom for this χ^2 is 3 cells minus 1, or 2 degrees of freedom.

Take a look at Table 15.3, which is a small portion of Table χ, and find the critical value of χ^2. To enter the table, find the degrees of freedom in the left-hand column and look across the row until you reach the $\alpha = .05$ column. Here you should find the value 5.991. If the computed χ^2 with 2 degrees of freedom is greater than or equal to 5.991, then we can reject the null hypothesis and accept the research hypothesis. In our cancer/social network study, the computed χ^2 equals 9.515. Because this is greater than the table value of 5.991, we can reject the null hypothesis and accept the research hypothesis. Our project confirms that cancer rates are not the same for the different types of social networks.

Question: This seems easy enough, but a while back you mentioned something about the degrees of freedom computation being different for two rows. What did you mean by that? And is chi-square much more complicated when there are two rows?

We were referring to additional rows in the experimental design matrix. When there are two independent variables, there are two rows in the matrix. Computing χ^2 for a matrix with two or more rows is exactly the same as computing χ^2 with only one row. You must calculate an observed frequency and an expected frequency for each cell and then use Formula 15.1 to compute χ^2. To illustrate, we'll extend our cancer study to include two independent variables.

As you may already know, smoking is the single most preventable cause of death and disease in the United States, according to the U.S. Department of Health and Human Services. So let's examine the relationship between cancer deaths and smoking behavior as well as social support networks. Now our table should look like Table 15.4, which is a 2×3 table with two rows and three columns. Note that the number of women is still 99, but we have further identified each woman by whether or not she smoked.

Table 15.4 Number of Deaths Per Thousand Women for Three Types of Social Networks and for Smokers and Nonsmokers

| | Type of social network | | | |
	Poor	Moderate	Good	Total
Smoker	25	26	18	69
Nonsmoker	20	8	2	30
Total	45	34	20	99

We will still use Formula 15.1 to compute the χ^2, but first we need to identify an f_o and an f_e for each cell. The observed frequencies are shown in Table 15.4, but we need to compute the expected frequencies based on the null hypothesis of no difference in the rate of deaths caused by cancer. This computation would be easy if the number of women were equal in all conditions, but in this case it is necessary to correct for the fact that more than twice as many smokers as nonsmokers die from cancer. A relatively simple formula compensates for differences in either row totals or column totals, or both, and enables us to compute the expected frequency:

$$f_e = \frac{(\text{row total}) \cdot (\text{column total})}{\text{grand total}} \tag{15.2}$$

Because this particular χ^2 has two rows and three columns, six different expected frequencies must be computed using Formula 15.2. Thus, the expected frequency for row 1, column 1 is

$$f_e = \frac{(\text{row total}) \cdot (\text{column total})}{\text{grand total}} = \frac{69 \cdot 45}{99} = \frac{3105}{99}$$

$$= 31.36$$

The expected frequency for row 1, column 2 is

$$f_e = \frac{(\text{row total}) \cdot (\text{column total})}{\text{grand total}} = \frac{69 \cdot 34}{99} = \frac{2346}{99}$$

$$= 23.70$$

The expected frequency for row 1, column 3 is

$$f_e = \frac{(\text{row total}) \cdot (\text{column total})}{\text{grand total}} = \frac{69 \cdot 20}{99} = \frac{1380}{99}$$

$$= 13.94$$

The expected frequency for row 2, column 1 is

$$f_e = \frac{(\text{row total}) \cdot (\text{column total})}{\text{grand total}} = \frac{30 \cdot 45}{99} = \frac{1350}{99}$$

$$= 13.64$$

The expected frequency for row 2, column 2 is

$$f_e = \frac{(\text{row total}) \cdot (\text{column total})}{\text{grand total}} = \frac{30 \cdot 34}{99} = \frac{1020}{99}$$

$$= 10.30$$

The expected frequency for row 2, column 3 is

$$f_e = \frac{(\text{row total}) \cdot (\text{column total})}{\text{grand total}} = \frac{30 \cdot 20}{99} = \frac{600}{99}$$

$$= 6.06$$

These expected frequencies, along with the corresponding observed frequencies, are listed in Table 15.5. Now we use Formula 15.1 to compute the χ^2:

$$\chi^2 = \Sigma \frac{(f_o - f_e)^2}{f_e} = \frac{(25 - 31.36)^2}{31.36} + \frac{(26 - 23.70)^2}{23.70} + \frac{(18 - 13.94)^2}{13.94}$$

$$+ \frac{(20 - 13.64)^2}{13.64} + \frac{(8 - 10.30)^2}{10.30} + \frac{(2 - 6.06)^2}{6.06}$$

$$= \frac{-6.36^2}{31.36} + \frac{2.3^2}{23.70} + \frac{4.06^2}{13.94} + \frac{6.36^2}{13.64} + \frac{-2.3^2}{10.30} + \frac{-4.06^2}{6.06}$$

$$= \frac{40.45}{31.36} + \frac{5.29}{23.70} + \frac{16.48}{13.94} + \frac{40.45}{13.64} + \frac{5.29}{10.30} + \frac{16.48}{6.06}$$

$$= 1.29 + 0.22 + 1.18 + 2.97 + 0.51 + 2.72$$

$$= 8.89$$

Table 15.5 Frequency Observed and Frequency
Expected for Three Types of Social Networks and for
Smokers and Nonsmokers

| | Type of social network | | |
	Poor	Moderate	Good
Smoker	$f_o = 25$ $f_e = 31.36$	$f_o = 26$ $f_e = 23.70$	$f_o = 18$ $f_e = 13.94$
Nonsmoker	$f_o = 20$ $f_e = 13.64$	$f_o = 8$ $f_e = 10.30$	$f_o = 2$ $f_e = 6.06$

The χ^2 is 8.89, but we still must look at Table χ to determine significance. We mentioned earlier that the number of degrees of freedom is the number of cells minus 1 if there is only one row. When there is more than one row, the formula for degrees of freedom is

$$df = (\text{number of rows} - 1) \cdot (\text{number of columns} - 1) \qquad (15.3)$$

Because there are two rows and three columns in the cancer study, the number of degrees of freedom is

$$df = (2 \text{ rows} - 1) \cdot (3 \text{ columns} - 1) = 1 \cdot 2 = 2$$

Now we need to look in Table χ for 2 degrees of freedom and compare our computed χ^2 value of 8.89 to the $\alpha = .05$ table value of 5.99. Our computed value is greater than the table value, so we can reject the null hypothesis and accept the research hypothesis that there is a difference between the frequencies in the various cells. On inspection of Table 15.5, it is evident that of the cancer victims with good social networks, most were smokers. The same result holds true for those with poor and moderate social networks.

The chi-square test is straightforward and easy to use. However, there are a few assumptions and limitations that you need to be aware of when you consider using it:

1. It is assumed that the sample is randomly selected from the population.
2. It is assumed that all observations are independent. (This assumption is usually met if only one observation is made for each subject.)
3. The χ^2 test is limited to nominal data.
4. The χ^2 test tends to be less accurate with very small expected frequencies. (This is especially true with expected frequencies of less than 5. A good rule of thumb is not to conduct the χ^2 test on data with expected frequencies of less than 5.)

5. The χ^2 test tends to be less accurate for small degrees of freedom and a small N. (A correction is available for $df = 1$. See, for example, Minium, 1978.)

C O N C E P T   Q U I Z

1. Chi-square can be used only on _____ data.
2. Which of the following are possible χ^2-values?
   -2.7 0.37 10.38 -4.77 -10.83 -0.47
3. To conduct the χ^2 test, it is inadvisable to have expected frequencies of less than _____ .
4. The number of degrees of freedom in a 3×4 χ^2 test equals
_____ .

Answers

1. nominal
2. 0.37 and 10.38 (χ^2-values are always positive because you always square the differences between the expected and observed frequencies.)
3. 5
4. $(3 - 1) \cdot (4 - 1) = 6$

THE MANN-WHITNEY *U* TEST

Suppose you are hired as a statistical consultant for a manufacturing company to evaluate the effectiveness of a job training program. The management of the company wants to know whether people who went through a training program designed and administered by the local community college are significantly better workers than those who did not participate in the program. Unfortunately, you were not hired until after the data from the first group of workers had been collected, so you have no control over how they were gathered. The data are shown in Table 15.6.

Question: Can't I just separate the data into people with training and people with no training and then conduct a *t* test to see whether there is any difference between the two groups?

The data you must work with, as you can see in Table 15.6, are not scores on a job proficiency test but *rankings* based on supervisors' evaluations of workers' job performance. A *t* test requires an interval or a ratio scale of

Table 15.6 Job Performance Rankings of 20 Workers

Worker	Rank	Training program
T. D.	1	No
M. K.	2	No
D. C.	3	Yes
R. K.	4	No
C. T.	5	No
M. O.	6	Yes
P. H.	7	No
B. S.	8	Yes
G. S.	9	No
A. G.	10	Yes
B. W.	11	No
H. D.	12	Yes
K. T.	13	No
M. S.	14	Yes
D. O.	15	Yes
A. H.	16	Yes
T. H.	17	No
M. V.	18	Yes
Z. S.	19	Yes
K. H.	20	Yes

Explanation: The best worker gets a rank of 20, whereas the poorest worker gets a rank of 1.

measurement. When you use rankings, the data are ordered by size, but there is no guarantee that the intervals between the ranks are equal. Thus, it is inappropriate to use a *t* test to analyze the data. You must use a nonparametric test such as the Mann-Whitney *U*.

Question: The title of this chapter is "Nonparametric Statistics," and now you say that the Mann-Whitney *U* is a nonparametric test, but I don't know what that means. What is a nonparametric test?

As we discussed in Chapter 1, statistics are generally classified as descriptive or inferential, and inferential statistics can be further divided into parametric and nonparametric statistics. **Parametric statistics** are those that are stated in terms of and make assumptions about population parameters (the characteristic elements of a population under study, such as its mean and its standard deviation). For example, the hypotheses for the *t* test and the analysis of variance are stated in terms of the population mean, μ, and we assume that the variances of the populations being compared are equal and the scores are normally distributed. It is impossible to compare such parameters as population means when the data are ranked, and often it is impossible to guarantee equality of variances or normality, especially when the samples are small. **Nonparametric statistics** are tests that do not compare population parameters and make fewer assumptions than parametric statistics. The major advantages of most nonparametric statistics are that they work quite well with data that are ranked or skewed as well as with small samples.

Just as with parametric tests, nonparametric tests are based on a null hypothesis and a research hypothesis, but the hypotheses are not presented in terms of population parameters. The null hypothesis simply states that the two independent samples come from the same population distribution. When the research hypothesis is two-tailed and nondirectional, it merely states that the two independent samples come from different population distributions. When the research hypothesis is one-tailed and directional, it states that one of the samples comes from a population comprised of ranks that are smaller than the population of the other sample. The nonparametric test used to analyze two independent samples is the **Mann-Whitney *U*.**

To compute the Mann-Whitney *U*, we actually compute two separate statistics called U_1 and U_2. The formulas for U_1 and U_2 are as follows:

$$U_1 = (n_1 \cdot n_2) + \frac{n_1(n_1 + 1)}{2} - \Sigma R_1 \qquad (15.4)$$

$$U_2 = (n_2 \cdot n_1) + \frac{n_2(n_2 + 1)}{2} - \Sigma R_2 \qquad (15.5)$$

n_1 and n_2 are the number of subjects in sample 1 and sample 2, respectively. The only new terms are ΣR_1 and ΣR_2. ΣR_1 is the sum of the ranks for sample 1; ΣR_2 is the sum of the ranks for sample 2. To conduct a Mann-Whitney *U* test with the data in Table 15.6, we first need to separate the data into two samples; one is the workers who took the training program and the other is those who did not participate. The reorganized data are shown in Table 15.7.

Once the data are separated, we sum the ranks for each sample and then compute U_1 and U_2:

$$U_1 = (n_1 \cdot n_2) + \frac{n_1(n_1 + 1)}{2} - \Sigma R_1$$

$$= (11 \cdot 9) + \frac{11(11 + 1)}{2} - 141 = 99 + \frac{11 \cdot 12}{2} - 141$$

$$= 99 + \frac{132}{2} - 141 = 99 + 66 - 141$$

$$= 24$$

$$U_2 = (n_2 \cdot n_1) + \frac{n_2(n_2 + 1)}{2} - \Sigma R_2$$

$$= (9 \cdot 11) + \frac{9(9 + 1)}{2} - 69 = 99 + \frac{9 \cdot 10}{2} - 69$$

$$= 99 + \frac{90}{2} - 69 = 99 + 45 - 69$$

$$= 75$$

Having computed both U-values, you can swiftly verify their accuracy because their sum must always equal the product of n_1 and n_2; that is,

$$U_1 + U_2 = n_1 \cdot n_2 \qquad (15.6)$$

Table 15.7 Job Performance Rankings of 20 Workers Separated Into Training and No-Training Samples

	Training	
No ranks (R_1)		Yes ranks (R_2)
3		1
6		2
8		4
10		5
12		7
14		9
15		11
16		13
18		17
19		$\Sigma R_2 = 69$
20		$n_2 = 9$
$\Sigma R_1 = 141$		
$n_1 = 11$		

Explanation: The best worker gets a rank of 20, whereas the poorest worker gets a rank of 1.

Let's verify the accuracy of our calculations. We know that n_1 is equal to 11 and n_2 is equal to 9, and we calculated that U_1 is 24 and U_2 is 75, so

$$24 + 75 = 11 \cdot 9$$

$$99 = 99$$

It checks.

Question: Now that we have correctly computed these two *U*-values, what do we do with them? Do we compare them to each other, compute a ratio, or compare them to a table value?

First, we compare our computed U_1 and U_2 values to each other and determine which is smaller. Henceforth, we refer to this smaller value as U. So, if

$$U_1 = 24 \quad \text{and} \quad U_2 = 75$$

then

$$U = 24$$

Next we need to compare U to the appropriate values in Table U in Appendix A, a portion of which is reprinted in Table 15.8. You need both n_1 and n_2 to enter the table. Because our n_1 equals 11 and our n_2 equals 9, we go over to column 11 and then down to row 9. At that place in the table we find the following numbers:

27   Regular type for a directional (one-tailed) hypothesis at the .05 level of significance

and

23   **Boldface type** for a nondirectional (two-tailed) hypothesis at the .05 level of significance

In order for U to be significant, it must be *less than or equal to* the number listed in the table. Our computed U is equal to 24. Our research hypothesis is one-tailed: It states that the sample of people who did not take the training program is from a population comprised of lower rankings than the population of people who went through the training. Thus, the U of 24 is significant because it is less than the 27 the table lists as the critical value for a one-tailed hypothesis. Had our research hypothesis been two-tailed, we would not have been able to reject the null hypothesis because our computed U of 24 is greater than the table value of 23.

Question: This isn't clear to me. Tell me again: When can you use the Mann-Whitney *U*?

Table 15.8 A Portion of Table *U*, Critical Values of the Mann-Whitney *U* Statistic

n_2 \ n_1	1	2	3	4	5	6	7	8	9	10	11	12	13	14	15	16	17	18	19	20
1	—	—	—	—	—	—	—	—	—	—	—	—	—	—	—	—	—	—	0	0
																			—	—
2	—	—	—	—	0	0	0	1	1	1	1	2	2	2	3	3	3	4	4	4
	—	—	—			**0**	**0**	**0**	**0**	**1**	**1**	**1**	**1**	**1**	**2**	**2**	**2**	**2**
3	—	—	0	0	1	2	2	3	3	4	5	5	6	7	7	8	9	9	10	11
	—	—	—	—	**0**	**1**	**1**	**2**	**2**	**3**	**3**	**4**	**4**	**5**	**5**	**6**	**6**	**7**	**7**	**8**
4	—	—	0	1	2	3	4	5	6	7	8	9	10	11	12	14	15	16	17	18
	—	—	—	**0**	**1**	**2**	**3**	**4**	**4**	**5**	**6**	**7**	**8**	**9**	**10**	**11**	**11**	**12**	**13**	**13**
5	—	0	1	2	4	5	6	8	9	11	12	13	15	16	18	19	20	22	23	25
	—	—	**0**	**1**	**2**	**3**	**5**	**6**	**7**	**8**	**9**	**11**	**12**	**13**	**14**	**15**	**17**	**18**	**19**	**20**
6	—	0	2	3	5	7	8	10	12	14	16	17	19	21	23	25	26	28	30	32
	—	—	**1**	**2**	**3**	**5**	**6**	**8**	**10**	**11**	**13**	**14**	**16**	**17**	**19**	**21**	**22**	**24**	**25**	**27**
7	—	0	2	4	6	8	11	13	15	17	19	21	24	26	28	30	33	35	37	39
	—	—	**1**	**3**	**5**	**6**	**8**	**10**	**12**	**14**	**16**	**18**	**20**	**22**	**24**	**26**	**28**	**30**	**32**	**34**
8	—	1	3	5	8	10	13	15	18	20	23	26	28	31	33	36	39	41	44	47
	—	**0**	**2**	**4**	**6**	**8**	**10**	**13**	**15**	**17**	**19**	**22**	**24**	**26**	**29**	**31**	**34**	**36**	**38**	**41**
9	—	1	3	6	9	12	15	18	21	24	27	30	33	36	39	42	45	48	51	54
	—	**0**	**2**	**4**	**7**	**10**	**12**	**15**	**17**	**20**	**23**	**26**	**28**	**31**	**34**	**37**	**39**	**42**	**45**	**48**

Source: Kirk, 1978.

Because the Mann-Whitney *U* requires fewer assumptions than the *t* test, you can use it on any independent two-sample data sets that can be ranked. Take a look at the data in Table 15.9. These data are scores on an algebra readiness test given to two math classes. Each class participated in a different math program during the past year. One class used a traditional program involving lots of paper/pencil and book work, and the other used a hands-on program with lots of manipulatives. Put yourself in the place of one of the district's math teachers who would like to determine whether there is any difference in the test scores of the two types of classes. This is a two-tailed research hypothesis because it asks only whether there will be a difference; it does not specify in which direction the difference will lie. When we examine closely the data from the two classes, we find that the distribution of scores from the traditional class seems to be relatively flat, whereas the distribution of scores from the hands-on class appears to be skewed toward the high end of the scale. Neither sample is normally distributed, so it is unwise to assume that

Table 15.9 Scores on an
Algebra Readiness Test Given to
Two Sixth-Grade Math Classes

Traditional class	Hands-on class
96	100
91	99
89	98
88	95
88	94
85	93
84	92
79	90
76	88
73	86
72	82
71	80
70	78
70	
70	
67	
65	
60	

their populations are normally distributed. This means that the basic assumptions for the *t* test cannot be met, and it is therefore best to use the nonparametric Mann-Whitney *U* to test the research hypothesis.

Question: The data in Table 15.9 are not ranked. How do we conduct a Mann-Whitney *U* on them?

The answer is simple enough. We *create* ranks by ranking the data. When ranking any data set, we always give the lowest score a rank of 1; when ranking the scores for a Mann-Whitney *U* test, we assign ranks as if the two samples have been combined. It is very important to remember to combine the samples when ranking and then separate the samples when computing ΣR_1

and ΣR_2. If you take another look at Table 15.9, you can see that the ten lowest scores (60 through 76) are all from the traditional class, but the 11th score (78) is from the hands-on class. Thus, scores 60 through 76 get ranks 1 through 10, 78 gets a rank of 11, and we continue to rank the scores in this manner until all scores have ranks.

Question: This seems easy enough, but how do we rank the three scores of 70?

Each tied score is assigned the same rank. You find the average of the ranks that would have been assigned to the scores and assign that average rank to each tied score. We'll show how to rank the three scores of 70. The previous score of 67 was assigned a rank of 3. The next three scores would normally receive the ranks of 4, 5, and 6, but because they are tied, they must all be assigned the same rank. The average of 4, 5, and 6 is 5, so we assign the rank of 5 to each score of 70. We assign the next score, 71, the rank of 7, and then we proceed to rank the remaining scores, dealing with ties in the same manner. (Large numbers of tied scores are a bit of a problem in the Mann-Whitney U test, but a few tied scores should not affect the outcome of the test.)

Table 15.10 shows the two samples with their corresponding assigned ranks. Now we can use the sum of the ranks for the traditional math class (ΣR_1) and the sum of the ranks for the hands-on math class (ΣR_2) to compute U_1 and U_2:

$$U_1 = (n_1 \cdot n_2) + \frac{n_1(n_1 + 1)}{2} - \Sigma R_1$$

$$= (18 \cdot 13) + \frac{18(18 + 1)}{2} - 208$$

$$= 234 + \frac{18 \cdot 19}{2} - 208 = 234 + \frac{342}{2} - 208$$

$$= 234 + 171 - 208$$

$$= 197$$

$$U_2 = (n_2 \cdot n_1) + \frac{n_2(n_2 + 1)}{2} - \Sigma R_2$$

$$= (13 \cdot 18) + \frac{13(13 + 1)}{2} - 288$$

$$= 234 + \frac{13 \cdot 14}{2} - 288 = 234 + \frac{182}{2} - 288$$

$$= 234 + 91 - 288$$

$$= 37$$

Table 15.10 Ranks for Scores on an Algebra Readiness Test Given to Two Sixth-Grade Math Classes

Traditional class	R_1	Hands-on class	R_2
96	28	100	31
91	23	99	30
89	21	98	29
88	19	95	27
88	19	94	26
85	16	93	25
84	15	92	24
79	12	90	22
76	10	88	19
73	9	86	17
72	8	82	14
71	7	80	13
70	5	78	11
70	5		$\Sigma R_2 = 288$
70	5		$n_2 = 13$
67	3		
65	2		
60	1		
	$\Sigma R_1 = 208$		
	$n_1 = 18$		

Using Formula 15.6 to check our computation of the two *U*-values, we get

$$U_1 + U_2 = n_1 \cdot n_2$$

$$197 + 37 = 18 \cdot 13$$

$$234 = 234$$

It checks out, and because *U* is the smaller of U_1 and U_2, we have

$$U = 37$$

Next we compare this computed value of *U* to the value found in Table *U*. Because the research hypothesis is two-tailed, we must use the two-tailed portion of Table U to determine the critical value of U. Using $n_1 = 18$ and $n_2 = 13$, we find a critical value of 67 in the table. Because our computed value of U, 37, is less than the table value of 67, we can reject the null hypothesis and accept the research hypothesis. There is a difference between the two classes on the algebra readiness test.

C O N C E P T   Q U I Z

1. The use of the Mann-Whitney U test requires _____ data and _____ samples.
2. In ranking unranked data, we always give the _____ score a rank of 1.
3. Tied scores always have the _____ rank.
4. The sum of the ranks for sample 1 plus the sum of the ranks for sample 2 is always equal to _____ .
5. If U_1 equals 35 and U_2 equals 57, then U is equal to _____ .
6. When comparing your computed U to the value in Table U, your U will be significant if it is _____ the table value.

Answers

1. ranked; independent
2. lowest
3. same

4. $n_1 \cdot n_2$
5. 35
6. equal to or less than

THE WILCOXON *T* TEST

Question: The Mann-Whitney U test requires independent samples. Is there a nonparametric test that can be used on correlated samples?

Yes; the Wilcoxon T test is a nonparametric statistical test that can be used to determine whether there is a difference between two correlated samples. Just like the Mann-Whitney U, the Wilcoxon T makes very few assumptions about the raw data that have been collected. The only major requirements for this test are that (1) the samples must be correlated and (2) it must be possible to rank the differences between the two samples. To illustrate when it is appropriate to use the Wilcoxon T, we use the following example.

As traffic congestion and air pollution become more and more pressing problems for large cities in the world, researchers and government representatives continue to search for solutions. As we all know, the reason for traffic congestion is that too many cars are on the road at the same time. Anyone who lives near a large city is aware that traffic is at its worst during the morning and evening rush hours. The rush-hour phenomenon occurs because nearly all business and industry workers arrive at their jobs between 7 and 10 A.M., and they leave their jobs between 3 and 6 P.M. One obvious solution to this problem is to stagger the arrival and departure times of workers throughout the day rather than concentrating them into just a few hours in the morning and the afternoon. Ideally, if one twenty-fourth of the workforce began work at, say, 6:00 A.M., another twenty-fourth began work at 7:00 A.M., and so on throughout the 24-hour day, traffic congestion would be significantly reduced.

In compliance with appeals from environmental groups and the traffic commission, a large accounting firm is considering staggering its workers' beginning and ending times throughout the day. As an initial step, the company hires you as a consulting psychologist to study whether work productivity is affected when working hours change from the traditional 9 A.M. to 5 P.M. to an earlier 6 A.M. to 2 P.M. shift. That is, you are to test the two-tailed research hypothesis that different work schedules will result in different productivity ratings.

To begin your research, you ask management to assign ten accountants to be your subjects in a small experiment. The accountants will have their productivity measured for 1 month on the regular 9-to-5 schedule and then have their productivity measured for 1 month on the earlier 6-to-2 schedule. Productivity is measured by the number of dollars produced for the company by each accountant, divided by the average number of dollars produced by all company accountants. Thus, an accountant who has a productivity measure of 2.0 is twice as productive as the average accountant, and someone who has a productivity measure of 0.5 is half as productive as the average accountant. The productivity measures for the ten accountants on the two different work schedules are listed in Table 15.11.

Because it appears that the intervals within these data are not equal, these data do not meet the minimum data type requirements for the *t* test. Consequently, we must use a nonparametric test to analyze these data. Moreover, because the same subjects were used in both conditions, the two samples are correlated. The **Wilcoxon *T* test** is the most appropriate to analyze these data.

So far, all of the statistical tests discussed in this book can be represented by one or more formulas. However, the Wilcoxon *T* test is best described as a procedure rather than a formula. When we conduct a Wilcoxon *T* test, we find the differences between the paired scores and then compare the ranks of those differences. Therefore, the first part of the procedure requires that we compute

Table 15.11   Productivity Measures
for Ten Accountants

| | Schedule | |
Accountant	Regular	Early
M. P.	2.0	1.7
D. Q.	1.7	1.6
O. D.	1.3	1.3
P. H.	0.6	0.8
D. M.	0.6	0.5
A. D.	0.5	0.4
W. A.	0.4	0.3
M. M.	0.4	0.9
C. L.	0.3	0.1
Z. Z.	0.3	0.1

differences between the paired scores, just as we did for the parametric correlated t. See Table 15.12. Now we see whether there are any zero differences. All
pairs that result in a zero difference are excluded from further analysis. Accountant O. D. had a zero difference, so her scores were not used in calculating the
ranks. This leaves us with the nine pairs of scores in Table 15.13.

Table 15.12

| | Schedule | | |
Accountant	Regular	Early	Difference
M. P.	2.0	1.7	0.3
D. Q.	1.7	1.6	0.1
O. D.	1.3	1.3	0.0
P. H.	0.6	0.8	−0.2
D. M.	0.6	0.5	0.1
A. D.	0.5	0.4	0.1
W. A.	0.4	0.3	0.1
M. M.	0.4	0.9	−0.5
C. L.	0.3	0.1	0.2
Z. Z.	0.3	0.1	0.2

Table 15.13

| Accountant | Schedule | | Difference |
	Regular	Early	
M. P.	2.0	1.7	0.3
D. Q.	1.7	1.6	0.1
O. D.	1.3	1.3	0.0
P. H.	0.6	0.8	−0.2
D. M.	0.6	0.5	0.1
A. D.	0.5	0.4	0.1
W. A.	0.4	0.3	0.1
M. M.	0.4	0.9	−0.5
C. L.	0.3	0.1	0.2
Z. Z.	0.3	0.1	0.2

Next, we rank the differences according to absolute value; that is, we ignore the sign and give −0.2 the same rank as +0.2. Remember that when we rank the differences, we give the smallest difference—according to absolute value—a rank of 1, and we give any tied differences the average of the ranks they normally would have received. Table 15.14 shows the final ranks of the accountants' productivity measures.

Table 15.14   Ranked Differences

| Accountant | Schedule | | Difference | Rank |
	Regular	Early		
M. P.	2.0	1.7	0.3	8
D. Q.	1.7	1.6	0.1	2.5
O. D.	1.3	1.3	0.0	
P. H.	0.6	0.8	−0.2	6
D. M.	0.6	0.5	0.1	2.5
A. D.	0.5	0.4	0.1	2.5
W. A.	0.4	0.3	0.1	2.5
M. M.	0.4	0.9	−0.5	9
C. L.	0.3	0.1	0.2	6
Z. Z.	0.3	0.1	0.2	6

Table 15.15 Signed Ranks

Accountant	Schedule Regular	Early	Difference	+ Ranks (R_+)	− Ranks (R_-)
M. P.	2.0	1.7	0.3	8	
D. Q.	1.7	1.6	0.1	2.5	
O. D.	1.3	1.3	0.0		
P. H.	0.6	0.8	−0.2		6
D. M.	0.6	0.5	0.1	2.5	
A. D.	0.5	0.4	0.1	2.5	
W. A.	0.4	0.3	0.1	2.5	
M. M.	0.4	0.9	−0.5		9
C. L.	0.3	0.1	0.2	6	
Z. Z.	0.3	0.1	0.2	6	

Having ranked the differences, we then **sign the ranks**. This is a process whereby we assign each rank to a category based on the arithmetic sign of the difference score for that rank. If the difference score is negative, we assign the rank to the minus category; if the difference score is positive, we assign the rank to the plus category. Table 15.15 lists the signed ranks. Next we sum the plus ranks ΣR_+ and the minus ranks ΣR_-, as shown in Table 15.16.

Table 15.16 Sum of the Plus Ranks (ΣR_+) and Sum of the Minus Ranks (ΣR_-)

Accountant	Schedule Regular	Early	Difference	+ Ranks (R_+)	− Ranks (R_-)
M. P.	2.0	1.7	0.3	8	
D. Q.	1.7	1.6	0.1	2.5	
O. D.	1.3	1.3	0.0		
P. H.	0.6	0.8	−0.2		6
D. M.	0.6	0.5	0.1	2.5	
A. D.	0.5	0.4	0.1	2.5	
W. A.	0.4	0.3	0.1	2.5	
M. M.	0.4	0.9	−0.5		9
C. L.	0.3	0.1	0.2	6	
Z. Z.	0.3	0.1	0.2	6	
				$\Sigma R_+ = 30$	$\Sigma R_- = 15$

Question: Shouldn't the sum of the minus ranks be -15, rather than 15?

No. You must remember that plus and minus are now *categories*. All the ranks have a positive value, no matter what category they are in.

After adding up the ranks, we determine the Wilcoxon T, which is the smaller of ΣR_+ and ΣR_-. Therefore, if the sum of the plus ranks equals 30 and the sum of the minus ranks equals 15, then the Wilcoxon T equals 15:

$$\Sigma R_+ = 30$$

$$\Sigma R_- = 15$$

$$\text{Wilcoxon } T = 15$$

To determine whether a T of 15 is significant, we use Table W in Appendix A, a portion of which is shown in Table 15.17. To enter Table W, we need to know whether the research hypothesis is directional (one-tailed) or nondirectional (two-tailed). We also need to know the number of signed ranks (n), which is the number of original pairs minus the number of pairs that have a zero difference. In our example, the research hypothesis is nondirectional and $n = 9$ because there were ten original pairs and only one of those had a zero difference. So we find the critical value of Wilcoxon T that corresponds to 9 signed ranks for a nondirectional (two-tailed) test. Referring to Table 15.17, we see that the critical value of T is 5. For T to be significant, it must be *equal to or less than* the table value. Our Wilcoxon T value of 15 is greater than the critical value from

Table 15.17 A Portion of Table W, Critical Values of the Wilcoxon T Statistic

n	Level of significance for a one-tailed test			
	.05	.025	.01	.005
	Level of significance for a two-tailed test			
	.10	.05	.02	.01
5	0	—	—	—
6	2	0	—	—
7	3	2	0	—
8	5	3	1	0
9	8	5	3	1
10	10	8	5	3

the table; therefore, it is not significant and we cannot reject the null hypothesis. According to this bogus research, shifting the work schedule back 3 hours earlier does not result in a significant decrease in productivity.

Compared to other statistical tests, the Wilcoxon T is a simple procedure. Here are the steps:

1. Compute the differences between the pairs.
2. Eliminate from further analysis all pairs that result in a zero difference.
3. Rank the differences according to absolute value, with the rank of 1 going to the smallest difference.
4. Assign the ranks to groups according to the sign of the computed difference for that pair.
5. Add up the plus ranks and the minus ranks.
6. Determine the Wilcoxon T, which is equal to whatever is smaller, the sum of the plus ranks or the sum of the minus ranks.
7. Determine significance: To be significant, the Wilcoxon T must be equal to or less than the value in Table W.

C O N C E P T   Q U I Z

1. The Wilcoxon T is a _____ test used to compare the difference between two _____ samples.
2. Pairs with a difference of _____ are eliminated from further analysis.
3. In the Wilcoxon T procedure, all differences are ranked according to _____ , with the rank of 1 going to the _____ score.
4. After the differences are ranked, they are separated into _____ different categories according to _____ .
5. Next you must compute both the _____ and the _____ .
6. The Wilcoxon T is equal to _____ .
7. The Wilcoxon T must be _____ the value in Table W to be significant.
8. Which of the following are possible T-values:
   25   −24   2   −6   −0.3   2.5
9. Is a Wilcoxon T of 26 significant for a two-tailed nondirectional test with 15 signed ranks?

Answers

1. nonparametric, correlated
2. zero
3. absolute value; smallest
4. two; the sign of the difference score
5. sum of the plus ranks; sum of the minus ranks
6. whichever is smaller—the sum of the plus ranks or the sum of the minus ranks

7. equal to or less than

8. all of the positive values: 25, 2, 2.5. Even though we sum the minus ranks, the ranks themselves are positive; therefore, T is always positive.

9. No. According to Table W, with 15 signed ranks and a two-tailed nondirectional hypothesis, the T-value must be equal to or less than 25 in order to be significant.

THE KRUSKAL-WALLIS TEST

Having discussed the nonparametric substitutions for the t tests, we now turn to the nonparametric counterpart of the one-way analysis of variance. Known as the **Kruskal-Wallis test,** it is essentially an extension of the Mann-Whitney U test to more than two groups. One of the examples we used when explaining the Mann-Whitney U test involved scores on an algebra readiness test given to two sixth-grade classes, one that had participated in a traditional math program and another that had used manipulatives in a nontraditional, hands-on program. Let's suppose that the school district adds still another level to the independent variable. In addition to the traditional and the hands-on classes, another sixth-grade class, known as the prealgebra class, is introduced to basic algebraic terminology, notation, and exercises. To compare the programs, instead of including all the students from the three classes, the math teachers committee decides to choose seven students randomly from each of the three classes and give them the algebra readiness test. The data from this test are shown in Table 15.18. The research hypothesis using these data states that the populations producing these three samples are different from one another.

Table 15.18 Scores on an Algebra Readiness Test for Samples from Three Classes

Traditional	Hands-on	Prealgebra
95	98	100
94	96	99
89	92	97
84	91	93
83	86	90
81	85	88
80	82	87

Table 15.19 Scores on an Algebra Readiness Test and Ranks for Samples from Three Classes

Traditional	R_1	Hands-on	R_2	Prealgebra	R_3
95	16	98	19	100	21
94	15	96	17	99	20
89	10	92	13	97	18
84	5	91	12	93	14
83	4	86	7	90	11
81	2	85	6	88	9
80	1	82	3	87	8
	$\Sigma R_1 = 53$		$\Sigma R_2 = 77$		$\Sigma R_3 = 101$
	$n_1 = 7$		$n_2 = 7$		$n_3 = 7$

As we mentioned earlier, the Kruskal-Wallis test is basically the same as the Mann-Whitney U, but it is used with more than two samples. With this in mind, what do you think is the first step in conducting a Kruskal-Wallis test? If you thought "combine the scores and rank them," you were right. The 21 scores from the algebra readiness test in our example are ranked in Table 15.19. We can refer to these rankings as we use Formula 15.7 to compute the Kruskal-Wallis test statistic, which is called H:

$$H = \left[\frac{12}{N_{\text{total}} \cdot (N_{\text{total}} + 1)} \right] \cdot \left[\frac{(\Sigma R_1)^2}{n_1} + \frac{(\Sigma R_2)^2}{n_2} + \cdots + \frac{(\Sigma R_k)^2}{n_k} \right] - 3 \cdot (N_{\text{total}} + 1) \quad (15.7)$$

The symbols in Formula 15.7 should be familiar to you:

$$\Sigma R_1 = \text{the sum of the ranks for sample 1} = 53$$
$$\Sigma R_2 = \text{the sum of the ranks for sample 2} = 77$$
$$\Sigma R_3 = \text{the sum of the ranks for sample 3} = 101$$
$$n_1 = \text{the number of scores in sample 1} = 7$$
$$n_2 = \text{the number of scores in sample 2} = 7$$
$$n_3 = \text{the number of scores in sample 3} = 7$$
$$N_{\text{total}} = \text{the total number of scores in all the samples} = 21$$
$$k = \text{the number of groups} = 3$$

If we substitute these values into Formula 15.7, we get

$$H = \left[\frac{12}{21 \cdot (21 + 1)} \right] \cdot \left[\frac{(53)^2}{7} + \frac{(77)^2}{7} + \frac{(101)^2}{7} \right] - 3 \cdot (21 + 1)$$

$$= \left(\frac{12}{21 \cdot 22} \right) \cdot \left(\frac{2809}{7} + \frac{5929}{7} + \frac{10{,}201}{7} \right) - 3 \cdot 22$$

$$= \left(\frac{12}{462} \right) \cdot (401.286 + 847 + 1457.286) - 66$$

$$= (0.026 \cdot 2705.572) - 66 = 70.345 - 66$$

$$= 4.345$$

Question: Do we now look up our *H*-value in Table *H*?

Actually, there's no need for a separate table for *H*-values because the χ^2 distribution is a very close estimate of the distribution of *H*. Therefore, we can look in the χ^2 table, Table χ in Appendix A, and find the critical value of *H* for $k - 1$, or 2 degrees of freedom.

The value in Table χ at the .05 level of significance and 2 degrees of freedom is 5.99. For *H* to be significant, it must be *equal to or greater than* the table value (note that this is different from the Mann-Whitney *U* and the Wilcoxon *T*). Our computed *H* is 4.345, which is less than the table value, so there is no significant difference and we fail to reject the null hypothesis. We found no significant difference between the samples drawn for the three different classes. In cases where the *H* is significant, the Mann-Whitney *U* is used to make comparisons between pairs of samples.

C O N C E P T   Q U I Z

1. The Kruskal-Wallis test is essentially an extension of the _____ to more than two samples.
2. In the Kruskal-Wallis test, all scores are _____ and then ranked, with the _____ score receiving a rank of 1.
3. The Kruskal-Wallis statistic is called _____ , and its distribution is very closely approximated by the _____ distribution.
4. The number of degrees of freedom for the *H* statistic is equal to _____ .
5. What different values are necessary to compute *H*?

Answers

1. Mann-Whitney *U* test
2. combined; lowest
3. H; χ^2
4. $k - 1$ (the number of samples minus 1)
5. The sum of the ranks for sample 1 (ΣR_1); the sum of the ranks for sample 2 (ΣR_2); the sum of the ranks for sample 3 (ΣR_3); the number of scores in sample 1 (n_1); the number of scores in sample 2 (n_2); the number of scores in sample 3 (n_3); the total number of scores in all the samples combined (N_{total})

S U M M A R Y

This chapter describes four statistical tests that can be used with nominal data or ranked data. Chi-square is used to analyze nominal data. The Mann-Whitney U is used to analyze ranked data from two independent samples. The Wilcoxon T is a nonparametric test that can be used to determine any significant difference between two correlated samples. The Kruskal-Wallis test is used to analyze ranked data from three or more independent samples.

Chi-square is a statistical technique that allows us to compare the observed frequencies in different categories to the expected frequencies from some theory or hypothesis. Once the observed frequencies are collected and the expected frequencies are computed or estimated for each cell in the analysis, it is relatively simple to compute chi-square. For each cell, calculate the value of the observed frequency minus the expected frequency. Then square this value and divide it by the expected frequency. Chi-square is equal to the sum of these values for all the cells. The number of degrees of freedom for a chi-square with only one column is the number of cells minus 1. The number of degrees of freedom for a chi-square with more than one row is equal to the number of rows minus 1, times the number of columns minus 1. For a chi-square to be significant, it must be equal to or greater than the appropriate value in Table χ.

Parametric statistics are those that are stated in terms of and make assumptions about population parameters, whereas nonparametric statistics do not compare population parameters and have fewer assumptions than parametric statistics. This chapter discusses three nonparametric statistics that can be used to replace either t tests or one-way analysis of variance.

The first of these tests is the Mann-Whitney U, which is a nonparametric test of the difference between two independent samples. To compute the Mann-Whitney U, combine the two samples and rank the scores (obviously, you do not need to rerank the scores if they have been previously ranked). The lowest score always gets the rank of 1, and all tied scores get the same rank. Once the scores have been ranked, sum the ranks for each sample individually and use Formulas 15.4 and 15.5 to compute U_1 and U_2. The Mann-Whitney U is equal to the smaller of U_1 and U_2. A significant U is equal to or less than the appropriate value in Table U.

The Wilcoxon T is a nonparametric substitute for a parametric correlated t test. You begin the computation of the Wilcoxon T in the same way that you would begin the computation of a correlated t test, by computing the difference between each pair of scores. After excluding all zero differences, rank the differences according to absolute value, with the smallest difference getting the rank of 1. Then assign them to either the plus category or the minus category depending on the sign of the original difference. Next, sum the plus ranks and then the minus ranks. The lesser of the two is the Wilcoxon T. The

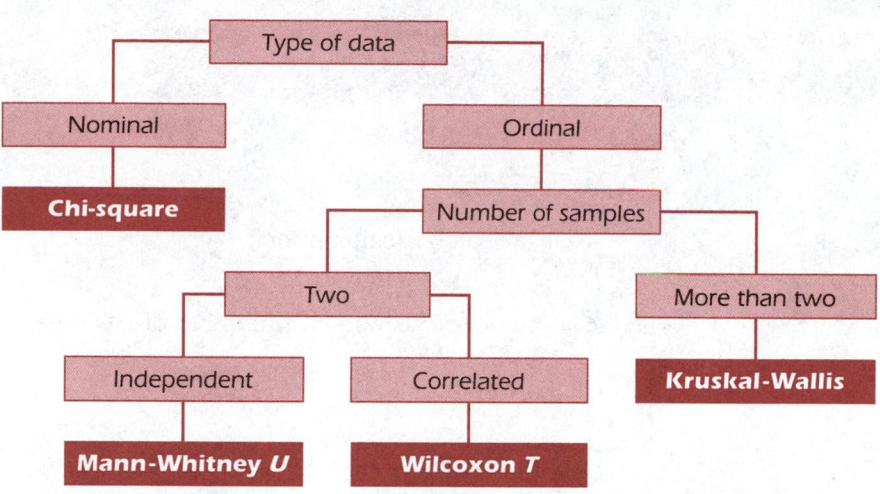

Figure 15.1 Summary flowchart for nonparametric statistics

Wilcoxon T is significant if the value of T is equal to or less than the appropriate value in Table W.

The last nonparametric test discussed in this chapter is the Kruskal-Wallis test. The Kruskal-Wallis test is a nonparametric substitute for the one-way analysis of variance. The Kruskal-Wallis test requires that scores be ranked. The sums of the ranks for the different samples are used to compute a statistic called H. The value of H is compared to the appropriate value in Table χ. In order for H to be significant it must be greater than or equal to the value found in Table χ.

The flowchart in Figure 15.1 is designed to help you choose the proper nonparametric statistic based on the type of data and the type of design of your research project. First, determine if the data is nominal or ordinal. If the data is nominal, the appropriate test is chi-square. If the data is ordinal, you have to determine the number of samples. If there are three or more samples, you can conduct a Kruskal-Wallis test. If there are two samples, you must determine if the samples are independent or correlated. If the samples are independent, you can use the Mann-Whitney U test. If the samples are correlated, you can use the Wilcoxon T.

KEY TERMS

nominal data

chi-square (χ^2)

observed frequency (f_o)

expected frequency (f_e)

parametric statistics

nonparametric statistics

Mann-Whitney U

Wilcoxon T

sign the ranks

Kruskal-Wallis test (H)

F O R M U L A S

$$\chi^2 = \Sigma \frac{(f_o - f_e)^2}{f_e} \tag{15.1}$$

$$f_e = \frac{(\text{row total}) \cdot (\text{column total})}{\text{grand total}} \tag{15.2}$$

$$df = (\text{number of rows} - 1) \cdot (\text{number of columns} - 1) \tag{15.3}$$

$$U_1 = (n_1 \cdot n_2) + \frac{n_1(n_1 + 1)}{2} - \Sigma R_1 \tag{15.4}$$

$$U_2 = (n_2 \cdot n_1) + \frac{n_2(n_2 + 1)}{2} - \Sigma R_2 \tag{15.5}$$

$$U_1 + U_2 = n_1 \cdot n_2 \tag{15.6}$$

$$H = \left[\frac{12}{N_{total} \cdot (N_{total} + 1)} \right] \cdot \left[\frac{(\Sigma R_1)^2}{n_1} + \frac{(\Sigma R_2)^2}{n_2} + \cdots + \frac{(\Sigma R_k)^2}{n_k} \right] - 3 \cdot (N_{total} + 1) \tag{15.7}$$

P R O B L E M S

1. A major fast food chain has hired you to do some market research. Given ecological and environmental concerns, they want to know whether the general public prefers their hamburgers wrapped in aluminum foil, foam plastic boxes, or paper. You have collected the following data from 3000 people. Analyze the data and tell whether there is a significant difference.

Foil	Foam	Paper
1230	740	1030

2. As a clinical psychologist, you have been testing three types of talk therapies on a group of 120 patients who have schizophrenia. Using the data in the table, compute a χ^2 to determine whether there is a difference among the outcomes of the three types of therapy.

	Outcome of therapy		
	Poor	Moderate	Good
Therapy 1	5	12	23
Therapy 2	20	12	8
Therapy 3	13	13	14

3. You are a social psychologist, and your current interest is people's behavior in relation to petty theft. In a crowded student union, your accomplice leaves his books and electronic calculator on a table while he gets a soft drink. While the accomplice is away, another person walks up and takes the calculator. You want to see how many people will stop the thief, and whether it makes a difference if your accomplice asks a student sitting nearby to watch his things. Using the data given here, compute a χ^2 and state your conclusions based on the data.

	Asked for help	
	Yes	No
Stopped thief	25	8
Did not stop thief	7	24

4. The chairperson of the Learning University psychology department is interested in determining whether the length of professors' teaching experience affects student rankings of the professors' teaching effectiveness. Based on student evaluations, the department chair assigns ranks to the 20 professors in the department and then divides the faculty into two categories: those with fewer than 5 years of teaching experience and those with 5 or more years. Use the appropriate nonparametric test and the data in the table to tell whether there is a difference between the rankings of the two groups of professors.

Rankings of professors	
< 5 years experience	5 or more years experience
20	17
2	13
19	1
18	4
9	10

(continued)

Rankings of professors	
< 5 years experience	5 or more years experience
16	6
14	8
15	12
	7
	11
	5
	3

5. Use the Mann-Whitney U test to see whether there is a difference between the visual acuity of a randomly chosen group of seven children and that of a randomly chosen group of nine adults. The vision test scores are listed in the table.

Children	Adults
22	19
23	16
13	22
16	19
21	17
14	25
24	20
	18
	15

6. Use the Mann-Whitney U to see whether there is a difference between the numbers of positive social responses per hour that are given by children who have autism and are undergoing two different types of therapy. One is a sensory deprivation approach known as "restricted environmental stimulation therapy (REST), and the other is a traditional behavior modification approach. The data are given in the table.

Number of positive social responses	
REST technique	Behavior modification
6	9
0	1
4	12
5	8
7	21
3	6
2	13
7	15

7. Ten pairs of identical twin rats were used in a study to determine whether diet affects brain development. The two members of each pair of twins were fed a different diet for 10 weeks after they were weaned; one received a protein-rich diet and the other a protein-deficient diet. At the end of the 10-week period, the brains of the rats were examined to see whether there was any difference in brain mass (measured in grams) between the two groups. Use the appropriate nonparametric test to analyze the data in the table and determine whether there is a significant difference between the two groups of rats.

	Diet	
Pair	Protein rich	Protein deficient
1	23	20
2	26	23
3	21	21
4	17	19
5	15	16
6	29	21
7	27	22
8	33	20
9	21	17
10	28	19

8. Ivan Pavlov III decides to replicate one of his grandfather's experiments. He classically conditions 12 dogs to salivate to a 1000-cycle-per-second tone by pairing the tone with a Tastie Bite Dog Yummie. Ivan III plays the tone and gives the dog the Yummie, thereby eliciting the salivation. Eventually, the dog salivates to the tone alone. Now Ivan III predicts that his dogs are more likely to salivate to a similar but higher tone than to a similar but lower one. To test this hypothesis, he presents a 900-cycle and a 1100-cycle tone and measures the amount of salivation (in milliliters). Use the Wilcoxon T to test his hypothesis using the amounts given in the table.

Dog	900-cycle tone	1100-cycle tone
1	8.7	8.8
2	8.9	9.2
3	12.8	7.2
4	19.7	18.3
5	11.9	15.6
6	12.6	12.6
7	21.9	16.3
8	31.6	16.5
9	8.7	22.6
10	9.8	9.3
11	15.6	16.1
12	4.6	3.8

9. Use the Wilcoxon T to determine whether there is a difference between the pretest and posttest scores of nine patients who have schizophrenia and are undergoing a new drug therapy. The table lists the numbers of delusional responses given in a structured interview before and after the drug is administered.

Subject	Pretest	Posttest
P. J.	10	7
O. C.	22	12
D. J.	18	19
S. R.	15	7
M. P.	22	21
D. T.	9	3
M. M.	4	0
L. N.	16	17
D. H.	8	2

10. Twenty-one subjects are divided into three groups of seven in a study of jealousy. Each group is asked to read a paragraph that describes a spouse flirting with either one, two, or three different people at a party. The subjects are asked to pretend that the paragraph describes *their* spouses and to evaluate how jealous they feel on a 10-point scale, with 10 being very jealous and 1 being not at all jealous. The table lists the data from this experiment. Use a nonparametric test to determine whether there is a significant different among the three groups.

1 flirt	2 flirts	3 flirts
6	7	5
4	6	9
5	6	10
1	7	9
3	8	10
2	5	6
4	4	5

11. If a person is deprived of REM (dream) sleep, he or she tends to spend more time in REM sleep when the deprivation period is over. Use the Kruskal-Wallis test to determine whether the amount of time spent in REM sleep the first night after the end of sleep deprivation is significantly different for people who have spent 1, 2, 3, or 4 nights being deprived of REM sleep. The number of minutes spent in REM sleep for each subject is given here.

	REM deprivation		
1 night	2 nights	3 nights	4 nights
100	120	140	160
122	137	145	173
97	129	147	158
110	122	151	151
109	121	139	144

12. Suppose we are interested in studying humor. We ask three comedians to tell the same joke to several different people. Each person listens to only one comedian and then rates the "funniness" of the joke on a scale from 1 to 100. A rating of 1 means the joke is not at all funny, and a rating of 100 means the joke is the funniest the person has ever heard. Use the Kruskal-Wallis test to determine whether there is a difference among the three different comedians based on the data listed in the table.

Comedian 1	Comedian 2	Comedian 3
75	62	56
68	66	2
99	45	46
86	65	54
76	69	55
69	59	
73		

13. A psychologist interested in interpersonal attraction asked 80 undergraduate students whether they prefer to date blonds, brunettes, or redheads. The data from that project are given here. Analyze the data and tell whether they are significant.

Blonds	Brunettes	Redheads
23	34	23

14. Suppose we ask 150 people whether they ever had an experience that they would classify as supernatural. At the same time, we ask them about their school experience and assign them to four groups: those who did not graduate from high school, those who graduated from high school, those who graduated from college, and those who have a graduate degree. Use χ^2 to analyze the data and tell whether they are significant.

| | Supernatural experience | |
	Yes	No
No high school	23	3
High school diploma	25	20
College degree	15	35
Graduate degree	2	27

15. In the process of revamping its curriculum, the psychology department at a small college surveyed its 200 psychology majors to see whether they preferred to have fewer courses, keep the same number of courses, or add more courses as a requirement for the psychology major. The results, grouped according to the respondent's year in

school, are listed. Analyze the data and tell whether there is any significance. If you were a member of the psychology faculty at this college, what conclusions could you draw from these data?

| | Number of courses | | |
	Fewer	Same	More
Freshman	35	15	10
Sophomore	25	10	20
Junior	15	15	15
Senior	10	20	10

16. An experiment was designed to compare the short-term memory capacity of 21 subjects randomly assigned to one of two conditions. In one condition, the subjects were asked to remember a list of words, whereas in the other condition, the subjects were asked to remember a list of numbers. The table lists the number of words or numbers each subject remembered. Generate a null hypothesis and a research hypothesis for this experiment, and then use the Mann-Whitney U to determine whether there is a significant difference between the two samples.

Words	Numbers
5	4
7	6
5	6
4	3
3	7

(continued)

Words	Numbers
8	5
3	8
7	9
8	7
8	7
5	

Errors in first 7 pages	No errors in first 7 pages
14	6
12	8
17	3
19	9
15	10

17. Given the computed *U*-value and the significance level for Problem 16, what conclusions can you reach about the experiment discussed in that problem?

18. A psychologist who is a proofreading expert has developed two ten-page manuscripts for an experiment. One manuscript has no errors on the first seven pages and then 20 errors on the last three pages; the other manuscript has an average of five errors per page on the first seven pages and then the identical 20 errors on the last three pages of the manuscript. The dependent variable in this experiment is the number of errors detected by each reader on the last three pages of the manuscript assigned. The psychologist predicts that the manuscript with the errors throughout will lead to more errors being noticed on the last three pages. Using the data in the table, compute a Mann-Whitney *U* and determine whether it is significant.

Errors in first 7 pages	No errors in first 7 pages
13	10
18	12
7	6
15	10

(continued)

19. State the null hypothesis and the research hypothesis for the experiment depicted in Problem 18. Given the *U*-value that you computed, what conclusions can you draw about these hypotheses?

20. A psychologist studying the human factors related to computer screens set up an experiment to compare the picture clarity of two different types of displays: EGA monitors and multisynchronous monitors. The experimenter set up 20 monitors, 10 EGA and 10 multisynchronous, with identical graphic displays in a room and then asked an art critic to rank the monitors according to clarity, with a rank of 1 being best. Using the appropriate nonparametric test, analyze the data. State what test you used, whether the value you computed is significant, and any conclusions you can draw from this experiment.

EGA	Multisynchronous
3	1
6	2
9	4
10	5
11	7
14	8
15	12
16	13
19	17
20	18

21. Thirteen subjects underwent an assertiveness training program. Before and after completing the program, they were rated as to their aggressiveness by an impartial observer. Use the Wilcoxon T to tell whether there is a difference between the before ratings and the after ratings for these subjects.

Subject	Before	After
1	70	81
2	55	66
3	36	47
4	56	53
5	77	76
6	93	99
7	37	48
8	22	47
9	82	93
10	83	81
11	84	92
12	77	88
13	47	84

22. Eight laboratory rats were trained to run a maze in the dark. Two weeks later each was tested in the maze, once in the dark and once in the light. The dependent variable in this experiment is the number of errors the rat makes in running the maze. The data for each rat are given in the table. Use the Wilcoxon T to determine whether there is a difference in the ability of the rats to run the maze in the dark as opposed to running the maze in the light.

Rat	Dark	Light
1	23	18
2	18	28
3	14	14
4	22	21
5	33	35
6	27	29
7	9	12
8	22	17

23. The accompanying data were gathered from three groups of eight subjects who participated in an experiment comparing long-term memory for three types of items: words, nonwords, and numbers. The dependent variable in this experiment was the number of items remembered out of a list of 50 items. Generate a null hypothesis and a research hypothesis for this experiment, and then use the Kruskal-Wallis test to determine whether there is a difference among the three conditions.

Words	Nonwords	Numbers
28	15	6
29	14	6
37	15	5
30	16	7
29	23	5
18	15	6
28	14	7
17	13	7

24. Given the results of the Kruskal-Wallis test conducted in Problem 23, what are your conclusions about the stated hypotheses?

25. Three separate groups of randomly assigned subjects were asked to list the number of words they recognized from a 100-word list spoken by a man, a woman, or a computer. State a null hypothesis and a research hypothesis, and then use the table data to conduct a Kruskal-Wallis test. Is it significant?

26. Given the results of the Kruskal-Wallis test conducted in Problem 25, what are your conclusions about the stated hypotheses?

Man	Woman	Computer
97	99	86
96	94	80
93	92	88
94	97	80
93	92	81
92	94	80
95	96	82
95	96	87
93	94	79

R E F E R E N C E S

Kaplan, G. A., & Reynolds, P. (1988). Depression and cancer mortality and morbidity: Prospective evidence from the Alameda County Study. *Journal of Behavioral Medicine, 11,* 1–13.

Kirk, R. E. (1978). Introductory Statistics. Pacific Grove, CA: Brooks/Cole.

Minium, E. W. (1978). *Statistical reasoning in psychology and education.* New York: Wiley.

Owen, D. B. (1962). *Handbook of statistical tables.* Boston: Addison-Wesley.

Tables

Table F The F Distribution

$\alpha = .01$

df_D \ df_N	1	2	3	4	5	6	7	8	9	10	12	15	20	24	30	40	60	120	∞
1	4052	4999.5	5403	5625	5764	5859	5928	5981	6022	6056	6106	6157	6209	6235	6261	6287	6313	6339	6366
2	98.50	99.00	99.17	99.25	99.30	99.33	99.36	99.37	99.39	99.40	99.42	99.43	99.45	99.46	99.47	99.47	99.48	99.49	99.50
3	34.12	30.82	29.46	28.71	28.24	27.91	27.67	27.49	27.35	27.23	27.05	26.87	26.69	26.60	26.50	26.41	26.32	26.22	26.13
4	21.20	18.00	16.69	15.98	15.52	15.21	14.98	14.80	14.66	14.55	14.37	14.20	14.02	13.93	13.84	13.75	13.65	13.56	13.46
5	16.26	13.27	12.06	11.39	10.97	10.67	10.46	10.29	10.16	10.05	9.89	9.72	9.55	9.47	9.38	9.29	9.20	9.11	9.02
6	13.75	10.92	9.78	9.15	8.75	8.47	8.26	8.10	7.98	7.87	7.72	7.56	7.40	7.31	7.23	7.14	7.06	6.97	6.88
7	12.25	9.55	8.45	7.85	7.46	7.19	6.99	6.84	6.72	6.62	6.47	6.31	6.16	6.07	5.99	5.91	5.82	5.74	5.65
8	11.26	8.65	7.59	7.01	6.63	6.37	6.18	6.03	5.91	5.81	5.67	5.52	5.36	5.28	5.20	5.12	5.03	4.95	4.86
9	10.56	8.02	6.99	6.42	6.06	5.80	5.61	5.47	5.35	5.26	5.11	4.96	4.81	4.73	4.65	4.57	4.48	4.40	4.31
10	10.04	7.56	6.55	5.99	5.64	5.39	5.20	5.06	4.94	4.85	4.71	4.56	4.41	4.33	4.25	4.17	4.08	4.00	3.91
11	9.65	7.21	6.22	5.67	5.32	5.07	4.89	4.74	4.63	4.54	4.40	4.25	4.10	4.02	3.94	3.86	3.78	3.69	3.60
12	9.33	6.93	5.95	5.41	5.06	4.82	4.64	4.50	4.39	4.30	4.16	4.01	3.86	3.78	3.70	3.62	3.54	3.45	3.36
13	9.07	6.70	5.74	5.21	4.86	4.62	4.44	4.30	4.19	4.10	3.96	3.82	3.66	3.59	3.51	3.43	3.34	3.25	3.17
14	8.86	6.51	5.56	5.04	4.69	4.46	4.28	4.14	4.03	3.94	3.80	3.66	3.51	3.43	3.35	3.27	3.18	3.09	3.00
15	8.68	6.36	5.42	4.89	4.56	4.32	4.14	4.00	3.89	3.80	3.67	3.52	3.37	3.29	3.21	3.13	3.05	2.96	2.87
16	8.53	6.23	5.29	4.77	4.44	4.20	4.03	3.89	3.78	3.69	3.55	3.41	3.26	3.18	3.10	3.02	2.93	2.84	2.75
17	8.40	6.11	5.18	4.67	4.34	4.10	3.93	3.79	3.68	3.59	3.46	3.31	3.16	3.08	3.00	2.92	2.83	2.75	2.65
18	8.29	6.01	5.09	4.58	4.25	4.01	3.84	3.71	3.60	3.51	3.37	3.23	3.08	3.00	2.92	2.84	2.75	2.66	2.57
19	8.18	5.93	5.01	4.50	4.17	3.94	3.77	3.63	3.52	3.43	3.30	3.15	3.00	2.92	2.84	2.76	2.67	2.58	2.49
20	8.10	5.85	4.94	4.43	4.10	3.87	3.70	3.56	3.46	3.37	3.23	3.09	2.94	2.86	2.78	2.69	2.61	2.52	2.42
21	8.02	5.78	4.87	4.37	4.04	3.81	3.64	3.51	3.40	3.31	3.17	3.03	2.88	2.80	2.72	2.64	2.55	2.46	2.36
22	7.95	5.72	4.82	4.31	3.99	3.76	3.59	3.45	3.35	3.26	3.12	2.98	2.83	2.75	2.67	2.58	2.50	2.40	2.31
23	7.88	5.66	4.76	4.26	3.94	3.71	3.54	3.41	3.30	3.21	3.07	2.93	2.78	2.70	2.62	2.54	2.45	2.35	2.26
24	7.82	5.61	4.72	4.22	3.90	3.67	3.50	3.36	3.26	3.17	3.03	2.89	2.74	2.66	2.58	2.49	2.40	2.31	2.21
25	7.77	5.57	4.68	4.18	3.85	3.63	3.46	3.32	3.22	3.13	2.99	2.85	2.70	2.62	2.54	2.45	2.36	2.27	2.17
26	7.72	5.53	4.64	4.14	3.82	3.59	3.42	3.29	3.18	3.09	2.96	2.81	2.66	2.58	2.50	2.42	2.33	2.23	2.13
27	7.68	5.49	4.60	4.11	3.78	3.56	3.39	3.26	3.15	3.06	2.93	2.78	2.63	2.55	2.47	2.38	2.29	2.20	2.10
28	7.64	5.45	4.57	4.07	3.75	3.53	3.36	3.23	3.12	3.03	2.90	2.75	2.60	2.52	2.44	2.35	2.26	2.17	2.06
29	7.60	5.42	4.54	4.04	3.73	3.50	3.33	3.20	3.09	3.00	2.87	2.73	2.57	2.49	2.41	2.33	2.23	2.14	2.03
30	7.56	5.39	4.51	4.02	3.70	3.47	3.30	3.17	3.07	2.98	2.84	2.70	2.55	2.47	2.39	2.30	2.21	2.11	2.01
40	7.31	5.18	4.31	3.83	3.51	3.29	3.12	2.99	2.89	2.80	2.66	2.52	2.37	2.29	2.20	2.11	2.02	1.92	1.80
60	7.08	4.98	4.13	3.65	3.34	3.12	2.95	2.82	2.72	2.63	2.50	2.35	2.20	2.12	2.03	1.94	1.84	1.73	1.60
120	6.85	4.79	3.95	3.48	3.17	2.96	2.79	2.66	2.56	2.47	2.34	2.19	2.03	1.95	1.86	1.76	1.66	1.53	1.38
∞	6.63	4.61	3.78	3.32	3.02	2.80	2.64	2.51	2.41	2.32	2.18	2.04	1.88	1.79	1.70	1.59	1.47	1.32	1.00

Table F The *F* Distribution (continued)

α = .05

df_D \ df_N	1	2	3	4	5	6	7	8	9	10	12	15	20	24	30	40	60	120	∞
1	161.4	199.5	215.7	224.6	230.2	234.0	236.8	238.9	240.5	241.9	243.9	245.9	248.0	249.1	250.1	251.1	252.2	253.3	254.3
2	18.51	19.00	19.16	19.25	19.30	19.33	19.35	19.37	19.38	19.40	19.41	19.43	19.45	19.45	19.46	19.47	19.48	19.49	19.50
3	10.13	9.55	9.28	9.12	9.01	8.94	8.89	8.85	8.81	8.79	8.74	8.70	8.66	8.64	8.62	8.59	8.57	8.55	8.53
4	7.71	6.94	6.59	6.39	6.26	6.16	6.09	6.04	6.00	5.96	5.91	5.86	5.80	5.77	5.75	5.72	5.69	5.66	5.63
5	6.61	5.79	5.41	5.19	5.05	4.95	4.88	4.82	4.77	4.74	4.68	4.62	4.56	4.53	4.50	4.46	4.43	4.40	4.36
6	5.99	5.14	4.76	4.53	4.39	4.28	4.21	4.15	4.10	4.06	4.00	3.94	3.87	3.84	3.81	3.77	3.74	3.70	3.67
7	5.59	4.74	4.35	4.12	3.97	3.87	3.79	3.73	3.68	3.64	3.57	3.51	3.44	3.41	3.38	3.34	3.30	3.27	3.23
8	5.32	4.46	4.07	3.84	3.69	3.58	3.50	3.44	3.39	3.35	3.28	3.22	3.15	3.12	3.08	3.04	3.01	2.97	2.93
9	5.12	4.26	3.86	3.63	3.48	3.37	3.29	3.23	3.18	3.14	3.07	3.01	2.94	2.90	2.86	2.83	2.79	2.75	2.71
10	4.96	4.10	3.71	3.48	3.33	3.22	3.14	3.07	3.02	2.98	2.91	2.85	2.77	2.74	2.70	2.66	2.62	2.58	2.54
11	4.84	3.98	3.59	3.36	3.20	3.09	3.01	2.95	2.90	2.85	2.79	2.72	2.65	2.61	2.57	2.53	2.49	2.45	2.40
12	4.75	3.89	3.49	3.26	3.11	3.00	2.91	2.85	2.80	2.75	2.69	2.62	2.54	2.51	2.47	2.43	2.38	2.34	2.30
13	4.67	3.81	3.41	3.18	3.03	2.92	2.83	2.77	2.71	2.67	2.60	2.53	2.46	2.42	2.38	2.34	2.30	2.25	2.21
14	4.60	3.74	3.34	3.11	2.96	2.85	2.76	2.70	2.65	2.60	2.53	2.46	2.39	2.35	2.31	2.27	2.22	2.18	2.13
15	4.54	3.68	3.29	3.06	2.90	2.79	2.71	2.64	2.59	2.54	2.48	2.40	2.33	2.29	2.25	2.20	2.16	2.11	2.07
16	4.49	3.63	3.24	3.01	2.85	2.74	2.66	2.59	2.54	2.49	2.42	2.35	2.28	2.24	2.19	2.15	2.11	2.06	2.01
17	4.45	3.59	3.20	2.96	2.81	2.70	2.61	2.55	2.49	2.45	2.38	2.31	2.23	2.19	2.15	2.10	2.06	2.01	1.96
18	4.41	3.55	3.16	2.93	2.77	2.66	2.58	2.51	2.46	2.41	2.34	2.27	2.19	2.15	2.11	2.06	2.02	1.97	1.92
19	4.38	3.52	3.13	2.90	2.74	2.63	2.54	2.48	2.42	2.38	2.31	2.23	2.16	2.11	2.07	2.03	1.98	1.93	1.88
20	4.35	3.49	3.10	2.87	2.71	2.60	2.51	2.45	2.39	2.35	2.28	2.20	2.12	2.08	2.04	1.99	1.95	1.90	1.84
21	4.32	3.47	3.07	2.84	2.68	2.57	2.49	2.42	2.37	2.32	2.25	2.18	2.10	2.05	2.01	1.96	1.92	1.87	1.81
22	4.30	3.44	3.05	2.82	2.66	2.55	2.46	2.40	2.34	2.30	2.23	2.15	2.07	2.03	1.98	1.94	1.89	1.84	1.78
23	4.28	3.42	3.03	2.80	2.64	2.53	2.44	2.37	2.32	2.27	2.20	2.13	2.05	2.01	1.96	1.91	1.86	1.81	1.76
24	4.26	3.40	3.01	2.78	2.62	2.51	2.42	2.36	2.30	2.25	2.18	2.11	2.03	1.98	1.94	1.89	1.84	1.79	1.73
25	4.24	3.39	2.99	2.76	2.60	2.49	2.40	2.34	2.28	2.24	2.16	2.09	2.01	1.96	1.92	1.87	1.82	1.77	1.71
26	4.23	3.37	2.98	2.74	2.59	2.47	2.39	2.32	2.27	2.22	2.15	2.07	1.99	1.95	1.90	1.85	1.80	1.75	1.69
27	4.21	3.35	2.96	2.73	2.57	2.46	2.37	2.31	2.25	2.20	2.13	2.06	1.97	1.93	1.88	1.84	1.79	1.73	1.67
28	4.20	3.34	2.95	2.71	2.56	2.45	2.36	2.29	2.24	2.19	2.12	2.04	1.96	1.91	1.87	1.82	1.77	1.71	1.65
29	4.18	3.33	2.93	2.70	2.55	2.43	2.35	2.28	2.22	2.18	2.10	2.03	1.94	1.90	1.85	1.81	1.75	1.70	1.64
30	4.17	3.32	2.92	2.69	2.53	2.42	2.33	2.27	2.21	2.16	2.09	2.01	1.93	1.89	1.84	1.79	1.74	1.68	1.62
40	4.08	3.23	2.84	2.61	2.45	2.34	2.25	2.18	2.12	2.08	2.00	1.92	1.84	1.79	1.74	1.69	1.64	1.58	1.51
60	4.00	3.15	2.76	2.53	2.37	2.25	2.17	2.10	2.04	1.99	1.92	1.84	1.75	1.70	1.65	1.59	1.53	1.47	1.39
120	3.92	3.07	2.68	2.45	2.29	2.17	2.09	2.02	1.96	1.91	1.83	1.75	1.66	1.61	1.55	1.50	1.43	1.35	1.25
∞	3.84	3.00	2.60	2.37	2.21	2.10	2.01	1.94	1.88	1.83	1.75	1.67	1.57	1.52	1.46	1.39	1.32	1.22	1.00

Source: From *Biometrika Tables for Statisticians*, Vol. I, Third Edition, edited by E. S. Pearson and H. O. Hartley, pp. 171 and 173. Copyright © 1966. Reprinted by permission of the Cambridge University Press and the Biometrika Trustees.

Table *N*   Random Numbers

24483	69647	24743	47325	91484	65438	40410	19209	66040	07336
55115	52788	63353	79385	99841	09039	79424	18900	54835	13192
78889	30435	68614	30981	62425	27889	60019	70207	04655	99728
45519	73480	03054	15411	34884	54035	57401	53172	78233	79048
65864	46289	03918	45376	80824	29437	81784	02749	18282	84189
36242	07308	67374	26574	80255	08058	20295	16041	01730	99304
78808	93258	22275	53594	40710	85067	68822	75412	41821	44602
99713	25076	97829	71678	97090	83687	48072	22145	93745	45550
59872	54369	79905	11491	16150	25307	85173	60238	76114	49311
53104	93300	55899	09603	32591	07156	66500	41276	00223	12682
48183	05389	11811	33781	95532	60559	76722	31156	45395	57629
91287	02779	64560	61047	54621	21072	25367	88578	98179	77593
73246	01192	81080	31504	48219	99909	44353	00536	63943	39475
91640	26925	50204	31859	38620	55718	02794	35024	00123	62576
64168	01945	24039	88922	05474	61924	66817	57246	51442	07277
50543	93393	04173	22806	47616	15719	93589	39927	13782	18723
90141	73368	99843	57475	77670	77813	82486	70834	39483	89162
88309	49559	02168	71179	11128	48848	13072	83781	69933	54171
50390	23556	12846	98722	01933	43433	87200	64651	27027	45562
68176	13514	82571	75940	00584	15786	59245	08720	89771	65606
22398	59779	22158	31364	29353	04533	50603	11530	22965	12813
31569	82262	31442	31350	76936	65029	12557	73810	75280	21615
97085	99017	68415	04704	19542	18358	63044	11028	48639	70205
51138	95399	02665	29551	12468	04793	11574	87288	98715	22039
28487	41186	22062	39748	35194	00054	11539	40367	93178	70035
77361	80511	23872	23768	04595	72294	78828	66226	21903	65215
50545	39002	56941	13042	93781	22444	46939	98420	74848	20140
02255	70355	15985	22300	53448	39101	44818	21404	28334	36643
76232	94410	04562	90230	25718	26144	31841	13189	45321	37933
77963	02032	48836	16550	16299	26160	34531	13959	03453	42437
89188	82741	74054	17693	34826	10423	34497	24042	04560	63990
34565	90604	52324	31749	01537	87840	24819	51175	86140	96059
41679	13067	75648	05828	87538	62162	85443	61156	77113	50132
27993	19385	10849	28667	42680	79842	34626	68201	87605	78575
34860	28281	91603	35590	15733	53073	37833	30389	13958	22059
01248	33549	80899	21943	62125	05684	79941	63953	70796	06071
99241	52891	20877	94660	02104	63178	09400	40076	28858	86346
88684	00717	65757	28115	55195	50651	00550	28971	74981	03843
41214	31334	60752	79907	85751	22153	31213	05799	00295	28045
25417	84610	69412	32876	12606	42529	99107	26526	37224	69405

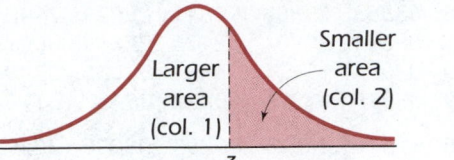

| Larger area (col. 1) | Smaller area (col. 2) | Smaller area (col. 2) | Larger area (col. 1) |

(Read z as a positive number)   (Read z as a negative number)

The larger area	z	The smaller area	The larger area	z	The smaller area
1	2	3	1	2	3
.500	0.0000	.500	.625	0.3186	.375
.505	0.0125	.495	.630	0.3319	.370
.510	0.0251	.490	.635	0.3451	.365
.515	0.0376	.485	.640	0.3585	.360
.520	0.0502	.480	.645	0.3719	.355
.525	0.0627	.475	.650	0.3853	.350
.530	0.0753	.470	.655	0.3989	.345
.535	0.0878	.465	.660	0.4125	.340
.540	0.1004	.460	.665	0.4261	.335
.545	0.1130	.455	.670	0.4399	.330
.550	0.1257	.450	.675	0.4538	.325
.555	0.1383	.445	.680	0.4677	.320
.560	0.1510	.440	.685	0.4817	.315
.565	0.1637	.435	.690	0.4959	.310
.570	0.1764	.430	.695	0.5101	.305
.575	0.1891	.425	.700	0.5244	.300
.580	0.2019	.420	.705	0.5388	.295
.585	0.2147	.415	.710	0.5534	.290
.590	0.2275	.410	.715	0.5681	.285
.595	0.2404	.405	.720	0.5828	.280
.600	0.2533	.400	.725	0.5978	.275
.605	0.2663	.395	.730	0.6128	.270
.610	0.2793	.390	.735	0.6280	.265
.615	0.2924	.385	.740	0.6433	.260
.620	0.3055	.380	.745	0.6588	.255

(continued)

Table P Values of *z* (continued)

The larger area 1	*z* 2	The smaller area 3	The larger area 1	*z* 2	The smaller area 3
.750	0.6745	.250	.900	1.2816	.100
.755	0.6903	.245	.905	1.3106	.095
.760	0.7063	.240	.910	1.3408	.090
.765	0.7225	.235	.915	1.3722	.085
.770	0.7388	.230	.920	1.4051	.080
.775	0.7554	.225	.925	1.4395	.075
.780	0.7722	.220	.930	1.4757	.070
.785	0.7892	.215	.935	1.5141	.065
.790	0.8064	.210	.940	1.5548	.060
.795	0.8239	.205	.945	1.5982	.055
.800	0.8416	.200	.950	1.6449	.050
.805	0.8596	.195	.955	1.6954	.045
.810	0.8779	.190	.960	1.7507	.040
.815	0.8965	.185	.965	1.8119	.035
.820	0.9154	.180	.970	1.8808	.030
.825	0.9346	.175	.975	1.9600	.025
.830	0.9542	.170	.980	2.0537	.020
.835	0.9741	.165	.985	2.1701	.015
.840	0.9945	.160	.990	2.3263	.010
.845	1.0152	.155	.995	2.5758	.005
.850	1.0364	.150	.996	2.6521	.004
.855	1.0581	.145	.997	2.7478	.003
.860	1.0803	.140	.998	2.8782	.002
.865	1.1031	.135	.999	3.0902	.001
.870	1.1264	.130	.9995	3.2905	.0005
.875	1.1503	.125			
.880	1.1750	.120			
.885	1.2004	.115			
.890	1.2265	.110			
.895	1.2536	.105			

Source: From *Fundamental Statistics in Psychology and Education,* 4th Ed., by J. P. Guilford, Appendix B, Table C. Copyright © 1965 McGraw-Hill, Inc. Reprinted by permission.

Table Q The Studentized Range Statistic

Upper 5% points

df_{wg} \ k	2	3	4	5	6	7	8	9	10
1	17.97	26.98	32.82	37.08	40.41	43.12	45.40	47.36	49.07
2	6.08	8.33	9.80	10.88	11.74	12.44	13.03	13.54	13.99
3	4.50	5.91	6.82	7.50	8.04	8.48	8.85	9.18	9.46
4	3.93	5.04	5.76	6.29	6.71	7.05	7.35	7.60	7.83
5	3.64	4.60	5.22	5.67	6.03	6.33	6.58	6.80	6.99
6	3.46	4.34	4.90	5.30	5.63	5.90	6.12	6.32	6.49
7	3.34	4.16	4.68	5.06	5.36	5.61	5.82	6.00	6.16
8	3.26	4.04	4.53	4.89	5.17	5.40	5.60	5.77	5.92
9	3.20	3.95	4.41	4.76	5.02	5.24	5.43	5.59	5.74
10	3.15	3.88	4.33	4.65	4.91	5.12	5.30	5.46	5.60
11	3.11	3.82	4.26	4.57	4.82	5.03	5.20	5.35	5.49
12	3.08	3.77	4.20	4.51	4.75	4.95	5.12	5.27	5.39
13	3.06	3.73	4.15	4.45	4.69	4.88	5.05	5.19	5.32
14	3.03	3.70	4.11	4.41	4.64	4.83	4.99	5.13	5.25
15	3.01	3.67	4.08	4.37	4.59	4.78	4.94	5.08	5.20
16	3.00	3.65	4.05	4.33	4.56	4.74	4.90	5.03	5.15
17	2.98	3.63	4.02	4.30	4.52	4.70	4.86	4.99	5.11
18	2.97	3.61	4.00	4.28	4.49	4.67	4.82	4.96	5.07
19	2.96	3.59	3.98	4.25	4.47	4.65	4.79	4.92	5.04
20	2.95	3.58	3.96	4.23	4.45	4.62	4.77	4.90	5.01
24	2.92	3.53	3.90	4.17	4.37	4.54	4.68	4.81	4.92
30	2.89	3.49	3.85	4.10	4.30	4.46	4.60	4.72	4.82
40	2.86	3.44	3.79	4.04	4.23	4.39	4.52	4.63	4.73
60	2.83	3.40	3.74	3.98	4.16	4.31	4.44	4.55	4.65
120	2.80	3.36	3.68	3.92	4.10	4.24	4.36	4.47	4.56
∞	2.77	3.31	3.63	3.86	4.03	4.17	4.29	4.39	4.47

k: The number of groups (or number of rows or number of columns)
df_{wg}: Degrees of freedom within groups

Table Q The Studentized Range Statistic (continued)

Upper 5% points

df_{wg} \ k	11	12	13	14	15	16	17	18	19	20
1	50.59	51.96	53.20	54.33	55.36	56.32	57.22	58.04	58.83	59.56
2	14.39	14.75	15.08	15.38	15.65	15.91	16.14	16.37	16.57	16.77
3	9.72	9.95	10.15	10.35	10.52	10.69	10.84	10.98	11.11	11.24
4	8.03	8.21	8.37	8.52	8.66	8.79	8.91	9.03	9.13	9.23
5	7.17	7.32	7.47	7.60	7.72	7.83	7.93	8.03	8.12	8.21
6	6.65	6.79	6.92	7.03	7.14	7.24	7.34	7.43	7.51	7.59
7	6.30	6.43	6.55	6.66	6.76	6.85	6.94	7.02	7.10	7.17
8	6.05	6.18	6.29	6.39	6.48	6.57	6.65	6.73	6.80	6.87
9	5.87	5.98	6.09	6.19	6.28	6.36	6.44	6.51	6.58	6.64
10	5.72	5.83	5.93	6.03	6.11	6.19	6.27	6.34	6.40	6.47
11	5.61	5.71	5.81	5.90	5.98	6.06	6.13	6.20	6.27	6.33
12	5.51	5.61	5.71	5.80	5.88	5.95	6.02	6.09	6.15	6.21
13	5.43	5.53	5.63	5.71	5.79	5.86	5.93	5.99	6.05	6.11
14	5.36	5.46	5.55	5.64	5.71	5.79	5.85	5.91	5.97	6.03
15	5.31	5.40	5.49	5.57	5.65	5.72	5.78	5.85	5.90	5.96
16	5.26	5.35	5.44	5.52	5.59	5.66	5.73	5.79	5.84	5.90
17	5.21	5.31	5.39	5.47	5.54	5.61	5.67	5.73	5.79	5.84
18	5.17	5.27	5.35	5.43	5.50	5.57	5.63	5.69	5.74	5.79
19	5.14	5.23	5.31	5.39	5.46	5.53	5.59	5.65	5.70	5.75
20	5.11	5.20	5.28	5.36	5.43	5.49	5.55	5.61	5.66	5.71
24	5.01	5.10	5.18	5.25	5.32	5.38	5.44	5.49	5.55	5.59
30	4.92	5.00	5.08	5.15	5.21	5.27	5.33	5.38	5.43	5.47
40	4.82	4.90	4.98	5.04	5.11	5.16	5.22	5.27	5.31	5.36
60	4.73	4.81	4.88	4.94	5.00	5.06	5.11	5.15	5.20	5.24
120	4.64	4.71	4.78	4.84	4.90	4.95	5.00	5.04	5.09	5.13
∞	4.55	4.62	4.68	4.74	4.80	4.85	4.89	4.93	4.97	5.01

k: The number of groups (or number of rows or number of columns)
df_{wg}: Degrees of freedom within groups

Source: From Biometrika Tables for Statisticians, Vol.1, Third Edition, edited by E. S. Pearson and H. O. Hartley, p. 192. Copyright © 1966. Reprinted by permission of the Cambridge University Press and the Biometrika Trustees.

Table R Critical Values of the Correlation Coefficient

df	.25	.10	.05	.025	.01	.005
3	.7071	.9511	.9877	.9969	.9995	.9999
4	.5000	.8000	.9000	.9500	.9800	.9900
5	.4040	.6870	.8054	.8783	.9343	.9587
6	.3473	.6084	.7293	.8114	.8822	.9172
7	.3091	.5509	.6694	.7545	.8329	.8745
8	.2811	.5067	.6215	.7067	.7887	.8343
9	.2596	.4716	.5822	.6664	.7498	.7977
10	.2423	.4428	.5493	.6319	.7155	.7646
11	.2281	.4187	.5214	.6021	.6851	.7348
12	.2161	.3981	.4973	.5760	.6581	.7079
13	.2058	.3802	.4762	.5529	.6339	.6835
14	.1968	.3646	.4575	.5324	.6120	.6614
15	.1890	.3507	.4409	.5140	.5923	.6411
16	.1820	.3383	.4259	.4973	.5742	.6226
17	.1757	.3271	.4124	.4822	.5577	.6055
18	.1700	.3170	.4000	.4683	.5426	.5897
19	.1649	.3077	.3887	.4555	.5285	.5751
20	.1602	.2992	.3783	.4438	.5155	.5614
21	.1558	.2914	.3687	.4329	.5034	.5487
22	.1518	.2841	.3598	.4227	.4921	.5368
23	.1481	.2774	.3515	.4132	.4815	.5256
24	.1447	.2711	.3438	.4044	.4716	.5151
25	.1415	.2653	.3365	.3961	.4622	.5052
30	.1281	.2407	.3061	.3610	.4226	.4629
35	.1179	.2220	.2826	.3338	.3916	.4296
40	.1098	.2070	.2638	.3120	.3665	.4026
45	.1032	.1947	.2483	.2940	.3457	.3801
50	.0976	.1843	.2353	.2787	.3281	.3610
60	.0888	.1678	.2144	.2542	.2997	.3301
70	.0820	.1550	.1982	.2352	.2776	.3060
80	.0765	.1448	.1852	.2199	.2597	.2864
90	.0720	.1364	.1745	.2072	.2449	.2702
100	.0682	.1292	.1654	.1966	.2324	.2565

Source: From *The Handbook of Statistical Tables,* by D. B. Owen, p. 510. Copyright © 1965 Addison-Wesley Longman Publishing Co. Reprinted by permission.

Table T Critical Values of the t Distribution

df	1-tail = .4 2-tail = .8	.25 .5	.1 .2	.05 .1	.025 .05	.01 .02	.005 .01	.0025 .005	.001 .002	.0005 .001
1	0.325	1.000	3.078	6.314	12.706	31.821	63.657	127.32	318.31	636.62
2	0.289	0.816	1.886	2.920	4.303	6.965	9.925	14.089	22.327	31.598
3	0.277	0.765	1.638	2.353	3.182	4.541	5.841	7.453	10.214	12.924
4	0.271	0.741	1.533	2.132	2.776	3.747	4.604	5.598	7.173	8.610
5	0.267	0.727	1.476	2.015	2.571	3.365	4.032	4.773	5.893	6.869
6	0.265	0.718	1.440	1.943	2.447	3.143	3.707	4.317	5.208	5.959
7	0.263	0.711	1.415	1.895	2.365	2.998	3.499	4.029	4.785	5.408
8	0.262	0.706	1.397	1.860	2.306	2.896	3.355	3.833	4.501	5.041
9	0.261	0.703	1.383	1.833	2.262	2.821	3.250	3.690	4.297	4.781
10	0.260	0.700	1.372	1.812	2.228	2.764	3.169	3.581	4.144	4.587
11	0.260	0.697	1.363	1.796	2.201	2.718	3.106	3.497	4.025	4.437
12	0.259	0.695	1.356	1.782	2.179	2.681	3.055	3.428	3.930	4.318
13	0.259	0.694	1.350	1.771	2.160	2.650	3.012	3.372	3.852	4.221
14	0.258	0.692	1.345	1.761	2.145	2.624	2.977	3.326	3.787	4.140
15	0.258	0.691	1.341	1.753	2.131	2.602	2.947	3.286	3.733	4.073
16	0.258	0.690	1.337	1.746	2.120	2.583	2.921	3.252	3.686	4.015
17	0.257	0.689	1.333	1.740	2.110	2.567	2.898	3.222	3.646	3.965
18	0.257	0.688	1.330	1.734	2.101	2.552	2.878	3.197	3.610	3.922
19	0.257	0.688	1.328	1.729	2.093	2.539	2.861	3.174	3.579	3.883
20	0.257	0.687	1.325	1.725	2.086	2.528	2.845	3.153	3.552	3.850
21	0.257	0.686	1.323	1.721	2.080	2.518	2.831	3.135	3.527	3.819
22	0.256	0.686	1.321	1.717	2.074	2.508	2.819	3.119	3.505	3.792
23	0.256	0.685	1.319	1.714	2.069	2.500	2.807	3.104	3.485	3.767
24	0.256	0.685	1.318	1.711	2.064	2.492	2.797	3.091	3.467	3.745
25	0.256	0.684	1.316	1.708	2.060	2.485	2.787	3.078	3.450	3.725
26	0.256	0.684	1.315	1.706	2.056	2.479	2.779	3.067	3.435	3.707
27	0.256	0.684	1.314	1.703	2.052	2.473	2.771	3.057	3.421	3.690
28	0.256	0.683	1.313	1.701	2.048	2.467	2.763	3.047	3.408	3.674
29	0.256	0.683	1.311	1.699	2.045	2.462	2.756	3.038	3.396	3.659
30	0.256	0.683	1.310	1.697	2.042	2.457	2.750	3.030	3.385	3.646
40	0.255	0.681	1.303	1.684	2.021	2.423	2.704	2.971	3.307	3.551
60	0.254	0.679	1.296	1.671	2.000	2.390	2.660	2.915	3.232	3.460
120	0.254	0.677	1.289	1.658	1.980	2.358	2.617	2.860	3.160	3.373
∞	0.253	0.674	1.282	1.645	1.960	2.326	2.576	2.807	3.090	3.291

Source: From *Biometrika Tables for Statisticians,* Vol.1, Third Edition, edited by E. S. Pearson and H. O. Hartley, p. 146. Copyright © 1966. Reprinted by permission of the Cambridge University Press and the Biometrika Trustees.

Table U Critical Values of the Mann-Whitney *U* Test

n_2 \ n_1	1	2	3	4	5	6	7	8	9	10	11	12	13	14	15	16	17	18	19	20
1	—	—	—	—	—	—	—	—	—	—	—	—	—	—	—	—	—	—	0	0
																			—	—
2	—	—	—	—	0	0	0	1	1	1	1	2	2	2	3	3	3	4	4	4
	—	—	—	—	**—**	**—**	**—**	**0**	**0**	**0**	**0**	**1**	**1**	**1**	**1**	**1**	**2**	**2**	**2**	**2**
3	—	—	0	0	1	2	2	3	3	4	5	5	6	7	7	8	9	9	10	11
	—	—	**—**	**—**	**0**	**1**	**1**	**2**	**2**	**3**	**3**	**4**	**4**	**5**	**5**	**6**	**6**	**7**	**7**	**8**
4	—	—	0	1	2	3	4	5	6	7	8	9	10	11	12	14	15	16	17	18
	—	—	**—**	**0**	**1**	**2**	**3**	**4**	**4**	**5**	**6**	**7**	**8**	**9**	**10**	**11**	**11**	**12**	**13**	**13**
5	—	0	1	2	4	5	6	8	9	11	12	13	15	16	18	19	20	22	23	25
	—	**—**	**0**	**1**	**2**	**3**	**5**	**6**	**7**	**8**	**9**	**11**	**12**	**13**	**14**	**15**	**17**	**18**	**19**	**20**
6	—	0	2	3	5	7	8	10	12	14	16	17	19	21	23	25	26	28	30	32
	—	**—**	**1**	**2**	**3**	**5**	**6**	**8**	**10**	**11**	**13**	**14**	**16**	**17**	**19**	**21**	**22**	**24**	**25**	**27**
7	—	0	2	4	6	8	11	13	15	17	19	21	24	26	28	30	33	35	37	39
	—	**—**	**1**	**3**	**5**	**6**	**8**	**10**	**12**	**14**	**16**	**18**	**20**	**22**	**24**	**26**	**28**	**30**	**32**	**34**
8	—	1	3	5	8	10	13	15	18	20	23	26	28	31	33	36	39	41	44	47
	—	**0**	**2**	**4**	**6**	**8**	**10**	**13**	**15**	**17**	**19**	**22**	**24**	**26**	**29**	**31**	**34**	**36**	**38**	**41**
9	—	1	3	6	9	12	15	18	21	24	27	30	33	36	39	42	45	48	51	54
	—	**0**	**2**	**4**	**7**	**10**	**12**	**15**	**17**	**20**	**23**	**26**	**28**	**31**	**34**	**37**	**39**	**42**	**45**	**48**
10	—	1	4	7	11	14	17	20	24	27	31	34	37	41	44	48	51	55	58	62
	—	**0**	**3**	**5**	**8**	**11**	**14**	**17**	**20**	**23**	**26**	**29**	**33**	**36**	**39**	**42**	**45**	**48**	**52**	**55**
11	—	1	5	8	12	16	19	23	27	31	34	38	42	46	50	54	57	61	65	69
	—	**0**	**3**	**6**	**9**	**13**	**16**	**19**	**23**	**26**	**30**	**33**	**37**	**40**	**44**	**47**	**51**	**55**	**58**	**62**
12	—	2	5	9	13	17	21	26	30	34	38	42	47	51	55	60	64	68	72	77
	—	**1**	**4**	**7**	**11**	**14**	**18**	**22**	**26**	**29**	**33**	**37**	**41**	**45**	**49**	**53**	**57**	**61**	**65**	**69**
13	—	2	6	10	15	19	24	28	33	37	42	47	51	56	61	65	70	75	80	84
	—	**1**	**4**	**8**	**12**	**16**	**20**	**24**	**28**	**33**	**37**	**41**	**45**	**50**	**54**	**59**	**63**	**67**	**72**	**76**
14	—	2	7	11	16	21	26	31	36	41	46	51	56	61	66	71	77	82	87	92
	—	**1**	**5**	**9**	**13**	**17**	**22**	**26**	**31**	**36**	**40**	**45**	**50**	**55**	**59**	**64**	**67**	**74**	**78**	**83**
15	—	3	7	12	18	23	28	33	39	44	50	55	61	66	72	77	83	88	94	100
	—	**1**	**5**	**10**	**14**	**19**	**24**	**29**	**34**	**39**	**44**	**49**	**54**	**59**	**64**	**70**	**75**	**80**	**85**	**90**
16	—	3	8	14	19	25	30	36	42	48	54	60	65	71	77	83	89	95	101	107
	—	**1**	**6**	**11**	**15**	**21**	**26**	**31**	**37**	**42**	**47**	**53**	**59**	**64**	**70**	**75**	**81**	**86**	**92**	**98**
17	—	3	9	15	20	26	33	39	45	51	57	64	70	77	83	89	96	102	109	115
	—	**2**	**6**	**11**	**17**	**22**	**28**	**34**	**39**	**45**	**51**	**57**	**63**	**67**	**75**	**81**	**87**	**93**	**99**	**105**
18	—	4	9	16	22	28	35	41	48	55	61	68	75	82	88	95	102	109	116	123
	—	**2**	**7**	**12**	**18**	**24**	**30**	**36**	**42**	**48**	**55**	**61**	**67**	**74**	**80**	**86**	**93**	**99**	**106**	**112**
19	0	4	10	17	23	30	37	44	51	58	65	72	80	87	94	101	109	116	123	130
	—	**2**	**7**	**13**	**19**	**25**	**32**	**38**	**45**	**52**	**58**	**65**	**72**	**78**	**85**	**92**	**99**	**106**	**113**	**119**
20	0	4	11	18	25	32	39	47	54	62	69	77	84	92	100	107	115	123	130	138
	—	**2**	**8**	**13**	**20**	**27**	**34**	**41**	**48**	**55**	**62**	**69**	**76**	**83**	**90**	**98**	**105**	**112**	**119**	**127**

Source: From *Introductory Statistics,* by R. E. Kirk, pp. 423 and 424, Brooks/Cole Publishing, 1978.

Explanation: Critical values for a one-tailed test at $\alpha = .05$ (regular type) and $\alpha = .025$ (**boldface type**) and for a two-tailed test at $\alpha = .10$ (regular type) and $\alpha = .05$ (**boldface type**)

Table W   Critical Values of the Wilcoxon T Test

	Level of significance for a one-tailed test					Level of significance for a one-tailed test			
	.05	.025	.01	.005		.05	.025	.01	.005
	Level of significance for a two-tailed test					Level of significance for a two-tailed test			
n	.10	.05	.02	.01	n	.10	.05	.02	.01
5	0	—	—	—	28	130	116	101	91
6	2	0	—	—	29	140	126	110	100
7	3	2	0	—	30	151	137	120	109
8	5	3	1	0	31	163	147	130	118
9	8	5	3	1	32	175	159	140	128
10	10	8	5	3	33	187	170	151	138
11	13	10	7	5	34	200	182	162	148
12	17	13	9	7	35	213	195	173	159
13	21	17	12	9	36	227	208	185	171
14	25	21	15	12	37	241	221	198	182
15	30	25	19	15	38	256	235	211	194
16	35	29	23	19	39	271	249	224	207
17	41	34	27	23	40	286	264	238	220
18	47	40	32	27	41	302	279	252	233
19	53	46	37	32	42	319	294	266	247
20	60	52	43	37	43	336	310	281	261
21	67	58	49	42	44	353	327	296	276
22	75	65	55	48	45	371	343	312	291
23	83	73	62	54	46	389	361	328	307
24	91	81	69	61	47	407	378	345	322
25	100	89	76	68	48	426	396	362	339
26	110	98	84	75	49	446	415	379	355
27	119	107	92	83	50	466	434	397	373

The symbol T denotes the smaller sum of ranks associated with differences that are all of the same sign. For any given n (number of ranked differences), the obtained T is significant at a given level if it is *equal to* or *less than* the value shown in the table.

Source: From *Introductory Statistics,* by R. E. Kirk, p. 425, Brooks/Cole Publishing, 1978.

Table χ   The χ^2 Distribution

df	.25	.10	.05	.025	.01	.005
1	1.323	2.706	3.841	5.024	6.635	7.879
2	2.773	4.605	5.991	7.378	9.210	10.597
3	4.108	6.251	7.815	9.348	11.345	12.838
4	5.385	7.779	9.488	11.143	13.277	14.860
5	6.626	9.236	11.071	12.833	15.086	16.750
6	7.841	10.645	12.592	14.449	16.812	18.548
7	9.037	12.017	14.067	16.013	18.475	20.278
8	10.219	13.362	15.507	17.535	20.090	21.955
9	11.389	14.684	16.919	19.023	21.666	23.589
10	12.549	15.987	18.307	20.483	23.209	25.188
11	13.701	17.275	19.675	21.920	24.725	26.757
12	14.845	18.549	21.026	23.337	26.217	28.299
13	15.984	19.812	22.362	24.736	27.688	29.819
14	17.117	21.064	23.685	26.119	29.141	31.319
15	18.245	22.307	24.996	27.488	30.578	32.801
16	19.369	23.542	26.296	28.845	32.000	34.267
17	20.489	24.769	27.587	30.191	33.409	35.718
18	21.605	25.989	28.869	31.526	34.805	37.156
19	22.718	27.204	30.144	32.852	36.191	38.582
20	23.828	28.412	31.410	34.170	37.566	39.997
21	24.935	29.615	32.671	35.479	38.932	41.401
22	26.039	30.813	33.924	36.781	40.289	42.796
23	27.141	32.007	35.172	38.076	41.638	44.181
24	28.241	33.196	36.415	39.364	42.980	45.559
25	29.339	34.382	37.652	40.646	44.314	46.928
26	30.435	35.563	38.885	41.923	45.642	48.290
27	31.528	36.741	40.113	43.194	46.963	49.645
28	32.620	37.916	41.337	44.461	48.278	50.993
29	33.711	39.087	42.557	45.722	49.588	52.336
30	34.800	40.256	43.773	46.979	50.892	53.672
31	35.887	41.422	44.985	48.232	52.191	55.003
32	36.973	42.585	46.194	49.480	53.486	56.328
33	38.058	43.745	47.400	50.725	54.776	57.648
34	39.141	44.903	48.602	51.966	56.061	58.964
35	40.223	46.059	49.802	53.203	57.342	60.275
36	41.304	47.212	50.998	54.437	58.619	61.581
37	42.383	48.363	52.192	55.668	59.892	62.883
38	43.462	49.513	53.384	56.896	61.162	64.181
39	44.539	50.660	54.572	58.120	62.428	65.476
40	45.616	51.805	55.758	59.342	63.691	66.766
41	46.692	52.949	56.942	60.561	64.950	68.053
42	47.766	54.090	58.124	61.777	66.206	69.336
43	48.840	55.230	59.304	62.990	67.459	70.616
44	49.913	56.369	60.481	64.201	68.710	71.893
45	50.985	57.505	61.656	65.410	69.957	73.166

Source: From *The Handbook of Statistical Tables,* by D. B. Owen, p. 50. Copyright © 1965 Addison-Wesley Longman Publishing Co. Reprinted by permission.

Table Z Areas Under the Normal Curve

Column 2 gives the proportion of the area under the entire curve that is between the mean ($z = 0$) and the positive value of z. Areas for negative values of z are the same as for positive values because the curve is symmetrical.

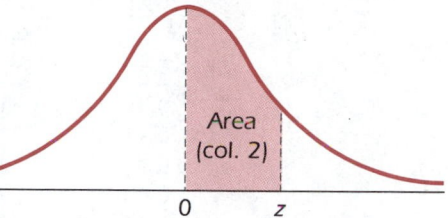

Column 3 gives the proportion of the area under the entire curve that falls beyond the stated positive value of z. Areas for negative values of z are the same because the curve is symmetrical.

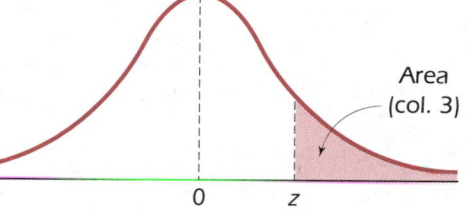

z	Area between mean and z	Area beyond z	z	Area between mean and z	Area beyond z
1	2	3	1	2	3
0.00	.0000	.5000	0.20	.0793	.4207
0.01	.0040	.4960	0.21	.0832	.4168
0.02	.0080	.4920	0.22	.0871	.4129
0.03	.0120	.4880	0.23	.0910	.4090
0.04	.0160	.4840	0.24	.0948	.4052
0.05	.0199	.4801	0.25	.0987	.4013
0.06	.0239	.4761	0.26	.1026	.3974
0.07	.0279	.4721	0.27	.1064	.3936
0.08	.0319	.4681	0.28	.1103	.3897
0.09	.0359	.4641	0.29	.1141	.3859
0.10	.0398	.4602	0.30	.1179	.3821
0.11	.0438	.4562	0.31	.1217	.3783
0.12	.0478	.4522	0.32	.1255	.3745
0.13	.0517	.4483	0.33	.1293	.3707
0.14	.0557	.4443	0.34	.1331	.3669
0.15	.0596	.4404	0.35	.1368	.3632
0.16	.0636	.4364	0.36	.1406	.3594
0.17	.0675	.4325	0.37	.1443	.3557
0.18	.0714	.4286	0.38	.1480	.3520
0.19	.0753	.4247	0.39	.1517	.3483

(continued)

z	Area between mean and z	Area beyond z	z	Area between mean and z	Area beyond z
1	2	3	1	2	3
0.40	.1554	.3446	0.75	.2734	.2266
0.41	.1591	.3409	0.76	.2764	.2236
0.42	.1628	.3372	0.77	.2794	.2206
0.43	.1664	.3336	0.78	.2823	.2177
0.44	.1700	.3300	0.79	.2852	.2148
0.45	.1736	.3264	0.80	.2881	.2119
0.46	.1772	.3228	0.81	.2910	.2090
0.47	.1808	.3192	0.82	.2939	.2061
0.48	.1844	.3156	0.83	.2967	.2033
0.49	.1879	.3121	0.84	.2995	.2005
0.50	.1915	.3085	0.85	.3023	.1977
0.51	.1950	.3050	0.86	.3051	.1949
0.52	.1985	.3015	0.87	.3078	.1922
0.53	.2019	.2981	0.88	.3106	.1894
0.54	.2054	.2946	0.89	.3133	.1867
0.55	.2088	.2912	0.90	.3159	.1841
0.56	.2123	.2877	0.91	.3186	.1814
0.57	.2157	.2843	0.92	.3212	.1788
0.58	.2190	.2810	0.93	.3238	.1762
0.59	.2224	.2776	0.94	.3264	.1736
0.60	.2257	.2743	0.95	.3289	.1711
0.61	.2291	.2709	0.96	.3315	.1685
0.62	.2324	.2676	0.97	.3340	.1660
0.63	.2357	.2643	0.98	.3365	.1635
0.64	.2389	.2611	0.99	.3389	.1611
0.65	.2422	.2578	1.00	.3413	.1587
0.66	.2454	.2546	1.01	.3438	.1562
0.67	.2486	.2514	1.02	.3461	.1539
0.68	.2517	.2483	1.03	.3485	.1515
0.69	.2549	.2451	1.04	.3508	.1492
0.70	.2580	.2420	1.05	.3531	.1469
0.71	.2611	.2389	1.06	.3554	.1446
0.72	.2642	.2358	1.07	.3577	.1423
0.73	.2673	.2327	1.08	.3599	.1401
0.74	.2704	.2296	1.09	.3621	.1379

(continued)

z	Area between mean and z	Area beyond z	z	Area between mean and z	Area beyond z
1	2	3	1	2	3
1.10	.3643	.1357	1.45	.4265	.0735
1.11	.3665	.1335	1.46	.4279	.0721
1.12	.3686	.1314	1.47	.4292	.0708
1.13	.3708	.1292	1.48	.4306	.0694
1.14	.3729	.1271	1.49	.4319	.0681
1.15	.3749	.1251	1.50	.4332	.0668
1.16	.3770	.1230	1.51	.4345	.0655
1.17	.3790	.1210	1.52	.4357	.0643
1.18	.3810	.1190	1.53	.4370	.0630
1.19	.3830	.1170	1.54	.4382	.0618
1.20	.3849	.1151	1.55	.4394	.0606
1.21	.3869	.1131	1.56	.4406	.0594
1.22	.3888	.1112	1.57	.4418	.0582
1.23	.3907	.1093	1.58	.4429	.0571
1.24	.3925	.1075	1.59	.4441	.0559
1.25	.3944	.1056	1.60	.4452	.0548
1.26	.3962	.1038	1.61	.4463	.0537
1.27	.3980	.1020	1.62	.4474	.0526
1.28	.3997	.1003	1.63	.4484	.0516
1.29	.4015	.0985	1.64	.4495	.0505
1.30	.4032	.0968	1.65	.4505	.0495
1.31	.4049	.0951	1.66	.4515	.0485
1.32	.4066	.0934	1.67	.4525	.0475
1.33	.4082	.0918	1.68	.4535	.0465
1.34	.4099	.0901	1.69	.4545	.0455
1.35	.4115	.0885	1.70	.4554	.0446
1.36	.4131	.0869	1.71	.4564	.0436
1.37	.4147	.0853	1.72	.4573	.0427
1.38	.4162	.0838	1.73	.4582	.0418
1.39	.4177	.0823	1.74	.4591	.0409
1.40	.4192	.0808	1.75	.4599	.0401
1.41	.4207	.0793	1.76	.4608	.0392
1.42	.4222	.0778	1.77	.4616	.0384
1.43	.4236	.0764	1.78	.4625	.0375
1.44	.4251	.0749	1.79	.4633	.0367

(continued)

Table Z Areas Under the Normal Curve *(continued)*

z	Area between mean and z	Area beyond z	z	Area between mean and z	Area beyond z
1	2	3	1	2	3
1.80	.4641	.0359	2.15	.4842	.0158
1.81	.4649	.0351	2.16	.4846	.0154
1.82	.4656	.0344	2.17	.4850	.0150
1.83	.4664	.0336	2.18	.4854	.0146
1.84	.4671	.0329	2.19	.4857	.0143
1.85	.4678	.0322	2.20	.4861	.0139
1.86	.4686	.0314	2.21	.4864	.0136
1.87	.4693	.0307	2.22	.4868	.0132
1.88	.4699	.0301	2.23	.4871	.0129
1.89	.4706	.0294	2.24	.4875	.0125
1.90	.4713	.0287	2.25	.4878	.0122
1.91	.4719	.0281	2.26	.4881	.0119
1.92	.4726	.0274	2.27	.4884	.0116
1.93	.4732	.0268	2.28	.4887	.0113
1.94	.4738	.0262	2.29	.4890	.0110
1.95	.4744	.0256	2.30	.4893	.0107
1.96	.4750	.0250	2.31	.4896	.0104
1.97	.4756	.0244	2.32	.4898	.0102
1.98	.4761	.0239	2.33	.4901	.0099
1.99	.4767	.0233	2.34	.4904	.0096
2.00	.4772	.0228	2.35	.4906	.0094
2.01	.4778	.0222	2.36	.4909	.0091
2.02	.4783	.0217	2.37	.4911	.0089
2.03	.4788	.0212	2.38	.4913	.0087
2.04	.4793	.0207	2.39	.4916	.0084
2.05	.4798	.0202	2.40	.4918	.0082
2.06	.4803	.0197	2.41	.4920	.0080
2.07	.4808	.0192	2.42	.4922	.0078
2.08	.4812	.0188	2.43	.4925	.0075
2.09	.4817	.0183	2.44	.4927	.0073
2.10	.4821	.0179	2.45	.4929	.0071
2.11	.4826	.0174	2.46	.4931	.0069
2.12	.4830	.0170	2.47	.4932	.0068
2.13	.4834	.0166	2.48	.4934	.0066
2.14	.4838	.0162	2.49	.4936	.0064

(continued)

z	Area between mean and z	Area beyond z	z	Area between mean and z	Area beyond z
1	2	3	1	2	3
2.50	.4938	.0062	2.85	.4978	.0022
2.51	.4940	.0060	2.86	.4979	.0021
2.52	.4941	.0059	2.87	.4979	.0021
2.53	.4943	.0057	2.88	.4980	.0020
2.54	.4945	.0055	2.89	.4981	.0019
2.55	.4946	.0054	2.90	.4981	.0019
2.56	.4948	.0052	2.91	.4982	.0018
2.57	.4949	.0051	2.92	.4982	.0018
2.58	.4951	.0049	2.93	.4983	.0017
2.59	.4952	.0048	2.94	.4984	.0016
2.60	.4953	.0047	2.95	.4984	.0016
2.61	.4955	.0045	2.96	.4985	.0015
2.62	.4956	.0044	2.97	.4985	.0015
2.63	.4957	.0043	2.98	.4986	.0014
2.64	.4959	.0041	2.99	.4986	.0014
2.65	.4960	.0040	3.00	.4987	.0013
2.66	.4961	.0039	3.01	.4987	.0013
2.67	.4962	.0038	3.02	.4987	.0013
2.68	.4963	.0037	3.03	.4988	.0012
2.69	.4964	.0036	3.04	.4988	.0012
2.70	.4965	.0035	3.05	.4989	.0011
2.71	.4966	.0034	3.06	.4989	.0011
2.72	.4967	.0033	3.07	.4989	.0011
2.73	.4968	.0032	3.08	.4900	.0010
2.74	.4969	.0031	3.09	.4990	.0010
2.75	.4970	.0030	3.10	.4990	.0010
2.76	.4971	.0029	3.11	.4991	.0009
2.77	.4972	.0028	3.12	.4991	.0009
2.78	.4973	.0027	3.13	.4991	.0009
2.79	.4974	.0026	3.14	.4992	.0008
2.80	.4974	.0026	3.15	.4992	.0008
2.81	.4975	.0025	3.16	.4992	.0008
2.82	.4976	.0024	3.17	.4992	.0008
2.83	.4977	.0023	3.18	.4993	.0007
2.84	.4977	.0023	3.19	.4993	.0007

(continued)

Table Z Areas Under the Normal Curve *(continued)*

| z | Area between mean and z | Area beyond z | z | Area between mean and z | Area beyond z |
1	2	3	1	2	3
3.20	.4993	.0007	3.30	.4995	.0005
3.21	.4993	.0007	3.40	.4997	.0003
3.22	.4994	.0006	3.50	.4998	.0002
3.23	.4994	.0006	3.60	.4998	.0002
3.24	.4994	.0006	3.70	.4999	.0001

Source: Values calculated by Myron L. Braunstein. Reprinted by permission.

Solutions to Odd-Numbered Problems

CHAPTER 1

1. 23,456.568
3. 0.240
5. 93,856.235
7. Research hypothesis: The job proficiency of National Guard soldiers is not as high as that of soldiers in the regular army.
   Null hypothesis: The job proficiency of National Guard soldiers is the same as that of the soldiers in the regular army.
9. Research hypothesis: The two management training programs differ in their effectiveness.
   Null hypothesis: The two management training programs are equal in their effectiveness.
11. Independent variable: the concentration of the nerve-blocking agent
    Dependent variable: the number of action potentials
13. Independent variable: the treatment—that is, suspension or physical punishment
    Dependent variable: the number of children's disruptive acts in the next 3 days
15. Interval
17. Ordinal
19. Nominal
21. Ratio
23. Ratio
25. Ratio

CHAPTER 2

1. 86   77   77   71   70   67   63   61   59   56   55   55   54
   54   54   52   50   49   46   46   43   41   39   34   33

3. $151 - 72 + 1 = 80$; $80/10 = 8$ intervals

5.

Real limits	Apparent limits	F
29.5–32.5	30–32	3
26.5–29.5	27–29	5
23.5–26.5	24–26	2

(continued)

Real limits	Apparent limits	F
20.5–23.5	21–23	6
17.5–20.5	18–20	6
14.5–17.5	15–17	4
11.5–14.5	12–14	6
8.5–11.5	9–11	4
5.5– 8.5	6– 8	3
2.5– 5.5	3– 5	3
−0.5– 2.5	0– 2	3

7.

Real limits	Apparent limits	F	Midpoint	CF	RF	CRF
224.5–229.5	225–229	2	227	40	.050	1.000
219.5–224.5	220–224	3	222	38	.075	.950
214.5–219.5	215–219	1	217	35	.025	.875
209.5–214.5	210–214	3	212	34	.075	.850
204.5–209.5	205–209	1	207	31	.025	.775
199.5–204.5	200–204	1	202	30	.025	.750
194.5–199.5	195–199	2	197	29	.050	.725
189.5–194.5	190–194	2	192	27	.050	.675
184.5–189.5	185–189	0	187	25	.000	.625
179.5–184.5	180–184	5	182	25	.125	.625
174.5–179.5	175–179	2	177	20	.050	.500
169.5–174.5	170–174	3	172	18	.075	.450
164.5–169.5	165–169	2	167	15	.050	.375
159.5–164.5	160–164	6	162	13	.150	.325
154.5–159.5	155–159	7	157	7	.175	.175

9. $147 − 65 + 1 = 83$
$83/10 = 8.3$; $83/9 = 9.22$; width of 9 gives 10 intervals
$83/20 = 4.15$; $83/5 = 16.6$; width of 5 gives 17 intervals
Choose interval width of 5.

Apparent limits
145–149
140–144
135–139
130–134
125–129
120–124
115–119
110–114
105–109
100–104
95– 99
90– 94
85– 89
80– 84
75– 79
70– 74
65– 69

11. $89 - 16 + 1 = 74$

13.

Real limits	Apparent limits	F	RF
118.5–125.5	119–125	1	.033
111.5–118.5	112–118	1	.033
104.5–111.5	105–111	1	.033
97.5–104.5	98–104	1	.033
90.5– 97.5	91– 97	3	.100
83.5– 90.5	84– 90	3	.100
76.5– 83.5	77– 83	3	.100

(continued)

Real limits	Apparent limits	F	RF
69.5– 76.5	70– 76	1	.033
62.5– 69.5	63– 69	3	.100
55.5– 62.5	56– 62	8	.267
48.5– 55.5	49– 55	0	.000
41.5– 48.5	42– 48	1	.033
34.5– 41.5	35– 41	3	.100
27.5– 34.5	28– 34	0	.000
20.5– 27.5	21– 27	1	.033

15. Compare the distributions using relative frequency. In this case, the distributions are not exactly the same.

17. Most players take between 72 and 80 seconds.

19.

Real limits	Apparent limits	F	CF	RF	CRF
47.5–50.5	48–50	1	30	.033	1.000
44.5–47.5	45–47	0	29	.000	.967
41.5–44.5	42–44	2	29	.067	.967
38.5–41.5	39–41	1	27	.033	.900
35.5–38.5	36–38	1	26	.033	.867
32.5–35.5	33–35	2	25	.067	.833
29.5–32.5	30–32	2	23	.067	.767
26.5–29.5	27–29	1	21	.033	.700
23.5–26.5	24–26	2	20	.067	.667
20.5–23.5	21–23	1	18	.033	.600
17.5–20.5	18–20	2	17	.067	.567
14.5–17.5	15–17	2	15	.067	.500
11.5–14.5	12–14	4	13	.133	.433
8.5–11.5	9–11	1	9	.033	.300
5.5– 8.5	6– 8	5	8	.167	.267
2.5– 5.5	3– 5	3	3	.100	.100

21.

Real limits	Apparent limits	F	CF
424.5–449.5	425–449	1	24
399.5–424.5	400–424	1	23
374.5–399.5	375–399	1	22
349.5–374.5	350–374	0	21
324.5–349.5	325–349	1	21
299.5–324.5	300–324	0	20
274.5–299.5	275–299	1	20
249.5–274.5	250–274	1	19
224.5–249.5	225–249	1	18
199.5–224.5	200–224	2	17
174.5–199.5	175–199	3	15
149.5–174.5	150–174	2	12
124.5–149.5	125–149	5	10
99.5–124.5	100–124	5	5

CHAPTER 3

1.

Real limits	Apparent limits	F	CF	RF	CRF
79.5–84.5	80–84	1	100	.01	1.00
74.5–79.5	75–79	4	99	.04	.99
69.5–74.5	70–74	8	95	.08	.95
64.5–69.5	65–69	17	87	.17	.87
59.5–64.5	60–64	9	70	.09	.70
54.5–59.5	55–59	11	61	.11	.61
49.5–54.5	50–54	3	50	.03	.50
44.5–49.5	45–49	7	47	.07	.47

(continued)

Real limits	Apparent limits	F	CF	RF	CRF
39.5–44.5	40–44	13	40	.13	.40
34.5–39.5	35–39	7	27	.07	.27
29.5–34.5	30–34	5	20	.05	.20
24.5–29.5	25–29	2	15	.02	.15
19.5–24.5	20–24	4	13	.04	.13
14.5–19.5	15–19	4	9	.04	.09
9.5–14.5	10–14	2	5	.02	.05
4.5– 9.5	5– 9	3	3	.03	.03

3.

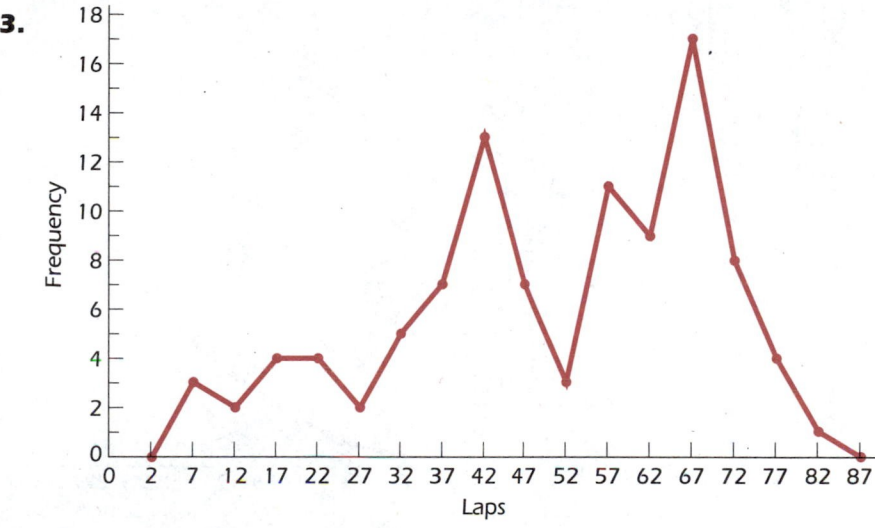

5. The graph for Problem 5 is the same as the graph for Problem 3, except the ordinate is labeled Relative frequency and numbers on the ordinate range from .00 to .18; that is, divide each number by 100.

7.

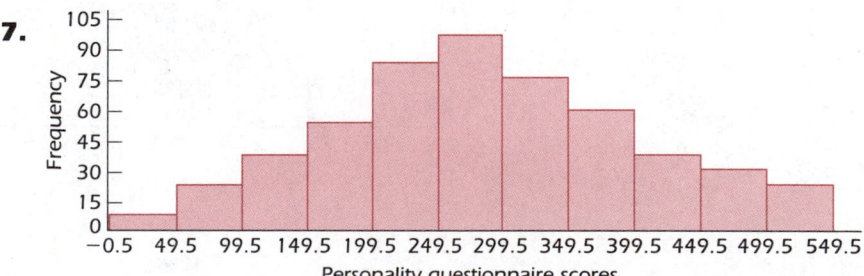

9.

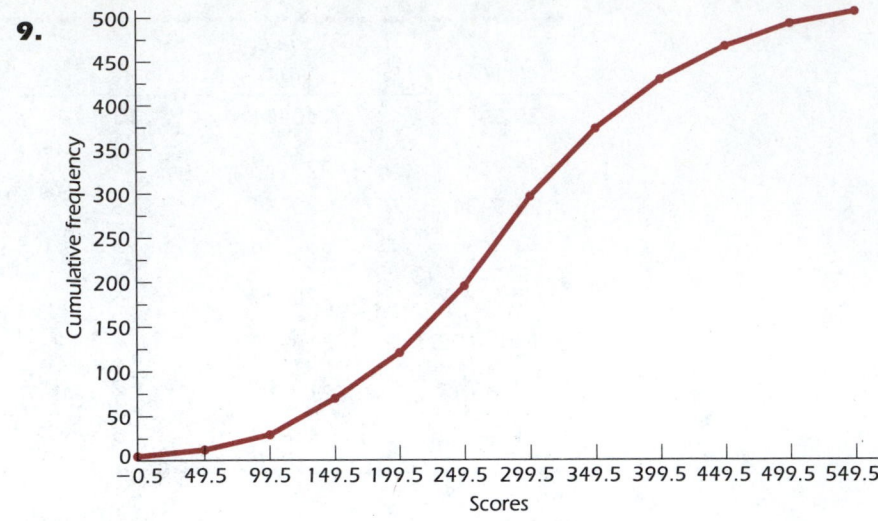

11.

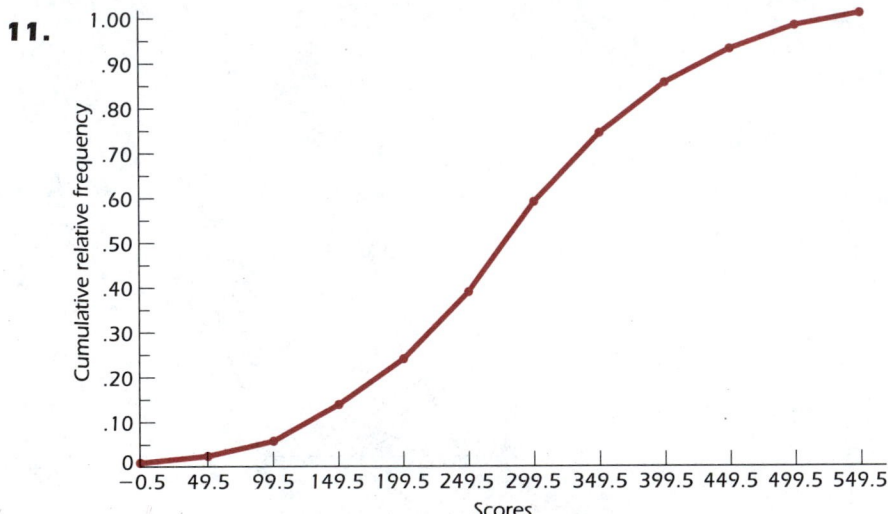

13.

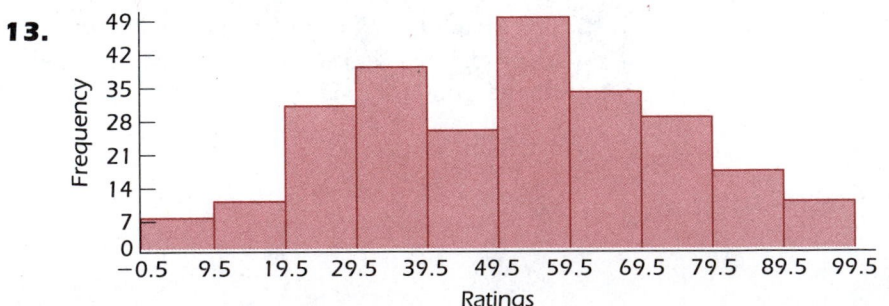

15–17. The following table is part of the answers to Problems 15–17. The graphs follow the table.

Apparent limits	F	CF	RF	CRF
90–99	10	250	.040	1.000
80–89	16	240	.064	.960
70–79	28	224	.112	.896
60–69	34	196	.136	.784
50–59	49	162	.196	.648
40–49	25	113	.100	.452
30–39	39	88	.156	.352
20–29	32	49	.128	.196
10–19	11	17	.044	.068
0– 9	6	6	.024	.024

15.

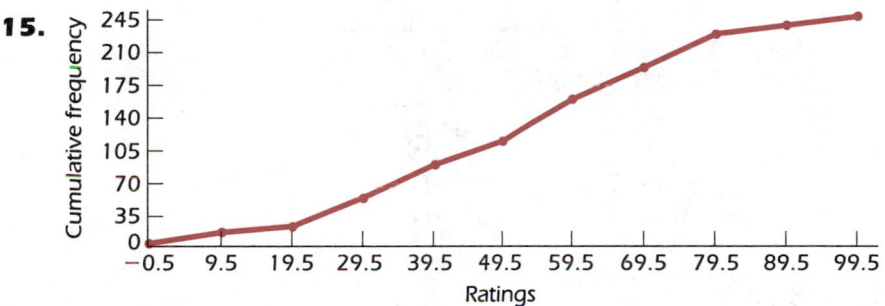

17.

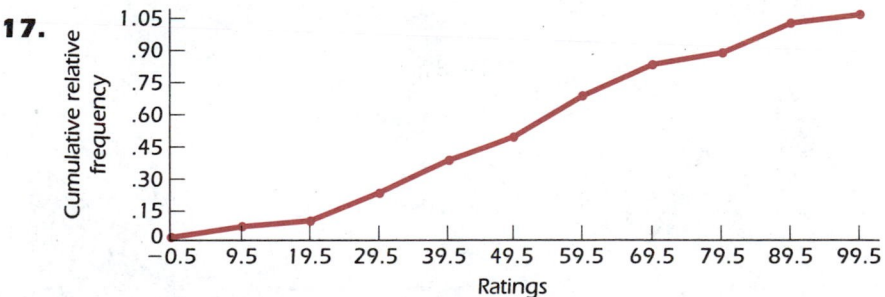

19.

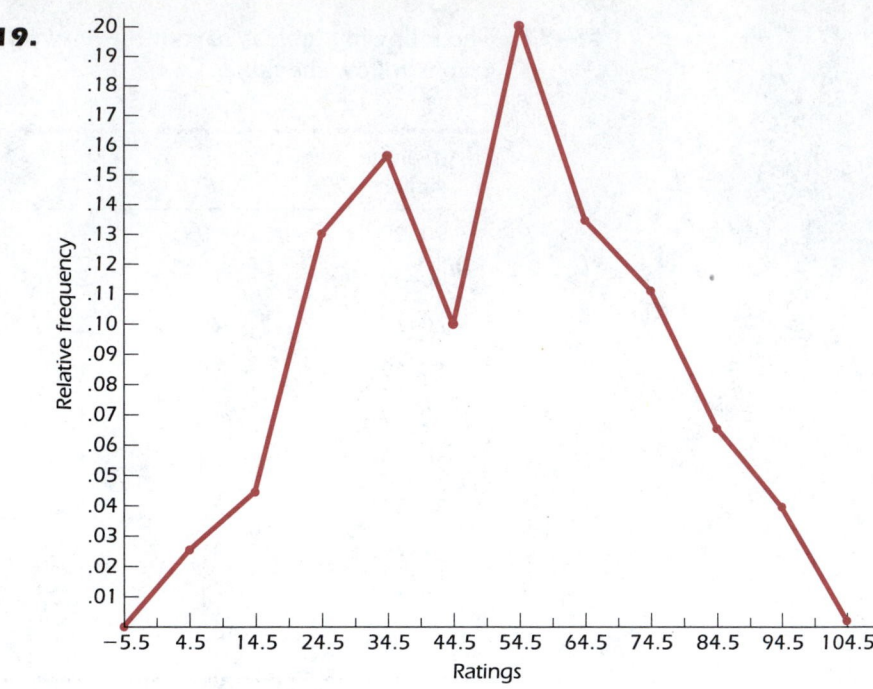

21.

Apparent limits	F
105–107	2
102–104	1
99–101	2
96– 98	4
93– 95	4
90– 92	9
87– 89	15
84– 86	8
81– 83	2
78– 80	5
75– 77	2

23.

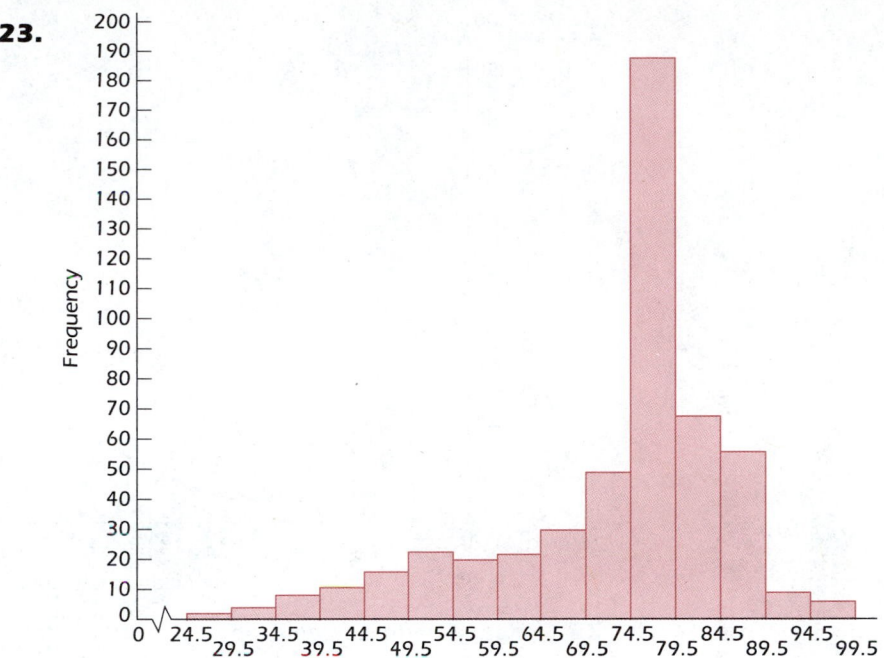

25.

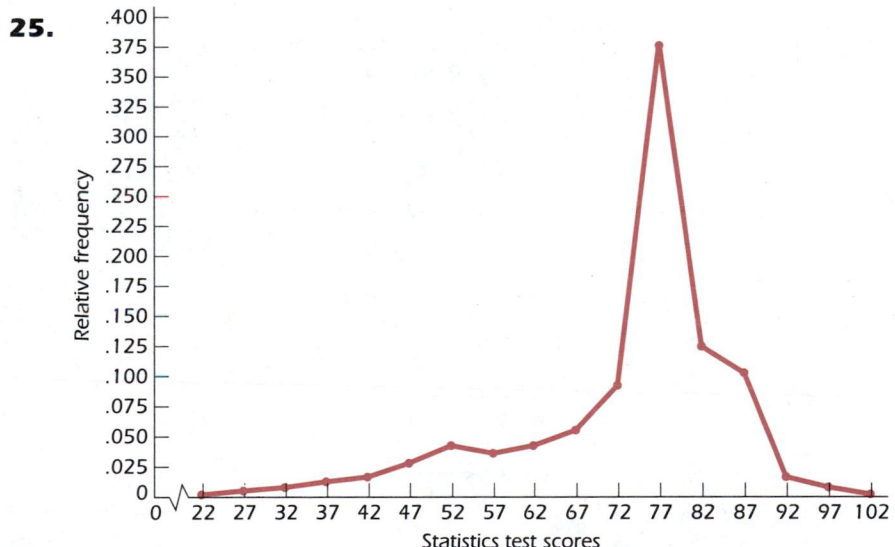

27.

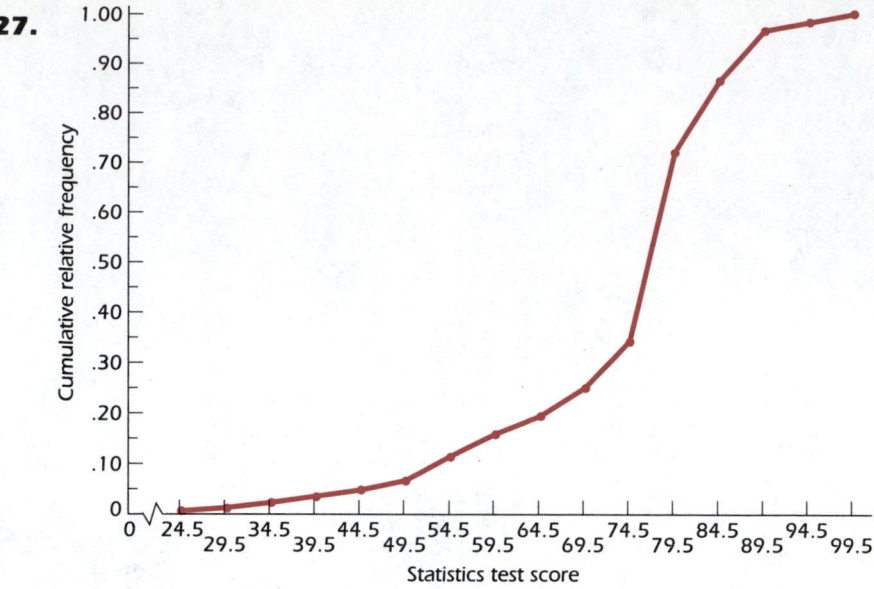

29. Relative frequency polygon

31.

Stem	Leaf
37	4 9 9
38	1 2 4 5
39	2 2 5 7 8 9 9
40	0 1 2 3 4 4 4 7 9
41	2 3 5 7 8 8 9
42	1 2 2 2 5 8
43	0 7 8
44	9
45	6 7 9 9

CHAPTER 4

1. Mean = 1877/18 = 104.278
Median = (99 + 103)/2 = 101
Mode = 74 and 93

3. Mean = 1228/30 = 40.933

Median = (40 + 41)/2 = 40.5
Mode = 38

5. Mean = 17,878.50/173 = 103.344

$$\text{Median} = 99.5 + \left(\frac{\frac{173}{2} - 76}{36} \right)(10)$$

$$= 99.5 + 2.9167 = 102.417$$

Mode = 104.5

7. Mean = 2335/58 = 40.259

$$\text{Median} = 39.5 + \left(\frac{\frac{58}{2} - 25}{13} \right)(2)$$

$$= 39.5 + 0.6154 = 40.115$$

Mode = 40.5

9. Mean = 12,675/250 = 50.70

$$\text{Median} = 49.5 + \left(\frac{\frac{250}{2} - 113}{49} \right)(10)$$

$$= 49.5 + 2.4490 = 51.949$$

Mode = 54.5

11. Mean = 346/15 = 23.067
Median = 21
Mode = 6

13. The best measure of central tendency depends on your purpose. The mode is the measure that is most descriptive of this distribution. The median is probably preferable. The distribution has a negative skew.

15. The median is probably the best measure, but the best measure depends on your purpose. The distribution has a positive skew.

17. They are equal.

19. Mean = 126/18 = 7
Median = 7
Mode = 7

21. Mean = 2728/11 = 248
Median = 245
Mode = 250 and 245 and 231

23. Mean = 12,768/294 = 43.429

$$\text{Median} = 41.5 + \left(\frac{147 - 136}{56} \right)(7)$$

$$= 41.5 + 0.196 \cdot 7 = 41.5 + 1.372$$
$$= 42.872$$

Mode = 45

25. Mean = 1578/20 = 78.9
Median = 78
Mode = 78

27. Mean = 120/18 = 6.667
Median = 6
Mode = 6

CHAPTER 5

1. Mean = 19/6 = 3.167
3. Variance = 6.834/6 = 1.139
5. Standard deviation = $\sqrt{1.139}$ = 1.067
7. Engineering majors:
Variance = (871/5) − 169 = 174.2 − 169 = 5.2
Standard deviation = $\sqrt{5.2}$ = 2.28
History majors:
Variance = (1051/5) − 169 = 210.2 − 169 = 41.2
Standard deviation = $\sqrt{41.2}$ = 6.419
9. The high brightness contrast produced more consistent results because the standard deviation is smaller for that condition.
11. Choose the high brightness contrast because it has a higher mean and a smaller standard deviation, suggesting that people tend to get higher scores under those conditions and there is more consistency in the results compared to the low brightness contrast.
13. Variance = 36,137.50/150 = 240.9167
15. ΣF = 115; ΣFX = 2149; mean = 2149/115 = 18.68696
17. Standard deviation = $\sqrt{42.006}$ = 6.481
19. Mean = 168/7 = 24
Variance = (4190/7) − 576 = 598.5714 − 576 = 22.5714
Standard deviation = $\sqrt{22.5714}$ = 4.751
21. Mean = 117/18 = 6.5
Variance = (891/18) − 6.5^2 = 49.5 − 42.25 = 7.25
Standard deviation = $\sqrt{7.25}$ = 2.693
23. Mean = 2770/11 = 251.818
Variance = (705,826/11) − 251.818^2
  = 64,166 − 63,412.305 = 753.695
Standard deviation = $\sqrt{753.695}$ = 27.454
25. Mean = 12,291/275 = 44.695
Variance = 50,934.34/275 = 185.216
Standard deviation = 13.609
27. Mean = 1568/20 = 78.4
Variance = (151,948/20) − 78.4^2
  = 7597.4 − 6146.56 = 1450.84
Standard deviation = $\sqrt{1450.84}$ = 38.090

29. Mean = $109/15 = 7.267$
Variance = $(827/15) - 7.267^2$
$= 55.133 - 52.809 = 2.324$
Standard deviation = $\sqrt{2.324} = 1.524$

CHAPTER 6

1. $\text{Mean}_{new} = 100 + 10 = 110$
Standard deviation$_{new}$ = 20
3. $\text{Mean}_{new} = (100)(7) = 700$
Standard deviation$_{new}$ = $(20)(7) = 140$
5. Mean_{new} = mean − mean = 0
Standard deviation$_{new}$ = standard deviation = 20
7. $\text{Mean}_{new} = 100/5 = 20$
Standard deviation$_{new}$ = $20/20 = 1$
9. Mean = $150/10 = 15$

Standard deviation = $\sqrt{\dfrac{3340}{10} - (15)^2}$
$= \sqrt{334 - 225} = \sqrt{109} = 10.44$

Client	Number of defense mechanisms	z score
L. V.	0	−1.437
P. D.	3	−1.149
O. S.	6	−0.862
T. J.	7	−0.766
T. V.	11	−0.383
M. Q.	18	0.287
I. S.	21	0.575
B. J.	26	1.054
K. S.	28	1.245
L. B.	30	1.437

11.

Tokens	z score
16	1.333
19	2.000
8	−0.444
9	−0.222
10	0.000

13. $Mean_{new} = 345 + 50 = 395$
Standard deviation$_{new}$ = 27
15. $Mean_{new} = 345 − 100 = 245$
Standard deviation$_{new}$ = 27
17. $Mean_{new} = (345 + 25)/6 = 61.6667$
Standard deviation$_{new}$ = 27/6 = 4.5
19. $Mean_{new} = (37)(2) = 74$
Standard deviation$_{new}$ = (13)(2) = 26
21. $Mean_{new} = 37/4 = 9.25$
Standard deviation$_{new}$ = 13/4 = 3.25
23. Mean = 719/9 = 79.8889

$$\text{Standard deviation} = \sqrt{\frac{58,133}{9} - (79.8889)^2}$$
$$= \sqrt{6459.2222 - 6382.2363}$$
$$= \sqrt{76.9859} = 8.7742$$

Woman	Self-esteem score	z score
T. D.	94	1.6082
B. C.	68	−1.3550
D. D.	78	−0.2153
P. F.	93	1.4943
N. Q.	85	0.5825
O. T.	80	0.0127
N. G.	75	−0.5572
V. C.	77	−0.3292
R. C.	69	−1.2410

25.

CAT score	z score
290	−1.7885
735	2.4904
666	1.8269
450	−0.2500
476	−0.0000

27. Ralph received the higher score relative to his fellow students because his score was more standard deviations above the mean of the comparison group.

CHAPTER 7

1. .0013
.1587
.3085
.5000
.4013
.0918
.0030

3. $z = \dfrac{140 - 150}{25} = -0.40$

Proportion = .5 + .1554 = .6554

5. $z = \dfrac{162 - 150}{25} = 0.48$

Proportion = .3156

7. $z = \dfrac{120 - 150}{25} = -1.2; \quad z = \dfrac{145 - 150}{25} = -0.2$

Proportion = .3849 − .0793 = .3056

9. $z = 0.6745; X = 150 + (25 \cdot 0.6745) = 166.8625$ msec

11. $z = \dfrac{36 - 42}{5} = -1.2; \quad z = \dfrac{48 - 42}{5} = 1.2$

Proportion = .3849 + .3849 = .7698

13. .1151

15. $z = \dfrac{50,000 - 68,000}{17,000} = -1.0588 \approx -1.06$

Proportion = .5 + .3554 = .8554

17. $z = \dfrac{35,000 - 68,000}{17,000} = -1.9412 \approx 1.94$

Proportion = .0262

19. $z = \dfrac{80,000 - 68,000}{17,000} = 0.7059 \approx 0.71$

$z = \dfrac{90,000 - 68,000}{17,000} = 1.2941 \approx 1.29$

Proportion = .4015 − .2611 = .1404

21. $z = -0.1764;\ X = 68,000 + (17,000 \cdot -0.1764) = \$65,001$

23. $z = \dfrac{5 - 9}{2.5} = -1.6$

Proportion = .0548

25. $z = 1.2816;\ X = 9 + (2.5 \cdot 1.2816) = 12.2$ min

CHAPTER 8

1.

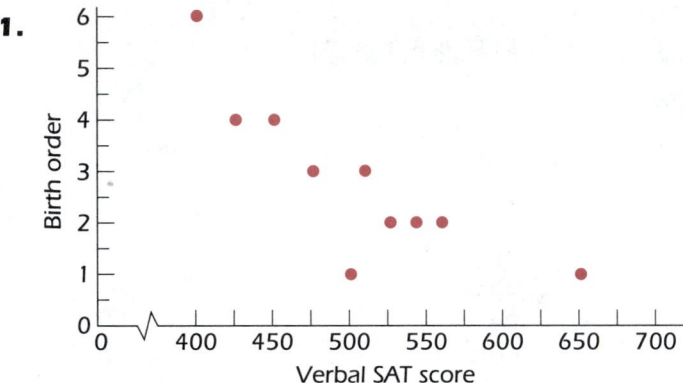

The correlation is negative.

3. $r = \dfrac{(5)(127,365) - [(3,493)(182)]}{\sqrt{[(5)(2,454,875) - 3,493^2][(5)(6,642) - 182^2]}}$

$= \dfrac{1,099}{2,511.182} = .4376$

$r = \dfrac{2.188}{5} = .4376$

5. $r^2 = (.8974)^2 = .8053 = 80.53\%$

7. $r = \dfrac{(7)(2,127) - [(341)(33)]}{\sqrt{[(7)(22,481) - 341^2][(7)(209) - 33^2]}} = \dfrac{3,636}{3,919.9699} = .9276$

9. $r = \dfrac{(7)(62.86) - [(19.4)(19.7)]}{\sqrt{[(7)(78.42) - 19.4^2][(7)(58.53) - 19.7^2]}} = \dfrac{57.84}{61.0834} = .9469$

11. $r = \dfrac{(6)(286) - [(12)(128)]}{\sqrt{[(6)(28) - 12^2][(6)(3238) - 128^2]}} = \dfrac{180}{270.2887} = .6660$

13. $r = \dfrac{(5)(485) - [(47)(62)]}{\sqrt{[(5)(537) - 47^2][(5)(918) - 62^2]}} = \dfrac{-489}{595.8993} = -.8206$

15. a. $r^2 = .0049$
   b. $r^2 = .1225$
   c. $r^2 = .5929$
   d. $r^2 = .4096$
   e. $r^2 = .1296$

17. $-.75$

19. high

21. If two variables, X and Y, are highly correlated, then it is possible that X causes Y. It is equally possible that Y causes X. And, most important, it is possible that some variable—for example, Z—causes both X and Y. A correlation coefficient does not provide sufficient information to infer causality.

23. $r = \dfrac{(12 \cdot 596) - (145 \cdot 41)}{\sqrt{[(12 \cdot 2155) \cdot 145^2] \cdot [(12 \cdot 183) - 41^2]}}$

$= \dfrac{1207}{1577.981} = .765$

CHAPTER 9

1. $\Sigma X = 27$
   $n = 10$
   $\overline{X} = 2.7$ $S_X = \sqrt{\dfrac{73.04}{10} - (2.7)^2} = \sqrt{0.014} = 0.118$
   $\Sigma X^2 = 73.04$

   $\Sigma Y = 4{,}715$
   $n = 10$
   $\overline{Y} = 471.5$ $S_Y = \sqrt{\dfrac{2{,}223{,}925}{10} - (471.5)^2} = \sqrt{80.25} = 8.958$
   $\Sigma Y^2 = 2{,}223{,}925$

   $r = \dfrac{127{,}205 - (4{,}715)(27)}{\sqrt{(730.4 - 729)(22{,}239{,}250 - 22{,}231{,}225)}}$

   $= \dfrac{-100}{105.99528} = -.9434$

3. $X' = \left[\dfrac{(-.9434)(0.118)}{8.958} \cdot (440 - 471.5) \right] + 2.7$

   $= [(-0.0124)(-31.5)] + 2.7 = 3.0906$

5. $X' = \left[\dfrac{(.55)(4.5)}{6.5} \cdot (47 - 52) \right] + 45 = 43.096$

7. $X' = \left[\dfrac{(.55)(4.5)}{6.5} \cdot (60 - 52) \right] + 45 = 48.046$

9. $Y' = \left[\dfrac{(.55)(6.5)}{4.5} \cdot (44 - 45) \right] + 52 = 51.206$

11. $Y' = \left[\dfrac{(.55)(6.5)}{4.5} \cdot (45 - 45) \right] + 52 = 52$

13. $X' = \left[\dfrac{(-.65)(10)}{0.003} \cdot (0.001 - 0.010) \right] + 75 = 94.50$

15. $X' = \left[\dfrac{(-.65)(10)}{0.003} \cdot (0.012 - 0.010) \right] + 75 = 70.667$

17. $X' = \left[\dfrac{(-.65)(10)}{0.003} \cdot (0.00 - 0.01) \right] + 75 = 96.667$

19. $S_{YX} = 10\sqrt{1 - (-.65)^2} = 7.599$

The following calculations are used in Problems 20–26.

$$\Sigma X = 29.5$$
$$\overline{X} = 2.95$$
$$\Sigma X^2 = 120.75 \qquad S_X = \sqrt{\dfrac{120.75}{10} - (2.95)^2} = 1.836$$

$$\Sigma Y = 28.9$$
$$\overline{Y} = 2.89$$
$$\Sigma Y^2 = 86.83 \qquad S_Y = \sqrt{\dfrac{86.83}{10} - (2.89)^2} = 0.5752$$

$$r = \dfrac{(10)(94.55) - (29.5)(28.9)}{\sqrt{[(10)(120.75) - (29.5)^2][(10)(86.83) - (28.9)^2]}}$$

$$= \dfrac{92.95}{105.639} = .8799$$

21. $X' = \left[\dfrac{(.8799)(1.836)}{0.5752} \cdot (1.7 - 2.89) \right] + 2.95 = -0.392$

23. $Y' = \left[\dfrac{(.8799)(0.5752)}{1.836} \cdot (2.7 - 2.95) \right] + 2.89 = 2.821$

25. $Y' = \left[\dfrac{(.8799)(0.5752)}{1.836} \cdot (1.6 - 2.95) \right] + 2.89 = 2.518$

CHAPTER 10

1. $\dfrac{900}{12,000} = .075$

3. $\dfrac{106 + 798}{1117} = .809$

5. $\dfrac{106 + 213}{1117} = .286$

7. If the two events are independent, then
$p = (.10)(.01) = .001$.

9. If the two events are independent, then
$p = (.10)(.20) = .02$.

11. If they are all independent, then
$p = (.65)(.01)(.20) = .0013$.

13. representative

15.
$$\Sigma X = 111$$
$$\overline{X} = \frac{111}{5} = 22.2$$
$$\Sigma X^2 = 2503$$
$$\text{est. } \sigma^2 = \frac{2503 - (5)(22.2)^2}{5 - 1} = 9.70$$
$$\text{est. } \sigma = \sqrt{9.70} = 3.114$$

17.
$$\Sigma X = 114$$
$$\overline{X} = \frac{114}{12} = 9.5$$
$$\Sigma X^2 = 1718$$
$$\text{est. } \sigma^2 = \frac{1718 - (12)(9.5)^2}{12 - 1} = 57.727$$
$$\text{est. } \sigma = 7.598$$

19.
$$\Sigma X = 635$$
$$\overline{X} = \frac{635}{8} = 79.375$$
$$\Sigma X^2 = 50{,}831$$
$$\text{est. } \sigma^2 = \frac{50{,}831 - (8)(79.375)^2}{8 - 1} = 61.125$$
$$\text{est. } \sigma = 7.818$$

21.
$$\Sigma X = 26$$
$$\overline{X} = \frac{26}{8} = 3.25$$
$$\Sigma X^2 = 98$$
$$\text{est. } \sigma^2 = \frac{98 - (8)(3.25)^2}{8 - 1} = 1.928$$
$$\text{est. } \sigma = 1.389$$

23.
$$\Sigma X = 1265$$
$$\overline{X} = \frac{1265}{13} = 97.308$$
$$\Sigma X^2 = 124{,}903$$
$$\text{est. } \sigma^2 = \frac{124{,}903 - (13)(97.308)^2}{13 - 1} = 150.667$$
$$\text{est. } \sigma = 12.275$$

25. $\dfrac{177}{500} = .354$

27. $\dfrac{123 + 177}{500} = .60$ *or* $.246 + .354 = .60$

29. $.354 + .40 = .754$

CHAPTER 11

1. hypothesis
3. independent variables
5. dependent
7. **a.** People who have had strokes and subsequent language impairment learn sign language more readily than they learn speech.
    b. type of presentation—spoken word or gestured sign
    c. number of spoken or signed responses made by the subjects on the fourth day
9. Dr. Hilo was using height as an independent variable, but it is a subject variable.
11. all
13. within-subjects
15. many subjects
17. **a.** completely randomized experimental design
    b. Infants spend more time looking at an organized array of lines than at a random array.
    c. type of array—random pattern or organized pattern
    d. amount of time spent looking at the card
    e. infant's age, room illumination, noise level, baby's body position, emotional state of infant (crying babies wouldn't notice cards), and others
19. completely randomized factorial; 2×2
21. extraneous variables
23. demand characteristics
25. statistical significance
27. In people who suffer from chronic headache, there is no difference between those receiving biofeedback and those not receiving it as to the number or severity of headaches.
29. People who have had strokes do not learn to communicate through sign language any faster than they do through oral speech.
31. Type I; Type II
33. two

CHAPTER 12

1. $H_0: \mu_X = 82$; $\Sigma X = 1286$; $\overline{X} = \dfrac{1286}{15} = 85.733$; $\sigma_{\bar{x}} = \dfrac{12}{\sqrt{15}} = 3.098$

$H_1: \mu_X > 82$; obtained $t = \dfrac{85.733 - 82}{3.098} = 1.205$; $df = 15 - 1 = 14$;

critical $t = 1.761$; fail to reject null

Data do not show that the new method is superior.

3. $H_0: \mu_X = 80$; $\overline{X} = 83$; est. $\sigma_{\bar{x}} = \dfrac{5.4}{\sqrt{65 - 1}} = 0.675$

$H_1: \mu_X > 80$; obtained $t = \dfrac{83 - 80}{0.675} = 4.444$; $df = 65 - 1 = 64$;

critical $t = 1.67$; reject null

Sample scored significantly higher than population.

5. $H_0: \mu_X = \mu_Y$; $\overline{X} = 135$; $S_X^2 = 552.25$; $\overline{Y} = 142$; $S_Y^2 = 1049.76$

$H_1: \mu_X < \mu_Y$; est. $\sigma_{\bar{x}-\bar{y}} = \sqrt{\dfrac{552.25}{26 - 1} + \dfrac{1049.76}{17 - 1}} = 9.365$;

obtained $t = \dfrac{135 - 142}{9.365} = -0.747$; $df = (26 - 1) + (17 - 1) = 41$;

critical $t = -1.68$; fail to reject null

There is no support to conclude that expensive dog food leads to a reduction in barking.

7. $H_0: \mu_X = \mu_Y$; est. $\sigma_{\bar{x}} = \dfrac{2.6}{\sqrt{17 - 1}} = 0.65$; est. $\sigma_{\bar{y}} = \dfrac{2.1}{\sqrt{17 - 1}} = 0.525$

$H_1: \mu_X > \mu_Y$; est. $\sigma_{\bar{x}-\bar{y}} = \sqrt{(0.65)^2 + (0.525)^2 - (2)(.64)(0.65)(0.525)}$
$= 0.511$;

obtained $t = \dfrac{13.4 - 12.7}{0.511} = 1.370$; $df = 17 - 1 = 16$;

critical $t = 1.746$; fail to reject null

There is no evidence to conclude that the type of lens coating improves reading speed.

9. $H_0: \mu_X = \mu_Y$; $\overline{X} = 17.667$; est. $\sigma_X = 3.339$; est. $\sigma_{\bar{x}} = 0.9640$
$H_1: \mu_X \neq \mu_Y$; $\overline{Y} = 20.167$; est. $\sigma_Y = 2.887$; est. $\sigma_{\bar{y}} = 0.8333$; $r_{XY} = .4495$;

est. $\sigma_{\bar{x}-\bar{y}} = \sqrt{(0.9640)^2 + (0.8333)^2 - (2)(.4495)(0.9640)(0.8333)}$
$= 0.9495$;

obtained $t = \dfrac{17.667 - 20.167}{0.9495} = -2.633$; $df = 12 - 1 = 11$;

critical $t = \pm 2.201$; reject null

Participants checked significantly more positive adjectives after undergoing assertiveness training.

11. The data do not indicate that there is a difference in the number of words or numbers that a person can memorize.

13. H_0: There will be no difference between the numbers of errors found on the two different manuscripts.
H_1: More errors will be found on the manuscript that has errors in the first seven pages.
Conclusion: Reject the null hypothesis.

15. H_0: $\mu_X = \mu_Y$; $\overline{X} = 10$; $S_X = 4$; est. $\sigma_{\overline{x}} = \dfrac{4}{\sqrt{10 - 1}} = 1.333$

H_1: $\mu_X \neq \mu_Y$; $\overline{Y} = 8$; $S_Y = 2$; est. $\sigma_{\overline{y}} = \dfrac{2}{\sqrt{10 - 1}} = 0.667$;

est. $\sigma_{\overline{x}-\overline{y}} = \sqrt{(1.333)^2 + (0.667)^2} = 1.491$;

obtained $t = \dfrac{10 - 8}{1.491} = 1.341$; $df = (10 - 1) + (10 - 1) = 18$;

critical $t = \pm 2.101$; fail to reject null, no significant difference
The data do not indicate a difference between the ability to understand computer-synthesized speech and human speech.

17. $\mu = 92$; $\sigma_{\overline{x}} = \dfrac{3}{\sqrt{36}} = 0.5$; $t = \dfrac{87 - 92}{0.5} = -10$; $df = 36 - 1 = 35$;

critical $t = \pm 2.03$; reject null, significant

19. $\overline{X} = 88$; $S_X = 23$; est. $\sigma_{\overline{x}} = \dfrac{23}{\sqrt{65 - 1}} = 2.875$;

$\overline{Y} = 97$; $S_Y = 41$; est. $\sigma_{\overline{y}} = \dfrac{41}{\sqrt{65 - 1}} = 5.125$;

est. $\sigma_{\overline{x}-\overline{y}} = \sqrt{2.875^2 + 5.125^2 - (2)(.38)(2.875)(5.125)} = 4.831$;

$t = \dfrac{88 - 97}{4.831} = -1.863$; $df = 65 - 1 = 64$;

critical $t = \pm 1.98$; fail to reject null, *not* significant

21. $\overline{X} = 227$; $S_X = 29$; est. $\sigma_{\overline{x}} = \dfrac{29}{\sqrt{10 - 1}} = 9.667$;

$\overline{Y} = 245$; $S_Y = 42$; est. $\sigma_{\overline{y}} = \dfrac{42}{\sqrt{17 - 1}} = 10.5$;

est. $\sigma_{\overline{x}-\overline{y}} = \sqrt{(9.667)^2 + (10.5)^2} = 14.272$;
$t = \dfrac{227 - 245}{14.272} = -1.261$; $df = (10 - 1) + (17 - 1) = 25$;

critical $t = \pm 2.060$; fail to reject null, *not* significant

23. $\overline{X} = 123$; $S_X = 4$; est. $\sigma_{\overline{x}} = \dfrac{4}{\sqrt{101 - 1}} = 0.4$;

obtained $t = \dfrac{123 - 122}{0.4} = 2.5$; $df = 101 - 1 = 100$;

critical $t = \pm 1.99$; reject null, significant

25. $\overline{X} = 3$; $\sigma = 30$; $\sigma_{\overline{x}} = \dfrac{30}{\sqrt{144}} = 2.5$;

obtained $t = \dfrac{3 - 0}{2.5} = 1.2$; $df = 144 - 1 = 143$;

critical $t = \pm 1.98$; fail to reject null, *not* significant

CHAPTER 13

1. Null hypothesis: The number of authors on a paper does not affect the number of negative comments received.
Research hypothesis: Papers submitted by multiple authors are less likely to receive negative comments than those submitted by a single author.

Source	SS	df	MS	F	p
Between	188.750	3	62.917	2.459	>.05
Within	307.000	12	25.583		
Total	495.750	15			

Conclusion: The *F* is nonsignificant, and we have no basis for rejecting the null hypothesis.

3. Null hypothesis: There is no difference between the grade point averages of students with full scholarships, partial scholarships, and no scholarships.
Research hypothesis: Students who receive scholarship money get higher grades.

Source	SS	df	MS	F	p
Between	0.150	2	0.075	0.146	>.05
Within	6.140	12	0.512		
Total	6.290	14			

Conclusion: There is no basis for rejecting the null hypothesis; the results were not significant.

5. Null hypothesis: There is no difference in moral standards between doctors in three specialty areas: orthopedics, pediatrics, and oncology. Research hypothesis: There is a difference in moral standards between doctors in three specialty areas: orthopedics, pediatrics, and oncology.

Source	SS	df	MS	F	p
Between	85.500	2	42.750	0.137	>.05
Within	2813.500	9	312.611		
Total	2899.000	11			

Conclusion: The results were not significant. There is no basis for rejecting the null hypothesis.

7. Null hypothesis: There is no difference in the ratings of beers made from 100% imported ingredients, 50% imported ingredients, or 0% imported ingredients.
Research hypothesis: There is a difference in the ratings of beers made from 100% imported ingredients, 50% imported ingredients, or 0% imported ingredients.

Source	SS	df	MS	F	p
Between	0.130	2	0.067	0.018	>.05
Within	43.200	12	3.600		
Total	43.330	14			

Conclusion: The results are not significant, and therefore we fail to reject the null hypothesis.

9. Null hypothesis: The percentage of correctly identified letters is not affected by whether the stimulus presentation is made at, above, or below threshold.
Research hypothesis: The percentage of correctly identified letters is affected by whether the stimulus presentation is made at, above, or below threshold.

Source	SS	df	MS	F	p
Between	23,286.670	2	11,643.333	523.950	<.05
Within	600.000	27	22.222		
Total	23,886.670	29			

Conclusion: The results are statistically significant. The null hypothesis is rejected.

HSD = 5.26

11. HSD = 1.239

Conclusion: The null hypothesis is rejected. The number of items remembered differs as a function of the type of items in the list. Words are remembered best, numbers are remembered second best, and nonwords are remembered the least.

13. HSD = 3.044

Conclusion: Men and women do not differ, but the number of words that can be recognized is significantly lower if the words are spoken by a computer than if they are spoken by a man or a woman.

15. HSD = 5.449

Conclusion: The null hypothesis is rejected. Only the control condition differs from the other three conditions. Hormone levels are significantly higher under the three stress conditions than they are under the control condition.

CHAPTER 14

1. Null hypothesis for columns: There is no difference in reading speed between the two different types of lighting.

Research hypothesis for columns: There is a difference in reading speed between the two different types of lighting.

Null hypothesis for rows: There is no difference in reading speed between the two different colors of the screen.

Research hypothesis for rows: There is a difference in reading speed between the two different colors of the screen.

Null hypothesis for interaction: There is no interaction between the lighting conditions and the color of the screen.

Research hypothesis for interaction: There is an interaction between the lighting conditions and the color of the screen.

Source	SS	df	MS	F	p
Columns	8.450	1	8.450	0.336	>.05
Rows	1170.450	1	1170.450	46.585	<.05
R × C	6.050	1	6.050	0.241	>.05
Error	402.000	16	25.125		
Total	1586.950	19			

Conclusion: There is a significant difference between the blue and orange screens. Reading is slower with the orange screen. None of the other hypotheses is supported.

3. Null hypothesis for columns: There is no difference in the scores on the DSM-KT between psychologists and psychiatrists.

Research hypothesis for columns: There is a difference in the scores on the DSM-KT between psychologists and psychiatrists.

Null hypothesis for rows: There is no difference in the scores on the DSM-KT between television and lecture presentations.

Research hypothesis for rows: There is a difference in the scores on the DSM-KT between television and lecture presentations.

Null hypothesis for interaction: There is no interaction.

Research hypothesis for interaction: There is an interaction.

Source	SS	df	MS	F	p
Columns	4.083	1	4.083	0.021	>.05
Rows	10.083	1	10.083	0.052	>.05
R × C	0.083	1	0.083	0.000	>.05
Error	1542.667	8	192.833		
Total	1556.916	11			

Conclusions: All *F* ratios are nonsignificant, so there is no basis for rejecting any of the null hypotheses.

5. Null hypothesis for columns: There are no differences in the numbers of days it takes a dog to learn to sit, to shake, or to roll over.

Research hypothesis for columns: There are differences in the numbers of days it takes a dog to learn to sit, to shake, or to roll over.

Null hypothesis for rows: There is no difference between old and young dogs in the numbers of days it takes to learn a trick.

Research hypothesis for rows: There is a difference between old and young dogs in the numbers of days it takes to learn a trick.

Null hypothesis for interaction: There is no interaction.

Research hypothesis for interaction: There is an interaction.

Source	SS	df	MS	F	p
Columns	366.067	2	183.033	70.397	<.05
Rows	124.033	1	124.033	47.705	<.05
R × C	28.467	2	14.233	5.474	<.05
Error	62.400	24	2.600		
Total	580.967	29			

Conclusions: Young dogs learn faster than old dogs, and there is a significant difference between the types of tricks. The interaction is significant. $HSD_{cols} = 1.800$; all three tricks are significantly different from one another.

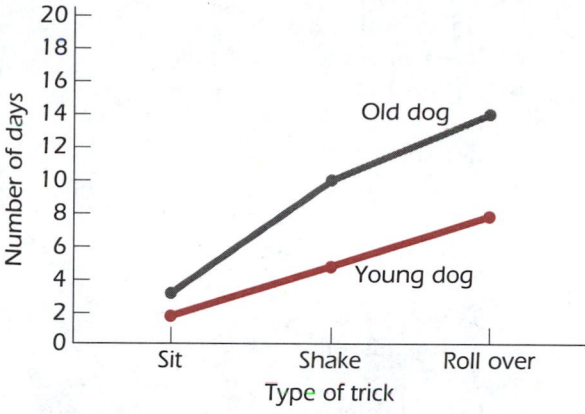

7. Null hypothesis for columns: There is no difference in the ratings of the effectiveness of the animal rights message whether or not the message mentions the institution.

Research hypothesis for columns: There is a difference in the ratings of the effectiveness of the animal rights message when the message mentions the institution, as opposed to when it does not.

Null hypothesis for rows: There is no difference in the ratings of the effectiveness of the animal rights message whether or not the message includes a picture of the researcher.

Research hypothesis for rows: There is a difference in the ratings of the effectiveness of the animal rights message when the message includes a picture of the researcher, as opposed to when it does not include a picture of the researcher.

Null hypothesis for interaction: There is no interaction.

Research hypothesis for interaction: There is an interaction.

Source	SS	df	MS	F	p
Columns	0.250	1	0.250	0.109	>.05
Rows	49.000	1	49.000	21.382	<.05
R × C	6.250	1	6.250	2.727	>.05
Error	27.500	12	2.292		
Total	83.000	15			

Conclusion: There is one significant *F*-value, showing that the presence or absence of a photograph affects the effectiveness ratings of the message. Messages are rated as more effective when photographs are used.

CHAPTER 15

1. $\chi^2(2) = 121.4$
Critical value = 5.99
It is significant.

3. $\chi^2(1) = 18.08$
Critical value = 3.841
It is significant.

5. $U_1 = 31$, $U_2 = 32$
Critical value = 12
U is not significant.

7. $T = 3$
Critical value = 5
T is significant.

9. $T = 3$
Critical value = 5
T is significant.

11. $H = 17.545$
Critical value = 7.815
H is significant.

13. $\chi^2(2) = 3.025$
Critical value = 5.99
χ^2 is not significant.

15. $\chi^2(6) = 20.764$
Critical value = 12.592
χ^2 is significant.

17. Based on the U computed in Problem 16, we fail to reject the null hypothesis.

19. Null hypothesis: People are able to detect errors equally well regardless of whether there were errors in the earlier pages.
Research hypothesis: People are better able to detect errors when there were errors in the earlier pages.
Conclusion: We reject the null hypothesis in favor of the research hypothesis. People detect errors more readily if there were errors in the earlier pages.

21. $T = 6$
Critical value = 17
Conclusion: The results are significant. We can reject the null hypothesis and accept the research hypothesis.

23. Null hypothesis: There is no difference in people's ability to remember words, nonwords, and numbers.
Research hypothesis: There is a difference in people's ability to remember words, nonwords, and numbers.
$H = 19.86$
Critical value = 5.99

25. Null hypothesis: There is no difference in people's ability to remember words depending on whether they are spoken by a man, a woman, or a computer.

Research hypothesis: There is a difference in people's ability to remember words depending on whether they are spoken by a man, a woman, or a computer.

$H = 17.506$

Critical value = 5.99

H is significant.

Index

TO THE OWNER OF THIS BOOK:

We hope that you have found *Behavioral Statistics in Action, Second Edition,* useful. So that this book can be improved in a future edition, would you take the time to complete this sheet and return it? We'd really like to hear from you.

School and address: _____

Department: _____

Instructor's name: _____

1. What I like most about this book is: _____

_____

_____

2. What I like least about this book is: _____

_____

_____

3. My general reaction to this book is: _____

_____

_____

4. Were all of the chapters of the book assigned for you to read? _____

   If not, which ones weren't? _____

_____

5. In the space below, or on a separate sheet of paper, please write specific suggestions for improving this book and anything else you'd care to share about your experience in using the book.

_____

_____

_____

_____

_____

Optional:

Your name: _____ Date: _____

May Brooks/Cole quote you, either in promotion for *Behavioral Statistics in Action, Second Edition,* or in future publishing ventures?

Yes: _____ No: _____

Sincerely,

Mark W. Vernoy
Judith A. Vernoy

FOLD HERE

FOLD HERE